EARLY DAYS
OF WORLD HISTORY

EARLY DAYS OF WORLD HISTORY

OSWALD SPENGLER

Reflections on the Past

TRANSLATED AND ANNOTATED BY
CONSTANTIN VON HOFFMEISTER

LEGENDBOOKS

Warsaw 2022

LEGEND
BOOKS

© 2022 Legend Books Sp. z o.o.

ISBN

PAPERBACK: 978-83-67583-02-2

HARDBACK: 978-83-67583-04-6

EBOOK: 978-83-67583-03-9

www.legendbooks.org

CONTENTS

TRANSLATOR'S PREFACE

BY CONSTANTIN VON HOFFMEISTER

THIS IS THE FIRST English translation of Oswald Spengler's posthumously published writings on the history of the ancient world. The often awkward structure and sometimes fragmentary nature of Spengler's notes in the German original were faithfully replicated in the English translation. He poetically describes the intimate nature of the bloody battles and seismic migratory wanderings that shaped the world before the advent of the Abrahamic order. The resultant boiling down of the primeval chaos and splendour of tribes and empires into a soup of mundane monotheism and nascent nations, not always representing a single and united seed, diluted the savage essence of the anarchic flow and clash between primal peoples moving amongst and against each other. The radical interpretation of historical events and processes that Spengler employs leads him to criticise the findings of his day's leading historians, presenting new hypotheses that topple established doctrine and challenge the very core of what it means to be a historian. By becoming a participant and seer instead of a mere observer, Spengler is almost a time traveller, gathering data and interpreting them on the spot in his deeply erudite and epiphanically expansive mind. Instead of merely chronicling the mainstream's established events, Spengler immerses himself in the actual unfolding of the twists and turning points in the world-historical narrative that the coming of the great races, with their propensity for violence and the unleashing of their creative faculties, engendered.

As a medium, Spengler channels the spectres of the past, turning them corporeal before our inner eye, so we can smell the rust of the armour and the gore caked on the combatants' blades. He describes culture clashes in the distant past, with Sea Peoples from Southern Europe raiding Egypt and mountain people from West Asia conquering Sumer. Beyond the horizon of dunes and fortresses, it was war and not peace that dictated the terms of existence, expansion and survival. Alternations of dynastic successions and regicides ensured the continuance of the empires' glory under blazing suns or nestled in the shade of hills. According to perennial tradition, people fight and people die, and new people fight and new people die — nothing new under the evening moon; yet hardly having uttered these words, the realisation dawns on one that Spengler wrote about the procession of rise and fall with gusto to illustrate humanity's endless repetition of tasting the apple — banished from the garden and forced to suffer everlasting struggle and toil on fields of honour and decay, in different climes and shifting landscapes.

Early Days of World History is a book that teaches us to remain calm when we crave impatience in the face of today's political and bellicose calamities. None of it is revelatory and nothing shall ever change. The line drawn in the sand millennia ago is still valid: stop and be devoured by the beast of time, or proceed and be slaughtered, replaced and then dutifully recorded in the annals of history. The ink collecting the dust of ages, we turn the pages to witness utter defeat followed by glorious victory and one brilliant invention nullified by another civilisational regression. The end is always nigh, they say, but in reality the end is always in the distance — over those yonder craggy cliffs. We can pursue the end relentlessly. Alas, it keeps marching away from us, camouflaged among the army that is always three swift steps ahead.

Moscow, Russia

March 11, 2022

THE CALL OF THE STEPPE

O F THE MANY MISCONCEPTIONS that exist about the works of Oswald Spengler (1880–1936), perhaps none is more prevalent, especially among English readers, than that which regards his worldview as having remained the same throughout his writing career. He is best known for the two-volume book *The Decline of the West*, the first volume of which was published in 1918, the second in 1922. By the 1930s, starting with 1931's *Man and Technics*, Spengler had reconsidered key aspects of his philosophy. This is not very well understood by most readers, partly because of Spengler's own dubious attempts to insist his thinking had never changed.

Spengler's otherwise mostly sympathetic intellectual biographer, John Farrenkopf, expresses annoyance at what he identifies as Spengler's unconvincing insistence that his philosophy had not changed. In the process, Farrenkopf reveals the nature of what he calls "the metamorphosis of Spengler's philosophy of world history."[1] Indicative of Spengler's later philosophy is his vastly altered attitude toward anthropology and prehistory.

---

1   John Farrenkopf, *Prophet of Decline: Spengler on World History and Politics* (Baton Rouge: LSU Press), pp. 231–232.

In *The Decline of the West*, Spengler had dismissed human prehistory as the "primeval spiritual condition of an eternal-childlike humanity," which qualifies as "history only in the biological sense."[2] By the 1930s, though, Spengler had developed a keen interest in anthropology. This fascination led Spengler to his mature philosophy of history, in which many of his earlier assertions are effectively reevaluated.

The Decline of the West, it should be remembered, appeared in two volumes that were four years apart in publication. The first volume was written and published during the First World War, although parts of it were conceived earlier than that. Spengler had written it under the assumption that his country would win the war, and compared to his later work, 1918's first volume does not much live up to Spengler's pessimistic reputation.

The first volume does portray civilizations, including the contemporary West, as thoroughly finite. However, its focus is mostly either on drawing a sharp distinction between the medieval-to-modern West and the cultures of antiquity, or else on defending the traditional German Idealist approach to the sciences from its English materialist nemesis. Its cultural pessimism is usually more implied than overt.

By the time the second volume was published in 1922, much had changed since the publication of the first volume prior to the German armistice of 1918. In addition to Germany's defeat in the war and humiliation by its outcome, as well as the violent internal political turmoil of the early Weimar period, the Bolshevik Revolution in Russia and the nascent Mussolini regime of Italy had clearly impacted Spengler's thinking. Farrenkopf reveals that Spengler's political thought during WWI, which is not much of a focal point in most of the first volume of *The Decline of the West*, was rather bourgeois-based and quasi-democratic compared to the political philosophy he had developed by the time the second volume was published. In the second volume, Spengler has adopted the political views he is known

----

2   Spengler quoted in Ibid, p. 217.

for, characterized by a hostility to democracy and the belief that the Prussian archetype had made Germany great.

Despite the differences between the first and the second volume, *The Decline of the West* qualifies as a single project with a focused thesis. The book presents models of high cultures which, according to Spengler, go through similar historical cycles. In Spengler's terminology, the word "Culture" ("*Kultur*") describes a civilization's creative epoch, in which the high culture in question is comparable to a living organism. During its "Culture" epoch, a particular civilization establishes its style of science, theology, politics, and art. "Civilization" ("*Zivilisation*") by contrast denotes the later epoch of a high culture, in which it is comparable to an aging or dying organism. This kind of epoch is marked by the increasing predominance of big cities, all-consuming economic considerations, and a critical culture in place of a creative one.

The words "*Kultur*" and "*Zivilisation*" had long been used in German thought to describe similar dichotomies; Spengler's innovation was in systematically applying the terms to historical epochs. *The Decline of the West* portrays the civilizations described in it as unrelated, but subject to the same cyclical pattern everywhere. The transition from "*Kultur*" to "*Zivilisation*" is always marked by a change in political economy, in which the formerly prioritized countryside is sucked dry by the ever-growing "megalopolis."

Spengler's civilizational forecast concludes with a deliberately vague and often poorly understood prophecy. According to Spengler, as the "Faustian" West descends into its epoch of empty modernization, just as the Classical culture did with the Romans, Western civilization will give way to a rising new culture he loosely associates with Russia. As Spengler sketches his incomplete portrait of this nascent culture, it is by no means limited to Russia proper, or even to any of the Russian nationalist models that include Belarus and Ukraine. It rather covers the huge territory of the historic Russian Empire, the European part of which Germany had recently conquered (as affirmed by the Treaty of Brest-Litovsk) when the first volume of *The Decline of the West* was published.

The unmentioned, yet-unknown, national vector of Spengler's prospective future civilization is therefore indeterminate; it could just as easily refer to Balts, Moldavians, or Central Asian peoples as to Russians and related nationalities. Spengler's attribution of "the Christianity of Dostoevsky" to this immanent new culture is almost as broad, referring far more to a philosophical and psychological ethos than to the Russian Orthodox Church. Whatever one makes of this prediction, it is indicative of Spengler's lifelong fascination with the steppe world, which would be more heavily emphasized in his mature work.

In *The Decline of the West*, Spengler names his primary philosophical influences as Goethe and Nietzsche. Additionally, the book owes much to the Hegelian historicist tradition, though with a Nietzschean psychological orientation in place of Hegel's emphasis on reason. There are other major influences on the book, such as Leopold von Ranke and the neo-Rankean tradition explored by Farrenkopf. Some early 20th-century influences on Spengler are also significant enough to draw intellectual comparisons.

Although an original thesis, the book's debt to two giants of the Wilhelmine era is evident. The first is the sociologist and economist Werner Sombart, whose ideas so inform *The Decline of the West* that even the notoriously citation-shy Spengler credits them in places. Spengler's 1919 political essay "Prussianism and Socialism" owes to Sombart the notion that the German tradition of militarism represents a historic and natural form of socialism, in contrast to the purely capitalistic traditions found in the Anglophone countries. This idea would be incorporated into the second volume of *The Decline of the West*. Sombart would later be cited in Spengler's last published book, translated into English as *The Hour of Decision*, so it is fair to consider Sombart a lifelong influence on Spengler's thought.

More often than its citations, *The Decline of the West* can be seen as engaging in "hidden dialogues," to borrow a term often used by scholars of the jurist and political philosopher Carl Schmitt for how Schmitt's works address opponents who dealt with the same themes. The term describes a thinker's response to another thinker's assertions, made without actually mentioning the rival thinker in question. One of Spengler's hidden dialogues probably seemed obvious when *The Decline of the West* was published, but has mostly been forgotten since the theorist in question was virtually erased from European intellectual history. Nevertheless, the influence of Houston Stewart Chamberlain's 1899 publication *The Foundations of the Nineteenth Century* is very apparent in Spengler's work.

Chamberlain, an English Germanophile who later became a German citizen, was an avid scholar of history and philosophy who had married into the Wagner family. He wrote in the tradition of the great composer Richard Wagner's essays, which are heavily influenced by Schopenhauer's philosophy. Chamberlain's bestselling work was promoted in German schools by Kaiser Wilhelm II, and as a schoolteacher in the Wilhelmine years Spengler would have absorbed Chamberlain's ideas. Since the end of the Second World War, Chamberlain's name has been so shrouded in black legend, his work so much more often proscribed than actually read, that a brief digression is in order before evaluating his influence on Spengler.

Although Chamberlain is known for his contribution to the racialist discourse of fin-de-siècle intellectual life, his ideas about race owed little to the English materialist tradition, and he was often almost as hostile to that intellectual tradition as Spengler would later be. While Wilhelm II and later Hitler both publicly held Chamberlain's work in very high esteem, in both cases their actual adherence to it is questionable. Chamberlain's controversial views on Jews contradicted the often Jewish-friendly policies of Wilhelm's government, but many of Chamberlain's statements on the subject of Jews equally contradict the outright persecutorial actions later associated with Hitler.

Chamberlain was also noted for his almost idiosyncratically high regard for Balkan nations like Serbia, combined with an unequivocal hostility to Turkey and Islam — sentiments that can hardly be said to have resonated with either Wilhelm II or Hitler.[3] Thus, despite the many nods to his influence by 20th-century German policymakers, it is best to view Chamberlain as a standalone thinker, not as the ideologist of any particular government.

The Decline of the West affirms some key arguments contained in *The Foundations of the Nineteenth Century*, while strongly contradicting others. Chamberlain had very emphatically argued against the traditional way of dividing European history into the standard categories of "ancient," "medieval," and "modern." Chamberlain had insisted that "if we draw one line through the year 500, and a second through the year 1500, and call these thousand years the Middle Ages, we have not dissected the organic body of history as a skilled anatomist, but hacked it in two like a butcher."[4]

Spengler not only clearly agreed with this view, but argued it more systematically than Chamberlain had. In Spengler's model, the "Faustian" Western culture spans the 2nd millennium AD, having fully come into being in the 11th century, and in the process of dying in the 20th century. This model is similar to Chamberlain's less developed proposal of the 13th century as the beginning of a new civilization.

This strident defense of a civilizational model similar to the one Chamberlain had argued, by the way, was what the German title of

---

3   Chamberlain's anti-Turkish sentiment would still be expressed as late as 1915, by which time Wilhelm II's government had sought friendly relations with Ottoman Turkey. In a book of that year, the publication of which was held up by German wartime censors, Chamberlain continues to lament the destructive historic Ottoman impact on Turkish-ruled lands. See Houston Stewart Chamberlain, *Political Ideals*, tr. by Alexander Jacob (Maryland: University Press of America, 2005), p. 62.

4   Houston Stewart Chamberlain, *The Foundations of the Nineteenth Century Volume I*, tr. by John Lees, first impression 1910, second impression 1912 (Revisionist Books edition, 2015), p. 34. (From Chamberlain's introduction.)

Spengler's first volume had originally described. Spengler's book was translated into English five years after the second volume was published, and only in light of the more pessimistic concluding volume's tone and content does the term "decline" represent a particularly accurate translation of the book's title. Only the second volume explicitly takes the book's focus in the direction of cultural and civilizational decline, giving the German title its famous second meaning and making the familiar English translation appear appropriate. The title's original meaning was a reference to Spengler's determination to end once and for all the standard historical model of the West, as criticized by Chamberlain in the quote above.

Spengler's German word "*Untergang*" literally means "twilight," an idiomatic term for "downfall." Nietzsche had published an 1889 book entitled *Twilight of the Idols*, a satirical reference to Richard Wagner's concept of a mythological "twilight of the gods." In Nietzsche's case, this meant the author's own attempt at toppling what he considered philosophical "idols." It was in the spirit of Nietzsche's title that Spengler had at first meant "the twilight of the West." The title initially referred to Spengler's own intended destruction, in a more rigorous fashion than Chamberlain's similar arguments before him, of the common "ancient-medieval-modern" model of Western civilization.

At the same time, a key difference between *The Decline of the West* and *The Foundations of the Nineteenth Century* exists on the question of the West's relation to Greco-Roman Classical antiquity. Both books portray the two cultures as fundamentally different civilizations, but Chamberlain had also emphasized their common roots in the same Indo-European ethnic family. *The Decline of the West* systematically downplays this affinity.

This and other differences in the two influential books can be attributed to the philosophical points of disagreement between Chamberlain and early Spengler. Chamberlain, writing in the Schopenhauerian vein, was a staunch critic of Hegelian historicism, while Spengler's early work propounds a variant of Hegelian historicism without Hegel's rationalism. In this way, *The Decline of the West* can be seen as the historicist answer to *The Foundations of the Nineteenth Century*.

However, as noted above, *The Decline of the West* does *not* represent Spengler's mature philosophy. Contrary to Spengler's own pretensions of lifelong consistency, parts of his worldview had very much changed by the 1930s. As Spengler's philosophy became less purely historicist and much more anthropologically grounded than the outlook articulated in *The Decline of the West*, his work became far more amenable to theories of common ethnological links between the civilizations of antiquity and the "Faustian" West, as emphasized by Indo-Europeanists like Chamberlain. That change is fully revealed in this posthumously published volume, *Early Days of World History*.

Philosophically, the shift in Spengler's work is noticeable in the early 1930s. The short 1931 volume *Man and Technics* is sometimes assumed to be a mere compendium to Spengler's earlier magnum opus, *The Decline of the West*. Actually, *Man and Technics* marks the first appearance of Spengler's mature philosophy.

In *Man and Technics*, Spengler largely abandons the constructivist view of nature articulated throughout *The Decline of the West*. In the much smaller former book's exploration of the significance of human technology, Spengler's previous ardent historicism gives way to the priority of anthropology. It would be a mistake, however, to regard this change as a turn to mainstream Darwinian physical anthropology.

As much as his philosophical priorities changed in many ways, in one respect Spengler remained consistent from *The Decline of the West* to his mature work. Spengler was a lifelong adherent of the view of the natural sciences bluntly expressed in Werner Sombart's 1915 WWI manifesto *Traders and Heroes*, an outlook that hearkened back to the time of Goethe. This view held the English tradition of scientific materialism to be alien to Germany, and called for alternative scientific theories to be promoted.

Latent even in some of Kant's work, and already in full effect in the succeeding generation of Goethe and the German Romantics, this traditional German hostility to Anglophone scientific materialism arguably originated as early as the age when Newton had libeled Leibniz as a plagiarist. Spengler's hostility to scientific materialism was thus deeply rooted in a German tradition. That intellectual tradition was more than simply a product of his time, because its origin far predates the era when actual geopolitical hostilities had arisen between Britain and Germany.[5]

His continuation of the German mission against English science explains Spengler's citation of German-Jewish anthropologist and fervent anti-racialist Franz Boas' now-discredited experiments in craniology in the second volume of *The Decline of the West*.[6] By contrast, in

---

5   Widespread Anglophone ignorance of the German tradition of anti-scientism, an ignorance which is more rampant in the English-speaking countries now than it was in Spengler's time, has often led to the habit of quite wrongly viewing Spengler's arguments on scientific subjects as idiosyncratic. In fact, rebellion against the established 17th-century philosophy of science was a highly respected historic German intellectual pastime. This philosophical tradition is usually either ignored or dismissed in contemporary English histories of science, despite its fruitful influence on celebrated mainstream scientists like Darwin, Mendel, and Einstein. Similar philosophies of science do exist in Anglophone intellectual history, such as that of George Berkeley or Edgar Allan Poe's *Eureka: A Prose Poem*, but isolated examples like those have gone virtually unnoticed in the Anglosphere. Much more typical of American discourse is the "Scopes Monkey Trial" of the 1920s, which pitted standardly accepted scientific theories against Old Testament literalism. In Germany, by contrast, unconventional philosophies of science have a long history of being viewed as a national calling.

6   Boas' work on craniology has been displaced by Corey S. Sparks and Richard L. Jantz in their 2002 scholarly article published by Proceedings of the National Academy of Sciences of the United States of America, entitled "A reassessment of human cranial plasticity: Boas revisited." The study's results are particularly devastating to Boas' theory of cranial plasticity where patrilineal inheritance of cranial characteristics is concerned. Strangely, Boas had based his craniological experiments on matrilineal inheritance of such characteristics, though most

Early Days of World History, Spengler cites the contemporary German Nordicist race theorist Hans F. K. Günther in asserting that "urbanisation is racial decay." That would seem quite a leap, from citing Boas to citing Günther. However, in the opinion of one historian of scientific ideas, Boas and Günther had more in common than they liked to think, because they were both heirs more of the German Idealist tradition in science than what the Anglo-Saxon tradition recognizes as the scientific method.[7] Spengler must have keenly detected this commonality, for his views on racial matters were never synonymous with those of Boas, any more than they were identical to Günther's.

Characteristic of Spengler's mature work is its multifaceted relation to the subject of race. Morally as well as scientifically, Spengler's works of the 1930s evince a nuanced attitude toward that issue. For all its expressed apprehension about the so-called "colored races," his political writing of that decade is also marked by Spengler's steadfast refusal to moralize against such peoples, distinguishing it from similarly-themed Anglo-American literature of the same era.

Spengler also annoyed the leaders of the Third Reich by articulating his stance against materialist and reductionistic notions of racial purity. Spengler himself had some distant Jewish ancestry, though not enough to get in any kind of legal or institutional trouble under National Socialist law. More importantly, he opposed racial purism of the skull-measuring type as an Anglophone cultural intrusion into the traditional German view of race. The German intellectual tradition of assigning transcendental meaning to different physical-anthropological types is proudly continued in Spengler's later work, so he cannot be accurately called an unequivocal enemy of racialist ideas. Rather, he sought to strip such concepts of English materialist

---

human cultures on Earth tend to view most genealogical subjects in patrilineal rather than matrilineal terms.

7   Amos Morris-Reich, "Race, Ideas, and Ideals: A Comparison of Franz Boas and Hans F. K. Günther," *History of European Ideas,* vol. 32, no. 3 (2006).

influence, which he outspokenly viewed as having crept into Hitler's movement.

If Spengler's views on race differed from those of Franz Boas, his underlying philosophy of anthropology can be seen as the polar opposite of the Boasian one. In one key way, the mature Spengler's anthropological theories not only contradict, but directly oppose those of the Boas school. The latter, drawing from cherrypicked examples of peaceful primitive peoples, attempted to deny man's warlike nature. Spengler's mature writing does anything but.

Spengler, who had written his doctoral dissertation on Heraclitus, applied the great pre-Socratic Greek philosopher's conflict-driven outlook to anthropology. In Spengler's Heraclitean anthropological approach, eternal violence is represented as more or less the only universal, axiomatic fact of human life there is, and virtually every other aspect of human culture as subject to flux and relativity. It is therefore a mistake to draw from Spengler's earlier choice of citation that his mature anthropology was in any way Boasian; it is more accurate to call it quintessentially anti-Boasian.

Having established this martial philosophy of anthropology in *Man and Technics*, Spengler expanded upon it in various essays of the 1930s. This interest grew into his main focus after the mixed reception of his last political tract, published in 1933 as *Jahre der Entscheidung* (Years of Decision) and translated into English a year later as *The Hour of Decision*. While that book was a bestseller, it was poorly received by the new Hitler regime, of which Spengler openly considered himself neither an enemy nor a supporter.

During this period, Spengler planned a full-length prequel to *The Decline of the West*. Although the project was cut short by Spengler's 1936 death of a heart attack, the surviving first draft of *Early Days of World History* already clearly outlines the book's anthropological theses. Posthumously published in Germany in 1966, this draft is unfinished as a book, but lucid and coherent enough that Spengler's penetrating arguments about prehistory and early civilizations are fully comprehensible.

In contrast to Spengler's earlier dismissal of human prehistory, *Early Days of World History* proposes four ages of human development. These are described as the "a," "b," "c," and "d" anthropological epochs. The fourth one, "d," is the age of high civilizations he had described in *The Decline of the West*. In place of Spengler's previous conflation of the earlier ages "into one lengthy epoch," explains Farrenkopf, the "a," "b," and "c" stages must be read as "corresponding to the Paleolithic, the Late Paleolithic and Neolithic, and the Late Neolithic and early civilization respectively."[8]

Despite his newfound interest in anthropology, *Early Days of World History* does not stray too far from Spengler's established domain as a philosopher of history. Notes Farrenkopf, "Spengler concentrated most of his research effort on the 'c' phase of prehistory, which laid the foundation for the early civilizations."[9] Whereas the settled civilizations explored in *The Decline of the West* had been described with botanical metaphors after the fashion of Goethe, Spengler compared the proto-civilizational cultures of the "c" period to the more mobile amoebae.

In his account of the development of early civilizations, Spengler conceived of three main culture complexes of the "c" age of mankind, each of them associated with a technological trademark. He dubbed these culture complexes with names borrowed from ancient mythological accounts. He applied the name "Kash" mostly to the Late Neolithic Middle East, and associated this culture complex with the construction of megaliths.

For the pre-Indo-European culture complex from Southern Europe, very similar to that which later Indo-Europeanists have often referred to as "Old Europe," Spengler's term was "Atlantis." He

---

8   Farrenkopf, *Prophet of Decline*, p. 217.

9   Ibid.

considered the original cradle of this culture complex to have been the area around southern Spain. Spengler chose the name "Atlantis" because he regarded pre-Indo-European Southern Europe as the prehistoric seat of a maritime culture responsible for building boats. He tied this technological innovation to the appearance of a European element in the ancient Fertile Crescent and Egypt.

This merging of the intrusive Southern European culture of "Atlantis" with the native Middle Eastern culture of "Kash," according to Spengler, resulted in what is commonly known as the dawn of civilization. This theory, which appears toward the end of *Early Days of World History*, has yet to be evaluated by anthropologists. If it is discovered that there is truth in this portrait of "Atlantis," such a finding would probably demand a reevaluation of the Platonic myth from which Spengler took the name. Perhaps the more recent archeological discoveries in the Danube Valley, and the hypothesis of the Black Sea flood of around 5900 BC, call for amendments to Spengler's placement of the "Atlantic" cradle in southern Spain.

The third culture complex described in *Early Days of World History*, the one depicted with the most obvious sympathy, is associated with the technological hallmark of the war chariot. In his analysis of this primeval proto-culture, Spengler came very close to what is now known about the original domestication of the horse, and the related Proto-Indo-European cradle to the north of the Black Sea. The heroic culture of his study of early history brings the reader to where *The Decline of the West* had placed the future, on the steppe lands of Eastern Europe and Central Asia.

Spengler's name for the horse-driven Indo-European culture complex was "Turan." Like "Kash" and "Atlantis," the term "Turan" has mythological origins. The word stems from ancient Persian chronicles, in which it had described the land of an Indo-Iranian people noted for its rivalry with Zoroastrian civilization.

In calling the Indo-European cradle and its associated culture complex "Turan," Spengler referenced a controversial subject in

European ethnological historiography. Since it was first coined in ancient Persia, the term has experienced many uses and abuses. Spengler's use of this name for his favorite "amoebic" cultural model draws attention to the fact that the word "Turan" originally described an Indo-European culture, not a Turco-Mongolian one. In so using the term, *Early Days of World History* dispels many historiographical misconceptions about both ethnic families, and also makes what have proven prescient observations about their histories.

The word "Turanian" was first misapplied to the Turco-Mongolian peoples by Muslim scholars in the Middle Ages. This inaccuracy was further abused by the 19th-century Hungarian-Jewish Turcophile historian Armin Vámbéry, whose work popularized the ideology of "pan-Turanism." Ideas like those of Vámbéry, a notable spy for Britain, influenced the late 19th century's historically inaccurate usage of the word "Turanian" in European discourse.

In reality, the Turco-Mongolians entered into history much later than the Scythian tribes associated with the ancient Turanians. The medieval Turco-Mongolians were easily conflated with ancient Turan because they both shared virtually the same horse-driven culture complex. Still, the Turco-Mongolians were markedly different people — if often partially descended from, and mythologically connected to, their Iranian-speaking Scythian predecessors on the steppe.

According to the ancient Zoroastrian Iranians, the first writers to use the term, "Turan" referred to their barbarian cousins from the steppes and forests to the north. In its original Persian usage, "Turanian" described the less civilized northern Iranians, the semi-nomadic pastoral peoples that had not adopted Zoroastrianism. "Iran" by contrast referred to the more settled Zoroastrians of the south. As a regional descriptor, the term "Turan" was associated with Transoxiana, in today's Uzbekistan; as an ethnic one, it referred mainly to the ancient Scythians and related groups.

That Spengler recognized the European character of the ancient Scythians was important to his understanding of the location of the

Proto-Indo-European cradle on the Scythian steppe. Indo-European scholar John W. Day has shown the physical appearance of the Scythians to have corresponded mostly with the archetype of the Celt. Ancient sources like Herodotus, Hippocrates, Callimachus, Zhang Qian, Pliny the Elder, Clement of Alexandria, and other writers of antiquity all describe the Scythians as having red or tawny hair and colorful eyes.[10] In affirming such sources on the subject of the Scythians, Spengler challenged the image of the Scythians that had developed for over a century in modern European discourse.

Oddly, the aforementioned common ancient description of the Scythians had been ignored or disputed in the 19th century. From the claims of the mid-19th-century race theorist Arthur de Gobineau, to the later 19th-century writings of explorer Richard Francis Burton, to the early 20th-century works of Romanian historian Nicolae Iorga, an erroneous image of the Scythians prevailed in modern European writings until around the 1930s. Such accounts deny the Scythians' strong links with Europe, and inaccurately describe the physical attributes of the Scythians accordingly. This typical 19th-century mistake derives from the preceding 18th century's notions of "civilization," which had darkened Europe's understanding of the Scythian world.

In the 18th century, the cultures of the Indian subcontinent were just beginning to be studied in Europe. From this discovery inevitably followed speculations about human ethnological and civilizational beginnings. Unfortunately, the resulting theories were diluted with 18th-century philosophical prejudices about "civilization" and non-"civilization," confusing the European understanding of Indo-European origins for over a century.

During that era, the region associated with ancient Scythia was emphatically rejected as any kind of civilizational cradle. "Nothing has ever come to us from either European or Asiatic Scythia," wrote

---

10   John V. Day, *Indo-European Origins: The Anthropological Evidence (Journal of Indo-European Studies)* (Institute for the Study of Man, 2001).

Voltaire, "but tigers who have devoured our lambs."[11] Voltaire instead placed the cradle of early humanity in the more settled and advanced region of India.

Voltaire's negative view of semi-settled peoples in the style of the Scythians was widespread in 18th-century discourse. For example, it was shared by two powerful admirers of Voltaire's ideas, Frederick the Great of Prussia and Catherine the Great of Russia. This disdainful attitude toward horse-driven peoples was evident in Frederick's opinion of the cavalry-loving Polish tradition, and in Catherine's dislike of the Cossacks as well as the Tatars.

Voltaire's ferocious above-quoted negation of the idea of a steppe cradle seems to point to the contemporary prevalence of a certain awareness of such a thing in some quarters, as if Voltaire was arguing against an entire school, and not just a single idiosyncratic suggestion. That was, in fact, very much the case. The 18th-century view of the subject cannot be totally excused as reflecting simple ignorance, because it actually obscured what had hitherto come close to the discovery of Indo-European origins by certain Eastern European intellectuals.

It is probably no coincidence that the 18th century's muddling of Indo-European origins occurred in the same era as the destruction of the historic Polish state. In Renaissance Poland, and into the 18th century, there had existed an impactful ideology known as "Sarmatism." Nietzsche may have had this famously freedom-loving, yet unabashedly elitist and militaristic, current of thought in mind when he dubiously claimed descent from the fallen Polish nobility.

The use of the term "Sarmatism" dates back to the works of the 15th-century Polish priest and chronicler Jan Długosz. It was Długosz who had proposed that Poland's prehistory originates from the ancient Scythian confederation known as the Sarmatians. This theory would be influential not only in the Polish kingdom, but throughout

---

11 Voltaire quoted in Joscelyn Godwin, *Arktos: The Polar Myth in Science, Symbolism, and Nazi Survival*, (Adventures Unlimited Press; Revised edition, 1996), p. 37.

Renaissance Eastern Europe. In contrast to the 18th-century Western disdain for historic horse-driven nomads, Sarmatism had inspired a widespread cultural trend of studying such peoples and glorifying them as the nation's ancestors.

In addition to the impact of the Polish Renaissance historians, the steppe orientation of *Early Days of World History* hearkens back to another influential early modern thinker from Eastern Europe. A distinguished foreign member of the Prussian Academy of Sciences, as well as a contemporary and correspondent of Leibniz, eccentric Moldavian prince Dimitrie Cantemir was a noted pretender to descent from Tamerlane. Cantemir left two cultural legacies to Western history, one of which distinguishes him as a forgotten precursor to Spengler.

Initially an Ottoman vassal, Prince Cantemir gave traditional Turkish music its first system of notation, ushering in the classical era of Turkish music that would later influence Mozart. Later — after he had turned against the Ottoman Porte in an alliance with Petrine Russia, but was driven out of power and into exile due to his abysmal battlefield leadership — Cantemir wrote much about history. Most impactful in the West was a two-volume book that would be translated into English in 1734 as *The History of the Growth and Decay of the Othman Empire*. Voltaire and Gibbon later read Cantemir's work, as did Victor Hugo.[12]

Notes one biographer, "Cantemir's philosophy of history is empiric and mechanistic. The destiny in history of empires is viewed... through cycles similar to the natural stages of birth, growth, decline, and death."[13] Long before Nietzsche popularized the arguments, Cantemir suggested that high cultures are initially founded by barbarians, and also that a civilization's level of high culture has nothing

---

12 See the booklet of the musical album *Istanbul: Dimitrie Cantemir 1630–1732*, written by Stefan Lemny and translated by Jacqueline Minett.

13 Eugenia Popescu-Judetz, *Prince Dimitrie Cantemir: Theorist and Composer of Turkish Music* (Istanbul: Pan Yayıncılık, 1999), p. 34.

to do with its political success.[14] Cantemir, the inventor of the grand civilizational genre of history book, can thus be credited as the lonely representative of proto-Spenglerian sensibilities in the progress-fetishizing Enlightenment epoch.

The influence of these precursors on Spengler's thought is difficult to ascertain. Spengler was famously sparing in his citations of his German influences; his work is even more barren of credit given to foreign ones. Even so, an avalanche of circumstantial evidence would seem to point to his possession of at least a passing familiarity with the ideas of the Polish Renaissance and the achievements of Prince Cantemir.

The eastward-looking orientation of Spengler's posthumously published book draws attention to an issue that demands clarification. Whereas shades of Western chauvinism can be read into the parts of Spengler's body of work that emphasize his "Faustian" civilizational model, *Early Days of World History* shows the opposite tendency in Spengler's thinking in full effect, displaying a strong affinity with Eastern Europe. To those half-educated in German history, it may come across as rather odd that the steppe world inspired awe in such an apostle of "Prussianism" as Spengler.

Actually, Spengler's Janus-faced attitude regarding the East fit his Prussian predilections perfectly. It is common, but quite inaccurate, to draw from Frederick the Great's 18th-century arrogance toward Easterners that this was the only prototypical Prussian sensibility on the subject of Eastern Europe. At least as quintessentially Prussian was the German unifier Field Marshal Count Moltke's curious admiration for the East, in his work as a historian and traveler.[15] General Erich

---

14 See Dimitrie Cantemir, *The History of the Growth and Decay of the Othman Empire vol. I*, tr. by Nicholas Tindal (London: Knapton, 1734), p. 151, note 14.

15 Field Marshal Moltke (the Elder) penned a mostly sympathetic history of the former Polish kingdom, translated into English as *Poland: An Historical Sketch*. Moltke also published a memoir of his early travels through Danubia, which is quite respectful of the Romanians, by 19th-century Western standards. See

Ludendorff's opinion is another example of the Eastern mystique in traditional Prussian culture. In contrast to Hitler's hateful dreams of *Lebensraum*, which constituted an underrated reason why Ludendorff eventually parted ways with his Austrian protégé, the enigmatic and misunderstood WWI commander always maintained a high respect for the peoples of the Northeastern European region he had once conquered — Balts as well as Russians.[16] That the famously pro-Prussian Spengler was drawn to the Eastern European steppe is thus not as surprising or idiosyncratic as it may seem.

Early Days of World History reflects a general contemporary trend in Indo-European scholarship, in which the above-described intellectual history of belittling the Scythian steppe was finally being questioned. "Horses gallop onto the world stage" in early 20th-century

---

Helmuth Graf von Moltke, *Moltke: His Life and Character* (San Francisco: Pickle Partners).

16 General Ludendorff's Eastern sympathies are partially documented in two illuminating English studies, Michael Kellogg's *The Russian Roots of Nazism: White Émigrés and the Making of National Socialism, 1917–1945* (Cambridge: Cambridge University Press, 2005) and Jay Lockenour's *Dragonslayer: The Legend of Erich Ludendorff in the Weimar Republic and Third Reich* (Cornell University Press, 2021). Lockenour notes that Ludendorff criticized the historic Teutonic Knights, whose regalia he proudly wore, for having vanquished what he regarded as the original and pure Nordic religion of the Baltic peoples. Lockenour also reveals that Ludendorff had learned the Russian language before the First World War, but Lockenour's otherwise comprehensive biography neglects Ludendorff's early Weimar-era Russian connections. Those are lucidly explored in Kellogg's book, which mistakenly describes him as "von Ludendorff," but nonetheless constitutes a crucial contribution to Ludendorff scholarship. Ludendorff's 1931 publication *The Coming War* portrays Hitler's bellicose war aims in the East as threatening to lead Germany to ruin in the service of secret societies and other "supernational powers." Even Ludendorff's Third Reich era work of 1935, *Der totale Krieg (The Total War)*, contains invocations of German racial solidarity with the Russians. As extreme as that book's contributions to military theory may seem, Ludendorff always insisted that his intense theories of total war applied only to what he considered defensive strategies, not to what he recognized as wars of naked aggression.

Indo-Europeanist discourse, notes David W. Anthony, because scholars increasingly observed that the earliest historic Indo-European languages "were spoken by militaristic societies that seemed to erupt into the ancient world driving chariots pulled by swift horses."[17] It was in this atmosphere that Spengler could portray the archetypal "Turanic" lifestyle not as alien to Europe, but as foundational to most of what is considered European culture. This view would take decades to catch on in Anglophone scholarly institutions, but it was already widespread in Central and Eastern Europe during the 1930s.

In the case of one popular political movement in 1930s Hungary, for example, the legacy of Vámbéry's "pan-Turanist" ideology appears to have been synthesized with a recognition of the term's original reference to a culture of an Indo-European character. Ferenc Szálasi's Party of National Will, later known as the Arrow Cross Party, differed from most contemporary Hungarian nationalist organizations in two ways. Eschewing the classist traditions that had loomed over Hungary's national development since the 16th century, Szálasi's group recruited mainly from the Hungarian working classes. Compared to the considerable Magyar chauvinism of the bourgeois Hungarian nationalists and aristocrats like Admiral Horthy, the Arrow Cross racial ideology was not as hostile to Hungary's Romanian and Slavic neighbors.

According to historian Nicholas M. Nagy-Talavera, Szálasi's ideology invoked a view of history based on "Turanian and Aryan nostalgia," and its proponents often used the phrase "Aryan-Turanian" to describe their country's national character.[18] This ideological modification of "Turanism" resulted in a different attitude toward Hungary's

---

17 David W. Anthony, *The Horse, the Wheel, and Language: How Bronze-Age Riders from the Eurasian Steppes Shaped the Modern World* (Princeton, N.J.: Princeton University Press, 2010), p. 18.

18 Nicholas M. Nagy-Talavera, *The Green Shirts and Others: A History of Fascism in Hungary and Romania* (Las Vegas: The Center for Romanian Studies, 2001), p. 499.

neighbors than the chauvinistic ones of that country's 19th-century thinkers, such as Vámbéry. Nagy-Talavera observes that "brotherhood within the Great Carpathian-Danubian Fatherland was the solution Szálasi had in mind for the nationality problem."[19] But it was not only in Hungary that ideas similar to those articulated in *Early Days of World History* were ascendent in the 1930s.

To Hungary's east, in Romania, historian and politician Nicolae Iorga's influence on the national historiography had gone unquestioned until the interwar era. Reflecting Romania's territorial rivalry with Hungary, Iorga coined a term later used by Allied newspapers for Hungary, "the jackal of Europe." Iorga's work opposed the sentiment of Vámbéry's "Turanism" with a marked hostility to "Turanic" cultures in the aforementioned tradition of 18th-century thought.

Iorga's priority of unequivocal hostility to Hungary was called into question by the more radical interwar-era generation of Romanian nationalists. The latter milieu balanced the Romanian position on the issue of the Transylvania region with an increasingly critical attitude toward the international legal order created by the victorious Entente of WWI. Rejecting Iorga's geopolitical views as too subservient to Romania's abusive and exploitative former allies, the younger Romanian nationalist movement was more open to a degree of international cooperation with Hungary. From this geopolitical difference with Iorga followed intellectual differences in the Romanian interwar generation's opinion of "Turanic" cultures.

This process appears to have started in 1925, with a trip by the respected law professor, parliamentarian, and Indo-Europeanist ideologue A. C. Cuza — who, by that time, enjoyed a much stronger repertoire with younger Romanians than Iorga did — to a welcoming Budapest conference in 1925.[20] Its implications for Romania's increas-

---

19   Ibid, p. 507.

20   For Professor Cuza's visit to Hungary, see Nicholas M. Nagy-Talavera, *Nicolae Iorga: A Biography*, p. 262 (Portland: The Center for Romanian Studies, 1998). On this 1925 trip, Cuza was accompanied by a young Ion Moța. Before being

ingly critical reception of Iorga's assumptions about "Turanic" cultures continued throughout the late 1920s and into the 1930s, with a young personal and political enemy of Iorga's named Mircea Eliade.[21] The latter thinker would go on to become, like Spengler, one of the 20th century's great challengers of the common notions of "civilization" inherited from the 18th century.

Eliade became a world-renowned scholar of Central Asian cultures, and of others sometimes grouped into the cultural super-family "Altaic." His works often deal with the same or similar themes as *Early Days of World History*. Notably, the writings of Eliade and mature Spengler display a shared interest in the cultural links between the ancient Indo-European peoples and their broadly Altaic successors on the steppes.

Much of Spengler's model of "Turan" anticipates more recent discoveries about Indo-European origins. In 2007's *The Horse, the Wheel, and Language: How Bronze-Age Riders from the Eurasian Steppes Shaped the Modern World*, anthropologist David W. Anthony convincingly places the Proto-Indo-European cradle on the Pontic Steppe, which stretches from north of the Black Sea eastward to the region around the north of the Caspian Sea. In arguing for this location as the original seat of the Indo-European cultures, Anthony demonstrates with archeological evidence that the Pontic Steppe was also the site of man's first domestication of the horse. In the process, Anthony affirms Spengler's association of the Proto-Indo-European culture complex with the use of the war chariot.

Spengler anticipates the later 20th-century arguments of Marija Gimbutas about the Proto-Indo-Europeans in somewhat exaggerating the truism that the invading charioteers possessed a culture of

---

killed in action fighting on the Nationalist side of the Spanish Civil War in 1937, Moța would become noted for his skills in international pan-nationalist networking, including Hungarian connections.

21 For Eliade's early feud with Iorga, see Nagy-Talavera, *Nicolae Iorga*, pp. 299–300.

a more patriarchal nature than that of the pre-Indo-European Old Europeans they conquered. However, the latter half of *Early Days of World History* reveals a difference in their hypotheses. Gimbutas painted the vanquished Old European culture as peaceful in nature. Spengler, remember, attributed to Southern European "Atlantis" the conquistador-like prehistory of having appeared in the Middle East and Egypt as an intrusive element, thousands of years before Old Europe itself was overrun by Indo-European "Turan."

Spengler's mature emphasis on anthropology and ethnology raises the question of how much his later theories effectively revise his key theses of *The Decline of the West*. Farrenkopf observes that Spengler's earlier portrait of the Greco-Roman culture is reevaluated by his mature philosophy. *The Decline of the West* often seems downright hostile to what it terms the "Apollonian" culture of the ancient Greeks and early Romans, and denies that culture's affinity with "Faustian Man." But while Farrenkopf is correct to note that Spengler's later work reconsiders these sentiments, Spengler's previous portrait of the "Apollonian" culture as having understood only a closed and purely empirical sense of space remains otherwise unchanged.[22]

Even less altered is Spengler's earlier model of the "Faustian" Western culture, not least because that had already been the most ethnologically oriented of the main civilizational models proposed in *The Decline of the West*. Conceptually rooted in German literature,

---

22 The metamorphosis of Spengler's attitude toward "Faustian Man," from triumphalist to pessimistic to downright apocalyptic, effectively changes the intent of his impressive history of mathematics in the second chapter of the first volume of *The Decline of the West*. Viewed in the context of his entire body of work, it is ambiguous and debatable whether his historiography of the physical sciences is supposed to be a belittlement of the Greco-Roman empiricism, or a rebellion against modern infinitesimals in the vein of Goethe and George Berkeley. Even his original 1918 account of the intellectual history of physical science, for all its apparent appreciation for the "Faustian" scientific achievements, portrays such innovations in constructivist terms, not as universal truths to be literally believed in.

the "Faustian" model quite obviously references the historic Germanic impact on Latin Western Europe as the reason for including the latter in the same category as the Germanic nations. Spengler's posture of completely rejecting historical causality is unable to obscure this premise. (Nor can this feature of his "Faustian" model be successfully divorced from it; neutered of the Germanocentric aspects that make the models of Chamberlain and Spengler concrete cultural conceptions at all, latter-day models of "the West" like Samuel Huntington's come across as sheer nonsense at bottom.)[23] The most famous civilizational model explored in *The Decline of the West* basically remains as described in that book, and is in no way upended by *Early Days of World History*.

Much more dramatically reconsidered in *Early Days of World History* is the third major civilization proposed in *The Decline of the West*. Whereas the "Faustian" West is the latter book's most beloved and influential cultural model, its most confusing and controversial one is the "Magian" civilization. This conception, spanning the first century AD as a living culture, encompasses not only the entire Middle East, but also the historic Constantinople and much of the Balkans.

In contrast to the Germanocentric overtones of the "Faustian" model, Spengler's proposed origin of the "Magian" culture substitutes an architectural style—that of the Roman Pantheon—for any

---

23 Doubly nonsensical is the tendency, tragicomically fashionable today in parts of Eastern Europe (of all regions), to conflate such empty definitions of "Western" with the much different concept "European." The latter term was conceived of, and very much remains, a definition that encompasses all the regions of today's Ukrainian state and the disputed regions equally; Transylvania is not and has never been, by definition, more European than the rest of the modern Romanian state. And even if we wished to mystically reduce entire civilizations to the influence of the great Christian Church theologians—as the Huntingtonians would have us do, insofar as their definition of "Western" is comprehensible at all—then we would still be left with the inconvenient fact that Chrysostom was a European, and Augustine was not.

concrete ethnological foundation whatsoever. That this supposed civilization appears to be a strange mishmash is partly Spengler's point, as shown by his portrait of it as a cultural "pseudomorphosis." Still, despite the great artistry of this concept, its total disregard for ethnological factors makes it the most often criticized feature of *The Decline of the West*. In *Early Days of World History,* Spengler clarifies elements of his "Magian" notion that had previously appeared fairly murky.

The first common point of confusion about the "Magian" civilizational model is the name itself. It must be understood that Spengler's use of this term does not refer to the original Persian Zoroastrian Magi, at least not directly. It is rather a reference to the Magi mentioned in the New Testament. To be sure, the term does invoke the residual ancient Persian influences on the 1st-century Near East, but its immediate reference is to the New Testament rather than the ancient Indo-Persian culture. That the "Magian" model thus takes the Christian religion as its chief focal point also explains why Spengler associates the concept with the Roman Empire's drive to the east — which, after all, is inseparable from the foundations of Christianity. *Early Days of World History* not only makes this Christian connotation obvious, but applies Spengler's earlier concept of a cultural "pseudomorphosis" to the figure of Jesus himself.

In his evaluation of 1st-century Galileans like Jesus, another reason why *The Decline of the West* uses the term "Magian" for Spengler's Christianity-centered civilizational model is revealed. *Early Days of World History* displays Spengler's interest in a theme introduced by some of Richard Wagner's essays to German intellectual (and popular) discourse. Continuing with Houston Stewart Chamberlain and renowned German-American Bible translator Paul Haupt, this tradition of Bible criticism concerned itself with the ancestry of Jesus, and that of the 1st-century Galileans generally.

Chamberlain and Haupt had argued that the Galileans in the time of Jesus were ethnically different from the people of Judea proper. Although not explicitly stated in the Bible, this difference is arguably pointed to in parts of the New Testament, especially the Gospel of Luke. Notably, in the Bible Jesus chooses only fellow Galileans for disciples except one — Judas.[24] In *Early Days of World History*, Spengler contributes to this school of arguments about ethnic differences in ancient Palestine.

In arguing for such differences, Chamberlain and Haupt had pointed to early biblical history, long before the rise of the Romans. In early antiquity the Kingdom of Israel was located north of the Kingdom of Judah. Some archeologists question whether the two kingdoms were ever fully united at all, but the archeological evidence does not rule out a federation.

When the Kingdom of Assyria — which had mastered the technique of population transfers — conquered the Kingdom of Israel, the Assyrians deported the biblical Jews and replaced them with a somewhat mysterious population. Chamberlain had been unable to identify it, speculating on the Phoenicians, but the more authoritative Middle East scholar Haupt argued that the population in question was composed mainly of Iranian Medes. Their descendants, the Galileans, were later forcibly converted to ancient Judaism, but were never fully accepted by their coreligionists in Judea proper to the south. In *Early Days of World History*, Spengler endorses this hypothesis of the Iranian descent of the Galileans.

In this way, another meaning of Spengler's earlier term "Magian" is revealed. In *The Decline of the West*, the word had already invoked the residually Iranian influence on 1st-century Near Eastern culture. *Early Days of World History*, by endorsing Haupt's hypothesis, firmly ties this image of an Iranianized Middle East to the person of Jesus himself.

However, *Early Days of World History* not only endorses this theory of Galilean origins, but expands upon it. In addition to the

---

24 See Richard Wagner et al., *Galilee Against Judea: Wagnerian Bible Criticism* (San Diego: Amory Stern, 2020). This anthology includes the writings of Richard Wagner, Houston Stewart Chamberlain, Paul Haupt, and A. C. Cuza.

hypothesis of a Galilean ethnogenesis proceeding from a population transfer involving Iranians, Spengler argues that racial differences had already existed between the peoples of northerly Israel and southerly Judah, even before the former was vanquished by Assyria. In Spengler's terminology, this would have been before the conquests throughout the Eurasian continent by "Turan."

In contrast to the south of early ancient Palestine, according to Spengler, the people of the north of that region reflected the intrusive element of Old European "Atlantis." *Early Days of World History* discusses the piratical "Sea Peoples" that menaced ancient Egypt as prototypical of this "Atlantic" element's prehistory in the earliest civilizations. In this way, Spengler amends the emphasis that Chamberlain and Haupt had placed on the Assyrian population transfer as foundational to the Galilean ethnogenesis. Spengler rather portrays that event as having added the Iranian element to the preexisting anthropological differences that had already previously distinguished Israel from Judah.

Spengler attributes not only racial differences but accompanying ethical ones to the north and south of early ancient Palestine. *Early Days of World History* emphatically asserts that the northern component of the ancient Israelites, in the times of early antiquity described by the Old Testament, had produced "kings" rather than "prophets." With this portrait of the prehistory of 1st-century Galilee, Spengler contributes to what had been Chamberlain's poorly understood central argument — not that "pure Aryan" ancestry was the norm in the Galilee of Jesus, which Chamberlain had in fact doubted, but that the Galileans were an inherently anti-legalistic people. By thus revealing to the reader his thoughts on the foundational starting point of his "Magian" concept, Spengler renders the latter notion altogether clearer than it had appeared in *The Decline of the West*.

One of the unchanged aspects of Spengler's older "Magian" model, that of Mohammed as comparable to Oliver Cromwell as a great agent of the megalopolis epoch within the high culture to which he belonged, may confuse or surprise some readers in our century. Since 2001, Islam has enjoyed an arch-traditionalistic and anti-modern mystique, both in a good and a bad way. The modernist and essentially liberal critiques of Islam that have come into fashion have fed into the perception stemming from the affinity felt by key paragons of the Perennial Traditionalist school toward the Islamic religion. In the process, virtually no one has bothered to question whether this image is even historically accurate. In this regard, Spengler's characterization of Islam provides a refreshing reminder of an overlooked feature of Islamic history.

It has been forgotten that the Islamic world, before the early modern rise of England, came much closer to modern urban capitalism than the whole of Europe did. Before being outdone by London in this regard, Ottoman Istanbul was the largest city in the world. Medieval Islam was very much a force for "*Zivilisation,*" in the German sense immortalized by Spengler. (Only one medieval Islamic empire provides a stark exception to this paradigm, namely the reign of the city-destroying steppe warlord Tamerlane.)

This part of Spengler's "Magian" model is therefore one of the more accurate aspects of it. A strong feature of the second volume of *The Decline of the West*, Spengler's characterization of Islamic history is more penetrating than many, if not most, contemporary portraits of that subject — in the overall picture, if not necessarily in scholarship. *Early Days of World History* does not alter this part of his body of work, though it perhaps invites his previous picture of Islam to be seen in a new light.

Early Days of World History demonstrates an early understanding of the ancient Indo-European incursions into East Asia. Spengler is aware of the proto-Tocharian presence in the early history of China, and he argues that Genghis Khan's Mongols resembled Indo-European peoples in physical appearance. This demonstrated knowledge of little-known aspects of East Asian history clarifies what had previously stood alone as puzzling remarks in *The Hour of Decision*, such as his ascription of a "Nordic world-feeling" to certain East Asian cultures.

Spengler covers not only China and Central Asia but also Japan. Elaborated upon in *Early Days of World History* is a theory mentioned only in passing in *The Hour of Decision*. Spengler argues that the Amerindian elements of today's Latin America, for whose history Spengler was noted for his respect, are anthropologically related to the Japanese. Spengler's impressive analyses concerning the history of Asia illustrate the links between the Proto-Indo-Europeans and the later Central Asian cultures, the beliefs of which have sometimes been grouped with Japanese Shinto in the ethnological super-family "Altaic."

During the interwar era, when *Early Days of World History* was written, the study of the Altaic group of cultures was popular in Northeast Asia. It was a central topic among Korean intellectual circles during the time when Imperial Japan occupied early 20th-century Korea. For one pioneering Korean historian from that period — who has since been accused of supporting the Japanese occupiers of Korea — this field of scholarship contributed to the consciousness of a Northeast Asian identity, distinct from Chinese civilization.

Early 20th-century Korean historian Ch'oe Namsŏn proposed a reconstructed prototype of what he considered a primordial Altaic religion. He called this religious tradition "The Way of *Park*" and located its prototype in ancient Korea. In this hypothesis, the region around Korea was the primeval cradle of both Shamanism and Shinto. It would be enlightening to compare Ch'oe's model with Spengler's identification of the Korea peninsula as, at one time, an easternmost range of Northern European peoples on the Eurasian continent.

One scholar of Ch'oe Namsŏn notes that at the time, Ch'oe represented a "new breed of Korean historian" with a tendency to hold ideas of a "Confucian or Sino-centric nature" under suspicion.[25] In

---

25 Chizuko T. Allen, "Northeast Asia Centered Around Korea: Ch'oe Namsŏn's View of History," *The Journal of Asian Studies*, Vol. 49, No. 4 (Nov., 1990), pp.

this way, the controversial Korean historian fused Altaic studies with an intellectual trope that was also popular in Imperial Japan. This trend propounded a Nietzschesque rebellion against Confucianism as a slavish and emasculating philosophy, a critique that was often contrasted with the heroism of the historic Northeast Asian peoples — including horse-driven ones like the Jurchens and the Mongols.

Accordingly, *Early Days of World History* bears a striking resemblance to attitudes and topics of interest prominent in Imperial Japan. In *Radical Nationalist in Japan: Kita Ikki, 1883–1937*, George M. Wilson provides an illuminating intellectual summary of the pan-Asian thinker of the study's title. "Rejecting future reliance on Western civilization," explains Wilson, "Kita turned his back on the Eastern heritage at the same time. Instead of the fundamental Chinese tradition of Confucianism and the civil society, he stressed the tradition of the warlike Mongol hordes."[26] This description reveals how Spengler's mature civilizational sentiments had influential counterparts in interwar-era East Asia.

Early Days of World History highlights another overlooked point about Asian history. Despite what was noted above about the Turco-Mongolians representing an altogether different ethnic family than their Indo-European predecessors in horse-driven semi-nomadism, there is conversely a case to be made for a certain cultural line of continuity between them. In *Empires of the Silk Road: A History of Central Eurasia from the Bronze Age to the Present*, Christopher I. Beckwith writes of a "Central Eurasian Culture Complex" spanning from the prehistoric Pontic Steppe to the downfall of the Central Asian cultures in modern times.[27] While this model obviously glosses over many im-

---

787–806 (20 pages), Association for Asian Studies.

26 George M. Wilson, *Radical Nationalist in Japan: Kita Ikki, 1883–1937* (Cambridge, Mass.: Harvard University Press, 1969), p. 87.

27 Christopher I. Beckwith, *Empires of the Silk Road: A History of Central Eurasia from the Bronze Age to the Present* (Princeton, New Jersey: Princeton University Press, 2009).

portant ethnic factors, it evocatively draws attention to the remarkable points of consistency in technological culture and social organization in the history of the steppe lands.

This unbroken cultural link, in spite of the historical ethnic changes, lends much support to an observation pointed to by Spengler in *Early Days of World History,* and later in much of Eliade's work: in all probability, the traditional "Altaic" religious attitudes represent the oldest and relatively purest prototype of the primeval Proto-Indo-European ones. For the purpose of any reconstructive effort, this discovery provides a crucial supplement to the older method of determining Proto-Indo-European spiritual inclinations by comparing and contrasting the Greco-Roman and Indo-Iranian civilizations.

For Spengler, this spiritual affinity with the steppe cultures also signifies a sentiment that his work had always evinced, a conviction that seemingly deepened with every book he wrote. His known disgust with the historical phenomenon he had deemed *"Zivilisation"* hardened in his mature work. Spengler's model of "Turan" provides his last answer to the questions he had raised by this hostile stance.

Early Days of World History depicts the Proto-Indo-European hordes of "Turan" as having laid waste to the comparatively urbanized settlements of the older cultures. Like many of the book's assertions, this one has since been proven accurate by archeological research. The Proto-Indo-Europeans apparently first established their reign of destruction in the region later associated with the resulting ancient Thracian tribes, in today's Romania and Bulgaria.

From 4200 to 3900 BC, long before the Indo-European peoples reached Greece or India, over six hundred Old European (pre-Indo-European) settlements, writes David W. Anthony, "were burned in the lower Danube valley and eastern Bulgaria." Their Old European inhabitants tried to escape to a settlement in Jilava (located in present-day Romania), explains Anthony, but "Jilava was burned, apparently suddenly, leaving behind whole pots and many other artifacts."[28] The Thracian region was completely overrun from the northeast by the horsemen from the steppe.

Regarding this invasion, which established the destructive style that would mark the later Proto-Indo-European expansions throughout Europe and Asia, Thracian Scholar R. F. Hoddinott observes:

> In favorable conditions this eastern infiltration might have given new impetus to the flowering Carpatho-Balkan civilization. Instead, the climate continued to deteriorate and the Yamnaya [Proto-Indo-European] trickle became a torrent, causing a general population surge southwards with increasing conflict for land capable of supporting fewer and fewer people. Complete destruction overtook the wealthy Chalcolithic [Copper Age Old European] settlements north and south of the Danube. Few ever recovered.[29]

In addition to its prescient prehistorical accuracy, Spengler's portrayal of the Proto-Indo-European invasions also invokes a trope stemming from what had already been well-known about medieval Central Asian steppe cultures and their conquests. The career of the great Transoxianian warlord Tamerlane, for instance, would appear to justify the image of "Turanic" peoples as lethal enemies of urbanized cultures. Although not the first example of this archetype's presence in written European history, which is older than Attila the Hun, Tamerlane apparently inspired the first influential European cultural trend to glorify it.

From Christopher Marlowe to Prince Cantemir to Edgar Allan Poe, Tamerlane enjoys a long cultural history as a Romantic figure, dating from centuries before the term "Romanticism" would have even been understood. Marlowe's notable astuteness about ideas and events from Continental Europe, together with Tamerlane's status as Europe's benefactor against the Ottoman threat, suggests that Marlowe's

---

28 Anthony, *The Horse, the Wheel, and Language*, p. 227.

29 R. F. Hoddinott, *The Thracians* (New York: Thames and Hudson, 1981), p. 24.

sympathetic late 16th-century portrait was partially of older origin. (It was Renaissance Venice, in Spengler's model a main "Faustian" force for the spirit of "*Zivilisation*" in its time, that had nearsightedly and fatefully foiled Tamerlane's aim of finishing off the Ottoman dynasty after he had defeated the latter in the late 14th century.) The image of a mighty conqueror from the steppe, destroying cities and with them comparatively urban civilizations, had thus already been celebrated in European cultures long before *Early Days of World History* was written.

As noted above, Spengler asserts in *Early Days of World History* that "urbanisation is racial decay." This statement summarizes a theme that had previously been explored in *Man and Technics* and *The Hour of Decision*. Spengler's work of the 1930s continues his dim depiction of the metahistorical phenomenon of "*Zivilisation*," which had already been articulated in *The Decline of the West*. His mature work expands this argument from a historical thesis to an anthropological one.

As Spengler's contempt for the onset of urbanizing "*Zivilisation*" grew even more pronounced in the 1930s, his literary depiction of its essence somewhat changed. *The Decline of the West* had likened the epochal shift from "*Kultur*" to "*Zivilisation*" to the aging and natural death of an organism. The book's systematic rigor in using this metaphor would seem to suggest that Spengler had intended its latent determinism to be taken more or less literally.

That deterministic attitude would be challenged by Carl Schmitt in his 1929 essay "The Age of Neutralizations and Depoliticizations," reprinted in the 1932 edition of Schmitt's *The Concept of the Political*. Naming *The Decline of the West* as representative of the kind of late Wilhelmine thinking criticized in the essay, Schmitt calls into question Spengler's notions about the differences between an organic spirit and a mechanical one. In particular, Schmitt criticizes the idea that such a difference can be attributed to a natural process like death of old age.

"The spirit of technicity," according to Schmitt, "is still spirit. Perhaps an evil and demonic spirit, but not one which can be dismissed as mechanistic… It is perhaps something gruesome… fantastic and satanic, but not simply dead, spiritless, or mechanized soullessness."[30] Life, concludes Schmitt, does not struggle with death; life struggles with life.[31] This critique illustrates a change in Spengler's later work, which portrays "*Zivilisation*" in even more sinister terms than Spengler had before.

The 1933 political polemic *The Hour of Decision* reflects this alteration in Spengler's depiction of an urbanized and culturally empty "*Zivilisation*." Spengler's organic metaphor of this phenomenon as comparable to a natural death is still sometimes used in *The Hour of Decision*, but this time the comparison comes across as far more poetical than real. In contrast to his earlier dismissal of historical causality, the book's political analysis singles out concrete culprits behind the proverbially Spenglerian dilemma of cultural death.

The Hour of Decision formulates a socioeconomic theory portraying urban capitalism and urban socialism as naturally inclined to collude against society's agrarian sectors.[32] Furthermore, the book ties

---

30 Carl Schmitt, translated by George Schwab, *The Concept of the Political: Expanded Edition* (Chicago: The University of Chicago Press, 2007), p. 94.

31 Schmitt's conclusion: "Whoever knows no other enemy than death and recognizes in his enemy nothing more than an empty mechanism is nearer to death than life. The comfortable antithesis of the organic and the mechanistic is itself something crudely mechanistic. A grouping which sees on the one side only spirit and life and on the other only death and mechanism signifies nothing more than a renunciation of the struggle and amounts to nothing more than a romantic lament. For life struggles not with death, spirit not with spiritlessness; spirit struggles with spirit, life with life, and out of the power of an integral understanding of this arises the order of human things." Schmitt, tr. Schwab, *The Concept of the Political: Expanded Edition*, pp. 95–96.

32 This is another point on which Spengler's thought should not be viewed as idiosyncratic. That agrarian interests were a priority for many in Spengler's time is best shown in Freikorps veteran Ernst von Salomon's *It Cannot Be Stormed*, a semi-fictionalized account of a farmers' revolt led by the author's own brother

these urbanizing forces not only to widespread infertility and the decline of public morality, but also to the increasing rampancy of mental illness and lack of physical fitness.[33] "*Zivilisation*" is still presented as a superhuman historical force in the Hegelian vein, but no longer as one comparable to the destined withering of a plant. Rather, per Schmitt's suggestion, the spirit of "*Zivilisation*" now appears as a malevolent force of darkness, as the mortal enemy of life-giving "*Kultur.*" In *Early Days of World History,* written in the years following the publication of *The Hour of Decision,* Spengler has found in the distant past his final answer to the menace of the megalopolis.

Early Days of World History is a mandatory and overlooked part of Spengler's body of work. It adds much to his already formidable record of achievement as a philosopher of history. Written in the mid-1930s, this posthumously published draft completes his career as

---

in the Weimar years. But whereas Salomon's brother's ideology was economically populist and fused contemporary National Socialist and Communist influences alike, *The Hour of Decision* expresses a socioeconomic elitism based on appreciation for "the country gentleman" as the historic bearer of high culture. For example, the book's depiction of ancient Rome is marked by obvious admiration for the Roman warlord Sulla, whose era is represented as parallel to the contemporary West (as of interwar times) in Spengler's cyclical historical model. *The Hour of Decision* glorifies Sulla as a defender of land-bound wealth against the increasing onslaught of usury-driven wealth, and portrays as Sulla's finest moment his annihilation of Rome's proto-capitalist equites for threatening to become a banking class. Within the Weimar generation of German nationalist intellectuals, the revolutionary populism of Salomon and his brother seems the perfect foil to Spengler's elitism — ironically, as Salomon came from a Prussian noble family of medieval Venetian origin, while Spengler was the son of a coal miner.

33 One of Spengler's lifelong inspirations, Werner Sombart, would in turn be heavily influenced by the arguments about population economics presented in *The Hour of Decision.* In particular, Sombart would expand upon Spengler's critique of modern medicine as aging Western populations produced more "graybeards" than children. A year after *The Hour of Decision* was published, Sombart would explore that theme in 1934's *Deutscher Sozialismus* (German Socialism), translated into English in 1937 as *A New Social Philosophy.*

a cultural critic and civilizational historiographer, which had begun in 1918.

Whether or not one agrees with Spengler's philosophical notions of "Culture" and "Civilization," his work invites the reader to think about what those words mean, beyond the standard dictionary definitions. In this way, Spengler's work is recommended for acquiring the understanding required to avoid the use of those terms as platitudes or empty slogans, which renders them meaningless. As the final chapter of Spengler's irreplaceable oeuvre, *Early Days of World History* is a vital contribution to the task of evaluating the concepts of culture and civilization critically.

San Diego, California
February 23, 2022

I. HISTORY AND HISTORIOGRAPHY

THE INTENTION OF THE BOOK

1

PREHISTORIANS LOOK for the epochs of human history in museum objects — equipment, fabric. I look for them in the epochs of human soul life. *That* is the fundamental thing. Everything else is [a] consequence of it.

2

Very sharply against the current direction, which has finally confused history with cultural history. World history is the history of states, wars and power, not the history of styles and intellectual currents. Everything only becomes historical when it is shaped politically: Church, not religion; commerce, not works of art; art and poetry do not count at all — they are an escape from reality.

I gave the theory of form in *The Decline of the West*. Here I give the story itself.

3

Introduction: 'World history' is the outcome of an insoluble conflict [between] soul [and] spirit, an image of mental turmoil, a hopeless, self-destructive struggle of the innermost life of the soul, whose temporal image are battles, kings, religions, techniques. Yet it is the life power that leads and *uses* the spirit, religion, technology, morality in its battles. Not the religions, [but] the *churches* are world-historical, not the inventors, but the political, economic *exploiters* of the inventions.

4

Introduction: To show in one great example — the only one that can be overlooked — how the 'two ages' [merge], a *high* culture [emerges] from a primitive world. The enormous connections to the Baltic Sea, the Congo and Ceylon.

How a crisis quietly appears, mystically, suddenly, birth of the soul.

5

Here, in broad outline, developing the sense of 'world history'. Sense of world history: the prerequisite is the 'human soul' of historical style, alienated from universal nature by the habit of the eye and the mind, and becoming detached around 5000. The predominant features of the spiritualised inner life, for which past — present — future have become conscious! As image, environment, goal. The after- and foreknowledge. Thus man becomes a historical being: c suffering history, d final thunderstorm. Ahistorical is the negation of an existing victory, historical the affirmation.

World history is organised events, with an ever clearer view of what has happened and what is to come. Mockery of itself: for nevertheless it is a suffering of a tragic doom! Hubris. Here the problem of the personal and the super-personal. The 'we' is culture, the 'I' is carrier, annihilator, decay. 'I' is linguistically hybrid, racially sterile. Individuality is the form of atomisation.

Soul of the landscape: epitome of all-nature, with which primeval man lives in alliance, alienated from historical man as a shell: in him (race) is also still a piece of 'landscape'. Thus the spirit stands, tearing itself apart, between nature inside and outside, poisoning the latter and the former, itself driven, succumbing. Grandiose perspective!

6

Accordingly, history is the 'public' history of the great multiplicities, borne by the significant individuals, and not the private fate of each individual without regard to his rank — whether by tradition, custom or his own force. But it is not the thin-blooded intellectuals who decide, but the thoroughbreds of the adventurers, fighters, stewards, victors.

World history is the history of human thoroughbreds that wither away in the spirit. It does not depend on the individual. The death of however many is replaced by the fertility of the mothers: the stream of life continues. And where this is not the case, it is over, even if every barren individual life remains. But the conflict is between the tendency of the masses and the strong few.

7

History as the stream of individual, irrevocable, unique deeds and perpetrators is what is told and can *only* be told. Historiography is therefore poetry, epic or tragic poetry, with an eye for destinies: otherwise one remains [stuck] in the auxiliary knowledge and foreknowledge of data collection. But one can only narrate what one sees vividly in front of one, not the form of the action, but the fact of the action. And where the data have disappeared, the history that actually existed but was forgotten can only be guessed at. The form is preserved, not the essence. It is little: but the deeper the poet sees the unforgotten, the more clearly he senses the forgotten in the remains.

8

Appendix and introduction: 'World history' in the narrower sense is the history of high cultures. The inner form, not the banal existence of documents, sets it apart from the preceding [stages]. A whole as an act, as an image, as a form, as a destiny. Whoever undertakes to describe world history must know what he wants. The mere reproduction of knowledge of what has happened is banal. Not the image, the meaning of the image is the task. The 19th century, banal to the point of unbearable, rationalistic, common sense, did that. But no one puts more into a picture than he has to put into it. A world history for a flat-head *is* flat[1]. Progressive philistines, democrats, evolutionists, utilitarian idiots.

World history is a tragic fate. Its scenes are battlefields of insoluble mental conflicts. Its legacy is corpses and ruins. It is stupid and cowardly to try to cover this up like the literati. Not their agony, but their greatness should be understood. No complaints, but pride! No evasion, but taking notice! As Aeschylus saw [the] Oresteia and Shakespeare saw Macbeth, the humanity of world history is tragic and great. When, in dark primeval times, human understanding invented fire, there was the doom in the march that was once fulfilled: the stepping out of the all-living nature, the defiance against it, the will to be different, stronger than it, and this rose up to the subjugation of nature, hubris. For despite everything, the human soul remained nature. In [man] himself the struggle broke out between nature here and the other there, in which he grew up to the immense greatness of suffering, victory and perishing, devastated the image of the earth, in order to finally succumb: the late man is again one with nature, a remnant, a corpse. But we, we today, who stand on the summit of one of these battles of the soul, victims and spectators at the same time, we should have the pride of the fencer.

How many are there — who can experience like this? The mass of men are mean. The common man wants nothing from life but length, health, entertainment, comfort — 'happiness'. Those who do not *despise* this should turn their eyes away from world history, for it contains nothing of the kind. Greatness in suffering is the best thing it has created.

------

1 'Flat' means 'superficial' in this context. — *Transl.*

9

World history is conscious history. The knowledge of aims, possibilities, means, the memory of successes and defeats, the presentiment or [the] hope of happiness, fame as the form of personal afterlife among personalities — all this distinguishes history from events, having history from merely suffering a fate, making history from mere instinctive acts. To history belongs the horizon of space and time, of distance, on which the willed, planned or past doing and suffering stands out. It begins with reflection in the form of speaking, first the small, daily, individual doing, growing over doing for life — life as an overall view of meaning, time, content — and rising from culture to culture to Faustian doing in the perspectives of the infinite, the universe and the millennia: Napoleon.

10

Reason why world history only begins in 3000. Until then, there is only a generic history of the human species. And even in the rise of primitive cultures there is only a history of forms. The individual event is indifferent, for it does not make an epoch. In these primitive peoples the distance of the best from the rest is not great. What happens, happens from the middle. The tribe acts, thinks, feels. The individual is only the scene and the expression of this action. The very fact that this action spreads over a wide area, is earthy, testifies to the impersonality even of individual life. At the beginning of all high cultures, the city stands as a symbol of the soul: people congregate at one point, and here 'history' comes into being.

It is the drive of the racial in the storms of life, of which every individual life contains a spark, but the being driven is grasped in deeds, resolution, aim, will, and here the individual is not only bearer but also leader. Here begins the decisive separation of peoples into subject and object of action: leader and victim, hero and mob. Each of these cultures is a struggle between them. The hero, creator, leader *begets* the culture, the masses gnaw at it, parasitise.

11

Always emphasise how the masculine history of deeds is thwarted by the feminine history of family (Napoleon, Servilia, Habsburg), i.e. marriages, protection, favouring of relatives. The 'history of ideas' is a fantasy. It only depends on who uses the ideas and how. Münzer, for example: how the ideas of democracy are used by only a few rich families. That is where the nepotism of the popes belongs.

12

Accordingly, I do not divide history into ages and not into geographical historical districts, but into forms: Prehistory, High History, Posthistory. All three are filled with states and battles, deeds and thoughts of individuals, except that they mean little at the beginning, much in the middle, and nothing at the end.

13

At the turn of the 5th/4th millennium it begins like this, from two points of human ascent, focal points of spiritualisation: dolmen[2] and Kash. There are no 'peoples' yet. Everything is nameless. But ideas of this kind seize populations, radiate on, drift past. In the north active, wandering, in the south passive, interpreting. All living creation comes from the north, from privation, from coldness. The south has the saturation, the sun. Life is flame. The south receives, the north begets.

I tell and leave the evidence for later.

14

Bringing out the overall situation of the book much deeper. The premise is the first age between the Ice Age and high culture. Since the great 'races' according to language, art, myth, etc. [record]. Now if it is a fact that in every culture a counter-soul is formed which is

---

2   A dolmen is a stone monument made of two or more upright stones with a single stone slab lying across them. — *Transl.*

very sharply characterised locally, this should be connected with the phenomenon of down-to-earth races. As well as the Yankee becomes Indian, so well is the true Frenchman caveman of the Aurignacian race.

The sadistic emanates from Florence (Etruscan) and Paris (Aurignacian), the Dionysian from the ancestral homes of the pre-Dorians. Think of the Dravida and Yangtse art, in the Magian of the Arab-Persian contrast, in Egypt of the contrast between Upper Egyptian and Western Delta art, which has only been preserved in Cretan form (the latter is ornamental and anti-plastic!). Epic, novella (*1001 Nights* is Persian) belong to the plastic (image), art lyric (Trovatore, Arabia) and fable to the ornamental. The German epic originates from homo alpinus (the pictorial dance of the *Schuhplattler*[3]), German music from the Germanic tribes (the ornamental dance of the waltz). The art of building belongs to ornamentation. Both are pure symbolism, priestly. Imitative pictorial art is more vital. But one must go deeper: the Constantinian portrait is ornament of the soul ('stylised')!

15

If science first [digs] and finds a rift between the 'Palaeolithic' and the 'Neolithic': if it finds shards, bones, ploughs, graves, it has remained blind: it has found traces of artificial life that has progressed from the organic to the organised, from the ancestral to the deliberate, from the useful to the making. The soul is different. A world of new feelings dominates life. The tree of knowledge! On it have grown hate and love, anguish of soul and exuberance, cruelty and pity, 'truth', 'justice', etc. The higher man is great and terrible. Over his existence — for how much longer? — there is an air of happiness and a fearful will of torment and suffering. For knowledge harbours suffering, and science

---

3   *Schuhplattler* is the name of a dance from the Eastern Alps. *Schuhplattler* also refers to the people performing this dance. The dance is characterised by hand strokes on the thighs and shoes. — *Transl.*

is the tragedy of this too-much-knowledge, which spilled over into in-finite suffering, which he inflicted on himself and others and received from himself and others.

16

What is world history? First of all, not human history in general, but its course in the age of high culture, where it is known, where it has epochs. So city, state. But then not history of the spirit (art, religion, science), but of life, of blood, of races. Not private history (biography), but 'being in form' of life itself in generations: political, whereby economy and spirit are classified as motives. State and history [are] interchangeable terms. War and politics [are] identical: against ideo-logical blather. Everything spiritual changes nothing. Facts and truths.

17

World history is [the] conflict of nature in man and apart from man, akin to the other great spectacles of nature in which its life cur-rents collide with one another — the earthquake, the thunderstorm, the storm. The beauty of destruction, the greatness of the will to win. It is stupid and disgusting to seek 'progress' in the pursuit of utility and usefulness in it. From the point of view of the philistine of prog-ress, history is meaningless — thank God. The man-made powers of nature race against the others.

18

World history is the history of beings and their deeds? Since every deed is directed against something that is to be overcome, transformed, inserted, extinguished, in order to assert one life against another, it is violent. Since it always and everywhere acts in a way that mild brood-ing cannot bear, it is criminal — criminal in the noble sense. Since it sets life against life, it is bloody and kills in order to promote life. It is not and cannot be anything else: there is no history as the evolution of ideas: 'intellectual history', as philosophers understand it, is the view over the changing conceits of individual schools and races, may they be called truths, thoughts or principles. It stands to the real history of the world no differently than looking at the waves.

19

Dark secret: Hebbel[4]: 'But never touch the sleep of the world'. The spirit does it — that is the great guilt in the tragedy of humanity. Nature takes revenge by destroying human beings. For it is the nature and task of the spirit to awaken the world; but this is precisely what brings disaster. Nature does not mock it. But the sleep of the world is its fault, measured against the idea of the spirit. The waking is the fault of the spirit, measured against the idea of nature — Hebbel's opinion.

20

What I am writing is a *tragedy*. The 'history of the world' in this aspect is tragic: man who has become 'free' in the struggle against the world — for himself, in himself, in the other man. The higher man is a doom. With his graves, he leaves the earth as a battlefield and a place of ruins. He has drawn plant and animal, sea and mountain, into his ruin. He has drawn the face of the world in blood, mutilated it, torn it apart. But there was greatness in it. When he is no more, his fate will have been something great. And blessed are those who live to see times of such greatness.

21

Even if I free 'world history' from the medieval scheme (antiquity — Middle Ages — modern times) and look at it independently of my own situation, the entire inner form of looking is nevertheless conditioned by the place and time of my individual life: no man can get away from it. What I see is only conditionally true for the Chinese and Indians. If the Chinese becomes a Christian, [his faith] is Taoism in a Christian version.

---

4   Christian Friedrich Hebbel (1813–1863) was a German playwright and
    poet. — *Transl.*

22

The higher historiography of German style (Ranke[5], Meyer[6], Taine[7]) is romanticism and will die out with it. I am the last. The English is rationalistic, shallow, causal, untragic.

23

As to disposition: In the first volume only a few large stages of time, hence the individual areas of the soul aphoristic, more questioning than answering. But immediately localised: on the globe as near the sun, near the ice, near the sea, far from the sea, plains, heights. From the beginning, there are leading and following or creatively accompanying and lagging regions — is the landscape decisive as the root of the souls or is the soul free from the power of the landscape so that it can also wander creatively?

Time limit for vol. I around 4000, thus concluding with the completion of grammar, metal casting, sun god.

24

'World history' in the proper sense does not begin with human beings. It describes the fate of higher humanity, even if it describes its more primitive age. A great deal has to happen before the soul's most important elements within the whole of humanity come to experience history instead of suffering events. But in the course of the destinies of the species *Homo* — humanity is nothing more than a presumptuous title for it — the point occurs only very late — here and there, by no means everywhere — when the structure of human works, spiritual as well as material, becomes a power for man himself, when 'culture' is

---

5 Leopold von Ranke (1795–1886) was a German historian and one of the founders of modern source-based historical science. — *Transl.*

6 Eduard Meyer (1855–1930) was an important German historian, Egyptologist and orientalist. — *Transl.*

7 Hippolyte Adolphe Taine (1828–1893) was a French historian and literary critic. — *Transl.*

thus not only an expression but an understood, omnipotent expression and thus becomes the environment. But I am still silent here about the long and rich prehistory, because it is metaphysical expression and can only be opened up metaphysically. Here the human soul is born and matures. From then on it is completed in its basic features and now begins to create. The epitome of this creation is the world whose story is told.

So there is a transition from the history of the soul to the history of the world: from the mysteries of the soul to the image of a world of human creation. This is how I understand 'world history'. This world of creation is meant.

25

What needs to be overcome today is the flint and potsherd materialism of the time when steam engines and telegraph wires were taken for the meaning and epitome of 'culture'. In this first century of descent, [the] nineteenth century, one confuses symptoms and the meaning of life, and if indeed for the white masses of our cities, the learned and unlearned, symptoms constitute the whole meaning of existence, this is only a symptom of the fact that existence has become meaningless, superfluous, has reached its end. But that was not the case here, in the beginning. If one chooses today's distinctions, then these first people were not technicians, but dreamers, foreboding, tormented, awakening dreamers. And what is significant about the fist wedges and bell cups is not that they made life more comfortable — that was not felt at all — but that the soul urged towards forms that were heavy with symbolism.

If the shard orderers lack metaphysical depth, the cultural circle theory lacks above all historical sense. 'Strata' are not ages. Tempo, duration and direction are the elements of historical time, not mere juxtaposition. But while the shard orderers only throw around millennia because the secret of becoming is closed to them, the ethnographers have forgotten the difference between *millennium* and *decade*.

And yet the whole secret of history, of the soul, of life lies in time, in when, how long, how fast, in why and where to. And though the why will remain an eternal mystery, which we only grope at, reverently or curiously, the when and where are the deepest symbol of what we suspect.

26

One can divide the history of humanity into two great periods: into a time of ascent, where the human soul is being formed, and where all external events, coming into being and passing away are meaningless in relation to the metaphysical construction of what underlies future events (as the expression of them), and into a time of inner possession, where this soul is finished in its structure and now life is to [take] shape, ever richer, finer, more dangerous: where, to an increasing degree, the single event has its significance.

I hope soon [to be able to present] [the account] of that first period, the early and youthful history of the soul. Here we shall recount what happened in the history of the effects of the mature soul. For this is the difference: the event gives fullness and meaning to the times. The inner prerequisites are there. So creation of the soul, with which life receives meaning, creation of life through the finished soul. Thus from the organic to the organised, [from] fate to causality. This is only to be hinted at here.

27

The world-view of the Faustian man of the Last Days, brave, sceptical, deep, not what is 'true', but what is real to us, the people of the late Occident, an image with which we grow, which we ourselves are, which each individual, insofar as he has depth, seeks, suspects darkly within himself, to make this clear to him, is my task.

28

And one must understand one's time! For there can only be a world-view out of a time; 'eternal' images are nonsense.

29

Looking and 'writing': Every creative urge is visionary — poetic. One sees an image into the woman (or man). Sexual love is added to the sexual urge. Likewise the poetic in the will to power: conquering, annihilating, cruelty. Lust in killing. Burning, destroying, creating. Alexander, Napoleon. Every great doer (Stinnes[8], Bismarck) is a 'poet'. (Kreuger[9], Borkman[10].) The 'deed' is born as poetry. Otherwise one is only subaltern: calculator, organiser, bureaucrat. To be poetic [is] to have ideas. Show is idea.

30

That most thinkers imagine they have found 'the' truth that all should find correct is grotesque. I content myself with describing my metaphysics in the hope of helping kindred souls to form theirs.

31

With every learned philosophy one must first scrape off the scholastic crust to see what kind of philosopher lies behind it; with most of them it turns out: none at all. In Eckart's case[11], for example, it is quite different from what the scholarly varnish suggests.

32

How this world has changed! A laughing world-spirit above the gears looks down today on respectable top hats, swords, stars of orders, and a breath earlier on state wigs and gallantry swords, where once the

---

8   Hugo Stinnes (1870–1924) was a German politician and industrialist. After World War One, he was considered Germany's 'business kaiser'. — *Transl.*

9   Ivar Kreuger (1880–1932) was a Swedish tycoon who built a global match empire. — *Transl.*

10 John Gabriel Borkman, a character in Henrik Ibsen's play of the same name, is a banker who speculated with his clients' money. — *Transl.*

11 Meister Eckhart (1260–1328) was a Dominican friar in Thuringia, Germany. He was a scholastic philosopher and theologian, and the main representative of German mysticism. — *Transl.*

stone axe flashed in the forest, — and somewhere in the corner of the stone deserts that are called cities, sit bespectacled schoolmasters, well guarded against the world's doings, and fiddle over the notions and conclusions, jealous of each other, tireless in words and writing, and communicate the result to disciples, that they may multiply it among themselves in the same important way. No one cares.

33

These professional views! What was originally the goal of all research, to understand human development, they have long since lost sight of. Each subject has its own conceptual world through which one only sees what fits in it. At a point where people lived and died, one sees a 'Neolithic station', another 'Linear Pottery'[12], the third a Neanderthal skull. The former knows only the series of hand wedges in undisturbed position, the latter the burner layer. As if from another world, concepts such as pre-Indo-European inflection resound — one no longer sees people, but letters.

I certainly do not want to create a 'new' method of cognition. There is no such thing. I only want to remind everyone of ways of knowing that everyone uses every day without realising it. The whole treasure of experience we have is based on such 'undiscovered' methods.

34

What the historian [is] not able to separate: history as the mental image before his inner eye with a mental order, and history as the moved in the universe. 'A people enters into history' — into the image or into the stream? The former changes through a found book, the latter through mutation.

12　The Linear Pottery culture is the oldest farming culture of the Neolithic period in Central Europe with permanent settlements, c. 5500–4500 B.C. — *Transl.*

35

To lose oneself completely in these distant times, one must be a poet — or a painter — on a late summer day in the south, and a glass of sunny wine in one's head. Then you see these millennia before you, in the middle of a landscape like a fairy tale. If you only ponder them at your desk and strain your poor logic, the glow of these early times will never shine on you.

36

Criticism of research: What lies before us, piled up, sorted, described by industrious collectors and folders, are the remains of works. Works are the results of deeds. Deeds are expressions of souls. Whether potsherds or genitives or traces of battles — they are always debris as witnesses of a life, of a series of deeds, of a soul. How little is left? How distorted, one-sided, conditional. What a mistake to want to deduce the extent of the soul from the sum of the remains: but there are no remains of ideas and resolutions. The debris is in itself banal, the most worthless of all. Where they determine the level of conclusions, science itself is worthless, insubstantial, soulless. Here, in echoing sounds, people speak to us. Only a poet relives them, who can awaken a world from a trace. For of [the] works only stone and metal survive, only the rest for the eye. The sounds, music, dance, the stories, scenes, deeds, the attitude, [all that] is missing, the will is lost. If we cannot call them up from the abyss of the past, research is worthless. It does not matter whether one collects weapons, skulls, shards or stamps. And carry into the destroyed image of the remains the little egoism of the day: progress, expediency, lack of physical knowledge as the origin of religion — how banal, how stupid it all is!

37

To show for prehistory a mistake which 'world history' has also committed, and which comes from the fact that today it is specialist scholars alone who lead the word, who have their 'material' to bully.

The word of Ranke that history begins where documents exist — no, my lord, that is where the box of notes begins, not history itself! Or did the Romans once begin to be historical exactly where we have the oldest scraps of manuscript? Hubris!

But so is the prehistorian. The 'finds' limit history, and according to the division of the finds they divide the periods. Poor people of a prehistoric age! If they make a scraper of wood instead of stone, they are no longer our business, for we do not find the scraper.

What I want, there as here, is the liberation of the historical gaze — the physiognomic tact — from the coincidence of preserved objects or testimonies, by training a kind of reasoning that excludes such nonsense. The history of the Romans is older than our testimonies, only we know nothing of it, but we must classify it as existing. The history of prehistoric man is much older than the Stone Age — in a quite different sense from the 'Eolithic problem'. It reaches into times and conditions where 'artefacts' did not even exist — but the development of the soul did. And it is the supporting factor; it is more important than the testimonies. We must learn that the division into the Stone Age and the Bronze Age was no wiser than if we wanted to divide the history of Europe into the Raven Keel Age, the Pen Age and the Typewriter Age. People confuse the expression with what is expressed. Corded ware[13] goes deeper than the fact of pottery. Metal casting is *one* consequence of a changed world-view, a symbol. We must make the sequence of stages independent of the classification of finds in museums. How incidental stone and bronze are to the inner epoch is shown by the Egyptian and [the] Babylonian cultures, which lie in the midst of it, without incision. Here the history is a history of the inner life, expressed in the style of buildings, ornaments, social forms, and not in a history of the material. The same is true of iron.

---

13   The Corded Ware culture is the name given to a culture of the Copper Age at the transition from the Neolithic to the Bronze Age, between c. 2900–2350 B.C. It is named after the characteristic decoration of vessels, in which grooved patterns were pressed into the clay with a cord. — *Transl.*

We want to write a history of the human being and not of the material, that is [a history] of the soul.

38

The idea of evolution only understood succession, and wrongly so, in that it considered stages to be modern — spiritual — rational; the theory of cultural circles, also outdated, only understood juxtaposition, which by no means receives chronological values through an 'earlier' or 'later'. The step remains to be taken to really write what 'prehistory' contains in its name, namely history, in which, in addition to place and direction, tempo and duration, when and how long play a role. History, however, is the narration of life, not the enumeration of its traces.

39

World history in the narrower sense [is] the history of the high cultures and their preparation, 10,000 years. Before that lies the region of the 'unhistorical', a continuous up and down of peoples, states, arts, without progress. Science proceeds here in a purely collecting and ordering way, i.e. in a natural scientific way: we are dealing with states of affairs. Because a great context is touched upon here: the history of ways of life, whose history refers to genres and times, which, seen from the latter, appears as a standstill.

Further from the history of life back to the history of the earth's surface of the planetary system! There [natural science] appears competent, because the relative times are monstrous.

40

Historical pictures:

1. The historical image, *world as history*: it is, as Goethe's *Dichtung und Wahrheit*[14] depicts his biography, the fact of memory symbolically shaped, enlivened, radiated through in a spirit of its own.

---

14 'Truth and Poetry' — *Transl.*

Thus every Western human being has such an own, incommunicable image of the world as history, into which the consciousness of one's own life is absorbed and which underlies all action and activity. Poetry and truth in so far as it is one's own greatness that animates mere data. Such images of history as individuals have, all individual groups, estates, strata, epochs also have. There is a Gothic, a Renaissance image of history, an image of history for the people of the 19th century. On the other hand, there is a German, a French image, specifically coloured, psychologically determined by the soul of such a people; an image of the socialist, the conservative, the liberal, the priest; of the peasant, the scholar of the great cities, the historian by profession; so that out of all these thousand [images] there finally emerges for each one a property which one shares with [no one] and which forms the never-to-be-eliminated basis of all dispute.

2. But the historical view of the world of ancient man is of a quite different kind.

3. The historical images are related to legend and fairy tale: in primitive man [they are] almost identical, in the peasant, in ancient man. Even in the highest Western European [the] image on the horizon [merges] into legend (according to form: Charlemagne, Napoleon, the Battle of the Nations[15] at Leipzig, Sedan[16] are today formed in the popular consciousness as legends).

4. This legendary form shapes the surface, the coincidence; the organic structure in the depth is feeling, intuition. Just as the 'image of nature' is only scientific to the educated (and that too only in the intellectual moments!), in other respects it too is and remains a myth

---

15   The Battle of the Nations near Leipzig from 16 to 19 October 1813 was one of the most important battles during the Wars of Liberation, in which the Coalition troops — essentially Russia, Prussia, Austria and Sweden, as well as smaller principalities — defeated the troops of Napoleonic France and its allies. — *Transl.*

16   The Battle of Sedan took place on 1 to 2 September 1870. For Prussia, the surrender of the French Army and the capture of Emperor Napoleon III was one of the most triumphant victories in its history. — *Transl.*

of nature. In the life of a higher man, the intellect highlights for moments a scientific image of nature, about whose constancy and duration one is mistaken.

41

On World History. Aphorisms: Hatshepsut[17] and Teje[18], the great empress and the Caesar mother from the depths, who can always be depicted along with her, — these are Livia, Agrippina and the women around Elagabal. Images are needed here: these women side by side, Akhenaten and Marcus Aurelius, Trajan and Ramses, Thutmosis and Augustus. Or Caesar. Such moments in an aphorism cycle under the title 'Perspectives' (comparisons and deep views of the highest kind)! A second cycle: *Sub specie aeternitatis*: last perspectives on cultures as a whole. And so arrange several things. Pictures to go with it! Create a new kind of illustrated book! Above all portrait heads! Ornaments to give a sense of the 'style of history'. A kind of graphology of history.

A cycle of aphorisms on the concept of solar and lunar civilisation. Here the types of peoples of the kind of the Romans, Prussians, Aztecs — and the Japanese, Carthaginians, Jews, who still project into later civilisations.

42

Historical method: The essence of the natural scientific method, the only pure scientific method there is, is very simple. All the more difficult is [the question of method] in history. The preparatory work (sifting the material, collecting) is namely of a systematic nature, an ant's work, which is the be-all and end-all of the lower historian, but which also often deceives the great historian about the essence of his achievement. He does not notice that the content of his creative,

---

17   Hatshepsut was the second female Egyptian pharaoh. She reigned from 1479 to 1458 B.C. — *Transl.*

18   Teje (1398–1338 B.C.) was the wife and co-ruler of the Egyptian Pharaoh Amenophis III, and the mother of Akhenaten. — *Transl.*

non-systematic-ordering achievement lies beyond this work and its method. In addition, as soon as a historian communicates himself and his creative insights and illuminations, he must of necessity use systematic means: language, concepts, judgements, conclusions. For prosaic spiritual communication is not physiognomic, but systematic.

Here, then, the form of communication is at odds with the content of what is being communicated, and profound thinkers have felt this painfully: how much of the best and deepest is lost there! How much the very individual, the fine must be ground down, coarsened, when it enters into the setting of language. A secret longing for artistic expression: poetic description, dramatic conception, image, vision, suggestion through lightning-like aphorisms (which only touch the means of language)! Unfortunately, even great historians have been seduced by this fact. Recognising the spirit of this form of communication, they thought they saw in it the specifically historical method, and they struggled to give their utterances the form of cause and effect, conclusions, judgements, concepts, instead of avoiding this necessarily heterogeneous sphere as far as possible.

Nevertheless, in every great historical achievement, the physiognomic-creative core will be very well distinguished from the scientific-systematic matter through which alone it became communicable.

ON HISTORY AND HISTORIOGRAPHY

43

Historical observation is Faustian scepticism. There are races and cultures of cognition. Even as a natural scientist, one only recognises in the manner of one's peers and only convinces people of the same kind.

44

Fate and causality: What fate is cannot be defined, only experienced with sight. Most people [are] too stupid for that. Then history is broken down into dates and one is called a cause, the other an effect. Those who do this do not know what history is.

Mussolini [is] destiny. Not an effect. Tragic. All humanity is a tragedy. To the wretch who thinks causally, history seems meaningless. But it has a meaning by which the small human standards and evaluations — right, wrong — become ridiculous. History has never taken such things into account.

45

What happens to man and how man makes history (cd) — his 'world history' — by becoming conscious of his horizon, situation, goal [and] means — and thus driven by the destiny in his soul. This conscious history begins with language. Difference between the great individuals and the crowd: the great have the greater physiognomic view of fact, but they are still in the service of fate.

46

The true statesman and historian feels himself to be an element in the stream of change that flows unalterably. [Politics is] the art of the possible. Feeling oneself as an element (Napoleon). Affirmation of fate, *amor fati*. The systematist who constructs chains of causes, numbers, laws [and] instead of looking, critically dissects, believes he can change the chain of causes — ideology, utopia.

47

The great historian forms the whole system (number, data, theory) without succumbing to it. As a means of clarifying what has been seen. The collector and file-keeper of data and numbers never gets out of the bare scheme to a view of the real, of the living change.

Data of space (number, statistics, chronology, map, table) are only means of expression, not ends in themselves.

The history of life — biographical or world-historical — can only be depicted pictorially, in succession or [in] artistic grouping (*Decline of the West*).

48

What is culture? 'Life' as a unity, human life above all a unity.

Cultures [are] the organic specimens of the totality 'human life'. Their inner form: youth, age, duration (1,000 years), tempo.

The concrete forms of these destinies [cannot be] foreseen, but the end of the inner form is certain.

49

The number kills the life — out of fear wanting to calculate — oracle, prophecy, horoscope. Chronology must never become the main thing, the scheme. The true historian and statesman foresees irrevocably the shape of what is to come (art of the possible), the systematist sees nothing. That is why he calculates, and always wrongly. He lacks living time. He speculates spatially, timelessly, law-like.

The systematist's fear is to discover data and rules in order to escape fate. The physiognomist is in awe of fate. He wants to suggest it pictorially, not avoid it.

50

Culture is the unconscious realisation of the possible, an urge, not a decision. All forms of culture arise involuntarily. No people creates culture, but is created by culture. The types of people are, like works of art and ways of thinking, expressions of cultures, symbols.

Whoever thinks or paints or writes poetry consciously only wants to create; *how* it will be does a power in him that drives him. 'It' next to 'I'.

Too great an awareness of what is intended kills creativity. All that remains is criticism, self-criticism. One knows how it should be, but cannot do it.

51

Addendum: How thinking develops analogously in every culture, in that one's own and only view of the world emerges linguistically and mentally in forms that proceed in the same way, most hidden in the respective logic, which at first glance is 'generally human'. What is fundamentally different is what is decisive, more real than all insights, namely the method of sensing, researching, looking: the ancient, Chinese, Egyptian method are the 'primordial phenomenon'.

52

A man of great deeds, like Napoleon, who wavers and doubts in moments of a difficult decision, experiences the point where the thinking of cause and effect proves to be insubstantial and fate reveals itself. Then no more thinking helps, only instinct, faith in the star.

53

The creator feels free. There is freedom in every deed. Every deed, even the unsuccessful one, is in essence a victory of free will. Only the shy person, the thinker, priest, tinkerer, does not know this real freedom. For him the word becomes a problem, like all reality. But this only speaks for the unnature of his existence.

54

'Soul' is a piece of history, a stirring in form: 'character' is what it is called. But character exists of individuals, peoples, estates, cultures, and finally of historical man in general: all these [are] soul-historical streams of place, duration, tempo, and kind.

History itself (the 'public', world history) is nothing but the visible, tangible, experienceable expression of this 'secret' history. Soul history and world history relate to each other like wanting and doing, urge to the sign and to draw, anger and blow.

55

But when does the sense of distance begin in this history of the soul's ascent? Among animals of race [it is] present, but as an instinct of belonging. Among human beings, however, it is finally conscious, comprehended, and therefore effective in terrible depth.

In all advanced cultures [it is] already old. But when does it arise? The exquisite types of imperious and holy consciousness, today felt as social and spiritual superiority — and aped. But culture is almost nothing but distance. It is *paucorum hominum*[19]. Most people have to work for the aims of the few — in politics, religion, art — otherwise nothing comes of it.

56

Ideas that do not have interest and passions of a vital kind behind them remain literature. Christianity only arose because it was the field sign of the poor, the rabble, the ones alien to the race, Lutheranism likewise as a weapon of the peasants, guilds, cities, princes, the idea of 1789[20], that of Marx likewise.

The spirit plays no part in history, only the instincts.

57

History depicts the human heart (Napoleon). In contrast, thoughts, even eternal ones, are different every century. And what a religion or a thinker presents as the meaning, the purpose of 'man' and 'history' is merely the taste of his time.

Man as the meaning of the world! What exaltation! This fragile creature that has 'spirit' for 5,000 years and then perishes from it! Man is a part, an element of the world, like plants, rocks, clouds. It is understandable that he feels important to himself. Every dog and frog does that and sees its world in relation to itself. That is a primitive prejudice. The mature man sees how accidental, superfluous his kind is in the world.

19　Latin: 'few men'. — *Transl.*

20　From the French Revolution: 'Liberty, equality, fraternity'. — *Transl.*

58

Age of the germinating, maturing, imperious spirit. So in the highest cases unconsciousness and foreboding, shudders of gloom and fear, orgies of noisy triumph and quiet disgust.

In general, [the] 'History of Mankind' is the tragicomedy of the spirit that forges man into the galley of causes and purposes, wonderful at dawn, stirrings of a beautiful child, games of the spirit, then searing, simoom, burying life under the sand dunes of his 'achievements'.

59

Introduction: It follows from this way of seeing history that the mind and the results of its brooding have no place in it. These results are practically important enough, but that does not depend on whether they are 'true' or 'false'. And in any case they only change the external forms of the event, not its deeper meaning. If the dagger [of Brutus[21]] had missed, the story would have been different. If Newton had never lived, nothing would have changed.

60

What greatness lies in history are the mighty passions of races, of peoples, families, estates, of individuals. What they cost, rivers of blood, the burning of cities, ruins, is not too dear. And only when the barren reason overflows from the cities, like a dirty flood, with humanity, peace or the striving to fill the rabble man with the happiness of the most: comfort, pleasure, bread and beer, does an immeasurable boredom settle over the world, so that men flee from passion to other parts of the world, become criminals, commit suicide — or smash this world to ruins.

---

21 Marcus Junius Brutus Caepio (85 B.C.–42 B.C.), often called Brutus for short, was a Roman politician during the late Republic and one of the assassins of Gaius Julius Caesar. — *Transl.*

61

The most original form of thinking about human history in Atlantis[22] and Kash[23] is the religious calendar fixation; only the hero culture thought big: the origin of real historical thinking is fame. To be famous, to be unforgotten, to live on in history. And one lives on in the form of names and deeds, mythologically, in the form of the heroic saga, which, in strict contrast to everything earlier (Gilgamesh[24]), means a real personality. And the oldest form of 'historiography' is the heroic song. The *skald*[25] is the forerunner of the historian: one should write poetry about history. And that is why historical writing of a high order always retains something of the heroic song. World history is a great saga of the happiness and end of Icarian man[26].

62

In c still long breath — a century does not mean much. Only in d [is] a century already much.

Hence the knowledge of the fleetingness of time, the fear of death, hence the need to use time, the calendar as an expression of the fear of the brevity of existence, the sense of history, chronology — recording

---

22 Atlantis is mostly synonymous with what later Indo-Europeanists call 'Old Europe', with the difference that it was a maritime culture that had once invaded the Neolithic Fertile Crescent. — *Transl.*

23 Kash was how Spengler defined the megalith-building culture complex of the Neolithic Middle East, which had been invaded by seafaring Atlantis thousands of years before the Old European seat of Atlantis was in turn invaded by proto-Indo-European Turan. — *Transl.*

24 Gilgamesh was a king of Uruk. According to legend, he had many adventures during his quest for immortality. — *Transl.*

25 The skalds were court poets in medieval Scandinavia, who formed a separate class that was held in high esteem. They died out on the European mainland at the beginning of the second millennium but survived in Iceland until the 13th century. — *Transl.*

26 Flying high but once repulsed by the sun starting to fall. — *Transl.*

events as something fleeting, lost. The historical sense [is] an expression of the rapid life towards a catastrophe.

63

What is culture? It has been understood in very different ways, depending on the weight of one's own personality: a sum of conveniences from the arrow to the telephone — abstractions of museum collections. I see in a culture a historical event, unique, irrevocable, and in it the fate of a being, the history of a soul, is realised, consummated. Culture *is* not, but *happens*, is accomplished in and through people, who are elements of its expression.

64

Against cultural circles: If the prehistoric way of ordering is superficial [because materialistic], so is [also] the ethnographic one of the theory of cultural circles for another reason: it lacks the instinct for the depth of time. One will find 'older' and 'younger' layers of cultural traits in every place, but that does not yet mean 'old' and 'young'. The measure of the size of the gap is missing.

If something is 'old' in Polynesia around 1900 A.D., but these islands were not settled at all until later times, 1600 is ancient, but that would be very young for Japan, and lacks sufficient value for the relationship to Babylon. In fact, however, Madagascar was only settled by Malays around 600.

Here it becomes clear: the ideas of tempo and duration are missing from the concept of culture. It equates today and yesterday with primeval times and the present — it is as if one wanted to compare the formation of the Alps and a sand dune. The bow, for example, is said to prove layers in Polynesia: but the compound bow occurs as a weapon in the Upper Palaeolithic of Spain, 5000 B.C. — in contrast, the bow forms of Polynesia are not ages, but ephemeral.

65

Counter-soul: The struggle, culture as battle, finds symbolic expression in this duality. In Egypt and Babylonia, where there is more mixture than subjugation, the contrast is not so stark. Both elements form 'peasantry' and 'society'. In the northern cultures, on the other hand, it is very abrupt: lower soul and upper soul.

Caution: the counter-soul is not identical with peasantry, the upper soul not with society. Instead, wherever victory remained in doubt, a seat of the counter-soul emerges: Sparta — Rome or Florence — Paris. The soul of victory forms the counter-soul as its pole.

66

Elements of the event: Cultures as organisms. Restriction of the theme to the c- and d-cultures. Rejection of the division into Neolithic, Bronze Age, etc. Rejection of the theory of cultural groups.

Overview of the c-cultures, today still enduring (besides still remains of humanity, solidified in a-b-cultures, at the southern end [of the continents] e.g.). Here we do not yet describe the soul of these c-cultures, but only the time, place and outer form. They all lie in their primordial amoebae in the old world, north of the equator, and form one group.

So group of amoebae and group of plants. Comparison from biology: the primordial forms of life are few: always the same in depth. There is only one 'life'.

Why I begin with the 5th millennium. Type and fates, number, pre-culture, place and time of the c- and d-cultures. Preliminary overall picture of cultural vegetation, whose upper layer is 'world history', whose lower layer is 'ethnology', whose humus is 'prehistory'. This is how the disciplines arrange themselves.

Major and minor amoebae, plasma with many nuclei. Naming, vocabulary, grammar, form and aim. Capsian sensual symbolic, Solutrean being and deed, Kash abstract.

67

Against cultural circles and prehistory: In the entire interpretation of culture, it is still a matter of finally getting rid of the inheritance of the previous century that still dominates all present-day systems: namely, the addiction, instead of starting from the soul of material and tool; and instead of comprehending the products sentiently, to evaluate them as results of modern-intellectual addiction to expediency. The history of prehistory appears to modern brains as the history of technology, the 'Bronze Age' is a concept like the 'time of the steam engine'. And the theory of cultural circles (cite Frobenius![27]) is, if one gets beyond mere words to intellectual foundations, nothing but the view that technical methods — bows, pottery, agriculture — decide the character of 'peoples'.

68

New concepts: There is something I want to call prehistoric tradition. This is a power that proves superior to any mature culture and captivates it. This tradition comes from the c-cultures which, as peasantry, 'people', 'land', form the foundation of all high cultures, which only have their cities above and founded on them. The eternal tendencies of movement belong to this. If, for example, there is one from Tunis to Molfetta, Crete, Caria, Etruria, Sardinia, Spain, the Carthaginians were spiritually subject to it.

So there are heirs to this tradition. And all high cultures have an ancient heritage. Thus the Persian kings, when they took up the ceramic Dimini path, like Sargon before them. Another is the tendency

---

27 Leo Frobenius (1873–1938) was a German ethnologist who came up with the term *Cultural Morphology*, which describes the external form of culture, whereby the individual parts of society are interrelated and thus form an organic whole, an organism. It is based on the assumption that cultures, analogous to the individual development of human beings, pass through the phases of youth, blossoming, old age and death, and do so according to an inherent programme over which human beings can exert only very limited influence. — *Transl.*

to develop the language of expression in a certain direction — direction of expression — in myths, stone, state.

69

One consequence of the division into materialistic stages of stone and metal use is that one set up a whole series of tool forms and classified them for all countries; if one found nothing somewhere, if there was no Neolithic in Spain, one believes in a time when the population had migrated. In fact, however, there has never been a human culture at all, but only individual cultures of individual form, and consequently always special developments. The Capsian, for example, is a piece of the outer expression of Atlantis, and it forms an organic whole with the Spanish Copper Age.

Thus the sequence of stages according to material dissolves into the time sequence of organic cultures, namely primitive cultures of different rank. The degree of primitiveness, however, like everything human, does not depend on time, but above all on humanity. Even in the Upper Palaeolithic, areas of higher and lower primitiveness are clearly distinguishable, and by the time of the pottery the differences in rank are already immeasurable.

70

What distinguishes culture in general from high culture is the greatness of the human being, the height and depth of the soul, which grows from the will and from suffering to the height of the sun of world history in the dawn of heroism. The great cultures are their battles: the victories until the sunset and then the view into the terrible all-for-nothing above the battlefield.

71

The purely coincidental circumstance that in the 'Neolithic' it is not the stone implements at all but the clay vessels that first catch the eye, because they are preserved in the greatest numbers, means that now all at once the division is made quite externally according to vessel forms and ornamentation, although both have quite different meanings. And it is only by chance that these characteristics nevertheless lead — in part — to the right paths.

The vessel forms are forms of the posture of life, that is, the posture of the body, the race and its moving style, its gesture. So they belong together with the forms of weapons, implements, tombs, huts, clothing; that is custom in the broadest sense. Vessel decoration, on the other hand, is an expression of world feeling and belongs to religion, cult, myth, rite, ornament. This, the form of race, the form of use, also indicates the political structure: the structure of family, tribe, clan. The lost art must also belong to this: dance, song. Forms of settlement.

72

Is it even possible to capture metaphysics in a scholarly scientific form? It is certain that it lives in the great works of art — buildings, music, painting, drama. And in the representation of great history. For historiography is design, creation, poetry in the highest sense. Only through historical, and not through systematic, representation can we communicate outside of art the secret that lies dormant in the world and in man.

73

What is needed, the real great task of the twentieth century in 'psychological' research, is not just any psychology (Klages[28]), but the his-

---

28 Ludwig Klages (1872–1956) is one of the most controversial German thinkers of the 20th century. As a prophetic philosopher, as a conservative revolutionary, as a radical pioneer of the ecological movement, but also as an innovative psychologist who gave scientific validity to characterology and the study of expression, especially graphology, Klages left behind a body of work of impressive diversity and range beyond the academic mainstream. His relentless critique of culture and civilisation revolves around the threat to humanity posed by the corrosive supremacy of the mind, i.e. above all of rational purposeful thinking, which manifests itself in science and technology that are hostile to life, obsession with money, psychological self-mutilation and widespread environmental destruction. — *Transl.*

tory of the human soul, its emergence, development, [its] decline[s]; how it heaps suffering upon suffering, for compared to the animal, human suffering, because it is inner and beyond the present and the body, is increased to infinity. Man is the soul-suffering animal. That is his depth, his greatness. That is why man's world history is a tragedy. For everything he expresses, his entire culture, his wanting and struggling, art, religion, state, war, has arisen from the suffering of the soul's existence.

74

What then is philosophy, as one feels at the word, without wanting or [being] able to define it? Not a science, even if, as in physiognomic observation of world history, knowledge is a prerequisite, but depth, foreboding of the ineffable. It is not the critical intelligence that decides, but the unworldly vision and horror, the awe of unsolvable riddles. Glowing wisdom, last shivers of a foreboding at the same moment.

75

What and how a thinker thinks — that is one question. But why he thinks the way he does is more important. If one subtracts from his thoughts everything that is determined by the language, the word-boundness of his thinking — the judgements, for example –, what he repeats after others because it is not possible for him to free himself from the schematics of his teachers in the church, the school, the environment, the specialist science, what remains is his personality insofar as it expresses itself in thoughts. Talking philosophically — lecturing, for example — is dangerous. Even more dangerous is written philosophy, the book, the system. What one really thinks in deep moments never comes unchanged into the sequence of linguistic sentences. And if you cannot read between the lines, you often do not learn what is decisive.

76

Turn by Schopenhauer, 19th century. Despite his Kantian half-measures. World as imagination. That is the new thing. Nietzsche rebelled against his own critical insight because as a pastor he needed ideals of the future: [the] superman, [the] Second Coming, in which he himself did not believe.

77

The 19th century, materialistically minded and Darwinistically enthusiastic about the Stone Age theory, moreover caught up in the faith of the progress philistines, established a scheme on the basis of the material of the finds, which is characteristic of the platitude of thought, which was to be valid for 'mankind' and into which everything found was now classified according to form and material. We are about to abandon this way of looking at things: there was no 'progress' and there were no stages of *human development*. There were only cultures, organic, local and temporal, with an individual language of expression. If such a 'stage' is 'missing' in a country, it does not mean that the people were missing, but that a culture, of which this not generally human stage was a part, did not touch that country. There is no 'hiatus'.

What is objectionable about the cultural circle theory, however, is its lack of understanding of duration and tempo. It is self-evident that in present conditions older and younger forms are together: but this applies only relatively, to these peoples, not to history. It is nonsense to speak of a 'primitive culture' in Australia and Polynesia when settlement does not begin until after 1000 A.D. Everything that this school has developed in the oldest and deepest layers on the basis of living contemporary observation is of the very youngest form, measured against what the history of Egypt and Babylonia teaches. There we are dealing with the last centuries, here with millennia.

78

Western culture [is] the least sunny. These wintry cities, these freezing people, the misery not only of hunger but of cold, the world-view of the long winter nights, the thinking in gloomy parlours, the existence in locked houses — all this sets the style of Faustian culture apart from all others.

79

Here a gap in the *Decline of the West* must be filled: the Common Human. The phenomenon of 'man' on the earth's crust. The eternal primeval human: instincts, love, hunger, fear, war, hatred. 'Life' [is] a primordial phenomenon of this planet. Meaning of life in itself. The 'unhistorical' human being as a moment of the earth's destiny. But in the midst of this event, the miracle of high cultures. Now work out how this stands out from the eternal primitive and yet is again like it. Just as in the highest cultural symbol there is only a sublimation of the primordial human, so in science there is the primordial fear.

But the reflection on this, the mechanisation of the world-view, is only an episode. And now the group of cultures as a whole, their relations, intermediate stages. Structure of this non-organic mixture, which itself has no development, but only represents a handful of individual developments.

'Life' is the almighty primordial fact. Everything else, culture, cognition, loving, hating, are only types of the expression of life. *Cogito ergo sum*[29] is nonsense.

80

The tiny number of human beings of prehistoric times, which completely changes the picture. The fact that Germania had 2.3

---

29 'I think, therefore I am.' This is the first principle of René Descartes' philosophy. — *Transl.*

million inhabitants at the time of Tacitus[30] must have been immeasurable compared to prehistoric times. What will it be like in the future, when the last culture has faded? Another reduction to tiny numbers?

King Gudea (c. 2340), one of the most powerful rulers in Babylonian culture, proudly gives the number of his subjects as 216,000. Under Urukagina it was only 36,000. The numbers must have been the same in the ancient Egyptian, Chinese and Indian cultures. The later cultures already reckon with quite different numbers, even among hostile primitive peoples. But that changes everything. The feeling of the world becomes different as soon as one has neighbours instead of infinite areas. War, intelligence as a weapon, the weapon itself, which is now necessary against human beings, the competition for physical, mental, technical superiority — in order to hold one's own. One must surpass oneself. Man has been standing under this aspect for 10,000 years; as a result, in comparison with earlier times, there is a rapid change in all conditions, all situations, moods, opinions, impressions (of others, of nature, of the relatively rarer animals). Until the high cultures appear in a flash. Think of the tragic destruction of the Maya by the occidental late period. Originally [one has] no feeling at all for the other people one sees occasionally. But then, as soon as they become 'neighbours', the primordial opposition of enemy and friend, hatred and contract [awakens]. Origin of law?

81

The 'great personality in history' is almost a phrase. One does not think about the fact that [their] significance bears no relation to reality, that it is chance that decides whether the great people of a time come to the fore — which presupposes a whole series of quite improbable coincidences and, moreover, a great epoch –, whether they merely participate or remain completely undeveloped, even for themselves,

---

30 Publius Cornelius Tacitus (c. 58–c. 120) was a Roman politican and historian. In 98, he published the most important written testimony about ancient Germania (*De origine et situ Germanorum*). — *Transl.*

while people of little or no significance crown the fact with their name. When a great situation is given, the first-born takes the place: when it is not, even the greatest man cannot find his place. Great men, then, are something different from world-historical personalities.

82

Genius, chance: Here, after all, a distinction must be made whether the famous name is that of a man like Hannibal or Caesar, who gives the shape of his being to a time, or a Danton[31] or [Robespierre], who only for lack of great persons imposes a chance name on an anonymous event, itself only pushed, not pushing.

Among the world-moving persons there are very few geniuses, and only a few of the geniuses have moved the world: mostly they were much lesser persons whom chance put in their place. Caesar and Napoleon also got into their places by chance — how many geniuses have remained undeveloped by negative chance! Rarely has a world-historical decision been made between two such insignificant people as Octavianus and Antony at Actium[32]: the pseudo-morphosis of Arab culture, the fate of the West, which was now no longer organised — for lack of energy in Augustus –, the form of the Principate: all this was here chance between mediocre people, while such important minds as Sulla and Caesar had little after-effect. But on the other hand

---

31 Georges Jacques Danton (1759–1794) was a French revolutionary and politician who was Minister of Justice and head of the first Committee of Public Safety during the French Revolution. He was thus one of the leading figures of the First French Republic. Because he spoke out against the continuation of the Reign of Terror he himself helped install, he was beheaded in 1794 as an alleged conspirator against the revolution. — *Transl.*

32 The Battle of Actium, which took place on 2 September 31 B.C. off the west coast of Greece, marked the end of the Roman Republic. Octavian, who later became the Emperor Augustus, defeated his opponent Marcus Antonius and the Egyptian Queen Cleopatra VII in this naval battle and thus secured sole rule of the Roman Empire. — *Transl.*

Hannibal! Only through him did Rome become great. And again the insignificance of the Diadochi[33]!

83

Myth and history: Myth is the primordial. Primitive people and children feel ahistorical. For them, the past is a low-perspective image that closes tightly behind the present and in no way offers anything 'different'. The atheistic man of early times also saw essentially mythically, although the individual wide perspectives already break through the picture. Note the costumes of the images from the biblical story that are present-day (Uhde is, of course, lying). No one can make himself completely free. Even we interpret the soul of ancient man, of tragedy, of art very 'currently'. Think of our judgements of Hellenic sculpture. Nevertheless, the historical sense belongs in a dynamic-perspective way to the ever-growing elements of the Faustian soul. A spiritual jolt is 1500, then again 1800. Today the maximum: seeing the effect *sub specie*[34] of the whole of world history! That will soon diminish.

The cult of the ancestors has something mystical about it; it thinks only of the lasting. The ancient historical thinker (Thucydides[35]) is static; everything is and will be as it has been, delimited by myth. History as universal development is a Faustian postulate. Ancient biography is a static compilation of anecdotes, Faustian [is] development proven only by anecdotes. Let us distinguish, then, the mere dimension (scope) and the functional variability of the historical image.

---

33 The Diadochi were generals of Alexander the Great who divided his empire among themselves and fought for supremacy after Alexander's unexpected death in 323 B.C. — *Transl.*

34 Latin: 'under the aspect'. — *Transl.*

35 Thucydides (c. 460–400 B.C.) was an Athenian general and historian who wrote a famous history of the Peloponnesian War. — *Transl.*

84

Myth and historiography: To the occidentally civilised aspect belongs a view of the (albeit nebulous) 'future of mankind' with a dimension of millennia, just as we would be embarrassed by a beginning, be it Homeric or biblical, purely as a whole. Such ideas would never have occurred to a Greek.

Two powerful final aspects are possible and both have been posited: an ideal state to be finally attained, or an indefinitely progressive development to unimagined possibilities. Ancient is only the idea that the present state could be replaced by another, even possible one — static. The sceptic recognises this [our 'infinite'] idea as a form, as a symbol.

85

Here carefully study Eduard Meyer I, 1.2 on the general kinship of the soul-being of the three Indo-European cultures, e.g. world-thinking, godhood, and of the three southern ones: Egypt, Babylonia, Arabia. Then the relationship of the high cultures to prehistory (Diluvium, Stone Age), their group and their fate as an ephemeral phenomenon of the earth's surface. The many individual problems of the original languages, original religion, original customs, in general the genetic preconditions of all high cultures.

Thus, for example, in Aryan primeval thought there always appears the Heavenly Father and the Mother Earth, the monism of world existence, the universal of the idea; in the other three, however, there appears the opposition of dead matter and living force, dualism, locally delimited, gods as opposed to the world, man formed, not begotten, etc.

It is only from this common ground of primeval times that the magnificent symbolism of the ancient, occidental, Indian special development arises. Thus from Indo-European world thinking first Vedic, Apollonian, Faustian myth — then physics: statics, dynamics. Egyptian, Arabic, Babylonian myths from primeval Semitic thinking.

86

Genius and private destiny: On the difference and conflict between general and private destiny: e.g. Nietzsche, who represents the epoch of 1880 to a large extent philosophically. Like Epicurus. In his place it could also be a kind of Leibniz, a philosophical Mommsen[36], calm, cold, with immense erudition in all fields and with a long series of thorough volumes. So it was the violent, dilettante, eternally self-tormenting, the artist without creative power. Or artistic epochs represented by one great figure (Aeschylus, Sophocles, Shakespeare) or many small ones.

'Causes' in history: The French Revolution was 'due' to the 'conditions' of the social situation, the Reformation even to economic conditions. That means doing physics in the wrong place. The fact that one follows after the other, not from the other, is confused. The mere organic development is confused with a causal nexus. Otherwise a rule would have to apply: because conditions are so, such a revolution must follow. In natural science, an effect is accompanied by a cause. In history, one fact is preceded by an infinite number of others. It is physics to assume here the same motive each time, e.g. economy.

87

Genius: Ancient thought does not possess this concept. Nor is it in the nature of ancient men to have such distancing impressions of a [person] as underlie the concept. In the West, however, there are two concepts of genius. One is Faustian. According to this feeling, only a very small number of purely Faustian natures can be called so, e.g. Dante, Michelangelo, Shakespeare, Goethe, Beethoven, Napoleon. The dynamic of the tendency towards infinity, towards space, away

---

36 Theodor Mommsen (1817–1903) was a German historian who was awarded the Nobel Prize for his work *The History of Rome*. — *Transl.*

from the body — that is 'genius'. Even the mere striving without effect is 'ingenious' — Jean Paul[37].

On the other hand, the sadistic concept of the *homme de genie*, people in great numbers who possess spirit, refinement, freedom: Voltaire, Larochefoucauld[38].

88

Destiny. Genius: multiple sense of the word:

1. Genius as Faustian soul in highest potency. So no ancient geniuses.

2. But genius as primordial human immediacy within a culture. So the genius moments of which every human being is capable (moments of highest excitement): anger, love, passion, where the 'spirit' is subordinate to the vital, where one becomes a prophet, poet, painter, where even the simple human being finds words that are high above his intellectual level. The genius from Gothic to civilisation becomes rarer and duller: Dante — Goethe — Wagner. Only among men, city dwellers, but in such high potency that 'immortality' comes into being, because the difference between the mere moment (possibility) and the production (reality) is more decisive. Those people with passionate moments of genius are only potential.

3. Finally, genius and fate: the relatively extremely rare moments when genius possibility really becomes epoch-making reality. Goethe, for example, could have become a diplomat, Napoleon a journalist — and their 'genius' would not have become epoch-making.

---

37 Jean Paul (1763–1825) was a German poet and writer. He was born Johann Paul Friedrich Richter and changed his name in honour of his idol Jean-Jaques Rousseau. — *Transl.*

38 François VI. de La Rochefoucauld (1613–1680), himself a nobleman, criticised the aristocrats' selfishness and lust for power. He failed as a leader of the Fronde, the bloody revolt against the monarchy, so he retreated to the flourishing salons, where he wrote aphorisms. — *Transl.*

89

Fate, chance, genius: I see it this way: the expression of a soul's way of being remains everything that is brought about — state, religious, pictorial, practical, industrial, military forms. The formal instinct that emerges in a Shakespearean drama and in a Napoleonic battle is one and the same. To enter the mind of a natural image, as Goethe did, and set a form before the eye in innumerable notes, or to enter the mind of a political image in order to direct a state — these are one and the same. Construct a steam turbine or design a symphony — you are doing one and the same thing.

And if I put in the man who is just becoming, the child — he is either capable of such things or not. In the latter case, it does not matter where fate throws him. We have seen thousands of incompetent kings, generals, poets. In the first case, it depends in which of the real forms, the practical possibilities of the time, the inner possibilities are educated. In the worst case, in none at all — and I believe that this is the vast majority of cases. Nature is wasteful. See the fate of the germs of all plants and [the] animal world. Kant as a dogged tax official annoying his superiors with his tricky bossiness, Beethoven as a mad schoolmaster and drunkard, Frederick the Great as an abbe, Napoleon as a shyster banker …

90

Fate, chance, genius: I see in every moment people who could have become great people. Genius lies as a possibility in almost everyone. I believe that at the time of Goethe, Kant, Napoleon, there were hundreds of thousands in Europe who could have become poets, thinkers, doers of the first rank. Fate picked out individuals and made their private nature the form of the times. German literature is Goethe. Strike him out and think of the epoch occupied by one or a few other names, and the 19th century would look different. Napoleon was not, when he was 10, the first p[olitician] of his time. Certainly he was not. Chance singled him out, unfolded his genius traits to the utmost reality, to the historical fact of the 'great man' — that eclipsed a thousand others for it, some of whom never suspected what might have become of them under other circumstances. When Napoleon was 20 years old, he had no idea of his great future. He and others only said so later. When Nietzsche was 25, he had no idea that he would become the philosopher of his time. It came over him. Certain of his dispositions matured into certain r[ealities]. I can very well imagine Shakespeare as an English admiral or as an evil brawler in a provincial corner.

To speak of born great men and to believe that they will achieve something as a result of their spirit is a delusion of causality. It is not the great man who makes time, not the great time that makes the great man — all that is causal [thought]. I can well imagine Napoleon as a Parisian money man with a dubious past around 1820 — officer, speculator, jobber. I can think of Goethe as the mayor of Frankfurt, universally esteemed as a witty man, occasional poet and somewhat ridiculed because of his weakness for ladies. How much was missing and he would not have written *Götz* and *Werther*! All it would have taken would have been other suggestions, a prince instead of Herder[39], and he would never have thought of turning his occasional poetry into something more serious.

91

Prolegomena to History: The Great Void of All Cultures. No 'eternal truths', no immortal art. History that has become is dead history. Antiquity is dead. What we call its survival — in us, the 'heirs' — is the history of a planned misunderstanding of a definite past: thereby it becomes mask and material for our own symbolism.

---

39 Johann Gottfried Herder (1744–1803) was an important German poet, translator, theologian and philosopher of history and culture during the Weimar Classic period. He was one of the most influential thinkers of his time and, together with Christoph Martin Wieland, Johann Wolfgang von Goethe and Friedrich Schiller, is part of the 'quadrumvirate' of Weimar Classicism. He started the tradition of collecting folk tales. — *Transl.*

Space, causality, system, natural law, necessity of thought — the rigid form of understanding and its alter ego, the world as nature. But now man, inasmuch as he is not only understanding, consequently the 'supernatural'. If the world is conception, then the laws of nature are suspended as soon as the word conception no longer designates the state. History as the eternally supernatural, the miracle (e.g. great thoughts, enlightenments). A miracle is the idea of Faust.

Here it is not intelligence that counts, but the great man. History, religion, ethics, art are the realm of the miracle. Here there is no causality, no natural law. The miracle as the accidental. All great men are coincidences: history takes on the physiognomy of a private fate.

92

'*Coincidence*': Napoleon's request to be allowed to go to the Orient to organise the Turkish artillery is approved 15 September 1795. On the same day, however, the Central Committee had struck him off the list of officers for insubordination. Three weeks later he became General of the Army of the Interior.

93

The most profound word about history is in Hamlet, in the actor's scene: history is the 'body of time', and the drama is to show it the imprint of its form.

94

No landscape becomes the mother of a culture for the second time. There is a deep meaning in this relationship between the epitome of the world, which we call the shaped surface of the earth (nature), and that other felt one, which is the unity of culture. [Culture is a] child on which its mother dies.

The West, too, with the mile-wide space of its cosmopolitan cities, its dilapidated railways, mines, factories, its dull residual humanity, will become a burnt-out crater and await new men.

95

On the problem of 'freedom of will': A worse name could not easily have been chosen for this question: the formulation alone already includes the methodological error that had to be uncovered. It is a question of the opposition of human beings as part of the world-view of nature or history. If someone says: I realise that freedom of will is impossible, but I feel free, he has already solved the riddle. For 'freedom' here, as always, is a counter-term; the word is meant to denote the non-validity of the principle of causality. And indeed: since causality is the form of intellectual thinking and thus the logic of the extended, 'man' (no matter what complex of facts one imagines under this very word) is unfree as long as one thinks exactly about him, as long as he is the 'object of thought', the alter ego of a concept. The causal colouring disappears from the image as soon as it changes intuitively. The inner certainty of becoming does not know the causal form. Fate is a logic of a different kind.

II. THE FOUR STAGES OF CULTURE

ON THE PREHISTORY SO FAR

1

LATE MAGDALENIAN ART of Central Europe adopted the preference for animals from the North Atlantic area, while High Capsian lifted scenes with humans, not the animal form per se. Late Magdalenian Altamira[1] art was destroyed by the victory of the Capsians in Western Europe (665), but the Late Capsian Alpine style also succumbed (from the south? Kash?) to geometrisation. Is this destruction or evolution? Perhaps to the sea from the Orient? The Solutrean in Eastern Europe has an anti-naturalistic, extremely schematic ('geometric' but not yet genuinely ornamental) art, Predmost, low-grade.

I protest against the Hoernes[2] comparison: geometric [art] = agriculture, naturalism = animal husbandry; that is wrong! Only in the Magdalenian does Western art strongly predominate; in the

---

1   The Altamira Cave in Cantabria, Spain, is famous for its Stone Age cave paintings. — *Transl.*

2   Moriz Hoernes (1815–1868) was an Austrian geologist and palaeontologist. — *Transl.*

Aurignacian, Central Europe is also substantially involved (concentration!). Menghin (670) [is] rightly against the assumption of a European bushman race. The steatopygia of the figures is 'idealisation', taste, not reality; just like the exaggeratedly large penis. Menghin[3] believes that both Aurignacian and Capsian man originated in Asia, ancient Palestine. Ego: in the Mousterian? Alpera (and 'bushman') art [almost always shows] hunting and fighting scenes, that is, joy in the display of force, not in form. Expressionist. Images of weapons, jewellery, clothing. Always reflex bow as weapon — so the first long-distance weapon (instead of hand axe) is an invention of Capsian?

2

Stone Age: These classifications come from the material in museums, so they are as insufficient as possible. But even apart from that, it would be better today to simply drop the term Neolithic, because between Late Capsian and Magdalenian, on the one hand, and the period in which copper utensils, bronze, seeds, breeding are present, there is virtually nothing left, neither temporally nor culturally — if one does not want to assume a great vacuum around 5000, the famous *hiatus*.

Neolithic art (Menghin 681): developed further in the Atlantic than in the Upper Palaeolithic. In the north, according to Scheltema, Indo-European, new and powerful. According to Scheltema, the Danubian style is the result of a balance between North and Near Eastern styles, but Menghin takes it as a continuation of a Palaeolithic style (Solutrean).

The 'older Neolithic' is completely absent from the Iberian Peninsula. Extensive geometric painting (Menghin 682f) — menhirs[4],

---

3   Oswald Menghin (1888–1973) was an Austrian prehistorian, university professor and Minister of Education in the National Socialist cabinet of Arthur Seyß-Inquart. In his book *Geist und Blut* ('Spirit and Blood') (1934), he dealt with 'fundamental issues of race, language, culture and nationality'. — *Transl.*

4   A menhir is a rough prehistoric monolith. — *Transl.*

bones, rocks in Liguria, Ireland — from the latest Azilian (Mas-d' Azil, relation to Maglemose) to the Bronze Age, especially Galicia and Sierra Morena. I believe that there is no hiatus here and that the Azilian just reaches down to 5000. p. 688 Ireland: no Scandinavian, only Iberian relations. In England, on the other hand, North Scandinavian influence. The South Scandinavian drawing Bronze Age, agriculture. P. 694: relationship of the Galitic bronzes in Russia with Japan (1st year B.C.). 695 Maikop: the treasure in the 3rd millennium B.C.: close connection between Caucasus and Babylonia, Egypt!

3

Palaeolithic (Menghin 657 ff): the French stages of the Old Palaeolithic (exist) only [in] Western Europe, are already missing in Central Europe (no handaxes). Only the Acheulean penetrates there fleetingly, but then [penetrates] the Mousterian from the East into Western Europe.

Beginning of the *Upper Palaeolithic*: Aurignacian dominates from northern Spain to the northern Balkans, at the same time Old Capsian in southern Spain, Italy, northern Africa, Syria. The Solutrean is Far Eastern and penetrates only late and weakly into France, nowhere into the Capsian area, missing in northern France, England. So it is Asiatic, as pre-Solutrean [reaches] Hungary early on, later Swabia, only in traces, late, [to] northern Spain, while the Aurignacian transforms itself here in the west into Magdalenian. This leads a backlash against the Solutrean as far as Eastern Europe (Hungary). Its origin, the Azilian, can no longer be traced east of Bavaria. The Capsian also developed further, growing microlithic tendency, which finally won (Tardenoisian) and thus broke through the old border south of the Pyrenees, mixing with the Azilian to the north-east until it reached the Maglemosian culture!

4

If Bayer[5] proves that in the eastern Mediterranean the Old Palaeolithic merges into the Neolithic (Campignian), if in Spain the Late Neolithic is missing and the Late Palaeolithic merges into the Copper Age, then something is wrong in this system of stages that was set up when one believed in a uniform 'evolution of mankind'. But even in the beginning, as we see today, evolution was aristocratic, not democratic: the *superior* types of men lead. Apart from that, these differences are merely based on the shape of the stone utensil — something very unimportant in the existence of that time! But what do we know of the work with sharpened wood, sticks, bow and arrow, of eating and drinking, of the life of the families, of the horde, of costume in the broadest sense, of the manner of housekeeping, of the life of the soul?

5

The wooden utensil was always more important than the stone! The oldest typical implements are wooden (Wooden wedge. That is why the stone wedge is missing in Central Europe). First hunting, fishing, gathering fruits. Then next to it, less important, some horticulture (hoe, woman). Next to both, some loose animal husbandry. (The acclimatisation of the animals to a feeding place.) Finally, next to all these in 'Kash' (Caucasus-Indus-Zanzibar) districts of cultic agriculture and animal husbandry. Wooden farming implements! The sacred arable land is originally common property of the *Gau*[6], temple property. Around 4000, however, agriculture already existed as an economic form (peasantry!). All high cultures are based on this peasantry. The 'invention' of agriculture is therefore older (5th millennium).

---

5   Josef Bayer (1882–1931) was an Austrian prehistoric archaeologist and anthropologist. He discovered the Ascalon culture while stationed in Palestine during World War One. — *Transl.*

6   *Gau* is a vague German term for region, district or landscape. — *Transl.*

'*Stone Age*' is nonsense. The typical implement is made of wood, only in individual areas is it imitated in 'stone'. Bow and arrow [are made of] wood.

'Upper Palaeolithic'. In the north, human portrait (Venus, movement types, single figures). [In] the south animals, compositional images, rest, *chthon*?

Capsian: Pygmies, likewise [is] the Capsian pushed northwards from Africa. The migration of the idea, not of the people. The place of fertile crossing is west coast of Europe (Magdalenian). Aurignacian and Old Capsian related (equatorial, no Sahara yet!).

Exit of Upper Palaeolithic — north lunar, south equatorial. Lunar: the 3rd full idea of 'powers'. Power of the moon. Real ornament. Totem. Clan (tribal state). Dominion over domains. Mask hunting and games, still pre-cultic. Advances of clans into southern kingdom (Egypt [and] Babylon). Light races. Aino to Cro-Magnon.

End of Upper Palaeolithic: emergence of horticultural cultures, hoeing, weaving, pottery. Ornamentation starting from the body (pondering on the meaning of the body), idea of the taboo Nordic, likewise the idea of the numen.

6

In the *Upper Palaeolithic* of the great currents of man [there was much space with] a thin distribution, that is to say, deserted [alternative] areas.

[The] beginning of the steppes [and] of the later desert zones [brings] displacement by primeval forest and aridity.

[In addition, the] expression of rigid races: light Nordic: Aino-Muzhik and 'Indo-European' types, etc. Black-Southern: the Negroes [who] stream in from Australia and become the new type in Africa? Cattle became important not for meat and milk but as draught animals and even earlier as sacrifices; sacred to the moon: horns [are] crescent. Farming is male, only hoeing [female]. It is nonsense to attribute such profound things as patriarchy and matriarchy to economic forms. The idea of life is the original. The deprived, longing, hard, dark life in the north and inland makes manhood, the saturated sluggish life in the south makes the woman's womb the meaning of existence. That was before all complicated economics. Cattle are useless for migratory instincts: only alpine, [i.e.] seasonal migration. The sheep [is] only bred for wool. Not needed in nature, likewise the goat. The cattle [is] imported in Africa, only became important with sacrifice and plough. The real migratory animals are the donkey and dromedary (Africa) and the horse (Asia).

7

'*Stone Age*': It would be better to divide the ages into *techniques* like beating, hammering and forging instead of according to the material. Hammered copper is treated in the same way as stone, but forging presupposes a different way of thinking: it is an organised technique like building with shaped stone (house stone, brick). So this is a revolution not of the material but of the thinking.

8

'*Neolithic*' can at best be used for a mental stage (as a designation). But not the Bronze Age. In Spain, probably also in parts of Asia, metal casting is already known at the beginning of the Neolithic. Through trade, the techniques of ore mining, smelting and forging were then widespread. And the *Iron Age* is a purely military epoch: a superior kind of warfare penetrates it, nothing 'economic'. This is already clear from the fact that the Sea Peoples[7] (Etruscans against Romans, Philistines against Jews) took the forges away from the defeated.

---

7   The Sea Peoples were aggressive seafarers who invaded the Mediterranean region, chiefly Egypt, toward the end of the Bronze Age, especially in the 13th century B.C. The origin of the Sea Peoples is still uncertain. Some have suggested they might have included Etruscans, Philistines, Sardinians, Mycenaeans and Minoans. — *Transl.*

9

In Europe, the *Old Palaeolithic* did not 'pass over' into the *Young Palaeolithic*, but weathered, whereupon the Young Palaeolithic shone in. Likewise, the latter is extinct, whereupon [the] *Neolithic* amoeboid pushes in. There is no connection between the Azilian and the Campignian, [but rather a] sudden break. [The] Neolithic comes suddenly, due to an improvement of the climate in Western Europe. Outside Europe [the] centre must lie where [the] Old Palaeolithic merges into the Neolithic and both are closely related.

According to Bayer, the 'Ascalon culture' (an identity of the youngest Old Palaeolithic and the oldest Neolithic) is spread over the whole of Africa, enormously in Somalia, Egypt, Tunis, and furthermore as far as the Near East. Therefore, according to Bayer

1. an oldest culture, Old Palaeolithic of the earliest kind, [exists] only on the western edge of Southern Europe, from there since Acheulean, radiating to Eastern Europe, perhaps as far as Asia, Central Africa, India.

2. The Aurignacian was highly northern and had decomposed the Old Palaeolithic from the Acheulean onwards, penetrating here as a highly developed Late Palaeolithic, decaying in the Azilian. Thus [the] hand axe [prevailed] [in] south-western Europe from the Old Palaeolithic to the Neolithic, Campignia, the blade [in] northern Europe, from the proto-Aurignacian to the Azilian.

3. Ascalon culture in the 'Orient' in the broadest sense would thus be unaffected by the northern thrust, the Old Palaeolithic spread and developed there from the west, now breaking back [returning] to its homeland as the Neolithic.

10

Neolithic: Here I have to introduce a number of new terms clearly and succinctly to replace the expressions Bronze Age, Brenner people etc. I distinguish between fluent and rooted culture. They differ not only in age, but in everything.

To start from the remains: Domes and pyramids have their history in the land of their birth. Megalithic buildings, on the other hand, migrate with their development.

11

Hoernes. Prehistory of culture. Three periods:
1. Palaeolithic: parasitic, hunters. Naturalism, male, aristocratic, secular (very important!), especially southern France and northern Spain. Male craft. Art as *forza di levare* (chopping away, carving away, engraving).

2. Neolithic — Bronze: symbiotic, peasants. Geometric, feminine, democratic, religious, mainly Central and Northern Europe. Feminine, *via di porre*[8], building up, assembling: weaving, braiding, pottery, casting.

3. Warrior. Gentility, fusion, Southern Europe, *forza di levare*[9], smithing. Difference between artificial design and expression and religious purpose.

12

Ice age: The word is familiar. The deeper meaning of the elementary events, of which 'ice age' is only a visible sign, has hardly penetrated historical thinking. Is the earth's axis of rotation subject to periodic or irregular fluctuations — a trembling and skidding — while the [distribution] of heat and pressure remains the same? Or does the overall climate of the earth fluctuate between hot and cold, wet and dry, with a rigid axis? In the first case, the hot and cold zones would change their position, not their size. In the second [case], the 'temperate' zone of today would soon have been icy, soon hot.

---

8   Italian: 'by adding on'. — *Transl.*

9   Italian: 'by means of removal'. — *Transl.*

13

Against the culture circle theory: They all start in the South Seas, where 'layers' can be observed, because they are quite young — the whole of Polynesia is a problem of the 2^(nd) millennium B.C. From there, without regard to time periods, they classify 'similar' phenomena of other parts of the earth. And through this method, whereby the South Seas remain the norm, the idea arises in their minds that the original culture was here: just as the Indo-European researchers, because they assumed this, finally considered Sanskrit to be the original Indo-European language.

14

Stone Age — Bronze Age: These are not times. Neither are railway times and car times: it is something quite different for England and Libya.

Mining is older than metalworking: Flint Age in Ireland, Belgium. Where there is a lot of metal, it comes naturally to try ores instead of hard stone. In metal-poor areas, the degree of use of metal tools depends on trade, [i.e.] price.

Inventing: e.g. in the 'invention' of the round arch construction to distinguish the mere *technical construction*, which was invented everywhere and certainly very often by thoughtful construction managers: in Sakkara, in Ur around 3000, always forgotten — and the *symbolic value* in Magian culture, where the technical became tradition and the main subject of technical reflection perfection. In Egypt and Babylon it was a completely meaningless special construction, because the style went completely different ways.

THE CULTURAL STAGES

15

The c-culture [brings] the idea of the house. [In] a-b [people live] somewhere in caves, under trees. Here — since c — people build. [The] house [is] a symbol of the feeling of life, [the] housing of life.

16

'Building' [is] an enterprise of several, organised, purposeful, linguistic understanding: commanding, discussing, obeying.

Like plant cultivation instead of gathering, animal breeding instead of hunting. [The] idea of creating something artificial against 'nature'. (Climate, animals, humans.) Caves (b-level), birds' nests, fox dens are results of libidinal actions genus-wise. To this genus instinct of the swarm is added the language-bound purposefulness of the tribe.

17

Every d-culture decays from the aristocratic formal early days to the democratic formlessness of the great cities. Home (c) [is] the countryside where you know everyone, a valley, a field. Rome, not Latium. What is called nation and fatherland today is an abstract thought of the metropolitan. Map, statistics.

18

Not every person of a cultured people is a cultured person. Culture denotes a rank. Many have something of it, some traits, a touch. Individuals represent it completely — Goethe, Frederick II, Leonardo. There are b-people among the c-people. In a d-culture — to which the peasants do not belong, as a stratum — [most] [people] are c-people.

19

There is no primordial language, but only a primordial type of thinking speech, which has nothing to do with pronunciation and vocabulary.

This archetype forms itself in c among wide populations, in many variations.

Later 'languages' are only newly coined groups from an early variation.

20

c: With speech-thought (new kind of 'consciousness') begins culture-history vis-à-vis natural man and events. History is a thoroughly spiritualised, word-conscious willing, organising — the tragedy lies in the fact that fate, blood (the unconscious) is stronger and directs.

21

c: Tribe, clan, family. The tribe [is] a union of families. Blood feud. Householder as judge in the house. Transition of families from one tribe to another, d: state as a fixed organisation. City, state.

The c organisation persists among nobility and peasants. The city destroys the families through the estate. Society [is] a sum of families with 'kinsmen' who no longer mean anything.

22

What is culture? Culture is like a rich house. Children 'see' nothing of the precious furniture, tapestries, vases. They live in their own world. Only slowly do you grow into the culture of such a manor. Lackeys, maids, the goat herder do not yet understand anything about it, but for other reasons. As a result of their upbringing — village education, church discipline — they remain on the c-level, which lives on underneath, as a foundation, also mentally. The blood and soul of the d layer is constantly replenished from c and is consumed. One can at any time regard the culture attained as a building which one person [inhabits] as belonging to, another hates, the third does not see at all.

23

c-Culture: First West, South, then North. d-Culture: first Egypt, Babylon, last West. The sun first hatched the hot souls. Slowly the winter-cold souls of the North also ripened. Late, spiritual.

24

c-d Cultures: Egypt (west). Babylon (south). India, China [and] antiquity [are founded] on W[est culture connected with the essence of the] South. Arab [culture is a] general mixture: West and South and North, [a] centre, radiating powerfully on all sides: religions, [up to] Islam; art, [up to] the art of the Roman Empire: dome, arch. [The] West [is] late, high Nordic: north and west.

25

I have already shown [in] *Man and Technics* the sequence of stages that man occupies inwardly. Stone and bronze are not spiritual values. But language separates primitive man b from c-d. High cultures (d) rest on the foundation of c. If today even the most primitive tribes possess languages, this is the consequence of c, just as they possess fire, tools etc. But it depends on the time of the creation of the language, about the 5th millennium. Until then, people had to communicate through signs and sounds or understood each other instinctively. This is where spiritual communication begins. Language in 'spiritual forms' as opposed to the hint, [the] sign. Language [is the] spiritual form of communication, extrasensory.

26

In b-c the distinguishing signs arise for the eye, [namely] distinguishing the people who belong to the 'we' and [those who are] enemies. These signs — ornaments, imitation, these strange soul-stirring geometric figures or animal images. Then the animal, the higher, perceived as equal to man: bull, stallion, lion, bear, etc., the destructive locust, the bee, strange creatures like snake, newt, shell. Slowly, as in thought, the sign becomes something else: what one carved or painted on the body, the hut, the weapon, passed into legend.

One called [oneself] wolves, the ancestor wolf; the feared or [the] mocked enemy [was called] something else. This is how ideas of the dead, tribal legends, cults came into being.

In the late totems that have become historical, the origin can no longer be determined. Skull hussars, wolf bellows, Picentes[10].

27

Race [arranged according to the four stages]:

a — Proto-race is natural race, somatic, archetype of the type of man. (We judge race almost only as visual images).

b — Mixtures, climatic-landscape s[wathes] of large areas. Mobile race.

c — Landscape race, occupational race: farmers, nomads, hunters, forest, desert, polar and equatorial varieties. Human type.

d — High culture type: nobility, selection. Spiritual race (face). Mass of cities.

28

Speaking begins with c: The 'language' [is] not yet there at first. Only names and gestures. Only slowly, in ascending cultural areas, do elements of a grammar sometimes develop. In the 4th millennium, certain units of form will already have developed here and there. The systems of Indo-European, Hamitic, Semitic etc. [were] only [formed] towards the end of the 4th millennium, perhaps later. (Only in Egypt, Babylon are they already developed.) In the 3rd millennium there are already language families.

---

10 The Picentes were a people in Italy that became part of the Roman Empire in the third century B.C. — *Transl.*

29

In stages a-b [the] event is without consciousness, without image, [in stages] c-d [begins the] history, [the] world as history, [the] image of one's own and other people's life. This is 'culture', the form of life conscious of itself, a-b [is] instinctive, cultureless activity. Only speech, which puts an intellectual distance in the place of instinctive connectedness, gives the thinking about it, thus detaches from the sensually present moment in which animals live, and gives the view from a distance over the streaming reality.

30

With culture, an iron armour is placed around life. [The] custom (since b) [is] obligatory lifestyle from within under the pressure of the landscape and its conditions. [The] custom of blood [is] unconscious, self-evident. Morality (since c, linguistic) [is] not a compulsion of the blood, but of the 'scholars' and their authority. In part [it works] against custom. Breeding and education (custom and morality). The indignant seeks to free himself, the servant hates only what he feels to be alien to himself.

31

[In] a-b [the] making of implements is still half instinctive. They belong to the genus *Homo* (like the honeycomb to the bees). Each [is] for itself. [In] c-d: now [special] cultures [arise]. Reflection. Long observed: Atlantis (Schuchhardt[11], Hoernes), Turan[12] (Strzygowski[13],

---

11   Carl Schuchhardt (1859–1943) was a German prehistorian and the director of the Prehistory Department of the Ethnological Museum in Berlin. — *Transl.*

12   Turan pertains to the proto-Indo-European steppe culture, very similar to what is now called the Yamnaya culture. — *Transl.*

13   Josef Strzygowski (1862–1941) was a Polish-Austrian art historian who highlighted the importance of Asia Minor, Egypt and the Near East for the development of Christian art. — *Transl.*

Scheltema). But only in their materially preserved remains. Excavation in China, Japan, Korea, South-East Asia, Indonesia.

[Since] c-d [man] becomes sedentary; therefore he differentiates himself psychologically. [The] power of the landscape binds the blood to itself.

Similarly [it is with] domestic animals: the race [is] transformed by the way of life. The c-man becomes [a] domestic animal. [He is] changed soul-body.

The nomad of sea and land is the protest of the human race against the effects of technical culture, of the 'spirit'. Cf. bohemian, adventurer, buccaneer, cowboy. The wandering peasant seeks only the place where he can put down roots again, the nomad flees from it.

32

I call the c-culture North Eurasian. It is lifestyle, world-view, soul. Not language and race. High culture (d) comes from the north. Starting in the south (Egypt, Babylonia). But never equatorial. Saharan culture was low (b more than c). Neither pottery nor language have sure results unless one can imagine (the historical-political). To make an image. To distinguish layers in a language — a questionable idea. Pots, after all, have been made. Lie in layers of earth. One forgets that there is actually no language, only speaking people. The 'language' lives in perpetual speaking through generations. We only know the writing of some of them, which cannot or will not reproduce the sound group. Letter writing is also conventional, not scientific. People learned to read, i.e. to think in terms of the written image of a familiar group of sounds, which changed from generation to generation, racially.

33

The b-man does not yet stick to the ground, he wanders. In c [comes] with the building of the soil and the keeping of cattle the settledness, with it [is] the changing cave transformed into the house.

The cattle nomads, having first emerged from sedentary husbandry, have again gone wandering.

34

1st millennium [B.C.]: the great ideas of movement emerge: ship — chariot — cavalry. 1st millennium B.C. — 2nd millennium A.D. they are widespread. Also bow, axe, metal.

2nd millennium A.D.: railway — steamship — automobile.

Psychology of weapons: cunning, courage, pride, caution, bravery. Courage of the sailor and courage of the swordsman are different. The one dares to win, the other dares for the sake of the carriage — because otherwise life is stale.

35

1. Ship, Hamito-Semites. Bow, axe. Egypt, Babylonia, Mediterranean. Bohuslän[14].

2. Chariot, Indo-Europeans. Sword, axe. Tripolye, Bronze Age. 2nd millennium, Hyksos, antiquity, India, China. Antiquity (Apollo — Dionysus). India (Vedas, Harappa[15], Shiva).

3. Horsemen, Indo-Europeans, Turks. Persians, Scythians, Borneo. 1st millennium.

4. Spread of means of locomotion. 1st millennium Polynesia, Japan, Peru, Mexico. Arabia, Turkic people, Huns, Germanic people.

5. West. Machine. 2nd millennium.

6. Russia.

36

b: Idea of the 'tribe' = blood relationship (blood brotherhood, adoption).

---

14   Bohuslän is a province in modern-day Sweden. — *Transl.*

15   This early high culture is named after the present-day village of Harappa in Pakistan: the Harappa culture. Harappa was a residential and working city. Its heyday was between 2600 and 1900 B.C. — *Transl.*

c: The 'state' [came into being] only with the 'nation': Units of power and war. Linguistic — thought. Notions of government, command, boundary.

The matriarchal tribe (Atlantean): becoming a member of the tribe by marrying a woman of the tribe. The patriarchal (Nordic): by adoption. Blood brotherhood. So [lies the] difference [in] the idea: the masculine-warrior line of deed and the maternal-bearing of mere 'generation'. Male and female succession — tradition and generation.

37

The difference between rich and poor is as old as that between powerful and powerless. Noble [is] possessive. The envy of the dispossessed since c. This begins with detached thinking (c), with reflecting on facts. Where instead of instinct seeking power, the purposive will is directed towards certain ends. The rationalist talk in late times (Sophists, Rousseau, Marx) is indifferent. The fact is that superiority expresses itself equally through treasures, possession of land, rulership, strength of arms, etc. In primitive times, he who has much property is thereby noble. Poor nobility is meaningless.

38

The great change of race and soul: 5th millennium: the 'peasant', the sedentary man, [has] the firmly established house — instead of the transient one. Change of food. Slaves of the soil instead of masters of the earth. [The] soul of the peasant [is] sly, mischievous, stingy, without much drive, the typical subject who does not leave the soil to remain free, but becomes a slave with it.

39

c-Culture: The 'peasant' is a slave to the soil, bound, disfigured by physical labour, oppressed mentally. Animal husbandry allows man to remain free: he rules over animals, not plants. He does not become a plant. From a purely physical point of view, warrior, hunter and nomad races are better educated than earth workers (mining and agriculture). Type of slave man. Pride is only in land ownership. Tendency of the possessor to emancipate himself from hard labour. The ideal types (Pergamenian goddesses, Germanic tribes of Tacitus, Naumburg Cathedral[16]) are warriors, not peasants.

40

The c-man becomes a planter, earthbound, sedentary, vegetative. Everything else: hunting, fishing, keeping livestock depends on it. With the spread of the desert belt through the old world, part of it is uprooted again: thus arises the nomad, who moves from watering place to watering place, becomes free from the command of the earth, master-man, conqueror. The contrast of peasant people and master people: obeying the earth — commanding. The born slave is the peasant. Hunter, fisherman. Nomads do not allow themselves to be subjugated.

The type of the peasant people emerges in the $5^{th}/4^{th}$ millennium, that of the conqueror people in the 3rd millennium. That is why Egypt [and] Babylon are not conquerors, but planters. Since then, all cultures emerge from ruling classes.

[There are] two types of the wandering man who is free from the earth: Bedouins and Vikings. From the Sahara arises the Atlantic seafaring to [the] North Sea and [to] the Black Sea, perhaps also East Africa — Arabia. From the [desert] Gobi perhaps Pacific shipping — from the Indus or Amur? Inca — chariot peoples. The cold of the far north also drives away the planters and leads to conquest. Scandinavia, Toltecs, Mongols. The master soul — free from the commandment of the earth — also knows community only in the form of violence: nobility, warriors, not peasants. Trade instead of industry.

---

16 The Naumburg Cathedral of St. Peter and Paul is the former cathedral of the diocese of Naumburg and dates from the first half of the 13th century. It is one of the most important late Romanesque buildings in Germany. — *Transl.*

41

The political unit in c is the 'tribe', of a number and limit that make rapid assembly at one point possible. Thus, for example, Benjamin, the Spartans, have been the Cimbri. So numerous that the armed men can also offer resistance. If the number sinks, the tribe joins stronger ones or is broken up; if it grows, it disintegrates. The tribe (elders or chieftain) breaks up into clans (family group), which have their own internal jurisdiction (*clientes, familia*). Franks, Tyrrhenians are tribal; Dorians only a modern abstraction based on language. Only in d was the political unit the nation (city, estate, law, state) with administration and government. The Ostrogoths, Lombards [are] a tribe (c) that tried to found a state (d) on ancient cultural soil. [The] Carolingians [are] likewise [a] tribal federation with the outward form of the Byzantine state. It is only in the 10th century that real Western-style states emerge. Was Kafti[17] a state or an amphictyony[18]?

42

In [the] c-cultures [there is] order according to clans. Patriarchy, matriarchy. Tribe. In the d-culture [the] city [is] society, [represented by the] estates. The more formal, the greater the distance between top and bottom.

Two estates. Third estate. Remainder, peasants. High cultures are aristocratic. Race [is] selection. Race and compatriot — [that is a] contradiction. Opposition to distance just recognises it by its attack. Intellect (programme) against instinct (race values). The healthy human being instinctively feels that distances are natural.

From time immemorial, racial mixture has been a matter of course, everywhere. Landscape, class always shape new types. Only the racially inferior preach race. Culture is form, is poetry. Culture

---

17   Spengler's own spelling of *Keftiu*, an ancient Egyptian term denoting Crete and its Minoan-Mycenaean inhabitants. — *Transl.*

18   An amphictyony was a loose association, on a religious-cultural basis. of cities in ancient Greece. — *Transl.*

is class, tradition, breeding. That is why [all] revolutions are against breeding, education, nobility. It is the outcasts of race, class, culture who bark.

43

What a c-people tenaciously retains is that which belongs to the world- and life-view, to the idea of existence: on the one hand, the custom of war, state, law — i.e. the weapons (ethos, idea of fighting), titles and offices of power; hunting, the house type (= style of the family), on the other hand, the taboo: funeral rite (although the artistic form of the grave is readily adopted), the idea of ornamental expression (not the means of expression), the idea of religion (not names of gods, cults, place, ritual forms). Little emphasis is placed on language, pottery, costume, gods, cults, practical implements.

44

[In] b-c [grows] out of the horde of non-speaking beings the language-connected tribe. Spiritual connection of practical action, enterprise. Spirit-guided instinct and instinct-guided spirit. Horde (swarm) [is] a natural, organic unity, instinctive. Idea of the we. Tribe [is] a conscious, somehow organised unit. Idea and knowledge of unity by end and means. Language rapidly changing, as it is only an aid. In very primitive state. Language with small vocabulary, primitive, grammar, easily learned. Whoever joined the tribe learned the language. The tribe gave up its language and learned that of its neighbour.

45

The seafarer and the horseman is man who has regained his freedom, against the sedentary culture. Culture emanates from the peasant, politics from nomads. Culture is spiritualised, domination is unspiritual. Culture is repugnant to the predator man — he has caught himself in his own fetters, the cunning hunter.

46

From a to d the contrast between insignificant multitudes and significant individuals grows: this is a measure of culture. In c there are still anonymous movements. In d they are hardly possible.

But since in prehistory and archaeology we know only potsherds, implements and weapons, no individual names and individual deeds, the history of such times is sunk into us for ever. Here the insatiable urge to know everything finds an insurmountable limit.

Consider the finds in Boghazköy[19], the Egyptian inscriptions, the remains of ancient Israelite literature: the excavations without this historical knowledge would report nothing of the states, wars, personalities. Only 'layers'.

47

Organisation: In the c-culture there is not yet a 'state', but only the power of a tribe, which can, however, extend over other tribes. A state is a political organisation with officials, administration, the need for written communication. It may be small in size, but the apparatus is essential. Tribal power, on the other hand, is based on personal contact, patriarchal or other cohesion.

A 'state' begins in Kafti around 2000. States were the basis of the Ostrogoths (Theoderic), Visigoths, Vandals, Franks. Powers were Huns. Arminius, Marbod[20]. Tribal organisms arise and pass away, through the death of leaders for example, states are founded and disintegrate. Artificial.

48

Art history: How does what we call art today, looking back, come into being? Surely our feelings and views are very different from what was felt in b [and] c. How do ornament and imitation come

---

19 The site of the ancient Hittite capital of Hattusa in modern-day Turkey. — *Transl.*

20 Marbod (c. 30 B.C.–37 A.D.) was a king of the Marcomanni in Bohemia. — *Transl.*

into being? The art of building is intellectual, enterprise, presupposes language, command, organisation, while everyone can knead and paint for themselves. Construction art therefore only in c. Painting, drawing probably already in b. Building art [is] therefore impersonal at first. Style of the race, because many belong to it. That is why the history of style (d) begins with building. Only when building begins with written designs does personal expression begin, very late. Thus also sculpture and painting: the separation of draft (idea, sketch, plan, i.e. 'writing') and execution (painting, chiselling).

49

In b (Altamira): Not the eye creates, but the playing hand, partly in the dark, instinctively. There is no mention of joy in the formed, but only [of] joy in the forming. That is important: joy in forming, not in the formed. Joy of the hand, not of the eye. As soon as the thing is finished, it is no longer of interest. And it only interested the creator, no one else. The joy of the spectator — if there was one — also goes out when it is finished. Like children who wipe the slate clean and start all over again. Like singing and dancing.

But Altamira is only the accidentally preserved witness of an art exercise that went much further — whooping, wordless, mimicking, dressing up, painting oneself, dancing. All this belongs together. The only things that have survived are paintings and carvings in *hard* material. The painted stone wall is something very secondary in itself. It gives a false image if one constructs steps from there. What we like should never be a standard for these times.

50

a-b Culture of the hand, c-d Culture of speaking, organised, spiritualised through and through, b: looking and foreboding: the eye sees the world under the aspect of the active hand, c: the hand is subject to the spirit, b: conflict fate — causality: nature — human hand working causally. Practical causality, c: conflict spirit — hand. The spirit, working at a distance, the hand near.

51

[The] world-view of c-culture expresses itself in construction, myth, ornament. Construction and adornment (ornament and imitation) originally emerged from different roots: construction is 'enterprise', adornment is 'handwriting', the former thus a 'we', the latter an 'I', the former approaching the language of grammar, the latter the innermost feeling (just as the construction of tragedy and the melos of verse are different). From the expressive activity of building emerges the architectural (also the composition of pictures), from that of jewellery sculpture and painting. Atlantis (stone) and Kash (brick) 'shape' life forms: animal, human, the body, in Atlantis according to its view of life, in Kash mythically shaped. In the north, pantheism corresponds to the predominance of ornamentation. Wooden construction is ornament. The soul of the ship, oar, sword, house, pot is interpreted ornamentally. In landscape painting, the soul of the plant world, mountains, sea.

52

c-Culture: Here 'knowledge' begins as a skill and then as the possession of certain types. With it, however, also the difference between learned and wise, the phenomena of the learned blockhead and the ignorant smart-head. Today, when the world of the learned is a craft with a specific aptitude for certain learned types, methods, areas (as [there is] aptitude for combining pieces of cloth into suits), the learned idiot is something commonplace. Learned thinking [is] often clumsy, stupid, shallow; unlearned very often deep, powerful.

53

The oldest means of transport is the river boat or whatever else you want to call it. Man feared the forest, before which he was powerless, and the mountains, unless they had wide valleys rich in game.

The fact that the 'cave man' was found everywhere in the mountains gave a false picture of his way of living. He survived there, but mostly lived elsewhere. The land route is more difficult than the river route. Every drifting branch showed how it could be done. Much later comes the pack animal, the carrier by land. Still much later the cart. But seafaring arose as a matter of course from river travel — at the mouths.

It is clear that c-settlements are located along rivers (Tripolye, Nile, Indus, Euphrates). A megalithic culture Elbe, Loire, Seine. All rivers could be navigated with sea ships of that time.

54

Culture and work: Activity is something else, is fulfilled existence. Bee, hunting, fishing, gathering, flint-splitting. Nothing about work. Only with c does 'work' begin as a conscious need, which the stronger unloads on the weak. With pure thinking (language), work: farming, animal husbandry, pottery, house building. Periphery of village work. In d the urban work, purely mental, not of the hands. Science, merchant, civil servant, disdain for manual labour, depressing life. Technical city work: slave labour.

55

How long a-b lasted we do not know.

1. Only the 2nd epoch. Long felt but misinterpreted: Neolithic [is] museum viewpoint. Abrupt, brief, fatal. External things. Testimonies: mining, navigation, crop farming, animal husbandry, stone building. Simultaneously 5th millennium everywhere. Reason? Work by several. Presuppose each other: animal husbandry presupposes plant cultivation, trade presupposes pottery, agriculture presupposes draught animals, barter presupposes boat, [the] wagon, [the] road. Language: this can be proved. From here on much faster, each century means something.

2.   What is 'speaking in words'? Suddenly emerged. Words crystallise. Crystallisation. Not the word, but the continuous sentences, sequences of sentences. The peasant rare, not our chatter, only necessary. Gossip, conversation purposeless, pointless, but: the purpose of speech determines the form. It must have had a purpose. Technique of speaking, sentence formation is not pointless. Again, two theories. Romanticism: poetry. Then grammar would have to be different. All poetry is wrestling with language as raw material. Both are wrong. One must start from the form of speaking, not from the language. Desk hypothesis. Conversation among several. Speaking presupposes listening. Answer. What are the forms of sentences? Command, answer, question, statement, negation, affirmation. Speaking is a connection of thoughts. Understanding — making oneself understood. Technique of speaking with the intention of the other person.

3.   Speaking and undertaking were there at the same time. Like hand and tool. Something like 'enterprise' is always plural. Doing to several, its technique.

   Complicated doing: shipping, wagons, mining, stone building, trade. Not 'the ship', but traffic on water; end — means. Creation, will to power over plant, animal, wind, water, God. Creative activity: creation of plant and animal forms, of buildings, ships.

   Marx sees the enterprise as far too banal, stupid. Inventing the car, no: road, driving. Organisation the means, end, arrangement of doing, genius. The 'process' is long, presupposes many individual acts: sowing, harvesting. Cattle. Trade. To devise procedure, to direct enterprise — engineer, director. Governing.

4.   Commanding and obeying. Guide, execute, think out, carry out. Separation of thinking and hand. Work of thought, work of hand: two deeds. Emergence of practical thinking. Creative action. Talent, learning, school, tradition, style, connoisseur. Free path for talent. The masses only instinct, without understanding. Triumph:

the first ship, the first building. Megalithic construction, ship, campaign. Heads and hands. Speaking — thinking.

5. Organisation, grouping into fixed forms. Overall action in battle. Organisation fight against everything. Troop of sailors, company. State: form of history, tribe in battle is army. Battle, strategy, weapons, orders, cunning. Division of the tribe: leaders, governing a technical question. Religion — struggle against the powers. Cunning. List. Interdependence of state, war, army, economic enterprise. A lasting effect. Technology increases work, does not decrease it. New needs. [It increases] therefore number of people downwards. Underclass. Number of noble natures remains, that of the insignificant grows.

6. Speaking, thinking human soul in the organism. 'Social'. Lonely, wanting to remain free, individual — mass, hiding, world-view. Envy, contempt from above. Ambition, pride. Historical feelings that are there once. Basic feelings that no religion, [no] idealism changes, too deep. This is where envy begins, the ambition of the little ones who cannot do anything, of the untalented. Mental conflict of the super- and sub-human. Lonely — herd. Russia, land of the knout.

56

New terms: It is wrong to call sedentary tribes 'agrarian' without further ado. Psychologically, the main thing is settling (house, village) as opposed to wandering. I therefore call c-cultures settlers. They can still be hunters, fishermen. Crop cultivation (not farming) can also be practised by nomads. Livestock, cattle, herd, stable cattle — these are very different things. Settler, home, house belong together. Nevertheless, the migratory instinct can be very strong (north). Settling and language: organisation of life. From hunting to herding, from gathering to planting.

57

New terms: I would like to bring new words instead of *Palaeolithic*, *Bronze Age*, etc. Likewise for *primitive*: difference whether a-b or to-day's 'pathetic tribes'. Clay vessels, cut, metal are inaccurate markers. Word language is more important.

58

Culture and sedentariness: Sedentary man (c) goes on to urban man (d). Sedentary through economy: agriculture, stable farming, mining, harbour, market. Herder 337: The soil no longer belongs to man, but man to the soil. Culture is the crowding together of people, whereby new ways of soul and life arise: envy, malice of merchants, politicians, buyers, scholars, i.e. city people (to soul, culture etc.).

The peasant soul in d as a reaction to the city soul.

Man and woman, father and son, friend and friend are soul relations.

59

'*The horizon*'. The animal has none: its strange world is purely present epitome of sensory stimuli that libidinously attract or re-pel, with life-magnetic certainty of the 'right'. Also the a-human. Indiscriminately (now, here). With the b-man, memory is added; he looks and suspects because the sensory stimulus enlivens the memory: inner images arise, imagination. His world is a 'world-view' as an inner life, free of choice, because the instinct of movement now not only responds to stimuli, but on the basis of past stimuli allows an image to arise as a new, inner stimulus (imagine): image of distant regions, times: yesterday evening, the island over there, the previous action. 'Once', 'there' instead of 'now', 'here'.

In c-man, this becomes knowledge. The reasoning instinct (be-cause, why). The looking memory (image) becomes moreover a causal one (reason, purpose). The horizon is now geographical-historical.

60

Here we show decisively that in all advanced cultures two layers lie one above the other, a peasant-Bedouin c[-layer] with peasant wisdom, proverb, custom, 'superstition', primitive religiosity, and a d[-layer] with philosophy, religious system, writing, school, state.

So that the Catholic Church is to be distinguished from the rural religiosity which adopted its doctrines together with the structure: a peasant and a scholastic textbook, the politics of Louis XIV and the political instinct of the Bretons. The latter expresses itself in peasant hatred of 'the state'. Revolt, particularism. A large part of 'Domestic Politics' consists in the cautious treatment of this fact: Rome and Italics, Germany and Bavarians.

61

Here rises the great eternal question of why, which shall not fade away again, ever more desperate, more urgent, more sharply conceived, with innumerable answers which only reveal the soul of the answer without satiating the torment of the question. Here, in the gifted minorities, thinking becomes a rage for causality, gnawing with grotesque features at eternal mysteries. The image on which this obsession, almost identical with religion, tried itself, in Atlantis ancestor, grandson, soul after death, in Kash life and world, heaven and earth. Genealogical: time, afterlife, ancestor worship. Cosmological: space, heaven, earth.

62

Wars, c: The forms of these wars are still preserved today wherever peasantry and Bedouinism have been preserved: in the Italian vendetta, in the *Haberfeldtreiben*[21], in the village feud of the young, the tribal feud of Arab tribes, in the Camorra[22].

The vendetta of the Bonaparte and Pozzo di Borgo families, who made politics 1800–1815, shows how deep this runs in people who are true to their race. Vendetta shimmers through in the *Iliad* in the feud between Achilles and Agamemnon, which at the time was closer to the listener in human terms than the battle for Troy. Homer himself no longer understood the motif. The feuds of the Israelite tribes, Egyptian districts.

63

Personality: In the b-cultures (Altamira) the human hands (bees, beavers) are organs of expression of a somnambulistic active body, more drawn towards than reaching out. This absolute instinctual painting [is] neither regulated nor hindered by any individual consideration. These drawings, like bee cells, are not at all the product of 'an' 'artist' and yet are already the expression of a heavy sense of destiny.

In c-culture, the 'abbreviated drawing' is made from such things as a symbol, glyph, by *one*, but as a carrier of the we-idea, not designed [or] willed, not as a concept of art above all: so still today the genuine peasant art. Here the I begins, but as an atom of a we, never subjectively. These styles are without individual deviations.

Only in d did the 'artist' (builder, painter, singer) emerge who, in contrast to the others (spectators), is aware of his role. The idea of the work of art and [the] artist emerges: they are the persons in whom primeval time (b-c) emanates, misunderstood, tragic, struggling. And

---

21 The *Haberfeldtreiben* is a custom in Upper Bavaria. A nightly field court is held near the residence of a person to be publicly reprimanded. Standing on a beer barrel by torchlight, the *Haberfeldmeister* recites the person's misdeeds and asks, 'Is it true?' The *Habers*, dressed in dark robes, reply with a deafening noise, 'It is true!' Finally, the criticised is told to come back next year if he does not improve his behaviour. — *Transl.*

22 The Camorra is an Italian mafia organisation in the region of Campania. — *Transl.*

so it is everywhere: the 'genius' personality is the isolated mendelized b-type, the man of destiny as commander, artist, seer. The talents are the special gifts of the 'I'-people. Genius is primeval type, talent is accidental (so there are genius and ingenious talents) as talent for talking, dancing, calculating, hairdressing. For now that everything that happens is consciously 'done', doing finds a technique, and talent is skill in procedure of some kind. Universal talent is nonsense.

In b all are 'brilliant', in c-d few. Art history (d) [is] the history of talents (school, style) with interspersed geniuses.

64

c-Culture: I want to get serious here for the first time about the distinction between race, language and people, which has often been found but never — never — practically carried out. I refer to *Decline of the West I*. I call a people a political unit which as such comes to the consciousness of its members. The Egyptians have been a 'people' ever since they formed an empire. Before that, the parts, districts, tribes were each a 'people'. There has never been a Sumerian people. It is irrelevant for the existence of a people whether several languages are spoken in it (Chatti, 'Sumir and Akkad'), let alone [several] 'races' are represented.

By race I mean an unconscious unity of bodily expression that was once soul expression but has become fossil in many traits and now mendelizes. But 'races' around 3000 are very blurred, mixed, abraded types. Then there is the notion of people — what a uniform landscape [or a] city produces in terms of its own traits.

Finally, language, which never creates conscious units as a type, always as a dialect: linguistic affinity ('Aryan' and 'Semitic') is a scientific fact, not a historically conscious one. Languages in the real sense are only those in which simple people understand each other immediately. All others are 'barbaric' languages for those who hear them, without distinction. Not linguistic but speaking affinity [counts].

65

b (Altamira): Instinct of the formation of the being, a result of the onset of cold, which awakens from a permanent bond with [the] fullness of nature. Not art, but a natural instinct that stands between the honeycomb of the bees and the symbolism of the figure, still impersonal, close to nature, already inspiring 'the foreign'.

c (Ceramics): Here already the separation of two worlds of form with different natures, the instinctive-organic (mountain form of the vessels = bee cells) and the spiritually organised (symbolism of lines and colour formations, 'ornament', to which belong megalithic grave and templum! Primeval song).

d: Only here the real 'art', namely the personal consciousness to express the inner, in 'works' whose purpose is not practical, but inner need in itself: thus beyond the megalithic grave to statue, relief. From ornament to the conscious imitation of world contents through word poetry, image poetry (epic, painting). Only this is artistic 'creation'. I call that poetry. A symbol or ornament is not poetised, but comes into being, super-personally. A poem has a personal author.

66

Ceramics: It is the graphology before writing, the actual handwriting of c-cultures, from the daily habit of 'ornamenting'. The language of the hand emerges as a conscious means of expression in c, from the alpera symbol to the cursive script: the great graphology of the we-personal peoples. This is much more immediate (drawing curves with the pen, practised, dexterous, daily) than weaving patterns and building. This expression of being rises to great heights in the North, where life honours itself, not ancestors or gods.

67

c-d-culture: The dominant form of spirituality, which we must presuppose in c, is 'common sense', peasant shrewdness, mother wit, today among farmers, fishermen, hunters, primitive peoples, [in] proverbs. But also among landed nobles, 'uneducated' monks. Only in the cities does erudition then grow, which goes well together with stupidity: learned fools, writerly fools. Something artificial out of which literacy grows, a bliss of writing, preaching, talking, debating, which disgusts the sane man.

68

(a) Race, life, blood = will to power. Language and thought: in palaver it becomes a syntactical tool, a concrete occasion of advance consultation of what is to be 'undertaken'. Speech only here as a deliberate communication of concrete contents (hunting expedition, building a ship, cult action, calculating, commanding, deliberating. From the instinctive 'we' to the 'I' and 'you'), which demand organisation.

b) Culture. From here on history is 'made' (on a small scale), although it is destiny. From the idea of the 'we' to organisation. Self-conscious majorities! Family, estate, band, guild, corporation, priesthood, gerousia[23], womanhood, young men. 'People', the consciousness of the organised, idea of situation, leadership, enterprise, habit of discussion, of task. 'Politics', 'war' as organised action. Skill as history. Landscape and history. Awareness of the causal relationship between land and man (climate, disfavour, opportunity, deliberate change of place, traffic, journeys).

c) Economy takes the form of enterprise: organisation of building a house, tomb, blacksmithing, shipping, expedition. Age of religion, its infinite power over the mind! Myth too must be discussed, narrated, the cult act organised as an enterprise.

---

23 The gerousia was the council of elders in ancient Sparta. It was the only Spartan court that could sentence people to death or exile them. — *Transl.*

69

The 'we': Even today, when individualism supposedly reigns, the power of the 'we' in its magical force is as great as ever. People just have different names for it. In a conference of ambassadors before a war, every individual wants peace, but everyone knows that it is useless and that war will break out for nothing. In every parliament this mood is overhead, everyone sees the nonsense, but no one can stop it. The 'we' is stronger than all the individuals put together. Likewise when in a party, a trust, the leaders meet. There is 'something in the air' and they do not come together, although *everyone* wants to. There is talk of inner inhibition — in fact the we, to speak with Freud, is only repressed (prejudices etc.). In any case, for the whole of higher history there is the fact that in a majority there is something stronger than all the individual wills together. And there it becomes apparent that the conscious will directed towards a logical goal does not reach nearly as deep as the dark, organically logical instinct of the 'we'.

70

It is only with c-d that the world situation arises, that people, organised as a people, therefore thinking in the categories of the 'human world', confront this with the rest of the world practically and theoretically: animals and plants and everything else are objects, the human world is divided into friends ('people', tribe, family, clan, class, etc., as the case may be) and enemies. Theoretically, this is expressed, for example, in religion, which opposes gods and humans, practically in the transformation of the earth's crust by humans.

71

Archetypal symbols of the cultural stages: The [primordial symbols] of the high cultures have arisen from interbreeding — defence of the lower by the victorious. Victorious in Egypt and Babylon was the southern hot, otherwise the Nordic. The proto-American also came from the north (Indians from Europe?) and was overlaid by the Pacific. Body, space, path are therefore symbols of defence and triumph, which is why they are so striking.

Much more general, shapeless are those of the a-cultures, not organised, but organic, such as 'striving', 'saturated', which expresses itself in ornament, building, grave, aristocracy, in numen, myth, eroticism. The a-cultures are only temperaments, unsymbolic; the b-cultures (destiny) mere tendencies, nuances of being judged. So also the 'soul' of these cultures is basaltic, crystalline, organic, organised. But only the high cultures are tragic, image of a duel, hard, dangerous, c is passing, displacing, merging, soul of villages and tribes.

72

Cultures: Important that the times become shorter and shorter: a — 100,000; b — 10,000; c — 3,500; d — 1,000. So one must not speak of ages, b-d together are short compared to a. Epic — tragic. Long breath — explosion.

73

Amoebae and plants: It belongs to the character of the amoeba that it does not reach peaks of vitality as a whole, but forms 'buds' everywhere again and again, which have a form-creating effect, short-lived, thus the Atlantic one in Portugal, Brittany, Crete, Sardinia. The early amoebae have long since died, leaving dead remains in the system of living languages and arts. Ethnology can no longer find anything living of Hamitism. What is perhaps still alive today are the young amoebae of the $3^{rd}/2^{nd}$ millennium: High Norse and Southeast Asian with buds like Peru, Japan, Haida.

So the amoebae's native soil must not be too narrowly circumscribed, especially by an area of highest design. So not 'Portuguese megalithic culture', but more generally the 'Atlantic West' to France and Tunis, and for Kash the northern edge of the Indian Ocean. Amoebae are creative possibilities that light up here and there into high realities.

74

Relationship of older and younger c-cultures: They form amoeboidly again and again, without it being possible to say exactly whether and since when they are separate individuals instead of one amoeba. Already in the Aurignacian-Capsian, around 10000, there is a North- and South-Atlantic crystallisation centre, the exact location of which is uncertain for this one, probably Africa. Likewise, a c-culture Alps — Shantung could be a younger Kash Amoeba ('Japhetic languages'?).

75

c-culture: Was there a periodic *diastole and systole of amoebae* here instead of an early and late period of plants? Are the large c-strains periodic?

Around 3500 shuffling of repelled

Kash and Atlantis elements

3000 the procreation

2500 Tuimah, end of the Old Kingdom.

Bronze Age. Upheaval? Emergence

of the c-culture of the North

2000 Hyksos, Kassites[24]

1500 Sea Peoples

1000 Dorians. Ionian Phoenician

expansion!

600 Celts, Medes, Scythians, Persians,

China, Sabellians?

200 A.D. Migration of peoples

600 A.D. Islam

1200 Inner Asia and Columbus.

---

24 Originally from the Zagros Mountains, the Kassites founded the second Babylonian Kingdom. — *Transl.*

Is there a rhythm in this? Is the Negro expansion a consequence of this? Can a Dravidian thrust be inferred in India? When? And the ceramic expansion? Bell beakers. Nuraghi[25]. Bronze Age.

76

b-c cultural streams (Menghin 658): The Late Capsian first breaks through the border between Aurignacian and Capsian south of the Pyrenees and, mixing with the Late Magdalenian, penetrates as far as northern Europe, Maglemose! Thus the proto-Atlantic trend is marked out. After that, the Capsian centre is in central and southern Spain and northwest Africa. This is where the term Atlantis is formed.

Apart from this, there is a Western European (Northern Spain, France, England) centre for Aurignacian and Magdalenian and a Far Eastern (Asiatic?) one with the Solutrean, which pushes in late and weakly between Aurignacian and Magdalenian east of the Rhine for a short time.

77

c-Cultures: structure: They too show a (slow) emergence, less birth than sprouting, then maturing, sprouting, dividing, asexual procreation, age. In contrast to the magnificent ascent — like a rocket — in the high cultures, here it is slow. Everything the ethnologist examines in today's folk culture is the remnant of it, decaying, blurring, without power.

At the beginning, a formidable comparison with botanical expression. The c-culture amoebae (a sprout is the bell cup culture), local lateral formations, division, creeping. Plasma. There is at least (there are no exact *tempi* here!) a millennium between emergence and height of the life force. The height at Kash-Atlantis in the 4th millennium, at North and South in the 2nd [millennium]. Amoebae can flow together. They have no sharp boundaries.

------

25 The nuraghi are megalithic tower-fortresses in Sardinia. — *Transl.*

Frobenius has discovered that today the Atlantean c-culture still lies in Spain, France, Britain, southern Italy in the folklore, which has Old Norse Rhine and Tiber as its border. This is where the Faustian late soul was conceived!

78

c-Cultures: The number of these cultures is small; besides two mighty ones, some smaller ones may have arisen, without significance. In any case, the emergence of 'Orient and Occident' is here for all time.

The number of 'eternal' ideas that created these c-cultures is small. The whole history of the world is based on a few very large concepts, e.g. the cosmological idea of Kash, the genealogical idea of Atlantis. Into these c-cultures falls the creation of the desert belt: the aftermath of the pluvial, the forest cover dying.

79

If already in the Upper Palaeolithic the differences in rank between the streams of developed humanity become great, to the point of complete impossibility of understanding each other, in the c-cultures the unity is lost for good. Here flowing cultures emerge high above the Palaeolithic rest, but among themselves they are by no means equal. The centre of gravity is undoubtedly the Mediterranean. What goes on in the Ranjun-Cambodia area or in North America does not have this height. Around 3000, when everything becomes narrower and steeper, the centre of gravity is on the Nile and Euphrates, around 1000 in Central Asia from Smyrna to Shantung, around 1000 A.D. again on the Euphrates, around 2000 again in Atlantis.

80

Northland: At the beginning, ch. 2. c-culture, only prove its existence. Draw the *soul* only in the hero chapter. *Nibelungen* film[26], longing for the sun. At that time Germanicism separates itself, the last saved treasure of the highest inward heroism: here honour and loyalty to the point of death (blood revenge) are taken to extremes, beyond the three previous cultures: this only appears in the migration of peoples. Kriemhild's revenge.

So draw this in three mighty stages: 1. plant 4000. 2. outbreak 2000, Roman legions. Similar in India and China is lost. 3. last and highest flowering 0–1000. World War. What remains is the Aino-style from Stavanger via the Russian Church to Peking, Northern Rim, muzhik[27] culture.

81

Of the strength of the c-movements and the subtleties of their last effects one has too little idea. The new souls took hold of the folklore up to the last frontiers of the old world. This can be proved from Spain to Scandinavia and Persia, from [the] Alps to China, from the Persian Gulf to the Baltic Sea: from this one can measure the force and the reach to other regions that have not yet been explored.

82

In the case of amoebae, one can really speak of influence; something of the form tendency or matter of the others flows into them (Linear Pottery), while plants only 'assimilate'. That is more than comparison. In the image of nature, i.e. the visual world of thinking men, synonymous visual processes appear again and again — 'going before the eyes'. Man, too, is 'nature' for the human eye. History, too, is the

---

26 *Die Nibelungen* ('The Nibelungs'), directed by Fritz Lang in 1924 and consisting of two parts: *Siegfried* and *Kriemhild's Revenge*. — *Transl.*

27 A Russian peasant. — *Transl.*

history of an element in nature. So elementary pictorial processes in plant, animal and human stories are symbolically identical.

83

The need for a divorce of ages of prehistory has always been there, but it has been satisfied, like everything in the 19th century, by materialistic division: the transition from cut stone to polished stone, from the cave to the hut — that is, the supposed 'achievements of mankind' on its way from hunter and fisherman to jazz, cinema and radio. The true epoch, around 5000, is the step from the organic to the organised, the emancipation of the spirit from life, which is now conscious, first 'recognised' by the spirit, then regulated. Life passes from the natural to the artificial. Instinct is to be subjugated — this is and remains an ideal — to the intellect. This tremendous revolution takes place only in individual districts and in these in some mental types of humanity. From now on there are lower and higher types of humanity, the former in what and how it happens — substance and sacrifice, the latter spirit and master. Individual cultures, organisms, arise instead of the primeval culture, and the question arises as to how they relate to older and younger types (b-c-d). Within this c-culture everything is and happens differently, fatally, abruptly, artificially, always endangered.

84

'Hunters', *'peasants'*: Psychologically extremely naive is the division of 'peoples' according to two economic forms. Firstly, the 'economy' does not distinguish people psychologically; secondly, choice of economy is an expression of character; thirdly, there are no peoples; fourthly, there are many more 'economic forms'.

It is shallow and materialistic to believe that the peasant was different from the hunter: because one is different, one becomes a peasant. But in reality there are, in colourful confusion, fishing tribes, seafaring tribes, mining tribes, tribes living in forest districts, in clearings, on high steppes, many tribes side by side, whose men are engaged in all kinds of activities. It is always the minority of the tribes that are economically one-sided, e.g. do not hunt, fish, farm.

III. BECOMING HUMAN

GENERAL CULTIVATION

1

THE DECISIVE THING is the world feeling, wordless, instinctive, which finds expression in custom, grave, weapon, state, religion, world-view. The 'racial' world feeling separates the pre-cultures. It is the felt relationship of the individual soul to others, to the world, to life. This is expressed in [the] customs (grave, battle, relationship to animals) and [in the] style of life. Nordic pantheism: individual names for domestic animals (the horse, the dog), implements (sword). Position towards animals. In the West [the animal is] a thing, in the North an associated being.

The religious primordial views (*Weltanschauung*[1]) [are] an expression of the feeling for the world.

2

There are two superior ways for human beings to overcome mere attachment to the earth: to free themselves from it through the sea (today the flight) and to master it through mobility (horse, car). A

---

1   This German term denotes how someone understands and explains the world. It makes clear what a person considers important and right. — *Transl.*

new spiritual air blows over this life, no longer the dull one of the slaves of necessity, of the soil.

3

Mutations are catastrophes that occur suddenly and mysteriously. They are forms of appearance that one does not understand. In human history they follow one another ever more rapidly from the beginning of the coming into being of man to the high cultures. One must not read 'cause' and 'effect' out of the succession of phenomena.

4

With the beginning of 'spiritual' wakefulness, an 'inner distance' occurs between the people of a 'we', and the sympathetic feelings that were once identical with the we-feeling, indiscriminate, all-embracing, now become elective affinities between lovers: the man wishes to embrace this woman, and between comrades: beginning of friendship.

Speaking as a bridge between I's.

5

Human earth': From now on, the aspect before the understanding eye changes: no longer only the background of a world, from which the situations and impressions alternately stand out, arousing attention, but two worlds: 'Nature' as earth with the sky above, plain, forest, river, sea, mountains with plants and the animals that fly, swim, roam — and secondly, in the foreground, as it were, the 'human world', the throng of 'my equals', engaged in an activity, as I myself do, that fills the earth, continues behind the mountains … This seen world: narrower, more daily, but the world that 'knows' man because it lives within natural limits in some felt community: the population of an island, a valley, a plain. Still today: Brittany, Bavarian Oberland. You see each other more closely, you understand each other better, you speak your own language with dialect.

6

Incipit tragoedia[2]: Theory versus practice: foreboding and looking become a tendency and intervene in doing. From imagining what has been and what is to come to the idea of 'future' and the means of knowing and changing it. From imagining the (beyond the circle of vision) to the idea of the human-inhabited world around the here. Here the We arises: I in the infinite world.

From theory to cult: taboo. Need of expressive language in symbols simultaneously with the rise of conceptual thinking (rare) [is] grammar. From grammar to syntax: habituation to abstract thought and communication: relating to what is seen instead of meaning of what is seen. An abstract conceptual world instead of the seen: syntactic speaking refers to this. Types of burial (rites).

Valuation of life. From the doing to the single act. Later to the cultic individual act. Taboo morality: 'good and evil' applied to behaviour.

From fear of possible misfortune to insight into the misery of life in general: life as fate. Soul, vision, foreboding in chorus. Sentient understanding each for itself. [From the] soul [directed] [towards the] world: centrifugal. [From the] world [directed] [towards the] soul: centripetal.

Mythical overall interpretation of the world (age of the fear of the gods, day interpretation, sun).

7

Ethics, literary history: The Nordic soul [is] noble, brooding. Only the male. Female souls (and minds) are different. Therefore only man understands man. Friendship. Therefore 'patriarchal' order, male state, male art. What is woman's art? Manual labour. The Nordic soul is extremely masculine. In action and contemplation. Woman does not know these struggles of the soul. Only the decadent, non-procreative

---

2   Latin: 'the tragedy begins'. — *Transl.*

woman, the non-mother, strains her little brain to occupy herself with men's questions.

8

The Nordic soul [is] by nature solitary, therefore brooding. In Kash and Atlantis one does not brood. One interprets the sensually tangible, from the outside, in space. Only the North — India, China, antiquity, the West — is mentally frayed from the inside out.

Egyptians and Babylonians do not know the suffering of the soul, only the external suffering, illness, death, poverty. These souls live in the sun. The lonely soul of the North broods in the night. Agony of soul. What is the meaning of existence, of suffering for me in contrast to the universe? Jesus had no idea of such questions. Conscience, repentance, penance have a meaning in the North whose depth remains inaccessible to the South. 'Soul' has a different sound. Soul struggles — where do they exist in Egypt and Babylon, in the Old Testament, in the Gospels?

It is nonsense, à la Ibsen and Nietzsche, to bring in the opposition between Christianity and paganism. It is a question of the opposition between nobility and priests. Both are priestly natures who envy the nobleman because he is a doer and not a brooder.

9

With speech and the habit of speech-bound thinking begins the punishment of curiosity, the hunt for novelty, revelation, wanting to know everything. The novelty, the gossip. The traders [are] welcome as the bringers of the new — lies. Sailors, hunters. Gossip from neighbouring tribes. Everything that the telegraph, [the] newspaper, [the] radio brings today [existed] then, only the pace is different.

Also curiosity — what is behind the mountains, beyond the sea. Wanting to know the invisible. What is behind the moon and the stars. What lies behind death and before birth. What 'once' was or will be. Once upon a time. Grandfather told — —

At last, what is behind things. Scientific curiosity.

10

Causa is 'power'. But in the way of thinking a causa, cultures divide as inner forms of the whole of human 'life'. Is the arrow the power, or does it sit in it, or in the fact of tensioning the bow, or in the arm, or in the will of the person shooting, or outside?

The human soul [is] different, changed, from case to case. Philosophy seeks to form uniformly, in vain. There are prevailing typical differences in causal thinking.

11

Cruelty: If there is 'something to see', fire, blood, wailing, destruction, even Peter and Paul would no longer captivate the crowd, even if they spoke with angelic tongues. This is a primal human instinct, but a purely human one. Sensation, curiosity, creepiness — what is that? A spiritual corruption of primal feelings? Poetry, the 'picture', public curiosity, social mores, diversions, events that sweep the soul away, film, gladiators are all based on this. We have used amusement for pleasure. This is how the dance of primitive races differs from that of the great cities.

12

'Spiritualisation of the drives': The drives become special — with the rise of language — technology — spirit — organisation. For example, the will to live for power in the sense of duty, acquisitiveness, commanding, cruelty, zeal for instruction, missionary fervour, proselytising, ambition, lust for power, urge for independence, sense of justice, love of truth, urge for research, will for knowledge, zeal for persuasion. And all these can come into opposition with each other: magnanimity against the will to justice, 'wanting to have' against pity (inner superiority over the comforted), struggle between duty and inclination, love and hate, tragedy material! All this is spiritualised. The unspiritual forms, for example, are the instinct of satiety, the instinct

of annihilation, the instinct of sex, the instinct of power, the instinct of destruction. Transmuted instincts belong to the transmuted will, elemental instincts to the elemental will. This is the difference between the cerebral inner life (cultural man) and the elemental: knowing desires and blind desire. The hero is the Nordic cerebral type, while the Egyptians and Babylonians are only the preliminary stage. The latter have world-consciousness, the former [has] self-consciousness: he sees through his position in the world. In peasantry (c) it remains undeveloped. High culture develops it in great form. Antiquity: will to be. India, China, Faust: the will to distance. History: the raging spiritual instincts.

13

Soul: It will no longer be possible to ask: Did this act correspond to the human soul? but: Did it correspond to the soul of that time? It turns out that the human soul has a history and that this is one with world history: in form. I will begin a historical psychology instead of a systematic one. I ask not only: What is ambition, but: When did it arise? The fear of the gods in the 5th millennium, ambition in the 2nd millennium. Soul greatness that flared up from one point to another from soul to soul. And if fame-seeking, bravery, a sense of honour arose at a certain point in time and from there helped to form history, then this history is the image of the history of the soul. It is not from contemporary people that one draws the development of the soul, but from historical people.

14

Soul: Pride, loyalty, arrogance and contempt belong to the spiritualised feelings. The last to appear are those which contain more spirit than soul and in which heroism is gnawed from within: doubt, mockery, contempt of the world of man, doubt of the self, of God, of everything. Hopeless melancholy, grinning, a sense of comedy. There is a scepticism that kills. Don Quixote, Mephisto emerged from it, so that the highest possible solution is still humour. Scepticism, disgust, doubt, ridicule, boredom: the hyenas that gnaw at the human heart. The depth of the capacity to suffer diminishes. The soul withers. There is only grief for lost money, joy at the gramophone, anger at bad stock prices, love of the bob cut.

15

Suffering is the great educator, the benefactor of humanity. It is from suffering that humanity has matured. From it it learned pride, glory, bravery, reverence. To overcome misfortune or to escape from it — this is where noble and base natures part company. For what follows on the heels of suffering, the bypassed suffering, is emptiness.

16

The great chapter on the tragic human soul of c-culture: The cerebral traits. Cruelty, pity, love (Romeo), hatred, pride. Still later, with the 'nevertheless' of heroism, the traits of honour, revenge, bravery. Melancholy: a caged animal goes to sleep, a hero suffers.

Cruelty and pity: pity, renunciation, asceticism as fine suicide, the tragic as self-torment. All the poetry of the 'people' (folk song, dance) with its melancholy is sweet torment. For no one rages against others who does not also torment himself. Here melancholy arises as a c-temperament. Here also the idea of crime — the conscious breaking of the sacred form.

17

'*Epoch*': This is the great concept without which the becoming of the knowing human being cannot be grasped. In the soul's being, around 5000, there is a great epoch: the emergence from the mystical all-connectedness (which conjured up images of the mammoth in the darkness) into the light of causal wanting to know — an impoverishment of man who has become unnatural, an expulsion. 'Epoch' [stands] at the beginning of every culture. Epochs are always mental mutations; historical epochs are only their spiritually comprehensible precipitation: a different appearance.

18

So I draw the picture of the soul not physically but historically: since it is not a thing but a process, and since all human souls of all times represent a single process of a higher order, in which traits appear, spread, change and fade through long sequences of generations, it has not parts but epochs. In general, it has animalistic, primeval, then humanly prehistoric, finally historical traits in its nature and activity.

There are animalistic, historical types of elementary fear and longing. Pride, a feeling of nothingness, cruelty and pity are historical traits. There is an animal-elemental will, a life tendency, and historical types of will: Faustian, Apollonian, Magian: for historical traits are not only conditioned by the stage of the type of culture, but also by the style of the individual culture.

19

Soul: What are actually the creative traits of the historical soul? Curiosity, mischievousness, cruelty, slander, lies: theatre, sport, newspapers, party life, conversation and social questions are based on these. The opposite of these is so rare that exceptions become proverbial.

20

Soul: The most terrible feeling of superior natures is contempt, for it indicates to the opponent his rank. Contempt does not ridicule the other, it does not insult, torment, oppress him, but *overlooks* him. He is no longer there. It seems that only heroism, not the Egyptian, Babylonian kings understood how to despise: perhaps the Hittites. To scorn is not to despise.

21

Soul: The Thersites[3] feelings belong to the feeling of distance: taking slaps in the face with a smile and taking revenge afterwards with one's mouth, lackey, rabble, prole, democratic feelings (even lying on one's stomach in front of money, the crowd, the majority).

Homer, as a man of letters, knew how to portray this brilliantly, but he did not know how to portray the contempt of the superior: for the skald is himself a Thersites nature. One calls him when one is bored, one sends him away when he becomes annoying. All literary money-making is based on this.

22

Soul: There are two kinds of egoism. 'I am valuable to the culture.' 'I am valuable to myself.' That is posh and mean. In world cities the second prevails: *panem et circenses*[4], Ibsen, Stirner[5], democracy, sophists. In the old lineage the first (Rome, England, Prussia, nobility).

The aristocratic attitude values the personality according to its value for the cause (status, lord, 'I serve'), the democratic one wants to ensure everyone the enjoyment of their person. Duty (attachment) — freedom. The aristocrat feels obliged by attitude, action, form to serve the cause to which he belongs. He is therefore obliged to preserve and increase his rank and wealth; in him the cause is elevated: representation. The parvenu[6], intellectual nobility, on the other hand,

---

3   In Homer's *Iliad*, Thersites was a soldier in the Greek army who participated in the Trojan War. — *Transl.*

4   Latin: 'bread and circuses' (bread and games). — *Transl.*

5   Max Stirner (1806–1856) is the most consistent and radical representative of the Own (the Self, the subject) as the analogue of alienation (reification) in the 19th century. His counterparts in more recent times are Julien Offray de La Mettrie in the 18th century, Wilhelm Reich and Arthur Janov in the 20th century, and Peter Töpfer in the 21st century. — *Transl.*

6   From French, derogatory: a simple person who has suddenly become rich or famous. — *Transl.*

lives himself for pleasure, imitates. Proud solitude — representing a lost cause.

All this is polarity of the Nordic soul alone (China, India, antiquity). The aristocrat demands with a clear conscience self-evident submission, obedience, because the cause lives in him. The extreme opposite is the world-view of the urban rabble, from the rich parvenu to the unemployed: enjoyment at other people's expense.

23

Laughter: The mere joyful laughter of the child, the antithesis of crying, is primordially human. In the age of speech, laughter has become more differentiated, more spiritualised than crying. The pleasing, mocking, gleeful, angry laughter: a whole language full of revelation of the soul that one does not like to admit. Desperate laughter and tears of joy.

24

The age of the great questions: This is where the riddles and joking questions belong, a main thing of ancient poetry, the charm of playing around the mysteries: one feels the answer as a pleasure, to have illuminated a darkness, spiritual relief; questions frighten. Especially number riddles: how much, how often, when: the mystery of the number is oppressive, enigmatic.

The animal fable paints soul traits for the first time: consciously awakening physiognomy. The riddle orders. Age of symbolic answers. Theory: looking and foreboding, sensually exact imagination. The foreboding of the numerical is descriptive. Likewise, the fable is a symbolism of mental processes in form and action. Animal symbolism. Likewise, the riddles are the result of urgent imagination.

25

Layers can also be distinguished in myth: Riddle-like myths in which things, processes, data appear as beings (animal, then human), without inorganic logic, at the very end only an ordered mythical world in which the narratives fit to some extent into a fixed overall picture. What the primitive view of the world looked like can be deduced from the most ancient fairy tales and fables: themselves enigmatic, full of contradictions, a nightmare, full of illogical horrors, a fever dream, not much different from the dreams of today's spiritual people. But how did people dream back then? Apparently, people did not find the waking world very different and transferred experiences from here to there.

The first question here is not: what *is* looking, but *when* does the early human being give himself over to looking? Therefore distinguish: looking of the active and inactive human being. What gives rise to the 'theory'? Satisfaction of urges: feeling of power, danger. Hunger, anger and fear: of natural forces and hostile beings, first only [of] animals.

26

Only with the loss of the all-connectedness does the urge for 'relationships' arise. The horde is connected to the universe and thus also to other hordes, animals, mountains, water. Now, with the expulsion from this oneness, the constant connectedness is replaced by the sought and produced, always artificial and solvable 'relationship' in the form of speech, intercourse, and later in the systematic forms of relationship of state and religion. Religion, too, is the relationship between beings within and beings outside (above, below). 'I and you', 'we and you' are relationships. Relationships have a causally conscious character. The primordial relationship is still symbolic, not conceptual in nature, thus recognised, but not yet 'explainable'. This is also true of primeval art, whose creation is understood but cannot be grasped as a work of art.

27

The doom of the number: As long as there was no I, only 'race', there was a very noble average with a small number. The inferior escaped. But the mass-like is the multiplication downwards, not of the top, but of the base. Hence the enormous difference of inner rank: while the noble, counted in absolute terms, was not common, it loses itself more and more in the mud of the common (the 'common' in the very correct double sense of average and meanness). Mass peoples. Mass cities.

Thus the value of the race *Homo* declines. Multiplicity is meanness (since the 'I' is in itself something exclusive): shallow, ignoble, stupid, narrow — measured against the ideal type.

28

What is quite decisive is the soul's formation through the constant impressions of density, of the 'human earth'. There is no feature of the developmental history of the soul as little as of 'world history' that is not co-determined by the fact of the number of human beings.

What is history and what are world affairs? History of the 'human earth' — - but for this the consciousness of the human world must not only be present, but must have become effective in the formal language of the expression of life: the fact that crowds of people dwell everywhere, touch each other, so that the lostness of a horde in space is already felt as an exception, liberating or frightening.

29

The 'we' is the experience of the unity of feeling and wanting, the 'you' is the experience of opposition in the dispute of opinions. Originally, the tribe to which one belongs is the world. Only slowly [does] the experience 'one tribe among others, something in the world' mature.

30

'Experience': It begins with the experience of the bird of prey, the breeding animal, the grazing cow, the hunter, warrior, pregnant woman, merchant, blacksmith, and ends with the medicine man and philosopher. For what is written in the books is the experience, cling-ing to words, of the professional brooding, the switchboard experience

of the naturalist. In judging, as in shooting, it is the point of view that matters. The 'place' determines the result. There is no other kind of criticism, and the end and conclusion of all wisdom is that one realises this. War and disputation (with 'intellectual' weapons). In the end, it depends solely on the tactics, not on the reasons, but on what [one] mutually acknowledges and advances as reasons; a commentary belongs to it, a point of honour, ticklish rules, preconditions, locations of the combatants; and over all this, in the end, the race decides again, because it chooses the means, the lists, the fencing moves. Animal traits everywhere (Brehm[7]).

31

'Mongolian' [is] a physiognomic type, not of bone but of muscle, thus originating in the soul. But the muscular form draws the bones with it. So this type of race arises in the epoch of world-view, of grammar. Hair, jaw, eye colour follow facial expression. Grandiose picture of how physiognomy not only teaches us to understand the races, but creates them. Thus, within the race 'human', the type 'human race' is created, which has then become rigid. Syntax only influences facial expressions, not gait and muscles.

So before Mongols and Caucasians lie the archetypes of physiognomic races, even earlier physiognomy-less masses. Influence of the landscape on these types, shape of the skull.

32

How in the moving body, already in the primeval times of animal history, the face triumphs over scent, hearing, etc.! The eye is the origin of the head, even in very low species. But the type of the limbs and vertebrates is completely dominated by it. In man the tyranny of the knowing eye now follows — in the South, in the age of the great mythology. After-thought has an optical character, inner images.

---

7   Alfred Edmund Brehm (1829–1884) was a German writer and zoologist who popularised zoological literature. — *Transl.*

33

The archaic 'cities' [are] castles or markets. Then special markets for certain articles at the place of discovery: salt, fish, metal, wood, skins. Development of market order, peace, law. Long-distance markets: Rhine Valley 1st half of the 2nd millennium, Danube valley around 1000, with direction there to the east, here to the south. Peddlers.

Under Dagobert I (628–38) the fair of St. Dionys (St. Denis near Paris) was world-famous in Western Europe. London [was] then the cattle market of Kent. Likewise, the ancient Egyptian and Babylonian 'cities' were in part great markets. Likewise Carthage, Massilia, Smyrna.

The whole history of settlement in the eastern Mediterranean, the Assyrians (Kültepe[8]), Hittites, Carians, Ionians — everything is market history.

34

Causes of migration, c-culture: In the end, they are always of a deeply spiritual nature. What is called 'overpopulation' is attributed by today's material thinking of purpose to economic hardship, but 'hardship' is a very fluctuating feeling in the soul. The most meagre standard of living in many Alpine villages is not perceived as hardship — the city dweller only imagines it. The riffraff concept of 'need' in the big cities arises from soullessness; deprivation thus refers only to food, housing and amusement. But a very deep moment is the psychological pressure of living too close, of the narrowness of people. In the North, with its sense of vastness, this is felt to be terrible. One leaves to be alone again with one's tribe. One fears the herd-like. This is the real motif of Nordic migratory tendencies, which is becoming more and more intense from millennium to millennium.

---

8   Kültepe is an archaeological site near the modern city of Kayseri in Turkey. It was the capital of the ancient Kingdom of Kanesh and an Assyrian trade colony in the second millennium B.C. — *Transl.*

RELIGION, ETHICS, MORALITY, LAW

35

Religion. Sacrifice: [For] primitive man, private property [is] robbery [of] cattle, weapons; 'peace' (hospitality) [comes] through voluntary surrender (gift of hospitality). Thus ['pacified' one] also the 'powers': one gives them gifts so that they do not rob. Sacrifice, votive gift, endowment. First things: treasures, cattle, slaves, sons. Then [only emerges] the concept of 'deprivation' (fasting, castration). [This is] morality.

Custom is the natural put into form, morality the unnatural put into legal demand. Morality is a technique; custom is attitude.

36

Northern Eurasian world-view: Personal, without priests; reverence, but without theology. (Overbeck[9] on the Teutons. Hackmann[10], Chantepie[11] on China.) [The] Occident [is] last struggle between West and North. Gothic: the strong West shapes the North. Baroque: the North emancipates itself. With Arabia, [the] South becomes strong once again. West: mother goddess, realm of the dead: Mary, Isis. Cult of the grave: relics, cathedrals, crypts; [everything] spiritualised by the North. [The] ancient priesthood of the West: Etruscans, Cretans, Delphi, Eleusis; Rome [is] Nordic [as] state, Western [as] priesthood.

37

Pantheism and polytheism: North — South. The one feel, experience the world as a whole with active forces, the other as a duality: active

---

9   Johannes Overbeck (1826–1895) was a German archaeologist and art historian. — *Transl.*

10 Heinrich Friedrich Hackmann (1864–1935) was a German Lutheran theologian, historian of religion and sinologist. — *Transl.*

11 Pierre Daniel Chantepie de la Saussaye (1848–1920) was a Dutch theologian, philosopher and historian of religion. — *Transl.*

subjects and passive world. From both, as soon as thought becomes sufficiently abstract, i.e. turns from looking to word-bound concepts, a monotheism can develop, but it is quite different in essence here and there: Nordic thought (the 'people' is never monotheistic) says God or 'the' Absolute, 'the' First Cause, 'the' Omnipresent — but that is pantheistic. In the tropical south they say 'the supreme God' who sits somewhere and is Lord of all. That 'absolut' can be expressed through music, not through sculpture.

38

Pantheism: Indo-European linguistic thinking [is] always individualistic — setting a numen: the wind, the clouds, autumn is coming, anger, fear — all powers, in the South [they become] persons. Boreas, Aurora, Roman gods of opportunity. Nyx, Eris (Hesiod). Everything is ['a god']: ghostly powers arise, disappear, merge; hosts of wild horses [that] thunder in clouds of dust over the plain — this is 'Poseidon', the power of the plain, of the waving grass.

The numen of the primeval forest [is] roaring, whispering, full of uncanny dangers, luring the wanderer astray, catching, corrupting. The lynx that steps out of the forest is the spirit of the forest that took this shape, suddenly.

39

In the non-Greek Athena there is a Nordic conception: Valkyrie. Friend of the warrior, not mother, but lover. Hera — southern Russian, not Dorian — is the motherly protector. There is less masculinity in her worship than in that of Athena. Sense of dependence. This is different from the 'mother goddess', *theotokos*. Hera, Leto, Turan, Baalat — 'mistress'. The Catholic Madonna is Tanit[12], goddess of birth. The Nordic 'dear woman' is goddess of protection.

---

12   Tanit was the patron goddess of Carthage. She was a mother and fertility goddess and probably the consort of Baal Hammon, the chief god of Carthage. — *Transl.*

Birth goddess, fertility goddess, mother goddess, love goddess — these are quite different conceptions. (Wilamowitz[13] I, 236).

40

Religion is originally action, not belief. Only from technique does theory develop. Theory: looking (fantasy, myth) and criticism (knowledge, systems, 'faith'). Only 'theology', the rationalist system, demands faith in its correctness. For that is what faith means in the mouth of the priest. Faith the holding of a certain system to be correct (eternal truth). Deep difference between religiosity (piety, looking, myth, world-view) and religion (rite, morality belongs to it), systems of gods, world plan.

41

The creation of 'gods' from 'powers' is done by imagining the power in the form of a human or animal body or as a monster: huge, dwarfish, beautiful, ugly, young, old, male, female, [as] a bull, ram, stallion, etc. One then transfers ideas of the soul to these bodies. God is originally neuter plural. Depending on the earthly circumstances, the male god 'above' is imagined as king, warrior, hero, householder, father, wise, kind, angry, strict, treacherous, the 'boy' (Jesus, for example) as hero, son, brother, crown prince. Karnos (Dorian), the ram of Thor, [is] certainly not the god, but 'his beast'. By contrast, βοῶπις; Libyan, Achaean: the sacred cow. Belongs to the bull: minotaur. A 'bodily' god, incarnate, can change shape like the sorcerous man (werewolf), appear as an animal. But the North thinks too patriarchally for that. There the animal serves the god, follows him: Odin's ravens and wolves, the Roman wolf to Mars, heraldic animals.

---

13   Ulrich von Wilamowitz-Moellendorff (1848–1931) was one of the leading philologists of his time. Through his work, he left a lasting mark on the science of philology in the 20th century, both nationally and internationally. — *Transl.*

42

The people of the North—from Northern Europe to Korea—thought differently about death than those of the South. Here in the South, the idea of the dead person's life in a land of the dead arose, which in the end became more important than this world, depending on whether the individual brooded or stood firm in life. This was banished into a theology on a grand scale most early in Egypt, most recently in the Catholic Church. The area from Ireland and [Brittany] to [North Africa] is the area of dolmens, menhirs and funerary buildings. This belief is 'eternal' because it is rooted in the soul of the 'race'.

Nordic man [is] different everywhere. To him life is a battlefield, and he lives on in the glory of his deeds and in sons and grandsons. He is separated from the world of life by the burial mound, so that he is not haunted. For he has nothing more to do here. The belief in Valhalla—if it was a belief and not a poetic image of the skalds who had heard of the Christian afterlife and now paid homage to their king in this imagination, [begins] around 1000 [A.D.], not earlier.

In the Protestant North, [in] Russia, [in] China, the belief in the importance of life clings.

43

Gender meaning of the celestial bodies and grammatical gender of the nouns: Life is everywhere viewed not only from the aspect of death and life, but [of] procreation and birth, the numina, like all beings, have a gender: begetting or receiving.

A cardinal question: Are the bearers of this creative development men, women or both? Who generates the procedures, styles, myths, petroglyphs? Men and women understand death differently: the pregnant woman, for example, from giving birth, the man from bearing witness. But whose influence is decisive in the individual areas? Where is the woman an accessory of the male group, where is she organised herself? Taboo and totem are male.

Possession: the man in the woman, the woman in the child. Matriarchy as intuition thus perhaps means that the show passes from the female to the male, patriarchy vice versa!

44

What is faith and superstition? Two quite modern, urban intellectual terms. Today — and thus in brightly conscious times — one disguises under faith that which one assumes to be correct, because it is proved according to the acquired principles of proof, i.e. by the statement of a holy book: Koran, Talmud, or of an authority: prophet, saint, apostle, God Himself in revelations, whereby each circle of training for a faith, be it, for instance, Catholicism, atheism (Russia) or Mormons, has its own method of proof, according to which one establishes the correct faith.

It is wrong to say that faith is knowledge of the unproven. On the contrary, faith is the proven. Knowledge, then, in the theological sense is equal to faith, in the 'exact' scientific sense the experimentally proven account, experiment of the only procedure that exists independently of the priest. For natural science lives in the belief that it is independent of theology. But it *is* theology. Only the historian (Polybios[14], Eduard Meyer, I) is *relatively* independent. He establishes *facts*. The physicist *believes* in his theory. So b-belief is definitely superstition. Modern superstition in the village [is] the last remnant of original religiosity.

45

Religious and religion. All not purely sensuous wakefulness, i.e. purely instantaneous-perception, is religious. It alone gives thinking in c-d the depth without which it remains mere intelligence. Religious [is] blood, race, instinct, in its deepest essence of organic

---

14 Polybios (c. 200–c. 118 B.C.) was an ancient Greek historian. He wrote *The Histories*, a universal history in 40 books for the period from 264 to 146 B.C. — *Transl.*

logic, set against causality, ratio, criticism for fate, mystery — seeing and foreboding. But — the religious is something *quite* different from dogmatic (and cultic) religion, denomination, church. That is *all* intellectualised, God as [the] eternal, [as] spirit, truth, critically isolated from nature. Religiosity and dogma are contradictions. That is why the great theologians and church leaders like Thomas[15] are very little religious, dry intellectuals.

46

Education: Man educates himself, the priest wants to educate him. All education through school amounts to forming the world-view of man, of the child, according to his own. It is the will to power over the spirit of others. Not 'Christian', but Nordic.

47

What Nietzsche, Ibsen, etc. mean by corruption through Christianity — they dream of southern freedom, but Christianity is southern — is the subjugation of life, of ways of life, of morality by spiritual statutes. One has the custom or one does not have it. One obeys the statutes or one is punished by hatred, servitude, shunning, taboo. It [is] neither Faustian man alone nor 'Christianity' (which one?) alone; it is 1. the spirit that atrophies instinct: c against b; 2. the North that forms the spirit, the language more strongly in the stronger struggle of life; 3. the city that kills the land. All this cumulates in the most northern of cultures. If Christianity had not come, the Nordic religion would have developed other tyrannical forms. Lutheranism is basically purely Nordic against southern Catholicism.

48

Morality and custom [are to be] distinguished. Morality is the expression of life in the organism of culture. There are c- and d-mores.

---

15 Saint Thomas Aquinas (1225–1274) was the most important Catholic theologian in history. — *Transl.*

In a and b, animal instinct [prevails]. One does not change morality. It changes because life changes. Nietzsche's error. Morality is theory, cult. It must be learned and is developed theoretically against custom (often also against other morals: Jesus), systematically. There is only systematics of morality and physiognomy of custom. The 'ethics' of the 19th century is a rationalistic system, morality, intellectually founded. Therefore [it is] against tradition, the nobility of old society, particularity by class, race, temperament.

I do not teach: you *should* become different, but the next generations will *be* different. Those who are not like that are not considered. Nietzsche's pastoral ambition to reform prevented him from completing his *correct* analysis of the times.

49

'Weltanschauung': Animals, free-moving beings have a sensibility understood [as] environment. The b-man has a world-view, looking, suspecting: there, behind the sensed and ordered environment, the mystery, the suspecting and looking emerges. Metaphysics, because the purely present environment loses itself in the future, the past, the invisible — as 'beyond the present'. But only in c — speaking-thinking, abstraction — does the causal-teleological construction come in: myth, theory, religion, knowledge (I believe that I know), the 'reasons'. World as history, world as nature: world-view.

50

Ethics, literary history: The Nordic (antiquity, India, China, Occident) soul alone frays itself. The southern one only the world. Compared to this infinite self-criticism (confession), the South is naive, 'primitive' (Egyptian literature).

The Old and New Testaments know nothing of the kind. Repentance for wrongdoing towards the external God, repentance for deeds that take revenge. Nowhere anything about agony of soul. Isaiah, Psalms, Gethsemane.

This self-criticism is evaluation. The born types of philanthropic and misanthropic people. Self-hatred and self-love in a very deep sense. It has nothing to do with self-respect. Self-hatred [is] common in priestly natures. A kind of optimism and pessimism. Types of egoism, altruism, suicide. Expression in deeds and musings.

Self-confidence, courage of action, determination, insecurity. Underestimating or overestimating oneself. Loyalty, submissiveness. Pride in one's own, lack of pride. To cope or not to cope with one's conscience, remorse.

51

After death: In b [there is] still no 'theory' about it, because the language is missing, the reflection. One does occasionally see the dead appear, one suspects something of his proximity, but that remains an isolated case.

Only speech-thinking develops theories of various kinds: life of the dead in the underworld (Atlantic): Egypt, Catholicism, purgatory, Osiris, Minos. Resurrection (on *this* earth): ἐκ νεκρων[16]. 'Immortality of the soul' — abstract, posthumous fame, remembrance (Achilles). Transmigration of the soul. The grave as a dwelling place, as a memorial, as a closure of the dead (rendering harmless, annihilation).

52

Myths and ghost stories are the same. The fear of the invisible, the 'supernatural', of the metaphysical. All fear of gods, dogmas and theology proceed from the fear of ghosts and the ghost story. The ghostly apparition, the phantom.

53

The divine — divinity — God. Depth of reflection. This gives quite different kinds of reverence, piety, faith. The ultimate root of these differences lies in the type of soul of 'races', [in the] soul of the North and

---

16 Greek: 'from the dead'. — *Transl.*

that of the tropics. Causal thinking ('unspoken grammar') sees *prima causa*, [in] clear light, *close* in the South. Personal gods are *close* gods.

In the misty north, the *prima causa* is assumed to be more distant, indeterminate: 'omnipresent' god, deity, impersonal. Already in c [forms] the difference of religion of the gifted (leading) and ungifted (performing). The inferior trembles before his god, the superior is his friend. Gods of masters and slaves. The religious thinking of the priests (philosophers, doers) and the doers (skalds). The b-shudders (ancestors, looking), layered by thinking (speaking), break through. Full-blooded, classy and anaemic, intellectual 'seers' (read Görres[17]): vision and abstraction.

54

Religion (beyond the religious) is personal; spiritual 'I': the organised anxiety of the individual, the sum of persons. Religious, wordless shudders are those of units in many copies, always forming again in ecstasy. Religion, however, is by its very nature the replacement of involuntary ecstasy by willed doctrine, view, action. The great mystics are therefore belated pre-religious beings who succeed in *unio mystica*[18], geniuses. Religion itself is a wordy system that wants to build the bridge from the understanding I to Mother Nature, selfish: banning nature, outwitting it.

The great ecstatics are *solitary*, the great religions are *folkish*. Religious primal shudders are wordless. Religions are systems in words (and word-directed procedures): be they words of doctrine, banishment, explanation (mythology, cult). The right words are the priestly secrets.

Throughout the history of religion goes the struggle of religiosity and religion, and again of popular faith and high religions: the religious depth that pervades life like a breath, wordless, formless,

---

17 Johann Joseph Görres (1776–1848) was a German Catholic publicist who wrote a four-volume work on Christian mysticism. — *Transl.*

18 Latin: 'mystical union'. — *Transl.*

simplicity of heart, appears to organised religion as heresy. Never will the great church teachers and the deep souls understand each other (b — c/d). And likewise popular religion in strict customs and manners is 'superstition' which must be fought — by theologians and philosophers. And yet the great religions, creations of the masters of spiritual immersion, are closed to the popular mind. The horseshoe over the door, the touching of the bones of a saint, the dove sacrifice of the Attic maidens — what do they understand of the profound sentences of the catechism, which are intelligible only to the gifted and the called? To be pious is not to be learned. The Church teaches, the people feel.

55

Religion, after it has penetrated all that is racial, is spiritualised, used by the powers of life as a means to an end: one invokes the gods in order to conquer, one takes away the god of the conquered in order to weaken him.

56

So wherever there are high cultures, there are two religions of quite different kinds on top of each other. They mingle outwardly, for instance in such a way that the higher gives its names and forms to the lower and that the lower communicates customs to the higher: but inwardly they remain two: the pious custom of the country and the written teaching of the city. What is a symbol in the higher religion is an amulet, a fetish (mass, image of a saint, etc.) in the lower.

57

Sacrifice: In Sumerian the sign for sacrifice is a pot with an ear of corn in it: thus one offered grain to the gods. Egyptian is the sacrifice of the dead, [the] gift to the deceased, who in return puts his strength in the interest of the family and renounces harm. In Babylon [there are] later (since 1900) only four classes of sacrifices: food, drink, animal, and smoke, no longer grain.

58

The religious side: In the c-cultures, what we now call primitive religiosity emerges. In all d-cultures it must be touched that the c-religions live on quietly in the peasantry, that there is above the class religion of the priests and the educated and in between a bourgeois-urban religiosity. Even in times of great pathos, the peasants are hardly moved. This is proved for Egypt, where the texts show only class belief, [and for] China by the many figurative gods. [One must] treat the 'higher' religion quite incidentally. *Judaism*, Arabia. In spite of all the prophets, the masses cling to their old peasant faith. In the Old Testament it shimmers through everywhere that king and prophets count for nothing. Likewise, the gods remain alive among the Jews.

59

Growing power of the Scriptures over language and therefore the mind. It is nonsense to speak of Egyptian and Babylonian literature. There is probably ancient, Chinese, Indian literature. Literature is Nordic. Religion, poetry, thought [are] at first non-literary, oral. Only the urban late cultures have the plague of literacy from which poetry dies. Poetry with the pen in the hand!

60

It is wrong to ask: What is religion? Religious thought is based on a need. The need is at least partly universal. 'Religion', on the other hand, is something different everywhere. Kash, Atlantis, the North. The argument about animism, magic, is ridiculous, because one takes local examples to prove what is 'generally human'. Father Schmidt[19],

---

19 Wilhelm Schmidt (1868–1954) was a German-Austrian Catholic priest, linguist and ethnologist. He travelled to Tierra del Fuego, Southeast Asia, East Africa and the Philippines and visited ancient peoples there. He developed the cultural circle theory and the theory of primordial monotheism, which asserts that all religions of the world go back to a common religion. According to Schmidt, this primordial religion was monotheistic. — *Transl.*

moreover, who wants to prove monotheism, which he values more highly than [polytheism], through inferior tribes.

61

Christianity, Arab culture: In a grandiose picture, show how a northern tendency has taken shape in a southern body. Southern in it is the celibacy, the hatred of 'nature', the personal God, sin, redemption, etc. Northern is the courage to take on fate, the sanctification of the deed, of the will. That is why Christianity is drawn to the North. It has lost the south. Luther stripped the rest of south.

62

The formation of law: Law as a totem in taboo form? See *Decline of the West*. Law of the stronger. Private and state law. In c, the idea of divine and secular law is formed. It is either divine law or lordly law: what is due to the powerful. There was a Kashitic, Atlantean, Nordic original idea: the god, the king, the lord. From then on, follow state, international, criminal and private law everywhere!

63

It is significant for the 'Neolithic' religion, e.g. in the Aegean, that there are almost only female idols. From this we can conclude that the celestial numina were not pictorially represented and that only the fertility spell demanded idols.

64

The religions of great style all arose under hot skies. The regions of winter are also those of the bald spirit of science: philosophy. The North, from Ireland to Japan, is not smart in the religious. The scientific spirit is the cold, the habit of freezing, in parlours, sitting behind books, doing intellectual work. A religion is creation of the sun, of nights in the open air, of fullness and warmth.

Science — or 'religion without talk' —, supposedly an advance of humanity, is only a fruit of the freezing spirit, which no longer longs for sun, south and fullness, but is conscious of its need and proud of it. The deeper to the South, the more science becomes a part of theology, and indeed the theology of ascetics, fakirs, stylites, who at least thus deny the fullness of the South around them: magical, Indian science as opposed to ancient, Chinese, to say nothing of Faustian, the coldest.

65

Against Lévy-Brühl[20]: 'Prelogical' thinking has by no means been in constant decline since prehistoric times. On the contrary, the trivial habit of thinking, which degrades thinking, makes it become superficial and conventional again: mass psychosis, modes of thinking, prejudices, superstitions. People of the c-culture are more independent in this than big city people.

Against P. W. Schmidt, *Ursprung der Gottesidee*[21]: In his endeavour to prove that his view of a personal supreme being is original, he makes a mistake when he thinks of pygmy tribes, south-eastern Australians, central Californians and Aino as the relatively oldest peoples. But they are not. The oldest we know more precisely are the Egyptians and Babylonians, 3000 B.C., and what we can infer from the Neolithic. What he brings in are modern peasant peoples, and he believes he can only find something of the sort there.

Not only is 'monotheism' inconceivable to very natural people — it is even inconceivable to the overwhelming majority of cultural people, the peasants, the common people, be they Buddhist or Catholic or Islamic educated. Their real religion, as it paints itself in the minds, recognises a very hazy complex of changing forms in which individual saints and gods — Mary, Joseph, relics — play an essential role and

---

20 Lucien Lévy-Bruhl (1857–1939) was a French philosopher and ethnologist who highlighted the structural differences between the world-views of scriptless cultures and modern Western civilisation. He devoted himself to the question of whether non-European societies have modes of thinking that have nothing in common with Western logic. — *Transl.*

21 'Origin of the Idea of God' — *Transl.*

'God' recedes altogether. The primitive religions in reality comprise the majority of people who publicly, by birth and education, belong to the higher religions.

66

Atlantis: Mother Earth, [the term does] not derive from agriculture, but [was] applied to it only later. Rather, the mother in general (birth, cattle, sheep, grain). The producer [comes] only second. Madonna (Isis, Mary). Female succession to the throne in Egypt (therefore sibling marriage? The sister, not the brother is important). Grave cult (cathedral as saint's grave. relic. pyramids). Therefore matriarchal forms (Laetitia Bonaparte[22]. Mistresses. Married women. Not Gretchen[23]).

67

Greek — Celtic — Germanic deity (Chantepie) 2000? By making comparisons, one may be able to better tap into the Old Norse conception of gods. The Norns, Loge, Wotan, Thor also seem to be Celtic: Lug[24], Gwydion[25], Tur. There is something hazy about them, a dark expanse, indeterminable. The figures are also blurred. Avalun, Arthur. These people are too strong not to feel the gods as their equals. But very much must be pre-Celtic, just as in their Danubian seats much that is 'Germanic' is Celtic. [Among others] certainly the goddess

---

22 Letizia Buonaparte (1750–1836) was Napoleon Bonaparte's mother. — *Transl.*

23 Gretchen is one of the most important characters in Johann Wolfgang von Goethe's *Faust*. At her first encounter with Faust, she is portrayed as well-bred, shy and pretty. Faust sees in her the ideal image of a woman and desires her with all his heart. At first it is pure sexual desire, which later matures into true, genuine love. Mephisto cannot exert any power over Gretchen because she is pure of heart and innocence personified. She is also a strong believer and lives strictly according to the rules of the Church. Due to these facts, Gretchen's character is the antithesis of the characters of Faust and Mephisto. — *Transl.*

24 Lug is a prominent god in Irish mythology. — *Transl.*

25 Gwydion is a magician and trickster in Welsh mythology. — *Transl.*

groups and the priesthood. In general, everything that differs from the Hellenic-Slavic view is probably pre-Indo-European and belongs to the Neolithic cultures. Cf. Japan, where the pre-Malaic stratum has the sun goddess.

68

Beginning of 'morality': Age of the sun god Babylon and Egypt. There is only custom of status (totem, sexual life in barriers) and taboo under mental fear. Has only the second millennium created an ethic: heroic and great in relation to the understanding of human life?

Morality is sacrifice: but here for the idea of man. Old Testament morality. This morality is idea, never realised, and different in essence from folk wisdom (peasant morality, proverb) and wisdom of life.

69

The c-human's reflection on himself. Self-evaluation. Very strong in the North: self-esteem, honour. To perish inwardly from something no man knows. In contrast, 'Spanish honour' (Calderon): what nobody knows will not hurt me. That is the Atlantic 'cutting a figure'. The Chinese 'saving face'. Only publicly, not in front of oneself. The Japanese, on the other hand, [are] Nordic.

70

Homer's Olympus and Valhalla in the texts of the 'Carolingian period' do not depict the religion of the time at all — but how the lords themselves lived and how little 'religion' they needed. He who is a hero in life needs no religion. He takes on fate himself. God is a cosmic abstraction to the temple culture, an ancestor, a powerful being of yore, king or ancestor to the tomb culture, a word for world to the North. If we know so little of the religion of the Indo-Europeans, it is because there was not much. Indian and Greek religion is essentially that of the subjugated, Germanic is a Christian poetry.

71

Landscape, climate of the soul: Since all reflection and forethought presupposes a drive to think and the world of vision as an object, all religion and wisdom is a reflection of the respective landscape and its soul. Therefore, one can speak of the climate of a religion — not [of] its abstract doctrine, but of the concrete form it [has] received in the place.

72

'Religion' is feminine-southern, birth of 'eternally right'. The North has religion, the South has 'religions'. History is *made* in the North, it *happens* in the South. In the anti-historical South, the chronological scheme emerges from the calendar: banishment of the spirit, of development. The North wants to record not so much dates as the physiognomy of persons and events. To the North belongs the personality and individual deed, to the South the typical event, the form of the event, ceremonial.

From the looking to the explaining myth: ancestral and nature myths as the original form of images. 'World as nature' and 'world as history' according to the degree of causal cosmology (North: history, South: nature).

Flowering of the meaningful ornament. The eternal, not change: 'eternity' is for the woman overcoming the flight of events: history becomes insignificant in relation to nature, the eternal form triumphs over the unique content. In Kash the great systems of being (character of languages, mythologies, cults, political forms).

Language habit: One only understands oneself completely through communication. The explanatory myth develops from the sign (symbol).

73

So the younger sun god has superimposed or (Mediterranean) broken through the moon god. Even older are sun and moon as twins

(Africa, South America, Australia). Lunar the continental, solar the maritime culture. In solar times, weaving migrated from Asia via Polynesia to America. All technology [is] of cultic origin. World myths migrated from South Asia to Finland (land) and West Africa (sea). A myth that presupposes the sea as known, originating from the early days of incipient seafaring. In Egypt and the Near East belonging to the early myths of the higher cultures, i.e. 4th millennium? Related in level and distribution [are] the service of fire with the Vestals from Rome to Peru (discovery of fire?) and cremation, in the primordial sense of rising in the sacred flame?

74

'Punishment' in b and in animals [is] killing the commoner who breaks custom. Punishment as revenge against the wrongdoer.

With the linguistic musing (c) on the causality of suffering, now thought back to and ahead of, belongs the concept of punishment for guilt and revenge for iniquity [together]: the individual or the tribe, humanity [has] a hereditary guilt (Hesiod's Prometheus, Christianity), as blood vengeance is hereditary.

The Nordic community (clan, then state) takes the revenge of the individual: penal law of the state. Belief that the powers (God) avenge guilt.

75

Demeter[26], Ge[27], Poseidon [are] the deities of the wide plain, the steppe. Naive man (c) perceives the environment in large units. The 'earth' only when it is visible from afar as a steppe. Otherwise the uncanny 'forest' or [the] mountains are perceived as the dominating unit. The Egyptians felt the 'Nile valley', not the 'earth'. Such units are

---

26 Demeter is an ancient Greek goddess responsible for the fertility of the earth, the grain and the seed. — *Transl.*

27 Ge is an ancient Greek goddess personifying Earth. — *Transl.*

the sea, the marsh, the desert, the plain to the horizon, the primeval forest, the mountains.

The god of the earth in China everywhere [is] *sehê*. The above and below — *Tinia, Ge — tien*[28], *sehê*.

76

Conceptions and names of deities have different histories. Everywhere and always other tribes have kept their idea of the divine and given [them] foreign names or vice versa. The Juno Regina of Carthage is Tanit. The Aphrodites of Hellas are Hellenic ideas. Under Jesus and Mary are Nordic ideas in the Protestant North.

77

In II only religious shudders, in III practical religion, which has a purpose. This practice is technical: invocation of the powers by gifts, sacrifice, prayer, magic. The cult is largely banishment.

The priests [are] the technicians of conjuring. The theory (legend of the gods) follows from the technique. Myth, cult legend. Omnipotent tendencies of the priesthood.

78

The pictorial representation of the powers is different among peoples in the plains (southern Russia) and in the mountains. There the great powers are those of the earth (in, not under the earth: Poseidon, Gaia), here they sit on mountains (Zeus). The atmospheric powers, thunderstorms, there from the clouds, the sky, here from the peaks. The violence of lightning, the nameless violence, mighty sounds, earthquakes. Man rethinks the powers in terms of persons. He experiences them in nature itself, where he either accepts them, nameless, or interprets them logically.

---

28   *Tien* is the old Chinese term for heaven. — *Transl.*

79

Polytheism of the Catholics: Not only 'God', the nameless one, then Mary, Christ, Holy Spirit, angels, saints, but also the devil as the evil god with his sub-gods. It is too easy to forget that this is the idea of a powerful but bad God, to whom cults also belong. To the Nordic 'pantheism' belongs the animal fairy tale, originally believed myth, reached Hellas from Central Europe (Wilamowitz I, 322), where it met animal-shaped gods, whom it quickly assimilated. But in Atlantis it was an animal god, in the north the general divine, which is in all beings. Tendency to conceal the names of the god, to call him simply Lord (Baal) or dear Lady (Leto[29], Hera). Father, Madonna.

80

Zoroaster religion without temple, without God, for Ormuzd[30] is a *principle*, not a person. Persons prove themselves by appearances and deeds. The principle lies only in things. The people cannot grasp such abstractions. Nor monotheism, which becomes pan- and polytheism. All northerners are against temples, priests, gods. Only powers, reverence. Custom has nothing to do with religion. It goes without saying. In the North, personal religion. Aversion to systems, to theological rationalism, to ritual laws. Free, to be alone with the powers.

81

If one wants to know the deities, one must know the people who believe in them. As long as 'religion' is something that is not dogmatically fixed, it goes without constraint in a formation with the history of the souls of men. It changes, even unconsciously, from generation to generation. But where there is a fixed stock, sanctified by tradition,

---

29 In Greek mythology, Leto is the daughter of the Titans Koios and Phoibe and was a lover of Zeus, with whom she fathered the twins Artemis and Apollo. — *Transl.*

30 Another name for the Zoroastrian creator god Ahura Mazda, personifying the power of light. — *Transl.*

fixed customs, rites, dogmas (i.e. a theology, professional science of priests = theory plus technique) as in all urban religions, there changes — again unconsciously — the way people understand these customs and dogmas into which they were born and brought up. There, too, is a difference from generation to generation, while some of the dogmas and rites eventually ossify, become soulless and fade away, or the religion suffocates.

82

The wordless seeing and foreboding is now 'comprehended', conceptualised, causally thought out, i.e. 'causes' are no longer seen or felt, but defined and given a name. It is now physiognomically significant how men systematically divide the seen and verbally apprehended nature according to cause and effect, i.e. what they 'believe', what they believe they know, are certain they know. The fact of the gradual situation of human life, the world and sudden devastating events lead to the consciousness of alien superior powers. It depends on whether one humanises them, thinks of them as persons, gods, giants, dwarfs, dragons, monsters, or honours them as a mystery, as fate, the course of the world, chance, etc. Both are mixed.

83

Theology [is] the rationalistic will to bring everything into a system. Religion is alogical. The usual 'history of religion' is the history of theology, not of religion.

84

The main difficulty of a history of religion — which no one has yet written, only Overbeck conceived in thought, Wilamowitz outlined for the Greeks — is that what the people really believe is not the same as what they do, and above all that they do not become aware of what they actually believe and do not believe. This is only noticeable in their actions, but who knows them? What is written today as the history of religion is a history of theological systems. That is very simple, but it is not a history of religion. Books on Chinese religion talk long and hard about the three systems. Not a word about temples, gods, oracles, customs of the dead.

Likewise in Christian countries. No Catholic peasant calls on God, but on his saint, not Joseph, but on Joseph of X. No Protestant thinks of Paradise when dying, but of the hill that becomes Sion. Popes wore amulets, had horoscopes; that is living faith. A printed 'confession' is only babbled. What Wissowa[31] writes has very little to do with the religion of the Roman people. He is a theologian.

Anyone who cannot find the difference between theoretical doctrine and living faith understands nothing of the essence of religion. Monotheism is only theory. No nation has ever believed in it, not even the Mohammedan peasant.

85

Systematic logic is alien to religious feeling and remains so, however strictly the priests seek to bring system into their rites and dogmas. That is why the real faith of peasants, sailors, petty bourgeois, warriors, nobles is completely illogical. E.g. the contradiction between the facts of fate and the idea of human-like gods who feel, think, act humanly — good or bad. The whim of the gods is still the best word for fate. So is the idea of what happens after death. The idea of a good god immediately comes into conflict with the fact — can he not or will he not? What reasons? 'Inscrutable counsel'.

86

It is wrong, even for this time, to speak of the religion of a people. Even then the difference between the warlike and priestly types is noticeable. There are pious to the point of holiness, often crippled, weak, sick; there are hypocrites, unpious (to whom this does not come to consciousness, but who, of strong race, have little sense for that

---

31 Georg Wissowa (1859–1931) was a German classical philologist and a historian of religion. He was the first to write a history of the Roman religion. — *Transl.*

in which the pious toil all day). There are mockers at last, within the limits of what was possible at the time. There are those who see apparitions, ghosts, revelations, portents, at every moment, others who are convinced of them, and others who laugh or scoff at them secretly or openly, and in any case despise them.

87

By 'religiosity' I mean the mere feeling, shudder, awe, conceptually indefinite. By 'religion' the world-view and self-conduct found in a definite way, by church the political organisation, by dogma, rite, cultus the conceptually definite kind of theory and technique.

In Spain, for example, religion has been the same for 3,000 years, the dogmatic definition, the cultic rules, the mythical descriptions are successively Phoenician, Israelite, Catholic —

88

The powers can basically only be experienced polytheistically or pantheistically. Monotheism is an abstraction. Poly- and pantheism merge into one another: Elohim, the 'Godhead', 'the' divine. Monotheism, once it is not a strict abstraction, merges into pantheism (omnipresence, omnipotence, nameless *deus sive natura*[32]) or polytheism (the true versus the false gods, Yahweh versus the Baalim).

89

The Atlantean knows only the idea of the mother, of the acting. There is no mention of a father-god: hence *conceptio immaculata*[33]. The contrast to the divine birthing woman is the lord of the dead, Osiris, seated at the right hand of God, Minos. In the north, it is not the womb of the earth that is 'worshipped', but nature, the earth itself with all that is on it. The ancestor-worshipping person somehow perceives the 'above' as paternal. But it does not include a deity. This

---

32 Latin: 'God or nature'. — *Transl.*

33 Latin: 'immaculate conception'. — *Transl.*

above is not a human-like being. The superficial way of seeing the earth as goddess everywhere, the sky, [the] sun, [the] moon as god, as is fashionable today, [is] nonsense. To the father of heaven belong the sons of earth. To the mother-goddess the god of death.

90

Atheism proves nothing against a person's religiosity. What matters is whether one has reverence for the mystery of the world, not how one thinks it. One can 'believe in God' and be the biggest scoundrel. The difference between [Germanic] atheism and that of the metropolitan literati from Paris to Moscow lies in the fact that the second is a negation, the first an affirmation.

91

Religion of the North — Northern Race: The 'Mongols' of Genghis Khan [are] blond, light-coloured. A jumble of racial types and languages. Religiously they are 'indifferent'. Whether they officially belong to Islam, Nestorianism — that is only a costume for them. They do not believe in the power of God, they have some themselves. But they believe in blind fate like Mohammed and C[alvin]. Their religion is only — as in Ireland — 'shamanism'.

Nirvana. No life after death as longing (Egypt, Catholics), [but] longing for the end. But life is to be fulfilled, to last in the memory of man. Buddha as a priestly nature naturally does not understand nobility.

92

Ethics: Man is free. That one could argue about this is the fate of the intellect, which thinks of what has happened only in terms of causality and for whom life thus becomes problematic. Its problem, that of indeterminism, is, like all problems, insoluble in terms of the intellect. Problems are always posed by the intellect and solved by life, never vice versa. Life solves the problem, but in the sense of freedom. For this means: causality has nothing to do with life. Think of Calvin's doctrine of predestination, which has become second nature to the Puritan Englishman. He believes that his life is destined. So fatalism would be the consequence. But no — his life solves the problem in such a way that he believes himself 'predestined' to Stoic resolutions and acts of will. Thus reason is led ad absurdum. And that is what I call fate. Fate is freedom, freedom from mechanical cause and effect. Freedom of will: reason poses problems, life solves them. All solutions of the mind are nonsense.

93

Morality: That there is something general which should determine personal morality — manners — has of course been known as long as one thought about these things at all and did not take them for granted, for a matter of instinct. In all primitive states the concept of punishment, and with it that of offence and judgement, does not exist. Men order their disagreements among themselves by a private or tribal law, and of the gods it is assumed that their wrath likewise knows where it feels itself offended. In actual cultures, however, one understands that an absolute standard of value exists par excellence; one feels this, one is certain of the fact. Searching for reasons, one finds either a statute given by God or commandments laid down by a mythical ancestor, or finally 'what is sacred to all men'.

Philosophy has hitherto known nothing better and has simply translated this mythical thinking into conceptual fetishism of an absolute morality: its propositions are illuminating because they obviously have something generally valid to confirm them, but it is equally clear that their results [do not] go beyond a rusty theoretical recognition within learned circles. I now note a limit to this generality. It is not 'mankind' that lays down absolute propositions. But to the Indian, Faustian, Apollonian-Magian human being, according to his soul being so and not otherwise, belongs a quite definite ethical ideal as well as a definite architectonic, logical, mathematical style.

It is understood that, on the one hand, the moral systems of the individual cultures are in touch with each other, and that, on the other hand, in every culture every epoch, [every] people, [every] class, every individual has a nuance of his real morality, really not in so far as his actions show it, but in so far as his inner feeling approves of just this nuance, although he often enough emancipates himself from it. Now tradition has brought it to 'artificial' morals, transmitted and imposed by literature. A strong example is the morality of the little pastor in the West; another is that borrowed from ancient writers and admiringly extolled. Where a system has achieved high recognition in literary and retrospective cultures — which in each case does not abolish its own morality, but devalues it theoretically — we have the very strong difference between theoretically real and practically real morality (with countless intermediate stages, e.g. Nietzsche), so that it is very difficult to create order here. With every moral proposition one has to add to the correctness the question: 'for whom'? It goes without saying that this eliminates all utilitarianism. This 'good and evil', as it underlies the life of every higher human being as an ideal of form, awakening at the same time with this soul as its meaning, as the style of its realisation, stands high above all practical details. Not the 'use' of one's own act, but the ideal of the possible perfect realisation of the soul is what underlies the values a priori.

This great concept of Kant's is therefore perfectly valid, provided that one does not speak of an abstraction of 'humanity' (which Kant did à la Rousseau and the Church à la Socrates), but rather takes 'culture' as the primal element of human history.

There is an ethical conscience just as there is a logical, artistic, scientific conscience: it is the feeling for the innate style of the soul in it that wants to be realised (which is identical with our life). The deeply felt conformity of empirically-theoretically developed norms to the style of existence is what we call truth.

94

Punishment: One of the strongest symbolic expressions of a culture is how it punishes and what it wants to hit. If we initially disregard corporal punishment and property punishment, prison as the actual centre of justice belongs to Faustian penal law. Faustian man knows nothing harsher than to deprive his fellow human being of the freedom of place, time and action (these are the Aristotelian units!) — in doing so, he eliminates his life, which is will, deed, movement, space. From the earliest times, castles and cities have been filled with dungeons and prisons. No other culture has known this. Especially for the ancient world — think of Diogenes[34]! — it would have been pointless. The concept of imprisonment gains a meaning here. There, [the] criminal is pushed out into the unknown, here he is imprisoned — in both cases his freedom is taken away. This is where ancient man puts the hardest thing he knows — exclusion from the polis, the exact opposite of the prison, banishment from the prison of the polis. He is forced to freedom in the occidental sense. No longer being allowed to stay there, having to avoid the customs, is the punishment — just what the Europe-weary emigrant wants. These are two opposing types of social death that exclude each other. This is the reason why the death penalty is gaining ground in antiquity and losing ground here. The purpose of this punishment is to take the content out of life, to let it exist as a mere animal function with the consciousness of it, but to exclude the higher human.

95

So when 'sacrifice' is made in front of ancestral images, graves, monuments, it is done as an act of veneration and remembrance — it can be in songs to glory, scenes, in the destruction of something valuable that thereby becomes the possession of the dead. In the West, however, the sacrifice is nourishment of the living dead, originally

---

34 Diogenes (died c. 320 B.C.) was a Greek philosopher who lived in a wine barrel. — *Transl.*

consisting in food and drink, in Catholicism in masses which cut short life in purgatory.

96

What all does the idea of burial presuppose! Much younger than the view of having to die, than the experience of the 'soul' (life force). Dark conclusions about duration, recurrence (for death is understood as that of life in the light, not as the end of the soul. The 'self' cannot be thought of as extinguishing). Burial already presupposes the order of the tribe, [of] custom, a great deal of technology, a genuine conception of life (sequence, beginning, end, return of life), an environment that is already ordered by experience, but not yet a mythical, cultic sense of the world.

The idea of building emanates from the grave-*building* type, felt sense in the form. From the unconsciously practised custom (racial expression, natural, rhythmic) to the awareness of the existing custom as something self-evident: customs seen in others are noticed without the thought that the like could be set or changed, finally the statute of rules for others, weaker ones: that one oneself follows a form is not noticed, of course.

This custom is first the order of forces: friend and foe, help, leading and following. Then the order of women: satisfaction of the sexual instinct, care for the children. Finally, the activity of nourishment: what man and woman have to do, how, when. The output is necessarily the order of the feeling of power. The first moments of self-control of the destructive instinct. The first setting of custom (law) is older than the inkling of the essence of custom. Primal law is simply the expression of the power instinct with the scent of practical expediency.

97

Mycenae. Shaft tombs: At last [one must] put an end to it: 'cult of the dead' [is] a blurred word. The Achaeans feared the dead, whose graves they did not want to disturb, hence the ring of walls. Something quite different from 'ancestor worship'. There is no cult of the dead at all, but either ancestor worship by [the] survivors or the tribe, or banishing dangerous spirits of the dead.

RACE, TRIBE, PEOPLE

98

'Unnamed', 'nameless' swarms. Sometimes they give themselves ephemeral names or they receive them from others. Until the people's name, like the proper name, is something about whose meaning one does not think. Research, however, nails down any name, to a language or landscape, and thus constructs 'peoples' that never existed. The fact that 'peoples' are fleeting associations, different in nature from one stage to the next, is forgotten. Wherever a name appears in the debris of written tradition, it is nailed down to the remnants of some language or the creation of some ephemeral people, and thus wreaks havoc in the imagination of centuries of history. But a 'people' around 1000 and around 2000 are, in essence, very different entities. What was called Germanic around 500 B.C. could not have existed in this structure in Greece around 1000.

99

'Pure race' [exists] only in human races that live outside of cities, cultures, [without] reading [and] writing, quite simply: matter. In [the] urban culture, the type disintegrates. [It is] ridiculous to depict a few splendid specimens (Bamberg Horseman[35]) ad nauseam. Did the gentlemen look like that? That was a somatic ideal of a noble lineage.

---

35 The Bamberg Horseman is a stone equestrian statue in Bamberg Cathedral in Germany from the first half of the 13th century. The horseman is considered the first monumental, post-ancient equestrian statue north of the Alps. Its outstanding sculptural quality and its unclear identity still occupy researchers today. — *Transl.*

Peasants were different. The ideal is the rare, the exception. What everyone has is not an ideal.

100

What is 'race'? What is expressed in active life and being — having race. Or what man, the scholar sees: blond head (not body) hair, skull shape. Physiognomy, not systematics. Race energy in the struggle between heritage, essence and environment (blood, soil). Not without effect: there are farmers, sailors, nomadic types. Priests, nobility, citizens. [The] masses of the big city [are] raceless. Nonsense [are] the race picture books. Superficial, stupid. Bamberg Horseman, Uta, not 'Germanic' but noble types. Ostade[36], Teniers[37]: peasants.

101

Urbanisation (Günther[38]) is racial decay. Infertility is intellect: shell, core. Sex drive as intellectual pleasure. Not intoxication (spring), but *circenses*. When individual racial creatures rise from the metropolitan mass — dancers, coquettes — they are without future, posthumously.

102

Patriotism and love of one's homeland are two different things. The earth-bound man, the peasant and the bourgeois, has a plant-like inclination in his soul for the patch of ground where he was born or later grew fast — his village, [his] town, even urban area, forest, coast, mountains, etc. Also the emigrant in [the] 'new homeland' (colonies,

---

36 Adriaen van Ostade (1610–1685) was one of the most important Dutch genre painters of the Baroque period. — *Transl.*

37 David Teniers (1610–1690) was the most important Flemish Baroque painter of his time. — *Transl.*

38 Hans F. K. Günther (1891–1968) was a German philologist and an influential race scientist. — *Transl.*

for example, Löns[39] the heath, like painters [in] Capri, Stendhal, Goethe). Those who are not — the bohemian, artist, etc. — love wide spaces. The masterful person (sailor and robber) loves the 'realm' of his power, the sea, the plain, *ubi bene*[40] — Vandals, Goths. Something quite different is the cerebral love of nature, language, state, an 'ideal'. Themistocles, Cicero. Today's nations. The less one talks about it, the more genuine it is, the more self-evident it is (England). Theatricality (*sono Romano di Roma*[41]).

103

Migration, colonisation: These words are too general and lead to shallow errors. To conquer [the] country [means]: to exterminate the population, to chase into the mountains, or to subdue. Colonisation by trade or agriculture. Types: Spanish Conquistadors: keeping the powerful empire of Spain as their homeland. Otherwise they would have been absorbed into the Indians.

104

Idiotic racial chatter, local patriotism, party-political tendency: the Lusatian culture proto-Germanic — proto-Czech, proto-Polish, proto-Romanian. [This is] deliberate confusion of German-Germanic — Indo-European.

Confusion of race and language. Language unit and change of race (Bulgarians). 'Germanics' [had] originally a different language.

---

39 Hermann Löns (1866–1914) was a popular German writer and critical journalist. He was also a passionate hunter who was committed to nature conservation. He is the world's best-known 'heath poet'. Löns detested the industrialisation of Germany. He hated the asphalt of the big cities and the endless descriptions of people's misery in the press, and always found this to be a symptom of a nation's decay. He volunteered for the infantry in 1914 at the age of 48 and was killed in the same year in a battle near Reims. — *Transl.*

40 From the Latin saying '*ubi bene, ibi patria*', attributed to Cicero: 'Where I am well, there is my fatherland.' — *Transl.*

41 Italian: 'I am a Roman of Rome.' — *Transl.*

In the ancient culture-man, who comprises only a part of the total population, [are] merged very many races, languages, c-cultures.

105

Human races are by definition something different from animal races. 'Man' as an animal is a *single* race. The finer differences are of a mental nature. Gross external (visible) characteristics, such as skin colour, [are] secondary. The structural types [are] dependent on diet, work (farmer, hunter, nomad, [a] degeneration [is] the sedentary city dweller), position of the infants. (Paudler[42], Luschan[43].) There are thousands of types (human breeds), i.e. circles of variation. Power of the landscape, of society. Nobility has a different race from the lower class (Poland, England).

New formation of races [arises] in [a] new landscape. English and French Jews. In the oldest Germanic regions [there were] already different races. Culture [is the] unity of the soul. Gradually [it] shapes an ideal form (not average form), [a] desirable form. Falsification [arises] from the race books that pick out photographs of nobility, spirit, peasants, and ignore the factory workers. If one were to add the crew of a tram …!

106

Foolish to determine the 'race' of peoples according to languages! The French are considered Romance, the English Germanic, because the Latin language prevailed there and the English language here: both peoples — peoples only because of political fates that could have been quite different — are of the same structure: western underclass, above them Celtic-Germanic conquerors. Where the Celtic language has survived, one speaks of 'Celts' and calls the Druids Celtic because they are native there.

---

42 Fritz Paudler (1882–1945) was a German ethnologist. — *Transl.*

43 Felix von Luschan (1854–1924) was an Austrian anthropologist, archaeologist and ethnographer. — *Transl.*

107

The racial type of the 'Aryans' (Persians, Indians) is closely related to those of the Turkic tribes: Persian relief figures. Much of it [is] with the ancient Greeks. The Turks [are] likewise [a] master race (Seljuks). Other types: [the] 'Mongols' (as far as Europe). If you call the Turks Aryans, you have the same right to call the Aryans Turkomans.

108

Just as the Saharan and Turanian expansion from deserts driving people away, also from Arabia ('Semites'); the Semites [are] the eastern group of the Hamites. Also master race, conquering. In contrast the 'Aramaeans' [are] Nordic (with Semitic language. [Of] Semitic race are the Arab sheikhs, noble).

109

How little we can know of these migrations. The 'Teutons', for example, [possess] two races: the 'Southern Germanic' — Saxons, Franks, Swabians — advancing only towards England, France. The northern Germanic tribes, first as Goths, Vandals, Burgundians via the Oder and Vistula to the Black Sea, Danube, Italy, Spain, Africa; then as Vikings and Normans to England, Sicily. These were the great tribes. The southern Germanic tribes [were] heavy, sluggish.

110

The predominant racial types in Scandinavia, Finland, Northwest Russia, Poland, Central and East Germany are pretty much the same, whether you speak Slavic, Finnish, Scandinavian, German dialects. The Greeks of Macedonia, close to today's Balkan types of Serbian, Albanian, Bulgarian — 'Nordic' types were rare and therefore considered beautiful — found the Persians and Indians much more alien than, for example, the Semitic-speaking Syrians. What were 'Persians' anyway? The name comes from a small tribal group in Zagros[44] that

---

44 A mountain range in western Iran. — *Transl.*

was close to the Medes, but the Persian countryside that was conquered by them largely had inhabitants of a completely different kind
who were allied with them (Xerxes himself), so that even the thin ruling class of the 'Persians' of Darius was very diverse in composition.

111

Whether a high culture politically forms a unitary state as an idea
or a reality depends on accidents of the beginning. In Babylon, the
temple areas did not tend towards unity. Only intermittently a total
state. Egypt realised at the beginning, therefore very often possible
again. There was no formation of the *Gaue* as 'nations'.

Occident: Charlemagne. Since then only idea. If Charlemagne's
successors had held on to unity for only a hundred years, it would
probably not have come to the formation of Germans, French, Italians,
English, but to the consolidation of the individual tribes as national
elements in a great political unity: i.e. Saxony, Bavaria, Tuscany,
Lombardy, Burgundy, etc.

The political nation destroys the community of tribes. 'German'
is opposed to Saxons, Franks, Bavarians, 'French' opposed to
Burgundians, Bretons, Aquitanians.

112

Athens was the centre in whose nationhood the Aeolian-Ionian
(Asia Minor) and Dorian-Northwestern Greek lifestyles met.
Therefore, it became the decisive place ever since the tribes were re-
placed by cities. Like Paris on the border of the Romano-Celtic (Old
Western) and Germanic-Nordic territories. (Jäger[45], *Paideia*, review
by Pfeifer in DLZ).

The polis [grew] out of noble associations. Polis means castle. Both
knights and ruling patricians (Tyrtaios — *Odyssey*) contrast of sea and

---

45   Werner Wilhelm Jaeger (1888–1961) was a prominent German classical philolo-
     gist. His main work *Paideia* idealises the Greek idea of education as the founda-
     tion of Western culture. — *Transl.*

land ideals. Phyles — originally only the nobility. As with us in the Gothic centuries, the city ('burghers') are [only the] *lineages*.

113

We must reckon in the North — again: by this I mean Northern Eurasia from the North Sea to the Sea of Japan — with very many and very diverse light-coloured races (Paudler). Above all, we must not confuse race with the somatic type of our sensory perception (in today's humans, that is, almost only what we see). What race is, we are only beginning to suspect, and much of it cannot be grasped scientifically at all. Race is soul, race is landscape; both can be visibly expressed 'bodily', but only to a certain degree, which allows for or gives rise to a great many exchanges, especially if one exaggerates the significance of externals such as the shape of the skull, the colour of the skin, the face. There is not one concept of race, but many. There are climatic races, occupational, urban, which interpenetrate.

114

Origin of the tribes (primitive peoples): These warlike racial barbarians beat the men to death and took the women who appealed to their erotic instinct — racy, erotically rich creatures. Thus a race of splendid warriors was born. They preferred to seek the opposite — the Teutons fiery southerners, Jewish women. The Arabs of Harun's time blonde, pale Germanic women who had been sold as slaves by their parents from Scandinavia through Russia. Many a crusader brought an Oriental woman with him. So did the Vikings, so did the Hanseatics.

115

A tribe was a warrior band with a self-naming (Danaans[46], Anak). A people was the totality of inhabitants, named after the land. Different languages of lords and subjects. For example, the Pelopians

---

46 One of the names that Homer used to describe the Greeks that besieged Troy. — *Transl.*

of Achaia, Dorians of Laconia, Rutulians of Ardea. Romans — a city name, Quirites. The land name was different. Tursha[47] in Umbria. Rasena.

116

Tribe and state: The size of the tribe is based on the need to know each other, to gather, to be able to talk to each other. The state depends for its possible size on the rapidity of intercourse, that is, on a script, on ships, on horses, on roads, on news runners. It is quite impossible that Egypt and Babylon could have incorporated [Syria]. Syria was only loosely connected with it, Byblos through maritime traffic. The Roman Empire did not develop until the type of ships and the building of roads made the organisation of power on a large scale possible.

117

A tribe is generally, not always, a unit of blood. A people is always the unity of an idea. Tribes, too, very often last in such a way that a community of men steals wives of quite different blood in order to reproduce themselves. The 'strong race' then proves itself by the fact that the type endures. Only inferior races are deprived of their type by foreign blood. But a 'people' is always a mental form, it has an 'idea', and the strength and duration of a people depends on the power of this idea. Romanism was an idea. It lasted [even] when there was not a drop of blood left from the old tribe.

It is the same with peoples as with people, as biology regards them: the body changes its element in the course of life, only the form remains the same, changing from youth to old age. So also the strong peoples: they can change the blood, the land, the language, everything, but the form remains the same. The Norman idea in the Englishman: beyond Saxons, Celts, pre-Celts. The Prussian idea from the Teutonic Order.

---

47 The Tursha were an ancient people, variously identified as the Lydians, Etruscans or Trojans. — *Transl.*

The strength of the idea, for example, in the strength of politics [is] instinctive. For the idea is instinct, not word-ideal, programme or the like.

118

Semites, Indo-Europeans is a language designation. Near Eastern, Nordic people — a group of racial types, *cultural* races. Germans, Jews an *ethnicity*. *Natural* race is *Homo sapiens* in varieties so mixed that the — perhaps — original elements can no longer be identified.

119

Race, hereditary units: Blond and blue, blond and grey (red-blond, flaxen), fair skin are units in themselves, dependent on winter (climatic). Completely different units lie in the skull forms, e.g. the different forms of the long skull (short and long face). Still others lie in the structure of the limb bones. The blond Libyans can therefore be Nordic types, among the Sea Peoples Aino types.

120

Race: The basic error from which all race research still suffers today is that of the time of its birth, the middle of the 19th century: materialism. It started from the roughly 'material', from what one could see, touch, and took it not as an expression, as a symbol in Goethe's sense, but as the essence of what one was investigating and searching for. Since at that time only the intelligence was recognised apart from the material. Rationalists as they were, they saw the bones of earlier human beings and in these the skull as their essence. In the case of living races, skin, hair and eye colour were added as superficially as possible. Part of materialism is that — à la Darwin — changes are only allowed causally, only physically. But living things change without cause, in themselves. The 'soul' of a life stream — 'chain of generations' — always reflects the soul of the landscape in which it breathes.

121

Connection of sexual (no, in general, of race) and intellectual potency. Expressed materialistically today: phosphorus in semen and brain. 'Sexual activity lowers brain activity.' No: the mind destroys life. All civilisations are diseases of the race. After the age of the mind (rationalism) comes the fellah age: mandarins, formal, the mass dull, unchanged, fertile, the mind uncreative, free, formal, frozen in old ties.

122

Race: An ideal of 'racial unity' has never existed. These warrior tribes chose the most beautiful wives of the subjugated. That their sons were worthy of the tribe was not determined by nose or hair colour, but by breeding and education in war. The prowess of the young man was 'race', not his nose.

123

We must not speak here of peoples in the sense of high cultures, but [of what] I called 'primitive peoples'. They are both expressions of one culture. Namely, the humanity of the c-cultures has an amoeboid form. These 'individuals from a majority of specimens', which I call tribes, are no greater than that everyone knows everyone. They are fused to a fleeting extent, split up, merge into others when fragmented: all that we still see of Indian and Negro tribes. Their land, in which they do not take root but flow, may be called *Gau, territory, pasture, Mark*[48]. Between tribes there may be a sense of togetherness that leads to fusion: all this is amoeboid and fleeting, formless.

Tribal groups, even with common names, are not yet a 'people', but only in moments of great destiny suddenly folkish units: 'Israel', in reality a plurality of changing individuals, 'Marcomanni'. What energetically gathers them together is always danger, war, conquest.

---

48 German, from Carolingian times: territory on the borders of the empire. — *Transl.*

ab cultures do not even unfold an organic tribal structure, but are animalistic 'hordes'. Thus: from horde to tribe (b — c), from tribe to state (c — d).

124

Peoples are fighting units in the stream of history. What fights as a unit is a people. That is why 'the Greeks' are not a people, but the Spartans, Thebans are [peoples]. That is why the Germans were not a people until 1870, but Prussians, Austrians. The Teutons, Celts, Slavs have never been a people. But every war party that goes out on land or sea contains c germs of a people within itself. Therefore the core of the people is the adult crew.

125

With the state, too, [a] precise distinction must be made: the act of state creation, will to power, and the technique of state organisation, which can emanate, for example, from a clever official. It is precisely c-states that have organised ingenious, yet primitive administrations, which one must not address as evidence of high cultures. It is not the practical ingenuity but the inner form that is 'culture'.

126

Population density in the Neolithic: Forests and swamps mean that many stretches were only inhabited at the edges and in clearings (*'Ebene'* means clearing in Old Germanic!), but these were very dense, e.g. Bohemia (*Reallexikon*), Bologna.

This must always be emphasised. There were walking routes, clearings and vast unexplored areas in the mountains as well as in the plains. The Neolithic tribes lived in patches and wandered from residential island to residential island in Pomerelia.

127

'The great history of small spaces': Density is of crucial importance: the whole psychology (world-view), thinking and doing of man is

different when he crowds or loses himself in space. The great historical events do not belong at all to the large number in a wide space, but to the small in a narrow one. With the organisation of traffic (commerce, news, roads) the horizon of the people, which is to be embraced as a unity, grows; nevertheless, the strength of proletarian parties, for example, is based on the fact that, in contrast to the peasantry, they always have their people together in one town. War, insurrection, the founding of the empire are different with five people per square kilometre than with two hundred.

LANGUAGES AND NAMES

128

How a name, whose typeface we know in a written language, must sound in a foreign language, is a question without meaning. There is no such must. There is a continuous speaking through generations, day after day, carelessly and carefully, meanly and educatedly in the same city, which slowly changes unnoticed and which is fixed by written signs only for those who are accustomed from youth to replace the written image with a group of sounds, not to 'read'. For no one reads letter by letter, but speaks according to his linguistic habit, and the written images only remind him of the accustomed phonetic structures. These phonetic structures, however, are not 'translated' in the case of foreign names, but adapted to one's own linguistic habit, similar-sounding words, etc., made bite-sized, inserted without rule, only according to convenience into the familiar sound rhythm, whereby sensual echoes play a role (plumbum, Milan, Bern, Berlin — bear). The 'folk etymologies' are largely unconscious. For once again, it is not 'language' that changes according to laws, but people take on different habits while speaking.

129

Names: Bessarabia does not come from Arabia, but from the boyar dynasty of the Basarab. Galicia does not come from Spain, but from galič. Karpathos[49] does not come from the Carpathians. The Eteocretans are therefore not Caphtorites, but Kreti, Carians.

130

Folk names: Originally only the small tribes [bore] names. One is not even aware of the fact of larger connections, since every neighbour is *hostis*[50]. (Dorians, Aeolians was originally [the] name for small individual tribes. Only legend expanded it). The tribe itself has no self-designation. It is too self-evident. One only calls the other, the neighbour, and almost without exception with expressions of derision, disgust, anger, but also fear, shyness, i.e. the folk names are names of opprobrium. Only when the designation becomes necessary and self-evident do people boast of their own names. Once every name had a meaning, but only for those who gave it. The next generation only hears the sound and changes it.

131

Language and dialect: Perhaps one may put it this way: dialects are ways of speaking that are mutually understood at least approximately by the speakers. Languages are not. The prevailing misclassification is based on political boundaries in which academia has settled at universities. That is why Sardinian, Catalan, Provençal are considered dialects of Italian, Spanish, French, *although* they are not understood, but Portuguese, Dutch are considered languages, although they are understood by Spaniards and Netherlanders. Umbrian could not be nearly understood by Romans, nor did Spartans, Ephesians, Boeotians understand each other.

---

49 Karpathos is a Greek island. — *Transl.*

50 Latin: 'enemy'. — *Transl.*

132

What then is part of the pronunciation? Let us distinguish the theoretical phonetic form from the actual *phonation*. The first may be quite blurred. 50 = fifty: that is theory, 'read aloud'. Spoken it is *fuffzge*[51], *fiffti* etc. Horse — *Fārt*[52], *Perd*[53].

133

Mankind in the north matures later than in the south. Therefore [the] Hamitic-Semitic language etc. is older than the Nordic linguistic types: Indo-European, Ural-Altaic etc.

134

Peoples' names: Celtic Boii, their land [was] called *Boja-heim* by the immigrating Germanic peoples, with a Germanic ending thus. The *Bojaheimers* emigrate — [and become] Bayuvarians. Thus Tyrrhenians, Etru-scans (Osker etc.), Hell-enes, Hell-oper. [Also] Dana-voi, Dana-ubis (Danube), Dan-oper (Dnepr), Tanais (Don). (Tripolye culture[54].) The great streams of traffic. Huns — *Hünengrab*[55] [in] Northern Germany! *Hüne* [is the] giant.

135

With each of these ancient linguistic remains one should first ask: Was the language named after the country, the country after an earlier people, the people again after a country? If one looks past this, one is in the dark.

---

51   German dialect for *fünfzig* (fifty). — *Transl.*

52   German dialect for *Pferd* (horse). — *Transl.*

53   German dialect for *Pferd* (horse). — *Transl.*

54   The Tripolye culture was a Neolithic European culture that spread across the territory of modern-day Ukraine and Moldova in the 5th millennium B.C. — *Transl.*

55   German: 'burial mound'. The word *Hüne* means 'giant' and *Grab* means 'grave'. — *Transl.*

The 'Lydian' language, for example, is called that because the country was *later* called Lydia. But earlier (and later) it was called Asia, Assuwa, Hesione, Sparda, Maionia. So where does this language come from? Etruria is called that because the Romans knew the land north of the Tiber by that name. But what was it called before the Tursha came? And was 'Etruscan' the language of the natives or of the conquerors?

136

What I said [in] *Decline of the West II* about race, peoples [and] languages has remained misunderstood and unheeded. If one had thought it through seriously, one would be further along. It is wrong to 'marry' a language to the names of the people, to press the name as a stamp on people, language [and] country. The first is a piece of political-historical events. If one knows them, one can find something about the history of language, which is largely political history.

One must not, for example, speak of the language of the Phoenicians, but must first ask: what kind of folk elements did the population consist of around 1500, 1200, 1000, 800, where does the name come from — were there several — finally: what did people speak around 1500, how, who? Who can do that?

137

Language: The oldest ways of speaking were done with a lot of gestures — facial expressions, intonation, movement of head and hands — and few words. It was impossible to communicate in the dark. So the vocabulary of languages of the 3rd millennium (without the cultural languages of Egypt and Babylon), such as Troy II or Tripolye, [comprised] about a thousand words (to give a figure, three digits), to which each village had a few local words. Such languages, which were only learned by adults, were easily changed. The tenacity of a language in a tribe is also due to its stock of words — it is difficult to learn a new one. Memory is not so elastic at that time.

The 'Hittite' language is an example of a tribe with an Indo-European language abandoning it and adopting a new one imperfectly. Some remnants remained. It is not the ruin of a structure, but a new structure with some stones of the old one built into it. (Yiddish is *not* Semitic, Pidgin is *not* Chinese). This actual 'Hi titte' language may well have had common ancestors with the present-day Caucasian languages. Of course, it is pointless to compare today's Caucasian forms.

138

Writing: There is an orthographic tradition, cultivated through learning, school. People write down letters that are not spoken without realising it. Writing has its own history, which is tougher than the sound group. The educated language adheres more to the conventional pronunciation of the written image.

Digamma[56] was written en masse when it was no longer spoken, certainly in wrong places, [same] h. The Phrygian inscription with αναξ; thus proves nothing.

139

'Pre-Greek personal names'. [I am] against the custom of trying to explain all the names of the epic Greek. Like the place names, the personal names are *not Greek* in masses. Especially those that look Greek — simply folk etymology. Examples: Eteocles[57], Agamemnon, Achilles, Odysseus.

1600 shaft tombs (ancient Indo-European) — 1400 tholos tombs (Libyan Achaeans) — 1200 Greeks. Agamemnon like Minos [were] annexed by Greek legend.

---

56 Digamma is an ancient Greek letter that is not used in the modern Greek alphabet. — *Transl.*

57 Oedipus' son in Greek mythology. — *Transl.*

140

To be and to have: Only Nordic linguistic thought knows the word 'have' — so strong is its property thinking. To be is: to be visually present. To have is: to belong to as property. We even say: the stag *owns* antlers. The colour is peculiar to the flower.

141

Language, writing: The division of science (sounds, consonants) is nothing more than a confusion of sound and letter. It simply divides the signs of the present alphabet into groups. In reality, there are hundreds of consonants and dozens of vowels that change from village to village. They are fundamentally different 'in German', in Upper Bavaria, Silesia, Franconia, Saxony.

Only speaking 'under the spell of the alphabet', the learned pronunciation of the written language, brings in a kind of common consonant treasure above the real peasant language.

The invention of the alphabet, then, is in fact the invention of a script which inaccurately summarises the hundred consonants *actually* spoken by means of a few signs, thus enabling those who have learned the pronunciation to speak on the basis of the text as it actually happens. The letter text is only a clue, not an actual reproduction of what is spoken, which would be impossible.

142

Vortex of language and races: It is useless to try to infer from much later or even present-day types of written remains. When the lordly tribes, often in a thin upper class, settled down, landscape-bound types of people formed everywhere, which dominated the racial image of the new tribes. In the stream of generations, echoes of the former elements appeared again and again — such as the 'Mongoloid' types in northern Europe, and very much in Russia, which can be traced back at least in part to this 'Bronze Age' conquest of the second millennium. Aino. And likewise the languages, e.g. in the Caucasus, are remnants of once large language families. Finno-Ugric. The tribes, which we group according to language, as Tatars, Huns, Turks, Tochars, Scythians, Mongols, but which were very close to each other in terms of landscape, way of life, world-view and are therefore presumably related in terms of 'race', blood mixture. What is considered a Mongolian characteristic today (Mongolian spot, eyelid fissure) should not be sought in Inner Asia at that time. It was certainly (ego) only spread from the south-east (such as Tonkin, Sikiang, Nanking) through the mixture in the Chinese empire since the Han period, through mixing.

143

China: Here one of the pre-Indo-European languages has established itself as the written language. Mutilated, abstract, intellectualised; apparently, because the inflection had a different soul, it disappeared altogether.

144

Apart from the names of persons, the important words for war and state also adhere more firmly than language. (Words of the priestly world adhere to place.) *Wer*, war, *guerre*, *wergeld*. Castle, *faubourg*, *borgo*, *boulevard*. *Meier*. *Palast*, *Pfalz*.

The names for special weapons adhere to the goods, i.e. trade names — *gladius, caballus, pilum, chako, kalpak*.

145

The ancient names of heroes (and gods such as Damater, Potidon) do not originate from the language group from which the 'Hellenic' dialect has developed and been preserved since Homer. If they were Indo-European, they have disappeared from one or more language families that have died out. What do we know of the Indo-European languages north of Hellas? 'Illyrians' and 'Thracians' are artificial fantasies. And Basque, Etruscan, Caucasian language families and others that have disappeared without trace?

Here, for once, we must object to the basic error of philologists in looking backwards from the written language remains as if there had been no written languages. What would we know of the Indian language up to Buddha if oral tradition had not preserved the remains of literature? Not one inscription. Of the many languages on the soil of China today? We know only the official 'Chinese' language of the literature and documents of the Zhou period. The bone oracles are word signs — of what language, we do not know.

146

There were no 'Hellenes' at all before 1200. The language unit — fictitious as it would be, for the Spartan could not understand the Ionian at all when he spoke — is formed from the young Indo-European group, which around 1200 formed a thin ruling class above many other languages, which were preserved, above all in cult, in the countryside, in the lower masses; starting from the Ionians, felt, experienced as a community of ruling dynasties, slowly extended to the whole countryside. The 'tribes' [were] originally only *phratries*[58], noble *phyla*. *Landsmannschaften*[59] is the right term for the cohesion: nobles and their retinue, *citoyens*[60], finally all in the country.

147

Names of persons and places, titles and words for arms, house, social order prove nothing for the language of the people. They are much more conservative than the language that is changed. The personal names in Romance countries [are] largely Germanic, in Germanic largely Hebrew, Romance. The Tatar Bulgarians speak Slavic, the names are Byzantine. [The] titles in Germany (army) [are] partly

---

58 From ancient Greek φρατρία: 'brotherhood'. A phratry is an association of several family groups that derived their kinship from a common mythical ancestor. — *Transl.*

59 A *Landsmannschaft* is a German fraternity. — *Transl.*

60 French: 'citizens'. — *Transl.*

French (General, Secretary), [partly] (Admiral) Arabic, (Hussars) Tartar, (Uhlans[61]) Polish.

148

Languages are quickly changed. Trade languages and peasant languages sit most firmly. Conquerors, nomads, administrators change languages much more easily. But the custom of naming is very tenacious. That is why personal names reveal more than languages (and place names).

In Boghazköy [there are] not only names of Indo-European character, but rather of West Asia. Therefore, the chancery language must have a different origin (has it only been in use since 1500?). Was it dragged along on the Galatian way from the Balkans by conquerors who were then destroyed and only left traces of their language in the chancery? Was this connected with the Hyksos?

149

Noth[62], *Israelitische Namen*[63], p. 41: It is even easier for a people to change its language than its proper names. Jews in Germany, Teutons in France, Old Rome, Old Hellas, Hittites, Asia Minor. It is not the sounds of names and rarely the components of the name that may be compared, but the general custom of forming names. The changes in this custom reflect history. Rome: death of the *praenomen*[64], emergence of the *cognomen*[65], its formation. Hellas: formation of two-part names Heracles, etc. Where? When?

Greek names: Wilamowitz II. originally secular, warlike. Later theological names. As with the Germanic tribes.

---

61 Uhlans were Lithuanian/Polish light cavalry units. — *Transl.*

62 Martin Noth (1902–1968) was a German Protestant theologian and biblical scholar. — *Transl.*

63 'Israelite Names' — *Transl.*

64 One's first name in ancient Rome. — *Transl.*

65 One's nickname in ancient Rome. — *Transl.*

150

The personal names, as long as one proceeded according to their sense and not merely conventionally, are of a religious nature in Egypt [and] Babylon (Israel), of a personal nature in the North. Names of gods did not occur in ancient Hellenic and ancient Germanic names. They are also absent from Old Italic and Old Celtic names.

151

Like the Hellenic-speaking tribes, the bearers of proto-Germanic and proto-Celtic found a population in north-western Europe with which they mixed — the blond race. Like the Turks, this creates an elite people, selection. The 'proto-Indo-European language' is quite simply the language of the Aryans in the land of Aria. From there [it is spread] with the chariot peoples. Here the type of the master and conqueror people emerges. The Tocharians also called themselves Aryans (Arsi). 'Persian' is only a tiny part of the widespread group (Scythians, Cimmerians, Pamir languages).

152

How many language types and tribal languages there have been is shown by the remains: Basque, Etruscan, Caucasian, Novilara, Boghazköy, etc. Hundreds of languages and linguistic types, which is childish to bring into systems! To call large areas Illyrian, Iberian, Ligurian on the map is silly: just as one could write the word Bushman or Swahili about Africa.

153

Here we find a naivety in linguistic research: in well-known languages (Germanic, French, Latin) one is always quick to identify foreign and loan words. In less well-known languages (Etruscan, Hittite) I have never noticed this. On the contrary, every word that one finds is considered a word of these languages without further ado. And in unknown languages, like Illyrian, Iberian — which never existed — every element (suffix, root) in a geographical area is considered an element of it. But what is a 'loan word'? Vocabulary migrates from one grammatical system to another, the earlier, the more. Only as the language becomes richer in words does the vocabulary become more solid. Speaking = thinking: one adopts the entire vocabulary of the foreign country, but thinks grammatically in one's own way.

154

What matters for race is not what language it speaks, but how it speaks it, 'dialect'!!! Pronunciation and syntax are race: this is how entities like Yiddish, Monk Latin, Pidgin English, *lingua rustica*[66] come into being. In part, the Greek dialects go back to this: they arose because a non-Greek population learned to speak Greek. (Gercke I, 523.) Above all, 'Achaean' is such an otherness (527). What peculiarities of pronunciation and sound change do Greek, Italic and Asia Minor dialects, Etruscan and Cretan have in common? Mark it out on a map!

155

Philologists always forget one more thing: that the difference between written languages and vernacular languages is not always dialectical, but very often that of completely different languages, one of which does not appear in writing at all and thus does not exist for the philological approach. If one then wants to read the existence of the peoples from written remains, large and important peoples disappear without a trace from the historical picture thus developed.

The Galatians still spoke Celtic (Jerome) in the 4th century, but there is not a single Celtic inscription. Those who learned to write wrote Greek or Latin. Likewise the Germanic peoples (Vandals etc.). In Hellas, pre-Greek languages were certainly still widely spoken in the time of Pericles, in Italy non-Italian even in the time of Hannibal, and in Etruria [the] development of writing was still quite different. If all inscriptions somewhere are written in *one* language, this is no

---

66 Latin: 'vernacular language'. — *Transl.*

proof that this language was also *spoken* by the people: Boghazköy, Normans in England, French, Visigoths in Italy, Spain.

156

I believe that the picture of the history of language is still wrong today: we involuntarily conclude for early times that there were relatively few original systems from which the languages we know can be derived. Surely it was the other way around. What we know are only the few languages that were officially used where people wrote, and it is clear that written languages in the mouths of powerful cultural nations caused the extinction of an infinite number of languages without writing. Wherever writing suddenly shines into another area, as in Boghazköy, nests of lost languages are suddenly uncovered. What do we know about the language of India, China around 1500 B.C.? Around the Mediterranean we know the written remains of perhaps 50 languages (including 'new' ones: from Cyprus, Novilara, Lemnos).

157

Zeitschrift der Deutschen Morgenländischen Gesellschaft[67] 1925, p. 301: Coptic is the vulgar, Demotic the written language of decline. Important that the fellaheen have a rigid language — Vulgar Latin, Kechua, Hindi. The final fate of cultural languages. In general: the history of language must stick to the written dialects and establish their grammatical genealogy. The written language shares the special fate in 'society'. The 'people' write little, in Egypt etc. perhaps they do not read at all. Reading and writing are exclusive.

This essay is crucial to the history of the Egyptian language, whose written side Sethe[68] compares to a canal, whose oral aspect he compares to a stream. Has Egyptian perhaps only been separated from Semitic-Hamitic by writing?

---

67 'Journal of the German Oriental Society'. — *Ed.*

68 Kurth Sethe (1869–1934) was a German Egyptologist who participated in the creation of the *Ancient Egyptian Dictionary*. — *Transl.*

158

Language: It is communicative (I and Thou). Genuine primeval poetry, however, uses it as a cosmic means, without regard to 'intelligibility'. That is why genuine poems are only comprehensible to the poet and often not even to him, if the experience has become foreign to him. Originally, all types of language are developed unconsciously. In high states, children unconsciously learn the language (several) of their environment, mimic signs, writing, often of several cultural languages. The adult is only aware of the 'written language', but not of the fragmentary sign language, which he also still possesses from childhood. The child draws by itself, but writing is work to it.

159

Language: I am talking about 'speech and thought types'. The practical thinking of the people of a c-culture has developed the system of, for example, Indo-European speech. It is the type of causal thinking that shapes the linguistic formation of the elements of things, of events, of 'property' in relation to something. The relational syllables (prefix, suffix, infix, determiner, inflection, article, preposition, etc.) are signs of thought.

160

All primitive fairy tales, folklore, legends, myths can be traced back to a few basic types, e.g. question torment (Laistner[69]), brother's tale, flight, defeat of evil, etc. They are also types of torment in dreams, especially in children. Psychoanalysis ('Mikosch') reduces all this to metropolitan sexual decadence; likewise everything can be reduced to hunger and thirst or dreams of power. I am only showing that here the human soul becomes pre-linguistically aware of its relationship to the world, waking and dreaming. These are the basic situations of the inventive, personal predator. Relationship to the other (enemy, friend), to woman, to animals, to the world, to day and night, to youth, age,

---

69 Ludwig Laistner (1845–1896) was a German writer and literary historian. — *Transl.*

past, future. These are the first foreboding, looking impulses of meta-physics. With language, they lose some of their depth. They exist alongside what can be spoken, even today, as that which cannot be put into words, which is put into music, painting, symbolism.

161

Language fate: Master peoples lose the language (Tursha, Normans); settler peoples hold on to it. No language proves anything for the origin of the people speaking it. [There are] three migra-tory types of languages: settler expansion (German), trade languages (English), administrative language (Roman). There is originally no 'pride in the mother tongue'. On the contrary: pride in understanding the foreign master language.

162

Language: Different 'languages' in the sense of 'Greek', 'Celtic' — i.e. language groups of strong peculiarity — arise through the extinction of the masses of other languages, so that now relatively different ones collide.

163

All theories about the origin of language, because they were devel-oped by theoreticians, have the error that they presuppose the think-ing and writing scholar, the poet and speaker — Herder, Hamann[70], Humboldt[71] –, and are therefore monological. Language, however, has a dialogical origin. One speaks to someone who answers. The series of sentence words [is] not the development of a thought as in 'speech',

---

70	Johann Georg Hamann (1730–1788) was a German philosophical-theological author who criticised the Enlightenment and postulated that there could be no reason before language and history. According to him, the ability to think is based on the existence of language. — *Transl.*

71	Wilhelm von Humboldt (1767–1835) was a German scholar, linguist, statesman and founder of the University of Berlin (now Humboldt University). — *Transl.*

but alternates as question, answer, command, etc. The sentence is originally not the version of a thought, but of an intention.

164

Not the concepts, the *sentences* come first. The conceptual words follow only from the purpose of the sentences. Here! Go! No! Is it so?

It is quite wrong for the language observers, the city scholars, to start from words for things: moon, sheep, table. The first is the sentence that addresses the other. And it is only in relation to the sentence that the words for things arise. Originally, a 'that there!' or 'these here' sufficed.

165

One must be clear about the fact that the words of abstraction — words without a picture, imagination — make things difficult for the speaker at first. 'The deer' is clear. 'The wind' (from blowing) denotes a fact, then it becomes a noun, subject, numen: 'The wind is blowing'. All nouns have a tendency to have a mythological effect on thought. Language, the mass of words present, is like a landscape, like sounds of the night, one smells 'powers' in it. Thus Zarathustra immediately personified his abstractions.

The personification of abstraction. 'Death' — *mors imperator*[72]. The Roman gods of sowing, sickling, grinding, etc. The door as god, the hearth, the marriage bed. Treachery of the object. The fire. Justice, wisdom, peace, war. (Transition from the visible to the abstract.)

166

Language, b: Looking, foreboding — emergence of phonetic formations of a vague kind, the symbolic expression, not yet an actual name.

---

72 Latin: 'emperor of death'. — *Transl.*

c: Even only the desire to communicate is relief. The agony of the soul, developed from insights of death, transience, threatening future, seeks communication — approach to the alien microcosm.

167

Place names: Today, one has recognised the importance of such layers of names for the determination of historical processes, but has completely overlooked the profound significance of this process itself. Nevertheless, it is precisely *this* that provides the historical information.

Now, in Egypt and Babylon, it is still possible to trace how the idea of the city name develops (example: Buto Ur): namely, one does not name the city itself, but something sacred, after which the settlement gradually receives its name. It is quite certain that the earliest real names for dwellings — whereby the place of origin and the place of residence are thus ideally separated, the inhabited and the residing, only develop at the end of the 4th millennium and only here, in the primitive culture, whereupon the custom gradually expands.

The Asia Minor-Mediterranean [nomenclature] certainly did not take place until the 3rd millennium, and that according to strict custom in every place. Thus the 'Asia Minor' place names on -ss and -nt are the oldest layer of names and are to be placed about 2500, when the Kassite-Atlantean radiation begins. Even the renaming by later layers of peoples is subject to certain rules which must be ascertained in order to see clearly: in many cases the heroic peoples left the name they had heard to the urban area, but renamed the castle — with them the naming is already more personal than cultic: no Pharaoh would have thought of naming a city after himself.

168

Proper names (excursus): We should not expect genuine city names in the late sense in the 4th millennium. The name is sacred (*nomen est omen*[73]), and only late does it become a mere designation for an object. If a settlement arose somewhere, there must always have been several names depending on the deep meaning: first the temple name, because the numen guaranteed protection, then the identical name, self-designation of the tribe whose centre was the settlement, then for instance the name of the settlement as a fortified defensive unit, often the customary name of the market. In political, mercantile and religious testimonies, various names will be mentioned, of which in the second millennium one will finally become widely dominant as a remnant from a time of solemn naming. Likewise, as is well known, one man originally bears several names. Mohammed had a lost 'baptismal name', as a husband he was called Abulkasim after his first son, in the city he bears the honorary name Amin. Muhammad is his self-designation as a prophet.

169

Names: The oldest, first naming was always a ceremonial act, a 'baptism'. With the name the youth, the association, the settlement received a numen, a being, and ceased to be a thing.

Language was something far too serious to be used for mere naming. So names also had a meaning (in Kash it was a whole sentence). Only later did they become polished and ordinary. So with every epoch that is perceived as such, the baptism into a new name occurs: the man is called differently than the youth, a 'people' is called differently ('Saxons') at the exodus, renaming of a city! This is why cultically important persons (Egyptian king) have several names depending on the role they play. Thus the pope takes a new name.

170

Antiquity: The strongest example of [the] disappearance of language while race remains are the Celtic languages, which dominated

---

73   Latin: 'the name is a sign'. — *Transl.*

almost all of Western and Central Europe and Asia Minor in 200 B.C. and then rapidly disappeared except for a few remnants.

171

Proto-Semitic split off from Hamitic in Africa in the 4th millennium and solidified insularly in Arabia. Since Guanche and Kabyle belong to Hamitic, the language may have originated in Spain-France (Upper Palaeolithic, migrating with the Megalithic). West-East pendulum. South-east: Somalo-Abyssinia. In the rest of Africa absorbed into the later languages (because [it was the language] of conquering minorities). The oldest Semitic is Akkadian (with the megalithic culture from Libya?). Much younger [are] Aramaic, Sabaean, Arabic. Did Germanic originate on a Semitic basis; or 'Iberian'?

172

Semito-Hittite languages: To finally dispel the impression that these are two groups of languages, it must be said: We know from this [group]:

1. Egyptian as the written language of a high culture, i.e. in a state of senile development. Only now does one (Sethe) suspect how different the languages of the peoples of the Nile valley were in this respect.

2. Semitic, in reality a high level language in many dialects, not a group of languages.

The differences are partly chronological: Akkadian 2500, Aramaic 500, Arabic even later. So a gap like Pyramid Texts and [Roman] I[mperial Age].

3. Very little else, [some] as Bedouin language, others from North Africa, which we treat as units without reasons: Libyan, Nubian.

173

How little the historically best-known area of distribution of a language proves for its history is shown by Celtic: about 500 B.C. half of Europe, about 0 almost disappeared, and Roman: about 500 a village, about 0 half the world.

174

Writing: Instead of 'taking over' the Phoenician signs, one has to reckon with stages: in the 2nd millennium, all over the Mediterranean, Nordic people, astonished by Egypt, tried to appropriate their signs somehow — as identifying words etc. This led to certain systems, until finally the Ionian Hansa made the fixed 'Greek' alphabet out of it. But one notices the older traces everywhere, where the signs were partly syllables. At that time, new tribes very often used the foreign script awkwardly — already as a result of negotiations. There must often have been very few people who got it right (Ulfilas[74]),

because they knew languages here. Is the 'Hittite' pictographic script that of a Sea People, i.e. an Indo-European language?

175

Language: The genealogical tree theory corresponds perfectly to the theory of biology of the time — Darwin! Outwardly it resembles the family tree of ancient families, but in reality it is a figure of logical inference designed to exclude chance. In causalism, each link is the effect [of the preceding] and [the] cause of the following. And from this family tree of language derives the picture of the history of peoples that still prevails today: aboriginal people, the 'Indians' 'migrated' from Europe to India, and more of such silliness. Convenient, but stupid.

176

Language: Begin this section thus: the great dividing line of two ages of human existence now lies where the thought/imagined, 'recognised' connection of two impressions as cause and effect begins to dominate awake existence. The original animal experience refers only to the fact of certain consequences: between the consequence of day

---

74 Ulfilas (c. 311–c. 382 A.D.) was a Gothic theologian and missionary who evangelised the Goths. He created the Gothic alphabet and thus was the first who translated parts of the Bible into a Germanic language. — *Transl.*

and night and that of wise and stupid there is a difference of kind. Now, however, the why is added to the that, to the knowledge of what has just happened as something known, habitual, the knowledge of the necessity also in the future, always and everywhere.

This epoch is synonymous with that of the habit of language. From elements of communication that only warn and indicate to actual speech that is continuously causal in the sequence of sentences and that represents and communicates causality. Here the stages a-b and c-d separate.

177

The influence of politics on the history of language: Whoever speaks the language of the master nation belongs to it. Whom one does not understand is the object. Hence the tendency of the subjugated to adopt the master language as quickly as possible. Only heroism knows pride in the language. This is how the fact arises that the great masses of a region speak a completely different language than the small upper class of officials, rulers, merchants and documents.

178

Language: Present a new theory here shortly. So far, pedigree and wave theory. Both [contain] the error of regarding the stock of language as single-layered and language itself as the essence (instead [of] a side of the expression of an essence) whose history lies resolved in itself. That is why there is still no history of language (world history of linguistic expression). But I distinguish: 1. dialects and social languages, 2. everyday and written languages, 3. language development and political development of language fates.

Decisive is the city: rural and urban languages; status: class [and] occupation; race; culture: the West Indo-European language of younger type ('centum[75]'), soul-formed in the 2nd millennium, belongs to a new cultural soul.

179

Original languages: When one sees the enormous fragmentation of languages especially in remnant areas (California, Caucasus), the thought suggests itself that the phenomenon of the great linguistic habit is late and belongs to the d-culture, possibly also c. But that something quite different appears before it: namely, a racial kinship in the emergence of grammatical principles, which found a different kind of realisation in each of the innumerable tribes. The 'kinship' therefore does not exist between the languages themselves, but [between] the principles of their emergence. This is rather convergence and certainly not genealogy. The accumulation of vocabulary must eventually have taken place in each village in its own right (just as even today in Europe each dialect, each area of land has its own property, cf. e.g. plant names!). The next step was the dying out of countless of them, with constant mixing of the word masses, but also of the pronunciation and endings, as soon as the language was taken over. Only historical causes and fates have then allowed very late, complex, convergent 'language families' to emerge over these masses, so that the assumption of an 'original language' is wrong. [What we consider to be an 'original language' is always a language that had the political fate of becoming widespread at a very late stage. Indo-European, for example, was certainly still some obscure dialect around 2000 B.C., of which we have no idea who and where [people] spoke it at that time.

180

Language: The great mistake of making the spread of 'languages' cartographically dependent on 'written languages'. Unfortunately, we

---

75 Indo-European languages have been grouped into 'centum languages' and 'satem languages' since 1890. The canonical centum languages are Celtic, Hellenic, Italic and Germanic. — *Transl.*

only know the oldest state of language from written languages. For this very reason, special attention should be paid to the erroneous inscriptions: papyri, gravestones, graffiti of the lower people, for they are more genuine. It is simply not true to divide the (Indo-European) language into Italian, Spanish, German, Russian, etc. There are hundreds of languages, all still segregated into human breeds, geographically precisely delimited, with transitions. The Spanish dialects, for example, are languages. Low German is closer to English and Dutch than to Upper Bavarian. German' and 'Italian' of the Alps have much in common in sentence structure, pronunciation, gender of the word.

181

Language: Even place names are only conclusive if they are supported by other evidence. The originators of a name are usually not the founders of the settlement and very often neither its inhabitants nor the victors in the battle for the vernacular. In the circle of the Aegean Sea, we know of many places with several names that applied one after the other; often none is 'Greek', but it was pronounced Greek. The Roman towns on the Rhine and Danube were inhabited by Celts and Germanic tribes; Latin was only the lingua franca, but the names remained Latin.

182

The basic error of linguistics is that it — as a specialised science — treats its object, 'language', as something existing in itself. However, there are no original languages, but rather basic types of thought that express themselves in infinitely internally similar language structures. But one will also find this in other worlds of forms: Hamites and Megalith, Kashites and Templum, Aryans and Spiritual Religion.

183

The linguistic virtuosity of the thin-blooded! Not Napoleon's speeches, but Kant's thinking, the philosophers' desire to know better, their desire to be right. Also the soul: that of the strong-blooded and the thin-blooded: to these belong the traits of pride, hatred, anger, devotion — and self-opinionatedness, pettiness, etc.

184

b: Primitive grammar: characterised phonetic formations denote the tense: 'now — not yet — not any more', the place, the thing.

c: The carrier of common speech becomes the 'sentence' of causal character: not 'that appears so', but 'that is so, because; should be so'. The types of sentences are no longer metaphysical but physical units and classes: Question — Condition — Confirmation — Statement — Syntax.

So b: gravity in the word-structure, c: [heavy weight] in the 'sentence' as a causally constructed word sequence. To b belongs suggestion of tense (past, present, future), place (there, here), characteristic (size, movement, number, male, female). Medium generality, not 'stag' but 'fawn, buck, grey horse, mare, black foal'. All this clarified by gestures. Inflection as a characteristic (symbolic) in the position and behaviour of the signified, primal grammar as the stock of characterising formations on the word. Syntax as the law of the process of sentence formation in speaking 'continuously'. Only the sentence turns word symbols into word concepts. A 'concept' is a constituent of a sentence, a carrier of causal sentence structures (an exclamation 'O God' contains a sound symbol, not a concept. 'God is — –': this is 'God' as a concept). The 'concept' exists only in continuous sentence speaking (also thinking as speaking to oneself).

185

The 'historical' languages are interspersed with fossils as only some limestone mountains can be. All the formerly living forms have 'settled' there, been smashed, ground down, mixed up: but the guiding fossils are recognisable everywhere. Basically, the whole grammatical system is fossil, because syntactic speech not only works with it, but also against its archaic rigidity. The skeleton of declension and conjunction is rapidly decaying, insofar as it is not held together by later mixtures. Fossil [is], for example, the gender of nouns, the medium, the dual, the difference between persons and things.

186

The syntactic, 'common' speaking and understanding of what is spoken is based on a kind of suggestion. Instead of the real terms and inflections, a dense torrent of sounds, relations, allusions penetrates the ear, which brings about the mental relations that are 'meant'. The ability to achieve this suggestion lies in the expressions: speaking forcefully, convincingly, clearly, irresistibly. It is the 'gift of oratory'. The opposite, the failed suggestion, is meant by the word 'chatter'.

187

Only with the habit of speaking to one another, from which follows speaking to oneself, does 'private life' develop as a quiet inner life first alongside and then in contrast to the public life of the general public. Besides the spiritual life of the tribe, there is also that of the estates, classes, clubs (totem clans, age groups), and then everyone has a thoughtful spiritual inner life for himself: but that is (personality). And only now does the strife arise: to reconcile everyone at the palaver, *quot capita, tot mentes*[76], because everyone wants to assert and enforce 'his' private spirituality. Strong personalities want to dominate public opinion, weak ones only want to assert themselves alongside it. Types of the know-all, grumbler, opponent, ruler.

188

There is a tragic difference between being able to speak and having to speak. As long as a swarm of people and animals feels, does, is as a whole, as a We, speaking is the accompanying expression of this being alive, as acclamation, confirmation, warning, as expression of

---

76 Latin: 'as many heads, as many opinions'. — *Transl.*

jubilation and pain, heat and energy. One could remain silent, but the heightened feeling of being alive urges one to speak up.

The swarm of higher people is different, in which everyone feels not only the 'we' but also the 'you and I' of the majority: here there is an urge to speak out, to talk before and after, to talk to oneself, in order to build a bridge between oneself and the others again and again, out of the pressure of being for oneself, the need to be together. The need to speak of lonely souls leads to the habit of dialogue, whose logical form is causal in nature.

And out of this need, this possibility that rises to the level of a matter of course, 'cultural life' develops, namely the formative life that only brings about the forms through dialogue between individuals.

189

The d-languages are without exception the result of convergence. They form from dialects, but they immediately disintegrate again of their own accord. The spiritual convergence, however, is syntactically — grammatically the life-unit of society, in word stock that of practical life. E.g. there was no original Indian language, only dialects. The various 'Hellenic' languages of 1100 are the product of the incipient high culture: languages of the chivalrous *Internationale* above the peasantry: dozens of courtly idioms above hundreds of village dialects, skalds, courts, merchants then bring the convergence further and further.

190

With high culture, the actual 'languages' develop *above* the dialects, e.g. the Indian, Hellenic, Germanic languages, but these are all professional languages, without exception. There is a priestly language of status and a noble one — Rigveda, Homer –, often recorded as a written language, which exists above the peasant and Bedouin dialect and is hardly understood by peasants. The language of the city: even there each for itself, for the lower class dialect remaining or becoming again (Berlin), because the c-thinking finds its syntactic style. Only the great state formations [and] political destinies result in the formation of genuine cultural languages as a linguistic fate: but these are ideal languages, which are described and demanded in textbooks, but are not really spoken in this way by anyone.

191

The form circles of language formation are nothing less than 'original languages'. Neither is one aware of this similarity, nor can one communicate on the basis of it. The prerequisite for being able to understand each other over long distances, despite village differences, is already a political and commercial grouping: the subordination of the village languages to one which is the language of the market, the trade route or the ruling class. Even [of these there are] still many hundreds. And it is only at the threshold and in the sphere of influence of high culture, of the city, of the state, of writing, that cultural languages such as Old Vedic and Sumerian develop, which now penetrate into the villages and create dialects there. So

a) Elementary form circles of language formation — ornamentation

b) Outgrowth of master languages (government, cult, trade) over the village language masses

c) Establishment of cultural languages (writing, memorisation, custom, education).

192

History of language: In contrast to the view prevailing today that formally related languages emerged from an 'original language' — a view which is purely philological, i.e. blindly technical, and which ignores the real picture of the whole culture including language custom, in short everything non-linguistic: settlement, society, race –, I want to give here a picture as actual history demands. I also point out that the 'pedigree theory' of languages bears a suspicious resemblance to Darwinism, that is, it corresponds to the materialistic way of thinking of the previous century, which fixed the method of reflection from the outset.

Indeed, one must imagine how the population was then organised in the age of the emergence of grammatically formed word languages from sign languages (UdA II). We are talking about the 7th-5th millennium, when the ability of personal causal thinking began to organise life. There is no mention of cities, nor of nations and nation states. The inner formal kinship of wide populations — what I call fluid culture — did not correspond to a consciousness of this kinship and even less to a state summary of it. The largest organised formal unit is the tribe, a village or a few, a narrow valley, what can be gathered in a day. Thousands of such units dwell where an 'empire' can exist in the 2nd millennium. They belong together religiously and politically and have only jealously and suspiciously treated relations against each other, where war is the state of nature and peace the artificial exception.

It is clear that a language develops in each of these tiny units by itself. Racial kinship corresponds to a kinship of pronunciation and sentence structure, intellectual kinship to a kinship of grammar and word construction. But no more than kinship! The natural condition, still to be found among Indians and Negroes today, is that no village understands the other and that for every intercourse the old sign language persists. Only gradually, as commerce and politics form larger units with their destinies, do these thousands of village languages begin to become hundreds of landscape languages: so it is still visible in the Mediterranean in the 3rd millennium.

Only the great movements of urban culture with its written languages cause most of them to die off as politically and mercantilely favoured 'official' languages; and only now does dialect formation begin: a regression to the natural state, so that finally every tiny region speaks the common language again in its own way, thus making itself something living out of the fossil material.

To take 'Indo-European' as a starting point, we have to assume the formation of innumerable village languages which are internally alike or similar, but in such a way that there are transitions to the neighbourhood everywhere and thus a sharp border to other 'original languages' does not occur at all. When tribes with such languages came to India in the 2nd millennium, a (relatively!) common migratory jargon developed, against which the oldest languages disappear. This then becomes courtly (Pali) and priestly (Veda) dialects, which much later come to a unified type through writing. In the same way, northern tribes that came to the Aegean spoke an infinite variety of dialects, which from one century to the next melted down to a few politically preferred ones, from a hundred to a dozen (1200), and finally, with writing, to a few groups.

But what is called 'Dorian', 'Aeolian', are only the results of the political formation of the state, where the ruling class elevates its synthetic language to the 'national language'. In fact, every village still has its own dialect in the inscriptions.

The only reason we do not know this about Egypt, Babylonia and China is that there is an official written language and dialects remain scriptless. How far this goes: we do not possess a line of Galatian and Macedonian (despite Alexander!). Everything written is 'Greek'.

193

What it looks like when someone speaks a foreign language with its own syntax is taught by every joke book, where, for example, a Negro speaks English, a Jew German, a Slav French. 'Germanised' populations speak with a different syntax that corresponds to their race: *lingua rustica*, the sentence structure of the East German, the Swiss. But this is rarely noticed, because they 'speak German'. A map of the grammatical and syntactical elements would look very different, but today's way of speaking only looks at the grammar. 'Horse mine'. 'Make a deal he did'. Language change of a race is only a change of grammar.

194

In the popular listing of language affinities, a little more mathematics would be in order: if two languages show agreement, say two dozen words, one should ask what percentage of the known word stock that is: 10%, for example, would not exceed the limit of coincidence. The same applies to the notion of phonetic stock and grammatical endings.

195

The high point of grammatical systematisation is already passed before the high cultures begin (in the late amoebae, that is), and a syntactic art of sentence sequences and sentence groups (subordinate clause architecture) begins, which abrades the fossil material of primitive grammar and uses it differently.

196

Language [is] not only spirit, but also world-view: it contains the first human philosophy and religion! All later philosophy is a reinterpretation of this first. Religion is therefore a deepening of language. Philosophy seeks to replace 'error' with 'truth', i.e. words with words.

197

Herder is right: language is the origin of culture (341/2). Languages put names and words in place of reality. Language is philosophy proper, metaphysical in its construction, in its material. The speaking man goes about only in a dream-image of his mind (342), and that in an impersonal one, lying in the tradition of speech. 'Dream-image of the spirit'. The genuine thinker frees himself from this: for him language is not a treasure of views, but a tool.

198

Only language as a habit turns sensual understanding into perception on the one hand, and into the spirit on the other. The history of language is the history of the emancipation of the spirit. Ancient languages are evidence of earlier spiritual states. Language and intellectual history are the same thing. Human consciousness was educated to 'spirit' through language. The sentence is the primordial precipitation of causal consciousness: subject — predicate. The phonetic structure (word) separates life from thought.

199

The sentence as an element of fluent speech contains in its structure all the elements of a primitive metaphysics. Logic begins with the lie. The ability to speak fluently seduces to play, which dominates the day for racy people from prehistoric times until today. Play of the imagination — fairy tale, lie, cutting open — play of the hand — ornament. Disguise, mimicry, imitation (voice, gesture), game of luck, fate (dice, bet, battle).

The lie is the first 'language for a purpose'. And it is only from this primitive play with facts that the concept of truths arises! Lying among primitive men is a sign of cunning, superiority, warfare, a pleasure, one does not take it amiss. Harmless. Only custom separates circles within which it is 'dishonest' to be duped. Only outwardly [is it permitted:] Jesuits. Northcliffe[77]. And morality demands an 'ideal', 'truth'.

200

What nonsense! Take the written language of the Vedas (1000 B.C.), Homer and the Aegean inscriptions (800 B.C.), Rome (200 B.C.), the Persian court (500 B.C.), the Gothic Bible (300 A.D.), [the] Celtic and Germanic manuscripts (800 A.D.), invent a 'people' for each of them, claim that these peoples formed a primeval people with a primeval language, without regard to the fact that these are written languages preserved by chance, that innumerable peasant languages

---

77   Alfred Charles William Harmsworth (1865–1922), 1st Viscount Northcliffe, was a British journalist and publisher. He owned the popular newspapers *Daily Mail* and *Daily Mirror*. — *Transl.*

have disappeared without being brought into written languages by accidents of political history. What nonsense! If we did not know that the languages of south-western Europe, America, the Philippines, the lower Danube, indirectly also of England, Canada, Australia, have emerged from the dialect of the small city of Rome, through historical, not linguistic events, we would long ago have invented a 'primeval people' out of Indians, Spaniards, French, Indians, etc., and would be looking for its 'seats' in France, for example. The intervention of political history in linguistic history is infinite.

201

Personal, artistic creative power, abstracting, explaining, critical: from language habit from sign to narration ('singer and listener'). Primeval form of poetry, creation of an image of the past. Explanatory myth (animal tale. It was once upon a time), sexual explanation and praising description (Cock-and-bull story. I was once upon a time. Meaning of the 3rd and 1st person). Here, signs of a detached spirit, humour (in the animal story) and wit (about others) already begin. A play with language, with logic, with laws of thought (humour = north, expanse; wit = south, narrowness?).

In narration, fate, coincidence, time finally find a form of expression. Has the *Perfektum*[78] developed from this? Real communication does not need this form at all.

202

Semito-Hamitic: The pace of language change certainly corresponds to the pace of change in life forms (everywhere? Indians?).

Very old systems like Semito-Hamitic can lead to astonishing immobility in closed earth spaces where nothing changes, as in Arabic. Arabic is almost immobile, while Egyptian, born on the soil of a rising high culture, undergoes rapid change.

---

78 Perfect form. — *Transl.*

But a new term should be introduced: just as to racial traits belongs Mendelian type, not a certain shape of nose, but a degree of variability, so also to grammatical systems variability from rigidity to light liquid is an element of form, which in the case of the Aryan systems tends to the last extreme, in the case of the Semitic to the first!

203

Among the motifs of diffusion in prehistoric times is the traffic along the ancient eternal trade and water routes, the Hun, Varangian, Vandal [and] Galatian routes. What do we know of the history, the trends, battles, leaders in the 3rd/2nd millennium in Europe! Along these roads, some language must have developed into the language of trade: first among the traders, then in the settlement, from there perhaps across whole tribes. For at that time there was no 'pride in the mother tongue'.

So if pottery proves relations from Elam[79] to the Adriatic — did languages of the Sumerian type migrate there and spread (Etruscan, Lemnos, Novilara ...)?

Thus Ionian, Punic, Spanish, Venetian have spread along the ports, Greek in southern Russia and [in] Provence.

204

With language, man seeks to outwit the superiority of the environment. To do so, he allies himself with his peers. Aspect of the 'human earth': man against the world. Language is cunning, weapon, power. Grammar. Fluent speech is prose, everyday life. The 'words' are partly prose, primal sounds. With language begins the arrogance against the animals.

Speech melody has played and [still has] an enormous role. In the developed use of writing expressed by punctuation: ? ! — are melody signs. Differences: sentence melody as a racial expression: singing (Thuringia), French; melodic sense use: question, answer.

---

79 Elam was an ancient empire in what is now southwestern Iran. — *Transl.*

205

Speaking among c-people is done with the whole body: face, arm, leg. When a Negro tells a story, he performs it at the same time, as does an old peasant woman who tells fairy tales to children. The grammatical sentences are short. The syntactic element is provided by (involuntary) gestures. Also in palaver, still today in southern parliaments and popular assemblies, street rallies. Only the 'educated' speak purely linguistically, without gestures. The 'chant' (tone of voice) is still a primitive remnant.

206

It is wrong to distinguish between poetry and prose, and possibly to make out the first as the older form. The first is a stammered speech without actual sentence structure, short, clarified by gestures. This is how the farmer still speaks to his farmhand today. But the linguists, who discuss, read and write all day long, consider their well-developed linguistic level — which the peasant would not understand at all — to be 'the' language. Cicero as a source for Latin syntax!

The first separation of two types of language lies in c: everyday and elevated prose, not 'poetry', but deliberate fine-tuning: salutation, cult speech, telling fairy tales and heroic deeds. Telling, reciting, solemnly speaking is different in essence from questioning, commanding, stating. It is only much later that the 'primeval song' — melody without words, la-la-la — is enriched by a 'text': the rhythmic art of speech develops, first hymnal, marching song, dance song, then 'song in itself'.

207

Every designation of things, qualities, activities arises in the opposition of the impression to another. Polarity of pairs of terms. The first term is always the expression of a hostile, unpleasant impression. Ugly comes earlier than beautiful, bad earlier than good. Language born of fear first establishes what is frightening. Language in b is speaking without language, like drawing without signs. Only in the transition to c do the fixed sound groups emerge as expressions of fixed learnable meaning. Language is an expression for an impression.

208

Primeval language: The 'sign' is never rigid. We believe it only because the written image seems to be. But one speaks even the simplest words differently again and again. What remains the same is, so to speak, the musical theme of the word, but every truly pronounced word is a variation on the theme (Sievers[80]!). Today, where the written word accompanies us and holds us, the variability is small; at the beginning — as today in dialect — it is infinitely large, so that the word is only recognised in the narrowest circle. That is why linguistic research must start from the dialect and not from the written word.

The oldest words were 'sung', purely musical, like laughing and crying. The consonantal side took a back seat to the vocal side. Even today, the deep meaning lies not in the 'word' but in the instantaneous use of the word in the tone (questioning, complaining, confirming, Sievers). The oldest written languages, therefore, really only emphasise consonantal fixation: vocalisation had to be learnt in use. It was not a fixed part of the word — as it still is today!

ART

209

Building *technique* and building *art* are two different things. The one can, as an instinctive expression of a spiritual urge, lead to enormous achievements, as the great stone buildings in the West testify,

---

80   Eduard Sievers (1850–1932) was a linguist with a focus on Germanic languages. With statistical methods and experimentation, he formulated laws for the melodic and rhythmic elements of language. He gained international attention for his exploration of melody in spoken language. Supported by experiments with test subjects, he put forward the thesis that authors consciously or unconsciously insert a melody into literary texts, which is reproduced by most readers. — *Transl.*

the other is conscious and deliberate artistic design. This only exists in high cultures — and as an imitation of them. Egypt had 'architecture', Crete did not. The tomb of Atreus[81] was built by Egyptian-trained stonemasons — like St Basil's Cathedral in Moscow by Florentines, the cathedral in Aachen by Byzantines.

210

Ornament Imitation
South (traces to Siam) (Ireland — Crete)
'abstract', symbolic 'concrete', realistic
significant.being.

All d-culture since 1500 [shows] the inner struggle between this fate of expression (Strzygowski, Renaissance, Chinese painting, animal ornamentation, prohibition of images). Imitation in surface formation, sculpture, construction (body of construction). Ornament in music, animal ornament, solution of the building in rooms, land-scape, etc. Addition, mechanical summation of individual motifs. Organisation, significant, the whole [seen] as a unity. Both possible in ornament as in imitation.

Organisation in ornament: Nordic (Scheltema), cathedral, sym-phony, Rembrandt. Addition in ornament: arabesque, mosque court-yard. Organisation in imitation: Raphael. Addition [in imitation]: Egyptian relief.

211

Art History: What is 'beautiful'? Ugly, hated, *haïssable*[82]? Beautiful — the *beloved*, [the] charming, alluring. A primal feel-ing. Creative impulse in eye and hand. To make something whose execution pleases. Today we always start from the feeling of idle

---

81 In Greek mythology, Atreus is a king of Mycenae, the son of Pelops and Hippodameia, and the father of Agamemnon and Menelaos. — *Transl.*

82 French: 'hateful'. — *Transl.*

contemplation. Even the 'artist' who wants to entice the viewer. Who himself contemplates his work in his mind, his 'idea'.

Originally, however, it is the voluptuousness of painting, chiseling, kneading. 'Beautiful' — like the lust of eating, drinking, loving, killing, winning. The lust in the wielding of brush, chisel, thread derives from that in the wielding of dagger, bow, lance. Above all the dagger! A good thrust! That is fine art. The performer is different — dance, mimicry. Voluptuousness of movement, rhythm, or the desire to mimic, transforming the I into the you, mask, cutting faces, caricature. This merges with painting and kneading into pictorial imitation. Singing is different again, discharge. Not hearing, but singing itself is the beginning. Wordless. The formation of melody (cheer). Again different the idea of the musical instrument. Bringing forth pleasant sounds. Bowstring, conch, tube. Not melody (cheer), but sound (always the same). There is no art of the eye, but art *for* the eye. But art of the hand, of the voice, of the body. From [the] art of the hand — painting, drawing — comes the art of writing, of writing down. Art of the word. Singing melody in words, painting a scene in sentences (cock-and-bull story), riddles.

212

Art is instinct, 'genius', creative play, nothing spiritual, A turn occurs in c: language, the spirit, the thinking of cause, effect, end, means the 'naive', instinctive art leaves in existence, but develops beyond it a 'conscious art', the end, [the] means, [the] process: from the art of the totem arises that of the taboo: the religious, ritualistic one of buildings, symbols, not of the significant, but of the manifold significant image.

The symbolism of religion, of ruling [and] of war. This art becomes [a] theology, [a] priestly art. Noble art lags behind it.

213

Poetry or classification of the language of words in art: Poetry is not the oldest [art]. Singing did not need words for a long time (la-la-la), the sounds were sufficient. The fact that one felt the need to use *sentences* when singing presupposes a high degree of habituation to speech. Likewise, scenes are by their nature only mimic, imitating. In both, the first sentences creep in surreptitiously, as it were. When singing, for example, a few real or half-words flow in, between la-la a group of words is involuntarily sung along senselessly (even today! If a boy sings la-la while a girl asks him something, he continues to sing 'I don't know' in the same melody).

The first type of poetry is *narration*. E.g. boastful adventures (showing off, cock-and-bull stories). These old primeval narratives have something monstrous about them. Therein lies their charm. The dreams often reflect the nature of the events, illogical, the charm of the wildly impossible. Pleasure when the other believes it: successes in war and hunting. Animal fables: symbolic content, the mysterious in the animal soul that one witnesses. Then the deepening of the memory of certainty is fruitful. One tells again and again what once was, at that time. Here, too, facts are transformed into the fantastical (legends, myths, fairy tales). Ancestral legend, haunting.

The first 'art in words' arises from the logical charm of invention, which here for the first time has a conscious effect, either boasting (vanity) or lying (to fool the other) or fable (joy in fantasising). In contrast, the charm of the metric is attached to the wordless song, to the mimic dance scene. The first 'singsong' is also merely recitative narration in a singing voice.

214

Art, poetry: Language (technique to several) is finished when the need for expression takes hold of it, like paint, stone, carving. A simply given material, but the deepest, because it is alive. Speech — not language.

215

Art History: Art has meaning only in the lives of people who have become distorted, ill, morbidly *tense*; only since the everyday practical way of thinking — the sober peasant — has been corrupted by literature (book, newspaper, theatre, novel, schoolbook). Since then 'art' — i.e. perceived as art — has been a need. In Egypt there was neither art nor artists, but crafts, religion. Only we perceived this as 'art'. I.e. we enjoy these things regardless of the purpose. A very artificial way of thinking! For the peasants there is no 'art'. Everything is self-evident, as there is only thinking. No 'artistic' reflection. The 'essence' of art.

216

The root of art: Surrendering to the rhythmic need of the body — swaying like a bird in the air, a fish in the waves, enjoying the primeval rhythm of everything, for oneself, without intention, without others — song and dance belong to this, for the exultation of the voice is overflowing rhythm, just like laughter and weeping. Only from this come imitative movements, mimicry, acting, 'playing someone'. This, however, is already art in the chorus, a sense of we in rhythm.

It is only much later that the art of pictures and sculptures is imitated in line and colour. This 'picture' should have a similar effect on the eye, 'represent', reproduce, so that it remains. Music [and] dance are only momentary and can only be repeated. But this takes time. Great in the younger Stone Age and in Egypt; otherwise, in the North, more ornamental. Great, furthermore, in antiquity, China, India, where the counter-soul is pictorial and is ornamentally regulated by the upper soul, e.g. in that Gandhara art immediately becomes rigid typicity as in Byzantium [and] Russia, thus again ornament. The deeper meaning of the after-image is: to want to hold on to, to perpetuate.

217

Epic and tragic: With a comparison that is more than such, because it reaches into the depths of formal affinity, one can call the human existence of the ab-cultures lyrical, insofar as lyric is song, word nonsense from floating feeling without causal word goals. Real lyricism, real, unprinted folk songs are like leaves in the wind, floating, without end, without fixed words. It is the sounds, not the content of sentences. Epic and tragedy are spoken, not sung, are logical sequences of sentences as means, organic described sequences as 'ends'. Lyric poetry does not describe: it is ornament as phonetic structure, not imitation through descriptive sentences.

And this is how epic and tragic culture, history, people differ: in the former the plane of facts is understood and organised, in the latter the 'ultimate reasons'. A leader of 4000 sees the goal from the facts at hand, a leader of high culture from the essence of times and spaces — whether he feels it like Sargon[83] or proves it like Napoleon.

218

The 'Artist': In the beginning, artistic expressive language is universally present, in the We. One understands each other, dancing, singing, miming, painting, without words. Personal art of the individual begins with rigid forming, painting, modelling. Each one does this alone, not in chorus. And even more so the writing of poetry. So in the rock drawings even a 'self' is a prerequisite. From then on, as the level of personality grows, the artistic language of expression withers away, as does the warlike, to become condensed into types.

219

Psychology of jewellery. Originally body painting. Scar marking, tattooing, shaving, tooth and skull deformation. Ear, lip, nose

---

83   About 4,500 years ago, Sargon, the king of Akkad, conquered the Sumerian city-states and founded the Akkadian Empire, which was possibly the world's first empire. — *Transl.*

jewellery, hangings, hairstyle. Jewellery [is] in inverse proportion to clothing. Jewellery [is] considered an expression of the sex drive: attraction, [appearing] beautiful. As an expression of rank, status, profession: originally absolutely impersonal, general. We-symbol of differentiated life. Look and foreboding. So, for example, symbolism of the warrior, mature youth, girl. Mother, old man, hunter ... It is the oldest symbolism of all, the oldest ornament.

220

Maximum artificial expression in the Palaeolithic, its 'decline' in the Neolithic. In between lies the emergence of the language of words, and the rigid image is now replaced by the animal fable. The power of imagination to the point of vision and hallucination must have been tremendous. What is this? There are people who act only under the impression of immediate perceptions, and others who always act under the impression of their imagination, realistic and fantastic natures. Passionate, dreamy, crazy. Having ideas, thoughts, living in imaginations.

221

Is the oldest jewellery an expression of the feeling for 'beauty'? Or is costume (painting, jewellery, clothing) dull, ornamental expression? Did the ornament (inkling of number symbolism in pictorial group-ing) originate long before counting, first on the body, then on the utensil? Since when has there been ('female') vanity on ornament?

222

Music (*Reallexikon*): Pipes made of bone and clay drums of the Stone Age certainly not for music, but signal, noise, ghost noise. Lurs[84] [are] not ancient. [The] lyre [is] Nordic, [came] to Hellas with

---

84 A lur is a long blowing horn. It dates to the Bronze Age and was made of bronze. Lurs were also called 'war trumpets'. — *Transl.*

the Dorian migration. Kithara[85] ancient-oriental, already [in] the 3rd millennium.

223

What we call art certainly does not consciously exist for early humans. 'The artist', 'the style', 'the beauty', 'the work of art' above all are literary inventions of great cities. *L'art pour l'art*[86] means art for the art trade. Only since works of art have been traded without regard to their practical purpose has there been 'pure art'. The healthy person is happy about a beautiful house, dress, piece of weaponry that he has in use. This is created by craftsmanship, which has nothing to do with 'arts and crafts' — i.e. the activity of people who want to be artists without creative power and therefore stick 'style' on all objects.

There is in c-cultures 'the building' of tombs, houses, temples, the chiseling and painting for ritual purposes, the singing and dancing, but 'the painting', 'the dance' does not exist. 'The court poet', 'the cathedral sculptor' is older and more genuine than 'the poet' and 'the sculptor'. The art exhibition is the end of art.

224

Imitative creation — telling, forming: Original fairy tales[87] (*Märe* = narrative), plus tales of gods ('myth', legend) and famous people (heroic saga): the essential thing is the psychological topicality of what is told. There are relatively few basic motifs, all of which erupt in primeval soul conflicts, experiences, and which are told in the same way by gods, heroes, people. This does not need to be borrowed, but has been

---

85 The kithara was an ancient Greek string instrument. The word 'guitar' comes from kithara. — *Transl.*

86 French: 'art for art's sake'. — *Transl.*

87 In German: *Märchen* — *Transl.*

created a thousand times over and over again: Potiphar[88], Nabob[89], Sleeping Beauty, Romeo and Juliet. This type of narration sticks to the process. The names are missing or invented or transferred to them.

The other type is the memory of what has actually happened: here the name of the place and person is the centre. The narrative slowly changes from the i[mitative] to the topical, symbolic. The names can also change or disappear at the end, then the state of the fairy tale is reached.

ARABLE FARMING AND LIVESTOCK BREEDING

225

The fact of progressive desiccation in relation to the dwindling ice exists in any case. It is superficial to say that 'man' has brought about the desert with a declining will to culture. Everywhere, on the soil of dying and dead cultures, ruins of great cities have remained — but in Yucatan, the Ganges region, Dahome, Java the primeval forest has taken possession, in Mesopotamia, Spain, Sicily, Asia Minor the desert. Culture, as long as it has lived, has constantly fought against these dangers, by continued clearing or by artificial irrigation.

226

Desert: The usual historiography tends to presuppose either the present-day picture of the landscape or what the oldest known documents reveal. But it must be taken into account that the landscape also has its history, not only the fauna and flora, but also the relationship of water to earth (climate). Today, the ruins of ancient cities in Spain,

---

88 From the Bible (King James Version), Genesis 39:1: 'And Joseph was brought down to Egypt; and Potiphar, an officer of Pharaoh, captain of the guard, an Egyptian, bought him of the hands of the Ishmeelites, which had brought him down thither.' — *Transl.*

89 A nabob was a provincial governor in the Mogul Empire in India. — *Transl.*

Africa, Asia Minor and Syria lie in areas whose desert character is usually described as steppe. That is why the average historian helps himself with the opinion that the landscape is 'deserted', that it has 'disappeared' with the cultural population. But this avoids the question of why the peoples died out, and the other, at least as important, question of why the land, after depopulation, was not taken over by the primeval forest but by the desert. There are two ways of 'cultivating' the soil, by draining or irrigating, by destroying the forest or by canals.

227

World consciousness and climate (soul of the *landscape*). World consciousness arises from the opposition of the self-soul to the soul of the landscape — I and world — nature inside and outside. In the south, the soul is absorbed in the hot landscape, more sensually shaping. In the north it struggles against the environment, more mentally determining. Powers, will, forces in nature. Will — fate. Will of the world.

Life as struggle. Struggle in nature. Ornamental landscape painting, music. In the south the body, the seen being. Body of the gods, sculptural group painting, relief.

North: disembodying, feeling. South: disembodied, seeing. North: heaven, earth, tien, sehê. Begetting spring. God as 'power'. South: father god, mother goddess. Procreating god, as person.

228

Livestock: Free-grazing herds that are driven on or followed. Buffalo of North America. Horses of Turan. Erection of cattle houses (dwellings) like human houses. Stables. Slave stables. There wild races become domestic races, cultural races — as with man himself. Human races [were] remade by change of food, kind of movement (farmers, nomads, horsemen, sailors), clothing (change of skin-breathing), living in houses.

229

The horse [is] felt to be a spawn of the steppe, 'divine', long before it was made a slave. As the eagle is the birth of the high mountains, the dolphin of the sea. Cf. lion, snake. Typical landscape animals symbolically experienced. The logical consideration of whether the animal is 'a god' or 'sacred to the god' [comes] much later. Originally pure feeling: the wild horses belong to the steppe.

230

Plant cultivation [is] something different from ploughing (grain). Plant breeding, animal breeding, human breeding. Field and plough belong together. Livestock farming. Wild herds as property (cowboys, peons), free grazing (gauchos). The tribe [is considered] the beneficiary of this herd of the countryside. Desertification: from plant breeding to herding in migration. Plant and animal breeding: plants [are] no longer collected, but grown, sown, grafted. In animals, ownership of wild herds, following them. Hunting. Ownership of wild plants, gathering them. Animal husbandry: Captive herds, 1) free grazing, 2) stable, hurdle, yard, 'domestic animal'. Cultivated land — livestock land.

231

Sedentary man, the domestic animal, the farmer raises domestic animals: cattle, donkey, sheep, goat. The wandering man, the swift animal, the horse. He understands the psychology of the horse, uses it. This is not necessary with cattle or camels. The quick, shy, irritable soul, which the horse expert must understand if he wants to steer. Type of rein (against cattle). The soul of the bovine is indifferent. It trots along. Here the soul remains free; it becomes subservient to the will of the man. Mental direction. The dog is only 'companion'. Man and horse, however, form a unity of will. The horse is stupid like all herbivores, but energetic, irritable. Madness: the horse's noble race. Horse 'race' means something different from sheep and human 'race'.

232

Nonsense, to begin an epoch with the 'horse'. 'Acquaintance' with the horse. To be distinguished: hunting and eating the wild horse, keeping herds of horses, wide plains. Milk. Horse, half-ass, etc. as pack animal (Mycenae), ass [and] mule [as] draught animal; mount. The cart [was] originally [a] team of oxen, Central Asia. Cart — chariot. Riding [was] the dominant mode of movement in northern Asia. In Western Europe (Celts, Teutons) only custom of the nobility, not for travel, but processions, scouting parties. Special weapons.

233

Landscape: Around 2000 the steppe must have been very advanced between the Danube and Lake Baikal, while Central and Northern Europe still had primeval forest with clearings. Meadows, thus more cattle and horse breeding. The steppe more sheep breeding above all. Steppe cattle. The chariot tribes, very mobile, come from the steppes; the Dorians were woodland loggers, sedentary. The real 'farmer' is sedentary, he cleared the land forever for his clan, possession as land. The steppe tribe migrates, even to the sea. His possessions are mobile, cattle, treasures, booty. The plough comes from peasant culture.

Transition from chariots to horseback riding. Strategically important: mobility as a weapon against standing and marching. Since when? Chariots as weapons since about 1800? Chariots were known longer, ceremonial procession, chariot of the gods. China — India — Eastern Mediterranean. Rider — not occasionally sitting on the horse, but consciously shaping it as a weapon: new breeds of horses.

234

Arable farming (cf. *Reallexikon I*!) [has] arisen from the most highly developed cult, first barley, then wheat. The plough [is] thought to be male, the earth female — hence the plough-animal the ox, castrated (priest-castration [arose] at that time!). Even older is the sacred chariot: the rolling wheel representing a star. The sacred ploughing acts are tied to the primordial calendar, which also originated here. This is 'Kash'. Even older, pre-cultic, is the hoe, a mere tool, while the primeval plough represents the phallus. The chariot belongs together with the idea of the draught animal: idea of the serving being.

To the hoe belong bean (in general pulses) and millet, fruit, vegetables. So (according to Hahn[90]) hoe-farming [is] horticulture. The garden is older than the cultic field (farmland, elongated, rectangular, templelike, quadruple and fourfold). The cult took the wild cattle and forced them to plough the wild barley. Only this gives rise to the seed and breeds, also cultic, in sacred captivity for 'service'.

The 'calendar' with fixed sowing and harvesting festivals (whereby the seed is there for the sake of the festival, not the other way around, the sacred moment of witnessing and bearing) with 360 days with dates that are the same everywhere (Easter, Pentecost), but only fit the climate of the Near East. Here [arises] at the same time the cultic artificial irrigation! This is simultaneous with metal casting (output of Neolithic copper) on the fire altar, more idea of the domestic animal (cattle, sheep, goat). With agriculture [is] first the crowding of people possible. The cultic metal casting [is] so rare that its absence proves nothing (the wooden plough is the rule!). And yet most people continue to live mainly from hunting and fishing. While in the pastoral regions agriculture is practised at least for a few months in random places (sowing, harvesting — two and a half months).

235

Dairy farming: Captive animals do not give milk. The breeding of permanent milk-producing animals is something late and refined, later than agriculture. In Babylon, milk production (cow, goat, sheep) plays a major role.

---

90 Eduard Hahn (1856–1928) was a German agrarian ethnologist, economic historian and geographer. He wrote the book *Die Haustiere und ihre Beziehungen zur Wirtschaft des Menschen* ('Domestic animals and their relationships to the human economy') (1896). — *Transl.*

236

Beginning of 'dairy farming': What is depicted in Ur is the milk sacrifice apparently to a goddess who protects birth and fertility. The milk is extracted from the cow in a strict rite. Only from this did milk drinking and rational milk production develop.

237

Cultivation and livestock breeding: Carefully build up: to this artificial relationship to nature, which follows from causal thinking as a partition between man and earth, also belongs the incalculable circle of phenomena which are summarised superficially enough as 'agriculture and stockbreeding', as if they were two 'technical advances, achievements' (note: this was then immediately trivialised to 'peasantry' and 'stockbreeding peoples'). On the one hand, it is something whole together with many others: one either thinks of all things in this way, artificially, or of none. On the other hand, agriculture and animal husbandry comprise an infinite number of methods, none of which occurs a second time.

There is also an enormous difference between the idea of a method, which always has the character of a symbolic, 'sacred' action, and an everyday economic practice that has arisen from it, in which again 'utility' can play a minor or decisive role. For example, herd ownership can be a mere sign of noble rank and very costly.

It is certain that signs of planned sowing and animal husbandry appear everywhere at the same time as building, pottery and many other things around 5000. But this does not mean an 'invention', but precisely a new way of thinking of man about himself and the world. Infinite procedures develop from this thinking. It is mentally impossible, for example, to separate the idea of sacrifice before the deities, of harvesting, of keeping slaves, subjects, from that of cattle. The idea is not 'use' but subordination, organisation of something living in the service of a higher life (king, state). The individual procedure, however, already belongs in its style to the formal language of an individual culture. It is something quite different in the soul whether one keeps animals captive or lets them graze, whether one performs the act of ploughing or digging the soil. Later, a selection of methods takes place. Originally, however, they are sanctified and separated by great symbols.

238

Livestock: The word is so misleading that it would be best erased. It is

1. the habituation of animals to the farm, which one does not exploit: rat

2. which are used as guards: dog

3. the taming of animals that carry loads: donkey

4. to accustom animals to be sheared: llama, sheep.

There is meat enough: not for this reason cattle have been tamed. Furthermore: herding has only arisen in stretches of land where cattle graze in the open year in, year out. The *paradeisos*[91]: game park. Like today: deer and sows.

This is an expression of the sense of rank and not the formation of a utilitarian economy! One remains far from the fact that every 'peasant' keeps cattle: the simple countryman donkey, goat, sheep. The great lords and the temples a herd of cattle. That is two things, and only one is 'economy'. But even this is not animal husbandry; even where meat, milk, wool are harvested, the life and reproduction of animals can be free, of course: in enclosures and territories. What all it takes before stables are built, animals fed and mated! As long as they look for their own food and reproduce, one cannot speak of cattle breeding. Cattle in a clearing surrounded by woods are caged and yet free. The herd 'stands' in a district like a human folk with self-searched watering and feeding places and resting places like the animals. The whole difference is that it belongs to someone.

---

91 *Paradeisos* is the Greek word for a royal garden in Persia. — *Transl.*

The transfer of the concept of property, nothing else, turns 'game' into 'husbandry', for the herd, it may be as free as it likes, may no longer be treated as free, thinned out, shot: it is 'spared': thus begins husbandry, with the feeling of rank: the herd is under my protection! With this, the territory becomes a 'protection park': but with this, the animal also feels safe. It knows its people and tolerates approaches: shearing, milking.

239

In the Rigveda and [in] Homer, much meat is eaten, but the slaughter of the animal is always a sacred act, a portion being due to the gods. This is proof that the breeding of cattle is of sacred origin and that the eating of beef was originally a sacrificial meal: the domestic animal was thus bred for sacred reasons. Milk and butter [are] very important to the Aryans. The original, non-sacred meat consumption [is] therefore fish, shellfish, game. Killing and 'slaughtering'. Slaughter is a sacrificial act.

240

Economy: *Domestic animal*: According to Hahn, the reindeer was bred by analogy by a people who, advancing to the north, lost the cattle and saw only reindeer around them. So where did the taming begin? Then the questions: What is the idea of domestication here, or the keeping of a particular animal? This can also refer to human slaves. Then: For what reason? Power [is considered] property? Or the performance of work? (Dog, cattle, horse.) Finally: What was understood by it: herd keeping (today deer, roe deer, at that time horse, cattle), stable keeping (pig), i.e. pasture or stable? And: With which animal species did this begin?

Sheep and goats [lived] wild between the Carpathians and Afghanistan. Donkeys from Egypt to Somaliland. Horses in Europe and northern Asia. In the Egyptian Old Kingdom antelopes, gazelles, cranes, etc. (Hilzheimer[92] 17) were kept as domestic animals, mostly abandoned again before the end of the Middle Kingdom. The cat remains.

According to Hahn (Hilzheimer 19) [domestication is] not to be explained by 'utility', since milk, wool, eggs only become productive in domestication, not before. Rather, because of religion (sacrificial meat): cattle, sheep, goats, pigs. Ego: grazing herds [in] Atlantis, stable cattle [in] Kash, dog tamed by hunter peoples.

It is added: man must become a breeder of animals. So the Kashites become breeders of herbivorous stable animals, the Atlanteans become shepherds. The idea of shepherding is Atlantean: so they adopt sheep and goats from Kash. The idea of stable life [is] Kashite: they accept all kinds of animals: it corresponds to the idea of the subjugated style and the domestic slave. The method was then adopted by others (North), transferred to other animals (fur animals, luxury animals, etc.).

In Atlantis it is the 'masters' (nobility), in Kash the priests who breed (slaves), without economic goals.

241

Fruit (*Reallexikon*): That is, arboriculture that is practised in the long term, i.e. demands full sedentariness. Date, fig, pear, apple, cherries, plums. Olive tree, vine. Many things (blueberries) today, others (raspberries) recently collected, not cultivated. So once everything. This [is] all proof that the South was the creator of cultivation. The North itself had to introduce the varieties first — this then together with the technique of cultivation. Refinement through grafting, on the other hand, is Nordic-artificial. The process of making fruit edible by fermentation, drying ('dried fruit'), in order to preserve and deacidify it, is very old. Intoxicating effect to boot!

---

92 Max Hilzheimer (1877–1946) was a German zoologist who wrote several books about domestic animals. — *Transl.*

TECHNOLOGY AND TRANSPORT, WEAPONS

242

[The] stone castle [is] firmly rooted — booty place of the island robbers, location. Likewise the stone tomb. Northern Eurasian fortresses are in idea ramparts, temporary *castra*[93], for mobile tribes who change their homes easily. Mycenae. Chinese 'palaces' [were] developed *from* the landscape, not *against* it. Gates and walls.

The isolated private house, dwellings as 'I', movable (tent, yurt, wattle). The essence is that each *pater familias*[94] has his own home. Caravan. Land gypsies and sea gypsies — the former has a movable, the latter a fixed location.

243

Stone building: It has been said that the mud-brick building in Babylon and the stone building in Egypt were due to the material available. This is a platitude of the 19th century, which wanted to explain the style of great art from the material. In reality, the Nile delta possesses as little stone as Sinear[95], and the regions of Elam [possess] as much as Upper Egypt. It is the different attitude to life and the difference in world-view that make the one material stand out.

244

Megaron: The importance of the house ground plans has been overestimated beyond measure. It was precisely what the excavator very often found and what suited his systematic inclinations, like the shape of the pots. Then, quite mathematically, a distinction was made between round and square and the square was soon called

---

93 Latin: 'camp'. — *Transl.*

94 Latin: 'head (father) of the family'. — *Transl.*

95 Sinear (or Shinar) is mentioned several times in the Bible. It is the location where the Tower of Babel is built. It most likely refers to Babylon. — *Transl.*

megaron, soon Lower Saxon farmhouse, whereby further reflection could be spared, since these two homely expressions sounded deep enough. But square buildings have been built everywhere and always. The Egyptian buildings of the early 3rd millennium already show an emphasis on the rectangular that could not be surpassed. The western Italian house (Etruria, atrium) likewise. China, Babylon.

Only the building technique! In the north — from the North Sea to Japan — we know log houses, half-timbered houses, wattle and daub houses — sunk into the ground, raised (pole), round (woven hut) = tent. And: the halls of Mycenae etc. are not living rooms but assembly rooms. Likewise the halls of northern European mansions. In the farmhouse, however, living and economic rooms are more important. Large farmhouses [are] related everywhere in the world, a living room, an anteroom (everywhere) and other [rooms] all around.

245

[A] superior weapon is immediately spread out. Sword, bow, chariot. If one did not want to or could not [use] [the weapons] oneself, one hired the subjugated: Balearic slingers, Cretan-Carian archers, chariots, cavalry (Celts, Teutons), Shardana, Hyksos, Habiri.

246

There were no 'houses' at all in the south. People lived and worked outdoors. Caves, huts, roofs were sufficient. The ideal form was the courtyard surrounded by covered halls, cells and corridors. The actual 'house', the private dwelling of the family, is only Nordic. In Gurnia, part of Amarna, Karun [there were] only narrow sleeping cells, no 'house'.

247

Building [is] only an activity, animalistic (bees, beavers). The symbolically meaningful building — the actual architecture, building art, building as a means of elementary expression of world feeling [exists] since c. Grave — temple — house: dead man — god — man.

Instinctive ('ingenious') like all real art, style. Mere dwelling (house, castle) [is] without symbolism of this kind, unmetaphysical. Only these three higher districts of metaphysical building: grave — stone 'eternal', beyond; temple — brick: 'high', stars; house — i.e. hall, private, closed against the world, I, door, hearth, seat, sleep. Outside — world of struggle. Inside: I, property. Possessive pronouns: mine, yours, his. The I and the My. Property [is] everywhere, also in animals. Nest, place, food, water, young. Here, however, metaphysically emphasised. Part of the I.

248

Objects of custom are the best markers of lost historical events: not pottery and language, but custom of fighting (type of weapons), burial, personal names.

Neither pottery nor language tell us anything about the spread of the Germanic tribes in the Migration Period: but the personal names in Spain, Italy, France do. Likewise, the history of the Christian Church is reflected in persons (Old Testament, non-Christian names, etc.).

249

Arms: The aristocratic time in Hellas despised the bow; that was a common weapon (Wilamowitz, *Ulysses* 166). This is the spirit of the geometrical time, Dorian (Dorians, spearmen). Before that, the older legends had valued the bow (Odysseus, Heracles, Philoctetes[96]). Apollo had the bow. Hera, Heracles 'Argivian[97]'. The Argeians (Argos = plain) [originally determine] [the] name of a wide area; later only transferred to the city. Heros and Hera [are] thus numina

---

96 *Philoctetes* is a play by Sophocles: on the way to Troy, the Greeks abandon Philoctetes on the desert island of Lemnos because of his incurable wound, which smells horribly. Years later, a seer foretells them that only with Philoctetes and his bow on their side can they conquer Troy. So, under Odysseus' leadership, a group sets out to get Philoctetes back. — *Transl.*

97 Adjective: related to the ancient city of Argos. — *Transl.*

of a widespread tribal group. The bow-bearing Heracles [is] thus pre-Norse, Sea Peoples period.

250

Hunting and war [are] identical. Weapons of hunting and war. Hunting ideals: in the north the brave fight with the animal. To wait for the game, with spear and knife, at one's own peril. Thus the ideal of the lords of Mycenae, Sparta, the Teutons. Hamites: killing without danger. Cunning, ambush. Pharaoh hunting ([different the] Assyrians). What kind of animals? Bullfighting Hamitic: Crete, watching the boys and girls succumb. The divine bull kills them, Minotaur. Cultic. In Spain ancient: Italy, in Roman circus prisoners with animals. Fighting game at the grave: Samnites, Etruscans, gladiators, since 300 B.C. mob fun as today. Until then, feast of sacrifice. In hunting: Hamites — attraction of killing; North — attraction of danger. Hamites: hunting traps, hiding, poisoning. North: hunting spear, knife.

251

Bow: The archer Apollo (southwest Asia Minor) [is] originally perhaps the god of death. Ἑκη —Ἑκατηβολος = Hecate. Likewise [wields] Artemis [the] bow. Both [are] fertility and death gods (Ephesian Artemis, plague sender). Ancient, pre-Greek Artemis cults in the Peloponnese. [Are] both Libyan? (Proto-Chattic?). Northerners made Artemis the huntress, Valkyrie, ποτνια θηρων, [the] demoness of the great forests.

Bow of Philoctetes: the ancient legend of Troy demands that the archer Paris be killed by an arrow. 'Philoctetes' came in later. Teukros was Asian, Meriones Cretan, Odysseus' bow shot is pre-Greek: not in the *Iliad* [Odysseus uses the bow], only in the *Odyssey*! (only because of the legend of the suitors' fight). The Mycenaean warrior vase [also shows] arrowmen, i.e. 'Achaeans'. Philoctetes [is] the owner of the bow of Heracles. Heracles, with club and bow, Libyan (Nimrod, the hunting giant), [is a] famous figure, right into the Old Testament (Meyer

II, 1) the lion hunter. [There are] vase paintings where he appears as a hoplite, but the bow must stand or hang somewhere. He is a Libyan Achaean, therefore at home in Argolis. He kills the Nemean lion with a club. Perhaps even older [is] the strangling of the lion by the giant, whose non-Greek name was senselessly tied to Hera by folk etymology (Kalinka[98], *Klio*[99] 22, p. 250 ff.).

252

Weapons: Nordic — individualistic is the separation of weapon against animal and human. It is cowardly and ignoble to outwit man; one fights man against man. Therefore arrow only against animals. Against humans battle axe, sword, spear. That is ethos. In the South (still today), fighting has no ethos. One wants to remove the opponent without danger — poison, arrow, hired assassins.

253

Transport: 'Chariot and horse' [is] nonsense. [The] horse [was] hunted (eaten) first, otherwise [it was] useless. Loads [carried] first the pack animals (pack mules), on which one also sat sideways. Only [for] short distances, from the field to the village. Long-distance transport [was] really only possible by water! Raft, boat. Caravan: carrier slaves, beasts of burden. Then [came] the term 'road', smoothed path (like the rails are older than the locomotive!). Plus the load sledge, [i.e. the] loop, a board that is dragged, short distance (e.g. statues, stones). Wheeled cart: four wheels or two rollers placed under the loop, in a paved yard. Short distance, because this chariot could not bear heavy loads or long distances, and above all it required a pavement. Then [came] the chariot, the two-wheeled cart, only as a weapon in battle, on the march, on the other hand, baggage. The horse as a swift runner

---

98 Ernst Kalinka (1865–1946) was an Austrian epigraphist and classical philologist. — *Transl.*

99 *Klio: Beiträge zur Alten Geschichte* ('Contributions to Ancient History') is the oldest academic journal for ancient history and was first published in 1901. — *Transl.*

[came] only here instead of the donkey and ox. Riding came much later: gallop. Again speed as a means.

254

The fact that a man sits down on an ass, [an] ox, a horse, does not yet make a tribe of horsemen. It requires more. As in late Egypt and [in] Babylon the chariots, so in late ancient, Chinese, Indian culture riding is accepted as a new weapon.

255

Weapons: Psychology. It is wrong to speak of arrowheads everywhere. For the most part these are points of javelins. The thrusting lance is Nordic. The sword [was] invented in the South, raised to the position of the ruling weapon in the North.

256

Conquerors are not in the habit of shaping pots and carving inscriptions with their own hands — that is what the subjugated are for. Of course, they use the style they have learned. So we can seldom infer race from pictures, nor masters from ornaments. That is why the more resolute a conquering party is, the fewer traces it leaves behind in the 'cultural layers'. But in weapons, implements, political institutions, titles, names.

257

The oldest technical theoretical traits are 'pre-religious'. From a certain stage onwards everything is derived from the cult: seeding, breeding, metal casting, etc. Probably also fire?

258

Theory and technique: The actual 'invention' does not consist in inventing the tool, but in the spiritual discovery of the process. The concept of 'cutting with something hard and sharp' emerges and, apart from understanding, can modify the ongoing actions. The device comes into being slowly through imperceptible transition — one picks out the natural stone structure better, improves a little, as every animal, when it wants to eat the other, turns it back and forth in order to touch it properly — but the understanding of the act is suddenly there.

259

Clay vessels: Schuchhardt's explanation is far too one-sided, modern. Kneading mud for all kinds of purposes: mud huts, lumps of clay (later bricks!) packed on top of each other, clay pits in which water collects, with raised rim, outlet (vessels). The beginning is not the vessel, but the mental activity of wanting to form, which extends to several applications at once. Clay kneading. Figure kneading.

Hut — vessel with lid — spiritual connection. [It is a] fact that after rain water collects in every hollow. Building the vessel from clay beads = hut. Likewise basket sealed with clay = reed hut.

260

Trade: Caravans — we associate with them the concept of desert and camels. But security forced the trader at all times (Gothic) to travel in groups with armament, never individually. So fleets and trains of pack animals. This includes custom — expressing each other, carrying boxes, storing together. Above all, languages with technical expressions for trade, traffic, security, description of goods, exchange. Specific storage places, storehouses, workshops, repairs, from where the peddlers move to the villages.

261

The chief priests of the ceramic sect! They have at last forgotten that men use and make these vessels. They let the pots marry each other, have children, talk of families, pedigrees, migrations; it is as if they wanted to divide the population of Europe of 1900 according to matchboxes or [according to] sardine tins. But there were pottery villages next to the house fire with good clay deposits. The distribution can prove migration of a tribe, conquest, change of taste, trade, competition. The vessels may have arrived there as packaging. They may have been part of the essential ornamentation of life or completely indifferent. Imitated or spread along the trade coasts by use of the traders — like tins. The colour may be intentional or accidental, the result of admixture or firing. Since clay is not found in every village, the pottery must be exchanged where it can be obtained best and most conveniently.

262

The potter's wheel (*Reallexikon* XIV, Vase) is first used for the production of cheap mass-produced goods. So only where gourds etc. were not to be had. This is a professional craft, not an 'art'. Pots [were] only available where other vessels were not cheaper. Besides wood, gourd, tube, basket.

263

Ceramics: To be distinguished [are] ornamentation and form. Then purpose: drinking, cooking, eating — or packaging ('export'). Then village wares and finds in trade centres where everything comes together. Coincidence of sites.

'Spread' across a country — from village to village or along the roads? Luxury and common goods. In Egypt, [in] the Old and New Kingdoms initially only the latter. The luxury ware is faience. The ornament [is] quite independent of the history of form (purpose), ornamental form, utilitarian form. Mode of diffusion: mass, scattered, isolated — immigration, trade, chance.

264

Ceramics cannot be separated from brick construction. The hardening by fire or air-drying for bricks is certainly even the older one. So first buildings, then fixed, then movable vessels of 'clay'. A *Kash* invention! The very idea of forming like pieces ('bricks') from clay is great! It is the earliest example of mechanical like-thinking. From there the

Etruscan-Roman brick technique with stamps. Bricks are something artificially abstract.

265

[The] chariot [is] unknown in [Old] America: the wheel must have been invented at *some* point in the old world. The chariot, as long as there is no road, is impractical. The sedan chair, pack animal, and boat perform better.

Holy sky chariot. Originally it was not intended for practical use at all, but in cult the image of the gods rolled along its processional track: symbol of the sun. So on a smooth road. The wagon of the gods has become a truck. The oldest wagons appear with the plough culture, which is of priestly origin. [The] draught animal [is] sacred! So the elements: rolling wheel, sacred track and serving bull came together. So the oldest wheel [is] a wooden disc. Wheel symbols with spokes [live] in all ornaments.

266

Lances: Made of flint (laurel leaf) in the Solutrean. Independently, older, of bone or wood in the Aurignacian and Magdalenian. These [are] probably throwing spears, those thrusting spears. (Close combat, courage, person.) Throwing spears [are good for] ambush. Then in the Late Palaeolithic — Neolithic flint lances recede completely: as the paintings testify, [they are] displaced by arrow-like throwing spears! Then in the Nordic circle in the Late Neolithic a highly developed industry of lance points of the finest type made of flint, partly sharpened. They spread with the Nordic train: Aegean obsidian as material as far as the Danubian area (3rd millennium).

267

As in the young Neolithic, so [also] in the Bronze Age the North possesses the greater wealth of lance forms, at first as imitations of the flint blade point. From the Nordic circle it [penetrates] to Western Europe, above all Britain, under whose influence Northern France stands; Spain rare; lance point with a cut-out in the blade invented in Britain, from there [penetrated] as far as Switzerland, [to] Italy, Hungary, Albania, [into] the Ukraine. Other forms [are found in] Troy II, Cyprus, still others since the Early Bronze Age (2200–1700) in Eastern Europe, Siberia. In prehistoric Egypt (hunting pictures of the slate) long throwing spear. The throwing spear [is] ancient Semitic, common (Egyptian image). Judah and Gad have thrusting spears (1 Chronicles often), thus under Norse influence, Naphtali javelins. Ennadu throwing spear from chariot. Naramsin[100] arrow-like short spear. Thus: the spear developed from or beside the arrow [is] Atlantean. The manly thrusting spear of open melee is Nordic.

268

The bow and arrow [occur] only [in] Atlantis. From Sumer to Peru spearthrowers. This includes the found 'arrowheads' (a small throwing spear). The sword [is] Norse.

269

The wars: As Homer and the vase paintings show, the bow and arrow was quite familiar to early Hellenic man. It is all the more significant that this weapon gradually recedes more and more, although it is precisely the most dangerous opponents who by nature use it with preference. It is quite astonishing that the Spartan and Athenian hoplite[101], like the Roman legionary, wields the lance as his main weapon alongside the sword, and that the cavalry, like the archers, who, as countless heavy defeats show, were indispensable, were recruited from foreign peoples. What a symbolic instinct speaks from this fact!

---

100 Naramsin was the grandson of King Sargon of Akkad and the fourth ruler of the Akkadian Empire. He claimed divine status and called himself 'God of Akkad'. — *Transl.*

101 Hoplites were heavily armed soldiers in ancient Greek armies. — *Transl.*

270

Building: The psychology of building is as yet undiscovered. The mere construction of sleeping, rain and storage places is not yet building in the significant sense. Building as a process of expression is not directed towards mere living accommodation. In addition, the southern climate of the Atlantis and Kash cultures did not make this question seem important: an earth pit, a shelter, a tent suffice. One lives in the open. One only sleeps [under roof]. Shelter! 'Architecture' as a symbol is culture: graves and temples: ancestors and gods are banished to sacred places.

Only the heroic culture also thinks of itself, if only because of the climate. There, the rich private house is banished first as a style.

Tomb and temple are ornaments, symbols. Castles and huts are only 'decorated'.

271

Firing technique: The essential is the purposeful construction of the kiln: smelting kilns for ore, firing kilns for ceramics. Kiln: fan, draught, increase and termination of heat. Hearth and altar are something else.

It goes without saying that the firing of clay vessels of a finer kind was not practised in every house, but only in the larger ones ('workshop'), while smithing was an exclusive craft. The artificial moulding of pots in the Campignia is perhaps an inconsequential coincidence. The term 'export' for clay vessels is unclear. The precious vases of Hellenic workshops [were] probably [exported]. But otherwise clay vessels are packing material on ships (*køkkenmøddinger*[102]) and trucks and as such were widely carried away. Varieties: lesser for mere packing, better for cooking, drinking, stock.

---

102 A Danish term for a prehistoric garbage pile, consisting of food leftovers, such as shells. — *Transl.*

272

Importance of pottery, ornamentation, weaving: It is wrong to value 'pottery' simply as it happens where technique, form and ornamentation are brought together. One must not separate ceramics from house building, clothing, utensils, etc. Art form and technique are two different things: carving and painting the same. Vessels have very different purposes.

1. Clay firing (brick, vessel) is Kashitic. Gourd, wooden bowl, shell etc. are other materials. Wood carved, especially in the north.

2. Vessels: drinking vessel, storage vessel (water, food), funeral urn, further: to put to the mouth, to spoon out, to pour out, to suck out with pipes: waves of various shapes.

3. Racial form: vessel and house, sense of bulbous, slender, etc., shape. Cottage urn, pear, spherical, dome shape etc. Longitudinal and cross section: race feeling.

4. Sense of life also in use: handle, carrying on the head, hanging on loops, leaning against the wall, saucer, foot, 'architectonics' of form.

5. Decorative technique: finger dabbing, drawing lines with a pencil (scoring), painting on, leaving out. Infinitely important! None of this is peculiar to the clay jug! Weaving and braiding patterns, single-coloured — ornamental or multi-coloured — carpet-like (willow rod, rushes, wool, flax), on wooden buildings beam patterns. Then notch carving on the house, wooden utensils. Then painting (body, fabrics, walls, house and vessel).

6. Where did the clay vessel play a role at all? Not in Atlantis, where it remained common furniture and the need for expression was satisfied by stone construction and relief.

The sacred dignity of clay vessels [exists] actually only in Kash: solemnly painted. An actual clay art for which there were professional artists: summit in Hellas. Turan emphasises the ornaments, the cults originated, the enveloping clothing, the intimate living quarters, the household utensils.

273

Inventing: Until now, science has imagined all this far too simply: 'inventing metal casting', 'origin of megalithic construction', 'discovery of the sea route'. These are always very many inventions, of which individual ones can be made here and there again and again without having any effect; but they must all be there together, with a corresponding forethought and will, in order gradually to reshape outer life.

To the sea route belongs the invention of something that can float (the raft), the deliberate movement (rowing), the discovery of regular wind directions and ocean currents, the cutting of wood, sealing, the shipyard, the rope, the anchor, the concept of the landing place (harbour).

Metal casting includes smelting, slagging, casting, hammering, mining, searching for deposits, means of transport. It is quite possible that ore smelting was invented in Almeria, and pure metal casting in Sinear. Copper Almeria, bronze Kash — that instinct, that business.

'Building' includes hewing, transporting, erecting, finishing, designing (orally).

274

It is one of the many rationalistic follies to believe that 'man' made 'the metals' serviceable to himself. 'Man' did nothing at all, and 'the copper' is a modern term. In reality, some circles of the Kashite culture — priesthoods of some temples — saw that these beautiful, heavy, shiny red materials were created by sacrificing malachite, for example. From there it is a long way to profane production in forges, and even further to the spread of knowledge of the whole process to remote places of need and ore regions (Spain, Cyprus, Ireland). It is nonsense to speak of the Copper Age when a few axes are found somewhere: as rare goods or booty they eventually came everywhere, perhaps superstitiously revered, often not used at all but kept as treasure, curiosity.

If the chief of a tribe keeps three axes, the tribe is not living in the 'Copper Age'.

275

Technical invention: The new, language-related thing is not the technical invention itself — the invention of clay pots and arrowheads, for example — but the technical idea, namely that something artificial is possible. That is why 1. there is no isolated invention, but always the whole of life is thought through in the same style: pottery, agriculture, cattle breeding, carts, boat, city, sacrifice — out of the same thinking. Trade thought of as business, just as cattle breeding, boating, etc., are thought of as business. War. 2. Thinking of this kind on the same level in different places of the human earth (c), but the style of the works [is] very different. Here more plant breeding, there more trade.

276

Navigation: Ocean navigation developed everywhere at the mouths of rivers from inland navigation. There were no harbours. People entered the rivers. That is why all types of ships developed from river ships: Nile, Euphrates, Loire, Volga. And they first developed as coastal ships. The 'Atlantic' type is not a type of shipbuilding, but of seafaring itself. Only from the idea of seafaring do ship forms of construction and navigation develop everywhere.

278

Technology: 'Invention of the carriage' — wrong idea. The idea of driving — that is what matters. It includes not only the idea of 'rolling' (wheel), but also of pulling and above all of the road. For this reason alone, the invention must have been made for a small area — temple courtyard. For 'roads' did not yet exist. Rolling instead of dragging.

Similarly, 'shipping' is a whole complex of inventions: boat, oar, mooring. Today one thinks too shallowly only of the construction of the means of transport, but the deep thought is that of the movement of place (road, railway, mooring).

279

Trade: The oldest vehicle [is] the raft (rushes, logs, tubes). Younger [are] bark boats and dugout canoes. The seaworthy longboat [is the] pinnacle of built plank rib boats. Sailing is Polynesian: originally probably double dugout canoes with one mast. To carry on land (in baskets, panniers); the pack animal [exists] only in livestock cultures. Snowshoe, from which sledge. The chariot is Indo-European-Nordic (Egypt and Babylon do not know it, only underlaid rollers!). The sedan chair. The passenger carriage [is] a combination of sedan chair and truck.

280

'Traffic' and 'horizon of life': Wandering is instinctive moving forward, without knowledge of whence, whither, why. Animal migrations. Traffic is organisation of locomotion: knowledge of purpose, destination (destination is a place, a country, not an abstract purpose, thus not 'wealth' but 'Rome').

Traffic: railways and points, trade routes, customs of traffic, hospitality, market peace, customers, contract. Life horizon is not worldview of abstract kind, causal system, but knowledge of mountains, countries, people, climates etc. up to a certain distance. A knowledge with which one lives and which is the background of the experiences of the day: one's own tribe is no longer the world, but something in the world.

281

'Traffic': The visual circle of primitive man reaches as far as his legs: and he walks only as far as is necessary. Walking here means that the grandsons sit farther than the sons, and the latter farther than the fathers. But there comes a time when many or individuals wander through or beyond others: for them then 'the world' is a perpetual new thing. However, one does not get far with herds of cattle and fields. Wandering is something different from spreading out.

282

Trade: A distinction is to be made between the border trade of the touching tribes, through which objects and processes can scatter randomly, i.e. (ego) neighbour trade and the scattering of goods, and (ego) directed trade, which presupposes ship, beast of burden, wagon and was probably first the metal and stone trade: obsidian. So rare things, ivory, amber, nephrite. The trade route becomes a communication route; along it the trans-shipment centres as the pillars of trade language and technical vocabulary, which penetrates into neighbouring languages. The traders, an 'international guild' of their own nationality, with customs, cult, language, often race (Assyrians). These paths become routes for peoples, Roman roads, the Great Wall of China, monsoon roads, railway and steamship lines.

283

Navigation in the Mediterranean: Köster's book[103] could lead to a misconception that Egyptian navigation is the 'oldest' here. But it is only the oldest of which the Egyptian monuments speak, and in view of the nature of these inscriptions, drawings and reliefs, we can only expect to learn of such things as directly concerned Egyptian officials, of ships, therefore, only when they were Egyptian or met with Egyptians, for instance, in a naval battle.

But that navigation is infinitely older, although we have not the slightest idea of these ships, is proved by the fact that already in the Upper Palaeolithic cultural forms spread unhindered across the sea. Today, this evidence is so clearly arranged on distribution maps that it would even be possible — a subject for a post-doctoral thesis! — to determine the lines of communication, which are perhaps as eternal as the trade routes of the mainland: e.g. from Tunis to Aquileia, Crete, Sardinia, from Morocco to eastern Spain.

---

103 August Köster (1873–1935) was a German archaeologist and maritime historian. — *Transl.*

284

Economy: The decisive transformation in c-culture is that the results of sacred causality become profane; the causality of fear (high
forces, evil, benevolent) becomes the causality of utility: warding off
not demons but discomfort, banishing not spirits but forces from the
plough.

285

Ceramics:

a) Atlantic to Egyptian: Syria.

b) Kash: Susa, Anau, Chaeronea, superimposed by genuine Sumerian.
    Ego: apparently Euphrates — South Asia Minor — Adriatic, per-
    haps Catalonia, much at sea, avoiding the Atlantic.

c) Linear Pottery: Lengyel, Cucuteni, Tripolye, Dimini — lies in
    Thessaly above Kash, so is younger. This includes Hoangho pot-
    tery and an element of Japanese Ko pottery.
    Painting style! Swastika, button seal, painting.

d) Rush mat pottery (Kamm-): Havel, Finland, Ural, Siberia, Japan,
    China (retarded races), shell heap! (in Japan) as co-type, also on
    the Riu-Kiu Islands.

c-d)   in Japan closely associated [with the] square stamp.
        On the other hand, Danish *køkkenmøddinger*, Western
    European Campignia, [in] primeval Egypt perhaps only ship-
    wrecked booty.

Furthermore, in Japan there is silex import from the Nordic megalithic culture. This is probably the echo of the Solutrean. Furthermore
Maglemosian harpoons.

c) has its centre of gravity in Central Asia, is under the influence
of b) in Eastern Europe and originates from the Solutrean of ca.
8000–5000 B.C.

I therefore distinguish the following form circles:

a) Atlantis: as far as Orkney, Denmark, Syria, East Africa (Capsia), North Arabia, Punt.

b) Kash: as far as India, Anau, Caucasus, Chaeronea, Pre-Sumerian, Switzerland, North Asia Minor.

c) Altaic: west to Lengyel, Dimini, east to Hoangho, Sahara, South Sea (Solutrean).

d) Arctic: from Baltic Sea to Japan, Central China, South Sea (Alps?), Aino, Bear Cult.

e) Nordic (tectonic [see] Scheltema), younger.

286

[The] origin of metalworking is only possible in such a way that luminous ore specimens were valued

for their beauty (malachite, copper!!!), polished, worked as stone, also sacrificed, until it was noticed that 'copper' 'arose' in the fire and solidified luminously in forms. The secret of the priests. This is the spiritual starting point.

There is no question that the place of ideas was the altar; the ores could come from far away, the rarer the more precious. So Kash was the origin of the idea of smelting; it was found somewhere far away, accessible through trade. What spread from there was first the rare finished copper tool (axe), then the smelted copper ingot, which presupposes that there were already places [with skilled smiths] elsewhere, finally the knowledge of the course of the entire process. Neolithic is the hammering, Kashitic the casting.

287

Economy and Cookery: The mistake has hitherto been made of paying attention only to the extraction of raw materials for food: fish, game, domestic animals, fruits — and not the culture of cooking, which also has its c and d stages. Originally, the consumption of food is in its natural state: milk, blood, eggs, raw meat, mealy fruits. Only then does the style of preparation begin, firstly for the sake of more convenient chopping: softening, cooking, warming, porridge, crushing, but then as an 'art', namely with regard to the enjoyment of it. Eating for the pleasure of tasting good. Here, too, nature takes revenge, rapes: bad teeth, stomach ailments. The art of roasting, seasoning. Intoxicating drink, sweet, sour, honey. The search for new means of enjoyment and cooking methods begins. The idea of the kitchen.

And from now on, agriculture is under the influence of the pleasure of culinary delicacies: one selects, plants, breeds. The 'food of the gods', the roast sacrifice, is added. Developed agriculture presupposes a developed culinary art. There is a baroque style of cooking, etc.: beefsteak. History of the art of cooking [is a] requirement.

288

Bronze: The oldest Babylonian bronze, pre-Sargonian, [consists of] copper and antimony. In Egypt arsenic seems to have been deliberately added. The oldest European bronzes have antimony, arsenic, lead, nickel in very different quantities: it seems that one only gradually arrives at tin with a certain percentage.

In this case, the starting point would be the observation that impure copper had advantages in smelting, and the development (not 'invention') of tin bronze would only be a slow, not cultic, but craft (smithy) refinement. For the profane use of metal is identical with the training of the blacksmith's craft with habits kept secret. It is important that bronze melts more easily: that is more essential at the beginning than the observation that it is harder than copper. But one must hardly assume international 'experience' there, but rather local custom, stubborn, self-confident, mischievous.

Troy II tin-rich, VI tin-poor bronze. In the Aunjetitz[104] culture, different tin contents were found for different purposes — according to the degree of ease with which complicated things (chains) could be worked. Ores were not melted together (which do not occur together anywhere except in Cornwall), which does not give a useful result, but the pure metals themselves, and indeed the tin is added at the end of the process.

---

104 The Aunjetitz culture (named after the site of Únětice/Aunjetitz in Bohemia, Czechia) was an Early Bronze Age culture. One of the most famous finds of this culture is the Nebra Sky Disk. — *Transl.*

IV. ATLANTIS — KASH — TURAN

ON THE NATURE OF THE THREE EARLY CULTURES

1

THE TRANSITION FROM the barge to the ship. With the barge, few people, one can row along the coast or [on] the river. The ship has a crew and can withstand the waves. It originated from that, but the idea of travelling is different. Not a locomotion along the land, a few steps, but a being free from the land, even if you keep an eye on it, and the decision to fight against the weather.

Primitive Western culture has created three things: — stone building, heavy, durable, powerful, the distance of time. — The ship, [to] reach the distance. — The bow, [to] keep the enemy at bay. The first is sacrifice out of fear, the second striving for prey, the third cowardice. From here [i.e. from the West] spread over the whole earth. North Sea, rock drawing, megalith. Idea of distance: distance is experienced as an advantage or obstacle, not yet as longing, second self, soul. Purely practical, not ethical!

Busy industriousness in order to be able to enjoy afterwards. Not the idea of the deed. He lacks the feeling of the *exegi monumentum*[1]; the Pharaoh [does not] look proudly on the achievement of the pyramid, but glad that it is finished and so large.

Despite the ocean voyage, the explorer's ambition to be the first is missing, the longing to go far away. Everything is business — sober. It clings to the earth. It does not want to rise above itself with giant wings. The hubris is missing. They invented the bow, but they did not become warriors with the ambition of the conqueror. They invented, the ship, but they discovered nothing. They invented the stone building, but the vertical was missing. It does not aspire to the clouds. The pyramid is so great as a mass, not as a vertical. [These] porticoes and domes are bound to the earth, they do not want to overcome a load with ease.

2

Nordic concepts of freedom of inheritance, division of inheritance, Nordic individualism, which makes a sacrifice with the insertion into an association (loyalty, allegiance) — eternal feud, breach of oath, disunity. Always the strong ego. Also in matters of property. What I have, I defend against the whole world. Pathos of property as part of the I.

3

Life feeling of the plain. Drive for restless movement. Dislike, contempt for the peasant roots in the soil, in the city. Always breaking out: wanderlust, longing for faraway places, adventure, travel. German wanderers, English world travellers, Russian migrant workers, crusades, Vikings, knight journeys. *Ubi bene* —

This is what the West lacks (Egypt, French, Spain, Italy). The conquistador type is Nordic. The stone building clings eternally to the place. The Nordic house is movable. The German, stunted by the

---

1   Latin: 'I erected a monument', the title of an ode by the Roman poet Horace. In it, he praised his own poetry. — *Transl.*

misery of centuries, at least dreams and raves in distant places, travels in books, reads about journeys, geography. Wandering becomes longing (Italy).

4

Thus the clash of the North and [the] West takes place in the north-eastern Mediterranean: the conquerors of the steppes subjugate the ancient Western peoples. The history of antiquity is based on this fact.

5

Nordic man is an 'I' in space — despite the soul-connectedness of blood and clans. The more one has 'race', the more decided is his sense of I. He can sacrifice the I to a cause, but voluntarily. It is compulsion that kills the noble and pleases the commoner because he wants to escape the ego.

Will belongs to the I. Property is will, decision. Whoever interferes with my free disposal of my property attacks my ego. Community feeling and herd feeling are quite different things. The one sacrifices the ego, the other crawls together for lack of an ego. In the Western tombs the dead are provided for a comfortable existence, in the Nordic ones an ego is respected for the last time.

6

3ʳᵈ millennium, the ornament: That the Eurasian North (Scandinavia — China) had ornamental symbolism — abstract, spiritualised — as its dominant expression, [has] long been noticed (Scheltema, Strzygowski). The old West had puny 'decoration' but no significant ornament. It built and formed, for the statue, especially the Egyptian one, is conceived architecturally, built up of heavy material, not from within (Gothic), not as a body in space (ancient), but bearing weight, from the bottom up.

7

In the south, clear outlines — that is, sculpture, drawing — [are] taken for granted, bright day, blue sky. You do not see it at all, but the sun. In the north — fog, cloud, ornament, impressionism — where the sky rarely shines through the clouds, the blue vault itself is divine. Sky instead of sun. And sky as anonymous power, sun as god, plastic. Gods thus plastically imagined, either [as] animal (bull, jackal, etc.) or as man, then either [as] father, son, child, or mother, virgin, old man, or ruler, judge, warrior, adviser.

8

In the North [the] tragic is the sense of all important poetry. One can determine the inner rank of the great poets according to this emphasis of their tragic conception. *Mahabharata* and *Iliad* are tragedies in the primordial form, to say nothing of Aeschylus. Unfortunately, we know nothing more about Chinese poets of the Zhou period. But in the Faustian North, where the basic tragic idea [realises] its law without compromise, not for the banal masses but for the great and strong individual, the greatest tragic idea ever conceived stands at the threshold of great poetry: *Götterdämmerung*[2]. And then Lear, Don Juan, Faust follow, until our present has become so soulless and superficial that it insults the tragic of history as 'pessimism' and warms itself to a shallow stupid optimism that corresponds to its puny horizon and strengthens its banal state of soul.

In the South, however, the idyll is the basic idea of the associated poetry and painting, the serene drama, the poetry of redemption.

9

The 'South Asian' culture: Plough [for] 'agriculture'. 'Arable farming' is not the extraction of grain, but a particular form of this extraction. The Egyptians also had grain — without tillage. Idea of 'pulling' — plough and cart, instead of pushing, carrying. The chariot

---

2   German: 'Twilight of the Gods'. — *Transl.*

for driving people was known long before it became a weapon. First hunting, then battle, the [weapon] of a steppe.

From here the idea of the brick and the clay pot (Egypt, stone pot and stone building): two tendencies from two different approaches: clay throwing and fieldstone packing, both of which occur together.

10

Westerners by ship from western France, England to western Sweden, Denmark, to Finland. Giant beds. Giant rooms. Non-Indo-Europeans. Subjugating still earlier races. Then since 2000 Indo-European conquerors (single graves, battle axe) advancing as far as Sweden and Italy (e.g. H. Güntert[3], *Deutscher Geist*[4] 1932, p. 44 ff.). These Indo-Europeans were cattle breeders who assigned agriculture as slave labour to the subjugated. The Westerners were connoisseurs of grain cultivation (perhaps without a plough?). [The] dwelling of the living was small [with them] compared to the palaces of the dead.

11

The Nordic peoples did not mean the sun as a heavenly body, but the light, the redness, brightness, warmth of 'the sky'. Dawn and sunshine were identical. Nothing astral, which is an abstraction, but a visual longing for brightness: day, sunshine, redness, bright sky. So instead of sun say sunshine. This is this, aether, etc. Likewise night, gloomy weather, cloud is the same: lack of brightness, gloominess. So the bright and [the] gloomy world. The Indo-Europeans and the Nordic people did not care about astronomy and 'sun worship'. The

---

3   Hermann Güntert (1886–1948) was a German linguist, specialising in Indo-European languages, and religious historian. His book *Der arische Weltkönig und Heiland: Bedeutungsgeschichtliche Untersuchungen zur indo-iranischen Religionsgeschichte und Altertumskunde* (The Aryan World King and Saviour: Studies in the History of Meaning in Indo-Iranian Religious History and Archaeology) and his religious research had a profound influence on such thinkers as Mircea Eliade and Georges Dumézil. — *Transl.*

4   'German Spirit'. — *Transl.*

bright sunny day was to them, pantheistically, the outer world in general. Sunshine.

12

Kash and Atlantis: Mutilating the dead enemies, ravishing women, from whose wombs a new generation grew forth, mocking the captive warriors, blinded, in the cage at the feast, so they went eastward, kings, slowly urgent from century to century, so that the grandchildren hardly knew that the ancestors had not yet sat here.

13

Heroism: Let it not be thought that hunger or want of land drove these tribes south. They were not shallow and they were not blind. They were consumed by a deep longing for a home in the sunlight. First appearing in world-historical form at that time, homesickness for the south, for the life-like sun. And they were not blind: trade along northern roads, rivers and coasts brought news of the sunlit worlds of the south: of golden Egypt and its pyramids, legendary Babylon, the Dravidian splendour of India, the yellow fertile land of China. That is where they were going. They were following a legend. They flew into the light like mosquitoes. All these paths of the Zhou [to China], of the Aryans to the Ganges, of the Mitanni, of the Sea Peoples were directed towards destinations that were known. And as the Germanic peoples to Rome and Byzantium, so they all wanted to go to Memphis and Babel, [to] the Indus and [to] the Hoangho.

14

Heroism: It is the ethos of the North, where nature itself is the enemy of life and makes every step a struggle, an overcoming. In the South, the barrel of Diogenes was possible. Here there is only struggle or extinction.

15

Europe [in] Neolithic, Nordic art, ribbon pottery, Aegean. In the north, a break around 2000. New ornamentation [towards] 1800: here the Germanic peoples are formed from a migration of peoples from the Danube to the north, where until then Nordic Hamites (megalithic graves) had sat. This formation of Germanicism is thus simultaneous with the advance of other tribes to Hellas, India, China! — Bronze Age. (Read *Reallexikon* 'Nordische Kunst'[5], Scheltema, Hoernes, Schuchhardt!).

16

Kash and Atlantis: To the inner form of the temple culture belong spiritual and business expansion, not streams of peoples: spirit (language, measure, calendar), business (not as if the economic sense were stronger than elsewhere, but it is directed with abstract certainty to distant things and invents the forms of expanded professional long-distance trade). In Atlantis, the merchant, the trader is not an occupational type.

Perhaps the hammering and driving of copper is Atlantean (Spain). But only Kash turns it into production for export purposes, carving, making ingots as a commodity.

17

The two great c-cultures: They explain everything in the Mediterranean (contents of the first chapter). The one [from] northwest [to] south-east: ancestors, care of the dead, tight state organisation, calendar: i.e. Libya, Rasena, Crete, Lydia, Egypt, Akkad, becoming weaker and weaker. Preserving corpse, tomb as monument. The other [from] southeast [to] northwest: abstraction, *templum*, cosmogonic structure, myth system, rite, omen: Sumer, pre-Egypt, Etrurians, Hatti. No ancestors, funerary monuments. The living is right. More church than state.

---

5 'Nordic Art'. — *Transl.*

These two cultures at the same time spread language types which correspond to the ornamental ones. Hamitic and Elamite. To which [language type] Basque, Rasena belong, [is] quite uncertain.

18

'Nordic' must be interpreted clearly:
In the 4th/3rd millennium, [the] focus of Nordic being is the Solutrean-Linear Pottery zone up to China, under Kashitic influence, fond of receiving and learning. Only in the 3rd millennium does the High Norse amoeboid emerge [at the] Baltic Sea, which incorporates the rest of Europe and finally really produces the three heroic cultures. These two amoeboid entities must be precisely distinguished.

19

Kash, Atlantis: If the Atlanteans avoided the impassable, still barely existing [Nile] Delta and went north via southern Arabia, then the lower class of Kash [and] Ur is also Atlantean-Akkadian and Sumer only the upper class. The Atlanteans would therefore have settled everything up to the Zagros. Kash, on the other hand, pushes forward [along the] shipping lanes: Indus, Persian Gulf, Red Sea.

20

We only know of Kash finds from random places: Anau[6], Astrabad[7], Elam, Harappa. It would be wrong to consider these as main points; we do not know where the centre was. But one clue is the direction of the Indian invasion towards 'Sindh'[8], whence the names Hindu, India and the 'Iranian' to Palestine [come]. Apparently, the whole of Iran and western India was 'Kash'.

---

6   The Anau culture was contemporaneous with Sumerian civilisation and was centred near modern-day Ashgabad in Turkmenistan about 7,000 years ago. — *Transl.*

7   Astrabad (renamed in 1937 to Gorgan) in modern-day Iran has been an important centre of Persian culture for millennia. — *Transl.*

8   Sindh was the centre of the ancient Indus Valley civilisation. — *Transl.*

21

1. Define here the great outlines, from the highest altitude, which will then be filled in in the following! On the edge of the ice and rainy season. Climate. 'World situation' — differences in rank —.

2. Building, temples, tombs. Thus the 'leitmotifs' are different. Religion, chariots, calendars and precursors of writing. Genealogical — cosmological. Sacrifice: slaughter, cattle breeding. (Here not yet the profane economic consequences.)

3. Language.

4. Idea of the state, people, status, leadership, idea of law, war as the original form of politics. Here 'peace' begins as the legal intermezzo of eternal war as the very 'life'.

5. Symbolism of the economy. Relationship to plant and animal (concrete or artificial). What is necessity there, what is expression (choice)?

6. Temperament: ideal of movement, wandering, acting (Punt[9] is Kash). Flow of people and flow of forms.

22

If the Dravidian languages 'belong to the Kash group', they have come to India like Latin to Romania, Greek to Bactria and Spanish to the Philippines, not by 'migration' but politically and economically.

23

Kash, Atlantis: Expansion due to desertification: [Was] the advance of the Eastern Hamites ('Semites') into Arabia, Canaan, Akkad — around   3000? — roughly   simultaneous   with   the

---

9   Punt was an ancient kingdom that traded with Egypt. It is not known exactly where it was located but some people believe it was in modern-day Somalia, Ethiopia or Sudan. — *Transl.*

occupation of south-eastern Spain, Malta, points of Italy and Greece? Simultaneously also with the megalithic culture in Denmark [on the] Elbe? With the migration of the Bell Beaker people[10]? With the occupation of Troy I? Before that, Kash had moved as far as Middle Egypt (4th millennium). It recedes as far as Syria and the Euphrates, but expands to the north. The drying up of Central Asia then leads to pressure on Europe (end of the Tripolye culture), China, Persia.

24

The Germanic peoples [are] a Hamitic mixed element. Bohuslän pictures are Western. Only the ornamentation is Nordic. And that is the infinite ornament of any kind — infinitely running, filling the surface, spirally moving. The deep meaning is always infinity. It is wrong to start from the finished motifs, like ribbon pottery, spiral. The ornament is solitary, personal. A picture, a statue is a you, a Nordic ornament is an I, it does not speak to others, it only speaks out. The fact observed by Scheltema that it emphasises the bodies of the vessel is symbolic. Thus: the infinitely solitary ornament.

25

Soul: Nordic soul [is] 'personal', i.e. solitary. I, never we. The 'we' is for them a sacrifice, ethical; for the South it is the normal constitution. Therefore [is] 'talking to oneself' Nordic. Accountability.

---

10   From c. 2,600 until 2,200 B.C., the so-called Bell Beaker culture can be identified in Europe. The name goes back to the German prehistorian Paul Reinecke (1872–1958), who first spoke of 'bell beakers' in 1900. The ceramic vessels look like bells when one turns them upside down. — *Transl.*

26

North: The graves at Ur[11] [are] 'Gutaean[12]' burials: with booty. The names on the vessels [are] therefore not those [of] the buried, but of the defeated.

Racial type of the Vedas, Persian, black-haired. [Are] perhaps the Ainu a remnant of this type (as far as the Alps)?

27

Wistfulness of all folk poetry, song, dance. Next to it intoxicating wildness. Melancholy of the plain — why? Russian steppe, prairie. Why do mountains, islands, seas, lakes comfort? It is because of the sense of infinity — the horizon consumes the soul, gnawing. Once, never again, future, endless passing. It is the home of heroic culture, Linear Pottery.

28

Building! This is true only of Kash and Atlantis. The northern cultures did not actually 'build', but wove the wooden wall ornamentally. Therefore, they 'looked' less at the overall appearance of the house than at the significance of individual ornaments (roof, beams). Cult buildings [are] therefore Hamitic and Kashitic.

29

Kash and Atlantis: There are no peoples yet. The great form of experienced and felt connection is the tribe, a few thousand 'souls', a few hundred 'heads'. Names exist only for these tribes, their territory ('*Gau*', 'territory'), not for rivers but for sections of rivers, not for mountain ranges but individual mountains and ridges, not for countries but a stretch of coastline, a valley, an island. The geographical horizon also limits the area of a tribe. Beyond that lies the legendary

---

11   Ur was one of the oldest Sumerian cities in Mesopotamia. — *Transl.*

12   Gutaean highlanders conquered Sumer and Akkad in the 23rd century B.C. — *Transl.*

distance with dark lore, ancestors, curiosity (experienced and known horizon).

30

Names: I want to introduce ancient mythical names for these two cultures to avoid confusing later entities with them. (Map!) Atlantis: the Greeks called two mountains by this name, the Mauritanian Atlas and the Ethiopian Atlas. The Atlantis saga is generally directed there, the ocean got its name from it: in all this there is an old tradition of something highly historical that ended early. Today, the traces can still be discovered in the depths: megalithic graves — death, life. Language — inflection. Rock paintings — ocular creation. Weapons, fortresses. Then Erythraea: as is well known, this was the name of the sea between Bombay and Aden in prehistoric times. Here lay Punt. Sumer is the Persian Gulf, Elam is the southern edge from Susa to Indus. South India and Somaliland filled with flint. Cult buildings. Astral teachings. Language. Agglutination. Bronze, ceramics: technique. 6-system abstract. Circle division, Hellespont[13].

Atlantis: building and management technique, 'overcoming', concrete.

Kash: Bronze, ceramics, sowing, breeding: exploitation, abstract. Ziggurat[14] (Dombart[15]).

31

The Far North: Here briefly, grandly give proof that we must draw no inferences from the peoples of today. Here, in the endless strip of mountainless plain with forest and swamp, bush and stream, hard winters and hot summers, a new kind of man awoke to

---

13   Hellespont was the ancient term for the Dardanelles. — *Transl.*

14   A ziggurat was a stepped temple tower in Mesopotamia. — *Transl.*

15   Theodor Dombart (1884–1969) was a German architect and local historian who wrote a book about ziggurats, *Der Sakralturm* ('The Sacral Tower') (1920). — *Transl.*

a world-historical mission. What they looked like we do not know. Too often storms of peoples have passed through this plain: Alans from Mongolia to Portugal, Tocharians[16] from Europe to China. And since then, through the inbreeding of closed cultural peoples, a type of city-dweller has developed in China and Europe that blurs every trace — we know nothing of the untouched peasants. What, on the other hand, is the 'Indo-European' language supposed to mean? Somehow this group of dialects existed in two branches around 1000 B.C. But what do we know of all the lost species of this language, extinct in the north, abandoned in the south — and of other language groups that are completely lost? In Africa and America there are hundreds of languages, and that it was once no different between the Atlantic and India, and in primeval China no less, is proved by the ruins of dozens in the inscriptions.

It is the rule that one language replaces the other. Western Europe has inherited the dialect of Latium, [the world from Iraq] to [Morocco] the one of Mecca. So the language is a happy heiress — but in what corners might it have slumbered before? And who, above all, were its preceding bearers? For with what right do we assume that the Aryans and Hellenes did not borrow this language? (On this Meyer, *Volksstämme Kleinasiens*[17] p. 256!) If today we distinguish the Western Europeans, Russians, Tatars, Mongols, etc., this is the result of historical events: the 'Russians' since the Golden Horde, the Mongols and 'Europeans' since the empires of the Romans and Chinese.

32

Kash [is] very old, [was] already in Egypt before Atlantis, perhaps even [came] by two routes, to the sea from Nubia down the Nile, from northern Arabia to the Delta. Then suppressed by the Atlantean wave of peoples, while 'Sumer' is the victor over the Atlantean-Semitic

---

16   The Tocharians were Indo-European speakers that migrated from the Volga-Ural steppe to China. — *Transl.*

17   'Ethnic Tribes of Asia Minor'. — *Transl.*

element. 'Kash' [is] thus pre-Sumerian, Sumer already the result of a fertilisation. In Arabia and Aram-Assur the human mass of Atlantis is victorious, only 'Sumer' is the result of a victory through replenishment. Sumer, however, is not only Sinear, but the whole perimeter of the Persian Gulf.

33

Greatness, high in the north, [stands] against the spirit of the sun. Heroic Fate. The fate is me. The gods [are] treated comradely, hardship sought, pride. Single combat, bravery. Killing the enemy [is] not simply necessary, but beautiful. Combat [is] considered the purpose of life. Ideal. Navigation [is] discovered as heroism, high seas, adventure. Burning palaces, rivers of blood, exultation of manhood. Nations are warlike unions of men, not [a] cultic unity.

34

Heroism: Here [applies] the genuine Nordic ornament, as the expression of a new soul. From China to the Rhine. Still in Faustian culture, French Gothic is Atlantic: stony; German ornamental: brick building. Ceramics are only a puny side branch! Above all wood, carved, painted, house and household utensils, then weaving, patterns. The house urns still betray the Chinese lineage in the landscape. Russian, Scandinavian wood and half-timbered construction. The heroic [does not show itself] in temple and grave, both of which are sacrifice, humility; life only wants itself. Very unreligious, little cult. The ornament is weaving infinitely, jubilant world feeling, dark foreboding, joy of fate.

35

Kash and Atlantis: During the maturing of these migratory cultures, as a continuation of the earthly fate that stands behind the word Ice Age, the unrestrained progressive transformation of the marginal zone from forest to steppe and [from] steppe to humusless sand takes place, from West Africa to China and at the southern tips of the three continents. And just as the ice once drove primitive, rare swarms of people southwards, so the desert now pushes masses of people in all directions: from North Africa, the later Sahara, to Spain, Italy, [the] Aegean, [the] Nile region, [the] Congo, from Arabia towards the Euphrates, from Turkestan to India and China. The whole history of Egyptian and Babylonian culture is under this pressure.

36

Feudalism: It is an elevated form of rural as opposed to urban economy. And also an expression of genealogical, not priestly, social feeling, thus closer to Atlantis than to Kash. It is, after warlike shocks, a natural relationship in which one must not judge with today's urban feelings. It was taken for granted. The revolt was either a real war to restore the old power of the defeated or later the confrontation from the city, from rationalistic motives. Protection in return for allegiance (not payment as in urban relations). The lord also gives, is hospitable. This is the meaning of Anax[18].

[It is] ridiculous to draw on the relations of primitive peoples. Here we are dealing with symbols. It is 1) a form of military service, 2) [a form] of economic order, 3) an expression of the idea of 'sovereignty'.

37

Social structure: In Kash a nobility is unthinkable: here as in the Magian culture (partly Atlantean?) a cultic social order, emphasis on the priesthoods, the king its exponent. In Atlantis, on the other hand, [the focus is] the ruling class. The social structure of strictest symbolism [is] different in each cd culture. The estates are there, but the superstructure is [in each case] differently founded: priestly or noble, that is, spatial-abstract or temporal-vital.

---

18   Anax was the title of the Mycenaean god-king. — *Transl.*

38

The amoeboid Kash culture (kinship of the Dravidian, African, Sumerian languages) penetrated early to the northwest, through the Red and [the] Persian Sea to Etruria (this very young, around 2000) — related way of naming, baptism of place and personal names. Lingam and Yoni (stone core in bowl-shaped base with spout) and the sacred bull 'Nandi' — all from the primordial Dravidian Shiva cult. From here the sacred bull penetrates to Etruria. This Kash culture is that of the sacred plough (plant cultivation in furrows), hence the sacred ground geometry, templelike, from which Babylon then makes a system.

Furthermore, [it is] from here that the exclusively sacred metal technology comes, which gives the impetus to the long-distance trade of the Nordic idea. For the need is southern, the form of long-distance trade is absolutely Nordic, proceeds from border elements (Assur, Minos, Tartessos) and therefore makes the 'face' of the two southern cultures turn towards the north, while the monsoon region withers away. To primeval Kash belongs the chthonic[19] goddess of sexual desire, [in] India Paravati, in Syria Astarte, 'Venus'. From primeval Kash [comes] the cosmology of the Indians, pre-Aryan, doctrine of the world-mountain (Sumerian land = mountain!), division of the world-building, monkey, Hanuman[20] — all also in Africa.

39

One c-culture has the direction of movement Indian world — Peru (with Madagascar as a later specialisation) — Japan. Another one around 2000 (Nordic) has the direction towards the South. Their expression of life is 'lifestyle', not abstraction in construction or thought: they are forms of living, not of inanimate objects. This corresponds to

---

19   Related to the Underworld. — *Transl.*

20   Hanuman is a monkey god in Hinduism. — *Transl.*

the new idea of the fateful: Achilles, not clay pots. But that is just not what the archaeologist can excavate.

40

The two southern cultures are clashes of simultaneous c-streams (Atlantis and Kash), whose need for expression was partly abstract (cosmological), partly critical (outline picture, burial chamber, building structure). In the three northern cultures, a young c-culture with [its] expression in [the] attitude to life lies on top of old ones that come through again: under antiquity, Atlantis cherishes, little Kash; under India, Kash; — [what] under China?

41

I *want* general names like Atlantis and Kash because I want to deliberately disguise the geographical location. For there can be no question of a firmly enclosed district as in the rooted high cultures. That is why Atlantis can mean Western Iberia or Morocco or the northern Sahara or all of them together or something else at any time. Kash is Persian Gulf, Oman, Balujistan to Hyderabad. Sumer stretched from Ur to Muscat, Elam from Susa to [the] Indus.

42

A third c-culture is the Indonesian. It is undoubtedly younger than the other two, of which Kash is the oldest. 5000 Kash, Lemuria[21]. 4000 Atlantis. 3000 Sunda, Polynesia from East Africa to Japan and Peru. (I must choose words that lie in the prehistoric period, nothing later that already has fixed meaning). This third c-culture lies strong in China, in India partly in the depths, and it has led around all the edges of the great ocean, where it became a very late witness as a high

---

21 Lemuria refers to a hypothetical sunken continent that was said to have been located in the Indian Ocean in a triangular shape, thereby touching India's southern point, southern Africa and western Australia. In H. P. Lovecraft's novel *At the Mountains of Madness,* the Elder Thing's buried city in Antarctica was compared to both Atlantis and Lemuria — *Transl.*

culture in Mexico and Peru. Is Indonesian culture a remnant of the Kash amoeba? Just as the heroic culture is a remnant of Atlantis?

43

Kash: I reckon that this primeval territory extends from Eastern Arabia to Malabar, but in the north deep into Turkestan. The great stream of peoples via Zagros and Kabul belong to it. Perhaps the Solutrean is at home here! Or locally generated from here.

The Old Sumerian religion knows above all the bison and the 'wild man' (not 'Gilgamesh'), who is naked, protector of the bison, Ur, stag against the lion, ringlets and chin beard like the bison.

Then Egypt would be: Atlantis over Kash, Babylon: Kash over Solutrean.

44

Art form: Atlantean is the expression in space: grave. The painting likewise: 'composition' of the scene. The apparent ornamental decorations (such as stars etc.) are imitations of some form (starfish), not symbolic forms. Sense of physiognomy (portrait, racial types).

Nordic: Everything is ornament of foreboding heaviness, also grave and house form, roof, half-timbering. Not the space, but the ornamentation, the play of lines has meaning. Not the vessels, but the play with its surface. Even then there must have been deep music, not loose play, major and minor.

Kashitic [is] the abstract, barely felt 'art'. Unartistic sect, sense of abstract thought-forms, mysterious numbers and measures. Ziggurat acts only as an embodiment of numbers. The statues were certainly only felt that way: seven rows of palm leaves. No sense of portraits. It only seems that way.

45

I call the two amoebae of culture which appear here, according to the predominant trait of their expression, the tomb culture and the temple culture. And I call the world-view that expresses itself here the genealogical and the cosmological.

46

Atlantis, Kash, Turan: Religion:

A: hot, mobile, genealogical. Grave building.

K: tropical, saturated, cosmological. Temple building.

T: cold, longing, nature soul, magic, mysticism. Without architecture. The artistic expressive instinct attaches itself in

A: to stone construction, stone relief, force, mass, overcoming. The ornamentation of vessels and clothing remains quite unkempt. 'Jewellery' as special adornment (diadem etc.): tectonic style, concrete.

K: temple, painting: pictorial style, abstracting.

T: House, dress, utensils: ornamental, mystical. Adhering to the need for dwelling and warmth: intimate culture of house and tent, warm clothes, carpets, interiors, beams, roof, windows.

Thus:

A: megalithic construction and rock drawing

K: brick building and colour overlay

T: tent and wood construction, carving.

47

The house is insignificant as a vehicle of expression in Atlantis and Kash. In Atlantis [it] even imitates tomb forms with the greatest magnificence. The Egyptian house [is a] 'tomb of the living', [the] Minoan [a] '*templum* of the present'. But Nordic heroism, in its first, purest ascent, builds the living, not the dead: dominions instead of palaces, a cv like Achilles instead of a tomb.

Dwelling huts are everywhere in c. But the house as a bearer of great symbolism is Turanian: first the house of the chief, then that of all. Tomb, *templum*, house is such that actually each tribe should have only one, that of the most powerful.

48

[On the] *spiritual culture of Turan*: I leave open the question whether there has been a fourth in America, *Pacific-Andean*, but I believe it. One concurrent with the heroic amoebae.

Turan: Investigate whether sacral prostitution is at home here! In general the forms which are 'Phrygian-Syrian'. The Chaldic, Bohemian and Aino would then have to belong to the marginal amoebae. Since new language types are no longer formed, because around 4000 all people already speak word languages, the Indo-European type of grammatical structure must be Turanian.

49

So also the idea of the humanless [is] different:

Atlantis: life after death, family

Kash: blessing in this world

Turan: *Amor fati* or contrition.

The first act of the unleashed spirit is the interpretation of the world in the image (seeing — thinking), an image of the fear of the freed, cast out of the all-life. Only around 2000 the pride in this confrontation with the All.

50

Atlantis: It is to be expected that the Capsian is younger than the Aurignacian and that both have a common origin: North and South crystals. Then the Atlantic amoeba is based on the humus of both and has its centre of gravity more in Spain and Morocco.

But then the Late Capsian is already the beginning of the c-culture itself. That the 'oldest Neolithic' is missing in Spain is therefore only the impression based on a wrong overall view. In fact, Late Capsian is already 5th millennium.

51

Two c-cultures: In this amoebaic period, state and religion arise as organised things, but not 'at all', but immediately in a few basic ideas, archetypal symbols, from which everything later in c- and d-cultures descends mentally, through solidification, decomposition [and] *interbreeding.*

The archetypes [are] the Atlantean state [and] the Asiatic religion! Atlantis is exemplary for everything state-like on earth, Kash is exemplary for everything highly religious. The original idea of Kash: the world exists for the sake of man, *macro-anthropos*[22] and microcosm. The world system has its meaning in man. The pride of Kash: the gods cannot do without man, who gives them meaning through worship [and] sacrifice. Heaven and earth are symbols of the human being. This is the original meaning of all great religion. Only 'Akkad' brings to pride the whimpering, the supplication, the contrition, the sense of sin (this is the reaction after the great time, around 2600, urban bourgeois). While the far north weighs man: chivalry, ancestry, race, distinguished, here he is *counted.* No genealogical distinction of rank.

52

c-Culture. Atlantis: The stretching power of this culture soul is tremendous. The current flows northwards to Orkney, Denmark, Germany (Bell Beaker), but then in 'pre-Saharan' times it has conquered Africa, [the] Sudan. On the line Timbuktu, East Africa, Chad — Nile — Arabia, Akkad partly from South Arabia because the delta was impassable, Zambezi, South, where the petroglyphs (much older than the 'Bushmen') show where mighty ruins must lie.

---

22 Plato calls the individual the *micro-anthropos* (the small human being). He can ultimately only behave within the cultural framework of his polis. The polis (the state as the big whole) is the *macro-anthropos* (big human being). — *Transl.*

53

Atlantis and Kash, [that is] '*Occident and Orient*'. These terms have already arisen here, as well as Northland and South Sea: these two are of a more recent type. The desert belt is then the great pasture belt. These are at the same time four original types of language formation (not 'original languages'), which become less and less typical towards the periphery.

Atlantic type: Occident: semi-Hamitic. Northland, younger: Indo-European. Kashitic type: Orient: Sumerian-Caucasian. South Sea: Austro-Asiatic. Occident and Orient [are] today still c-amoebae among decayed d-cultures.

54

Atlantis: The word has fallen into disrepute and yet denotes a reality. That is why I would like to rehabilitate it.

55

Atlantis Kash
Concrete abstract
political-social idea religious-social idea
State World Mission
Egypt The four world regions
Order, administration Redemption, improvement
Administrative practice Private law
National universal
no expansion, borderless
National border

56

Atlantean art: The stylised and yet naturalistic art of the Alps stands at the end of the Palaeolithic, is local, 5000. To this 'idea' belongs Negade[23] art, but also Minoan art with its naturalism, which originated in Libya and reached as far as Asia Minor. Its essence is a sketch of the vital: not the body at all, but the living body — running, looking around, flying. Kash is more abstract.

57

Kash, centre of gravity somehow Turkestan — Persia — India, thus also a land mass, still very indeterminate. Solutrean as an advance. Indian Palaeolithic. Anau. Linear Pottery as marginal zone, partial amoeba as far as China. On the other hand, traces as far as Spain: Malta, Molfetta, Dimini.

There are still two zones: Linear Pottery and Elamite. The fact is that the primeval Babylonian culture (Elam, Sinear) extends from eastern Arabia to Punjab. The key lies in the prehistoric exploration of Arabia and Turkestan.

58

Kash and Atlantis: To Kash, where the gods determine the cosmos of things, belong the *omina*[24]: in abstract and calculable form everything is rigidly predetermined. All of Hellas is awash with oracles. Mathematics. To Atlantis, where the meaning of life is felt not mathematically, [but] world-rhythmically, what is to happen is not mathematics of the cosmos, but rhythmic result, organic-logical, of the tendency of life. It is not the time and place of the punctual event that is important, but the overall result of the event, and one knows this inwardly in advance, not through *omina*. Precisely because this stream of life is the meaning of the universe, it cannot suddenly cease with death, while life as the conclusion of a mathematics of the gods becomes indifferent after death.

---

23 The Negade culture is from the predynastic period of Egypt during the Copper Age. — *Transl.*

24 Latin: 'omens'. — *Transl.*

Inner kinship of Faustian and Egyptian culture, first and last flowering of Atlantis. Just as Sumer and Arabia [are] first and last flowering of Kash. In antiquity Atlantis and Turan intersect as in India Kash [and Turan], in Faustian culture North and antiquity (in this again Atlantis in depth), very complicated. In China the ancient Munda[25] culture with North.

59

Amoeboid 'tendencies': The megalithic culture is the only one that 'thinks in mass', not only in stone, but in the cubic, voluminous, already on the Atlantic coast, then classically in Egypt, more weakly already in Babylon (while the three northern cultures think abstractly in space instead of [in] substance and thus create the most transient, ideas of form, but no monuments). So the Semito-Hamitic grammar must testify to something similar, be massive, become sated and inert southwards, bathed in light, without longing.

The monsoon amoeba 'Kash', on the other hand, of which traces [live] in Sumer, Dravida, Sudan, brought with it a different tendency (pre-Sumeric, Oannes[26]), namely earth mother, agriculture and animal husbandry as an expression of a chthonic thinking. Harappa [belongs] here. The amoeboid cultures continue to mature, without prejudice to the high culture built upon them locally. The kinship of the Germanic systems is not to be understood causally from an original language, but convergently from a simultaneous world-view (*Paideuma*[27], amoeboid, cultural soul). The Vedas and Homer [are] strongly Nordic, the [respective folk] faith (as in Rhoda[28]'s psyche) peasantly southern.

---

25   The Munda people are an indigenous tribe in South Asia. — *Transl.*

26   Oannes is a mythical creature from Mesopotamia, a hybrid of a fish and a man. — *Transl.*

27   *Paideuma* is a Greek term for education. — *Transl.*

28   From the Bible (King James Version), Acts 12:11–14: 'Then Peter came to himself and said, "Now I know without a doubt that the Lord has sent his angel and rescued me from Herod's clutches and from everything the Jewish people were hoping would happen." When this had dawned on him, he went to the house of

60

The North c. 2000: [It is] to be distinguished: the North man is mobile, active. He advances by storm, his tribal associations chasing before them what lies in the way, or if it holds fast, subduing or exterminating it.

The southern man — Gaia — advances very slowly, individually, in troops, from village to village, tenaciously, firmly on the ground. Thus he has [moved] slowly northward from the Indian Ocean (Kash) along streams and coasts.

Nile Valley — Mediterranean (coastal travel, North Africa, Crete, 'pre-Indo-European' settlements with the place names). Sinear to Caucasus and Bosporus. Indus, Ganges — Dravidian. From Tonkin to the Hoangho (Yueh) and Japan and Polynesia.

From here comes the somatic type of Chinese and Japanese, the 'eternal' peasant class, *Homo dinaricus*[29], *mediterraneus*[30].

4000 B.C. Northern man is creative in the south — all cultures! — but he dies for it. Upper class, even as a peasant! For in Italy and Hellas the Oriental slave formed the new peoples! The oldest thrust from the north is the semi-Hamitic one via North Africa to Egypt and Babylon!

61

West-East push of the 4th millennium: From Spain to the South Seas. The new thing is a brave life tendency, courage. But not conscious courage, not a courageous world-view. One dares, but not for the sake of daring, and one suffers from the necessity of having to

---

Mary the mother of John, also called Mark, where many people had gathered and were praying. Peter knocked at the outer entrance, and a servant named Rhoda came to answer the door. When she recognised Peter's voice, she was so overjoyed she ran back without opening it and exclaimed, "Peter is at the door!"' — *Transl.*

29 Latin: 'Dinaric man', meaning a man of Dinaric race. — *Transl.*

30 Latin: 'Mediterranean man', meaning a man of Mediterranean race. — *Transl.*

dare. This determines the inner form of this mighty train of an amoeboid culture. The proud individual does not yet feel like a person. He knows nothing of himself. And one gropes one's way with the ships from coast to coast into the unknown, one pushes forward through endless steppes, but not with the epic face of the discoverer and conqueror. Even if the Egyptian warrior, the ruler, slays the enemy, he is not a hero, but redeemed from a danger. One dares or one dies, but the pathos of daring and heroism are unknown experiences.

62

Northern cultures: The contempt of the northern soul for everything that the southern culture had chosen as its highest ideals can be seen in the heroic no to everything: nothing has survived from this first period, neither astronomy nor law (Babylonian), neither construction nor administration (Egyptian). One lived the defiant nevertheless before oneself. Life needs no testimonies. It feels itself, that is enough. Only then does the crushed sub-soul regain consciousness and assert itself as a 'people',

first religiously, then also politically.

63

The northern peoples [around] 2000 bring the idea of competition and the esteem for personal danger, courage, contempt for death. The idea of competitions, *Agon*[31]—also at Stonehenge? Another idea is that of watching cruel games, gladiators (Osker? Rasena?), bullfights in Crete, ancient in Spain.

64

Kash and Atlantis: How many amoebae were created in this millennium around the middle of the ten millennia B.C. we do not

---

31 *Agon* is an ancient Greek term meaning 'contest' or 'struggle'. According to Friedrich Nietzsche, agon was the foundational principle of Greek culture. Only the struggle among equals before the public could lead to the creation of exemplary cultural works. — *Transl.*

know and never will. What is certain is that several of them never rose to prominence. Two, however, rose to the utmost height possible for such a culture, and they, more than others and later ones, have determined the course and substance of world history. They arose at about the same time; they have each inwardly seized only a part of the human world, and they prove by the history of their existence, which is not yet extinct today, that primitive culture of a higher style is not 'culture of mankind', but of a part of mankind.

65

Neolithic and Bronze Age [in Europe] fall in the sub-boreal dry period, where the loess soil was free of forest. That is why all the Linear Pottery settlements are on the loess: farming, village. The Corded and Zonal Ware, on the other hand, had hardly any real agriculture, no habitation sites found, therefore little sedentary. That means: more livestock farming in free herds, Atlantic! Cattle, pigs, sheep, goats.

66

Expansion of Atlantis: It proceeds so slowly that there is no consciousness at all of expansion in certain directions: one extends the pastures from father to grandson, occasionally leaving the territories of the grandfathers. The grandchildren sit a little further west. [This is] very different from the Nordic heroic urge to go far away.

67

I assume a flowing Neolithic culture from Morocco, moving along the old traffic routes through the forest and steppe landscape to the Nile with an ancient maritime centre in Tunis (Phratria, pre-Carthaginian, Atlantic). These Tehenu (Hamites) of Egyptian complexion also reached Crete and Sicily, also Sardinia, Liguria, Nubia. They have the custom of cultic rock carvings, the *tumuli*. Furthermore, a culture of younger, Kashitic style flows from Sinear to Crete — Etruria, with related language types, templelike, priestly. Around 2500 Tuimah appear, perhaps warlike tribes, not a mass of peoples.

The emptying of the Sahara brings a rush of peoples to the north (Europe, Mediterranean) and south (rock drawing of the 'Bushmen'). Capsia in Palestine. Navigation in the Mediterranean [is] pre-Egyptian.

GRAVE CULT — MATRIARCHY — PIETY

68

Pantheism: Western polytheism is 'egoism of human life'. — It recognises only humans and human-like gods (with intellect, compassion, wisdom, wrath, etc.). Plant and animal are merely object. Nordic pantheism sees 'the divine' in every animal, plant, mountain and river.

69

Pantheism: The idea of 'powers' [becomes] here the necessary expression of polarity: God and devil, Yang and Yin, Ormuzd and Ahriman[32], while in the south the colourful picture of a multitude of figures prevails. Polarity [is] the sensual primal experience in the opposition of forces; two opponents belong to the struggle. The world as a battlefield. In evaluative reflection, the difference between good and evil is brought in, lived in, not morally, but vital: friendly — hostile. The opponent is not evil, but an enemy. Aesir[33] and giants. Only the moralising systems bring in good and evil instead of good and bad in the aristocratic sense: low, cowardly, mean.

70

Pantheistic powers ('gods') are originally powers of the landscape — *tien*, *schê*, Poseidon, Wotan. The western and southern gods are numina of cult sites, of individual tribes: Helen of Therapne, Hera of Argos. Not a single Egyptian or Babylonian deity is placeless. As

---

32	Ahriman is the spirit of destruction and the lord of darkness in Zoroastrianism and thus the main adversary of Ormuzd. — *Transl.*

33	The Aesir are the main gods in the Norse religion. They live in Asgard. — *Transl.*

gods of territories, Re, Amon become gods of the *state*. Where place-bound gods appear in Greece, Rome, India, China, they are either pre-Nordic or de-Nordic. 'Henotheism[34]' of western nomads. Yahweh. Bogus monotheism. Allah. 'He of Tonent'. Kamos, Baal, El.

'Powers' [dwell] in every weapon, [in] implement, stone, animal, plant. Soul of 'property' [in the north]. Hence the power of famous weapons in Nordic sagas (Philoctetes' arrows, Roland's horn[35], Siegfried's sword[36]).

71

Patriarchy: The conception of the West rested on the knowledge of the stream of life from mother to mother. The genealogical view prevails. The North is more 'spiritual': it wants the man, the son as the bearer of the tradition of the name, the call of the ancestors. The daughter follows the mother bodily; this is seen. But the father chooses and recognises the son by his will. To this male succession, then, belongs the recognition of paternity, adoption, repudiation, denial, and the demand of the virginity of the woman whom one has chosen as the mother of the hereditary son. The jealousy of the West — Spanish, French — is directed towards the sole possession of the beautiful body — therefore the question of the child is excluded. The jealousy of the North is the need for the certainty of possessing the self-begotten son as heir. It does not come to consciousness in the midst of sexual intoxication, but clearly underlies it: jealousy fears there the theft of ownership of the body, here the forgery of the blood. There it clings to the present, here to the future. The jealousy of the woman is something quite different.

---

34 Henotheism is the belief in a supreme God, which, in contrast to the monotheism of the Abrahamic religions, does not exclude the worship of other subordinate gods. — *Transl.*

35 In *The Song of Roland*, written around 1100, the encircled Roland calls Charlemagne's main army to aid with his horn. — *Transl.*

36 In Germanic mythology, Gram is the name of Siegfried's sword which he used to kill the dragon Fafnir. — *Transl.*

72

Community: Growing together (male alliance): bonds, army, warrior peoples. (Loyalty, attachment — hatred of the individual against the community.) Estate, nobility. Patriarchy. In the West more blood community, genetic: matriarchy. In the South 'community' (Buddhists) by experience and deeds. Community of fate. Huns, for example, [were] warrior swarms of diverse blood (the only recently found inscription of a Hunnic gold helmet [is] 'Caucasian').

73

Since the essence of Kash culture is abstract and cosmic, not vital and pictorial, i.e. without a cult of the dead, there is much that the Italic tombs cannot reveal, namely everything that came from the ancient Orient. The burial culture comes from the southwest, from Africa. One must distinguish between the mere fact of hiding and the symbolic greatness of the idea of burial. Only here have the dead demanded the service of the living. They are the masters of the family as well as the tribe. The ancestor, not the tribal god as in Kash, rules. From the East, on the other hand, comes a tendency that places not life but the world at the centre of thought: orientation, cosmology, personified god systems, *omina*.

This comes from the southeast to Apulia and Sicily, from the northeast (Danube) to Tuscany and Picenum[37].

74

Religion: As soon as the sensual understanding, the musing, shapes gods, they must take the form of living beings: animals, monsters, hybrid beings, humans, and as such again they must be father, son, mother, daughter, youth, child, old man. They marry, procreate, are born and die. In the north, the shape is blurred. The little spirits weave. Fate, heaven, remains abstract. Providence, destiny, the will of God — all impersonal.

---

37   Picenium was the ancient name of a landscape in central Italy. — *Transl.*

75

Matriarchy — patriarchy: The feeling of life [is] the first. Only from this [becomes] world-view (religious), only from this language-bound ideas. Father in heaven. Mother, Madonna. Gods and sculpture. Powers and ornament. Building as sacrifice, cultic. Not in the north. There one has the house for oneself. West: palace for the divine chief. Offerings. The others only 'dwell'. No type of house. Cells, honey-combs. To the north, the single house.

76

The North Eurasian primal ethos: I and the world, with the de-mand therein: self-conquest for a great cause (deed, glory, merit). Various versions: the ancient, Indian, Chinese, etc. Imperative. Stoic philosophy, Confucius, English individualism, Prussian [socialism]. Romanesque (Spanish, French) anarchism and English-Scandinavian (Ibsen).

77

Pantheism: The powers of the landscape: 'the' storm, the inunda-tion of water, fire (lightning, forest fire, steppe fire). Soul of the forest, sombre, eerily silent, roaring. The swollen stream in spring, [which] sweeps away huts, animals, people. The soul of the wide plain with the dusty horizon.

Poteidaon. In the south, the unmediated lost presence, became corporeal: the soul of the plain, storming along in hordes of wild horses, becomes the 'god of horses', finally that of the sea: the water storm with the wave heads. How the silence of the forest condenses into shapes. Böcklin[38]. Cloud Spirits.

78

Real monotheism is an abstraction of learned minds. It does not exist in historical reality. In the South polytheism: genealogically

---

38 Arnold Böcklin (1827–1901) was a Swiss symbolist artist. — *Transl.*

Madonna, cosmologically gods of heaven. But even the pantheistic North does not tolerate a monotheistic conception. Protestantism has retained not *one* God, but *two*: God and devil. It is Ormuzd and Ahriman, Yang and Yin, necessary opposition of the polar powers. one cannot refrain from one. And when in Protestantism the devil dwindled as a power, God also dwindled to a word, a concept. They had reality only one through the other. God [and] the devil: [*the*] good — [*the*] evil — [the] positive, [the] negative [are] powers that assist the individual in the struggle — helping, hindering.

79

The Nordic need for survival is tradition, reputation, legend. Names and deeds live on in memory, in monuments, in buildings, works — and in succession from father to son — for the son is the bearer of the reputation of the ancestors — that is Nordic nobility as an idea. Ancestor worship is only one sign of it. The *imagines*[39] in Rome. Ancestral table in China. Nordic sense of adoption, of possession as success of the ancestors, which the son is to multiply.

80

In the North [pantheism] has always really prevailed in spite of [Christianity]. We do not even notice it. The 'will of God' ([i.e.] destiny), 'heaven', God in heaven, 'God' in general, all meant abstractly. In contrast to the 'Madonna of Altötting[40]' or the Bambino[41], Crucifixus, Joseph. Theism means the idea of incarnate beings, 'gods', not the thinking of abstract 'powers'. What has neither arms nor legs [and] no face, what is neither naked nor clothed, is not a 'person'. But

---

39 The *imagines* were Roman death masks. — *Transl.*

40 The Shrine of Our Lady of Altötting in Bavaria is the oldest Marian shrine in Germany and one of the most important pilgrimage sites in Europe. — *Transl.*

41 The Bambino Gesu of Arenzano (Child Jesus of Arenzano) in Genoa is a Catholic devotional image depicting the Child Jesus. — *Transl.*

'gods' are embodied forces of nature, powers — bodies (only as a result souls, spirits with human-like reasons for effects: wrath, goodness).

81

Nordic soul: In Japan the ancestor cult is Chinese, i.e. Nordic import (Chantepie I, p. 296). The Indian religion hardly knows it. Hence the faith originally has no nature gods of high rank. Man is god enough for himself. The Germanic religion [is] usually wrongly judged, because we know it from the noble view of the professional warriors. But after all, the tribes lived from hunting, agriculture and animal husbandry, so they had above all religious views that related to whether we know them or not. If you divide the 'natural' world [into] *earth* (on, in the earth), the *subterranean* ('underworld' is a special idea) and the *celestial* (clouds, peaks, sky), the earth was the most important. China (Chantepie, 196): deity of the earth: hypaethral[42] opening in the cult room, hole in the floor. Sanctity of the door and the hearth (Janus, Vesta). This must have existed among the Teutons. Yang and Yin (p. 197). Pantheism: the powers. Whether one counts them — 1,3, many — or not, [whether one] thinks of them humanly as gods, is a secondary matter. (p. 199: Poseidon and Demeter also in China.)

82

Nordic are the reshaped infinite powers. The idea of a corporeal-human-like God with a humanly one-sided soul and human thinking is a narrowing of the idea. But if, in the North, the divine person is Father and Son, [in] the West, Mother and Child. Therefore [there is] no figure painting in the north, but ornament, landscape. Dissolved animal ornament against Egypt (Ireland — China). Tendency towards body design Hamitic (Altamira, Bohuslän, Egypt) against pure ornament (Nordic Neolithic). Cave drawing — Egyptian reliefs. Atlantean

---

42 'Having no roof in the centre'. — *Transl.*

world-feeling [is] southern-bodily. Nordic-spatial-spiritual: meaning, not image.

83

The Atlantis [worships the] highest female deity. According to Tacitus (Germ. 45), the Aesirians on the Amber Coast found worship of the mother of the gods and a language similar to Britannic. There the stone circles of Odry (them!). In Asia Minor, too, the Magna Mater came from Libya, as did Hera from Argos.

84

Nordic [is] the will to power over the future. By permanent works, laws. Effect of personality. Monument, legend, memory. Sons and grandsons. Ancestor worship [is] Nordic conception. From this, as a mere abstraction of urban thought, the 'immortality of the soul' has developed, not an experience (like the haunting of the just dead), but a concept. Something quite different is the Atlantean belief in the 'life in the hereafter' (Osiris). Catholics and Protestants, [that is] Atlantis and Nordic. Grave dwelling and grave monument.

85

The tomb of the nobles [is] the centre of tribal life. Grave cult as a summarising act. The 'gods' [are] somehow related to it. Grave temple, cult of the deified noble ancestors. Dome construction, menhir, dolmen, cromlech[43], Etruscan chamber.

86

The survival of the dead, elsewhere annoying, feared as haunting, reappearance, ghost, perceived as annoying, is here [in the South] elevated to a value. It is the actual focus of the beautiful life. Whereas in the conception of Hei and Hades there is the unpleasant feeling that it is now over, here the opposite is emphasised. 'Immortality', an abstraction of Nordic thought, appears as eternal rest, memory in saga

____

43   A cromlech is a circle of monoliths enclosing a mound. — *Transl.*

and song. It is not life that is eternal, but what one has done in it. And the sons are there to preserve the memory of the ancestor, not to feed him.

87

Here and only here has the entire world-view, dull contemplation of life, of the world, from mythical foreboding to the highest theology, gathered around the riddle of birth and death. Only here has the idea of 'life after death' become a dominant force in reality. In the North, dead ancestors are honoured through memorial customs and the cult of remembrance, but it never occurred to anyone to devote their lives to preparing for life after death. In world history, this only happened here, in the area of the great funerary constructions from Ireland [and] Brittany to Spain, Egypt and Palestine — precisely the area of Catholic doctrine. Here, it is not the judgement of the dead, but life afterwards, in paradise and hell, that is the decisive thing, 'eternal' life. These thoughts are already clearly perceptible in the theology of the Old Kingdom. Here one feeds the dead.

88

'Immortality of the soul' is an inconceivable abstraction. In reality one has need of ideas, not concepts; one sees oneself physically similar in the hereafter, recognises oneself again, 'new body and new soul'. But in the North [the] ideal of the noble and the common man is different. The first: 'Possessions die, clans die ...', so in order: Possession — Blood — Glory. [The noble mind]: to do a deed that is spoken of even in later times. The common mind [clings to] domestic animal [and] cattle. But property is important. It is what gives a man his value. The propertyless man — something speaks against him: the lack of earning power, of happiness.

89

The idea of God is either plastic or not, concrete or abstract. There it demands an image, here a symbol. [The] North [knows] weaving powers, not concrete figures. Thou shalt not make thyself an image. These are the northern tribes. The West always did: ancient Christian art. In Hellas only very late. The 'Apollos' are not gods, but men. So here the southern landscape worked.

Personal god versus concept of god. Person — i.e. gender, age, character.

90

Pantheism: No personal gods. The Aeolian rhapsodes[44] already incorporated the ideas of the landscape (cf. *Heliand*[45], Krist), because the heroic sagas come from non-Greeks. Edda only Viking Age. Christianity and ancient paganism since the migration of peoples. Latin poetry model.

Nonsense to jabber of the sun-god of the Teutons [and] Teutonic astronomers. Likewise [of] Chinese primeval astronomers. There are people who consider the possession of astronomical knowledge a characteristic of culture — like dinner jackets and lipstick — and therefore attribute it to all peoples they wish to compliment. So of course the Germanic peoples had 'astronomers'. How they are supposed to have done it, you do not ask. As people of primitive outdoor life, they naturally knew the duration of winter and summer [and the] revolution of the moon, as a marker, without thinking about it. Astronomy is applied mathematics and nothing else, i.e. priestly secret science.

91

For Westerners [there is] life on this side and life on the other side. Gods, devils and ghosts are beyond. For the Northerners [there are] I and Thou in *one* world. All — animal, plant, thing — have soul, dark perhaps and menacing, but not 'other'. So are Celtic, peasant, Chinese ghost stories, the Homeric gods, the Roman numina, Indian, Persian,

---

44 A rhapsode was a person in ancient Greece who recited epic poems. — *Transl.*

45 The *Heliand* ('Saviour') is an early medieval Old Saxon epic poem. It is about the life of Jesus. — *Transl.*

Andersen's fairy tales. Companionship with animals. Everything is 'divine', θεός, powerful. *Religio* [and] attachment.

The most natural thing [are] ghosts. Grimm; *tat tvam* asi[46]. Man is like, not opposed to, these powers. Even tools and works (paintings, buildings, deeds, thoughts, works, names) of men have a soul in them that works. Therefore, property here is a metaphysical relationship. These things contain my soul. The sword, the soul of the sword, is a part of my own power. Only through gift does my soul withdraw to make room for the others. The thing stolen is hostile to the thief.

The soul of the field and that of the farmer are one. Roman: to ask the numina to leave the land. To move the boundary stones [means]: to offend the power. Lares. Janus, Vesta, property gods. Every deed has become a numina that perpetuates.

92

Atlantean [is] '*matriarchy*'. In addition, the 'Dionysian' of the Greek lower class: the woman moves into the cult. The North knows only male cults. In France, the woman is the mistress of the household, the man servant, accessory. The woman chooses the lover, already with the troubadours of the 11th century. So [there is] an opposition between marriage (socio-economic form of the home) and love. According to [the] troubadours and Stendhal, 'love' for one's wife is ridiculous.

93

Matriarchy: In the North, perpetuity (not of the soul, but of the blood, psychically it is glory) is determined by the succession of sons and grandsons. The woman is the property of the man for this purpose. The son is worth more than the daughter. The conjugal fidelity of the wife alone is a side of true blood. Monogamy means [having] an equal wife belonging to him alone. The purpose of monogamy is

---

46 Sanskrit: 'you are that', meaning that the individual is partly or completely identical with the Absolute. — *Transl.*

to secure the paternal blood and property. In the South, life is considered an existing fact, a casual enjoyment, as a dog in the sun is the centre of thought. Life is given by the woman, the mother. He who is father to it comes second. The man enjoys the woman. Pride in his blood is senseless. Man is free from the silent bondage of the 'family' to which the pedantic North man easily falls. The family is the mother with the children, not the man with the sons. One should not use the harem as argument. This kind of polygamy is an expression of nobility and wealth among all races and all times. Germanic, Persian, Indian, Chinese. This does not contradict monogamy at all.

94

The southern high cultures of Egypt and Babylon, which abstracted dogmas from the religiosity and world-feeling of Atlantis and Kash, theoretically conceived the tropical sun, which had to be felt as the world-dominating elemental power, in very different senses: as life-giving — genealogically — or as astronomically dominating the heavens. In the north they are other forces: thunderstorm, rain, storm, frost. Soul of the landscape.

95

For the Uranian religion, which knows no 'gods', only 'powers', without personal ideas, the name Zeus is characteristic (Wilamowitz 225).

Indo-European grammar! Personal gods can only be imagined in plural. Monotheism is an abstraction, again impersonal: world-soul, deism, pantheism. The Jews imagined Yahweh not as the only God, but as theirs, the best, most powerful God.

96

Idea of suicide: Since when? In the Kash-Atlantic [area it is] very rare, in the Pacific Ocean (Japan, Bali, Malaya) often. In the Occident, everyone who can think has had the thought, whether they suppressed it, defeated it, despised it, nursed it, succumbed to it. Types of suicide: adventure, war, daring.

97

Atlantis: The Catholic Church corresponds to rationalist-scholastic philosophy. Descartes, Voltaire. Lutheranism: the heroic way of forging one's own destiny, not using redemption but perhaps a helper. No saints, because the individual has to fight for himself: Edda like Luther. The priest is superfluous. He is only described as a connoisseur of spells in the sagas of Iceland, among the Nordic peasants, where he understands the magic of baptism and consecration (consecration of young men). The Puritans did away with this altogether.

Thomas Aquinas and Loyola[47] [are] Atlantic. Luther wanted to free himself from this scholasticism through it — he only half succeeded. He remained a theologian. But he completely liberated the peasants, the people, inwardly.

98

Atlantis: In the funerary temple (cathedral, Islam) the architecture of the gate is of outstanding symbolism (the 'way' is life, Egypt, Occident). Pathos of the 3rd dimension. Hence the Egyptian pylon. The hundred-gated Thebes — this refers to the countless temple gates. Tomb of Atreus, Lion's Gate. Front of the French cathedrals: the portal between two menhir towers [is] the decisive thing. Therefore 'Pillars of Hercules', a sanctuary in Tunis. Temple of Janus.

99

Everything Klages says about the Secret Consecrations belongs to the area from Etruria to the Euphrates, at least in this form, and it finds its final expression in the early Arabic period with its magical mysteries. The Lord's Supper, as a rite of Christianity that has become

---

47 Ignatius of Loyola (1491–1556) was one of the founders of the religious order of the Society of Jesuits. — *Transl.*

rigid, has preserved the act, but the inner form of the rapture has become a completely different, spiritual one. Consequently, this is part of the *Paideuma* of Kashitic culture. It is the idea that through the symbolic food one takes in the god. Traces of this go to Mexico!

100

Nordic religion: The Nordic man has no gods, but infinite demons and indeterminate figures — ancient Rome, for example, has a lot of them. As he develops the 'custom' strongly, all these spells, incantations, in the strictest manner (old German folk customs at death, birth, etc.), so the Roman religion seems very formal, because the customs are all official and the actual style-sayings represent the Roman religion, while in the North abstract Protestantism represents the 'religion' and the customs are almost all considered superstition. In the South, the gods are the centre of religion. All the motifs of superstition, folk tales and animal legends merge into mythology, so that the customs do not stand out on their own, but disappear into a larger whole.

101

The feminine in the cultures: As completely unconscious as this may be, a deep sense of the metaphysical difference between the masculine and the feminine, far beyond human relations, is everywhere, and in it is symbolically reflected the way we see and feel the world.

'Matriarchy' is a superficial conception. The Atlantean idea of the world sees in the feminine the metaphysical centre of gravity of the whole. There is something feminine about everything, including kingship. The mothers are important. In Kash indifference: two mathematical halves of the world being. In the north, shivers of mystery in the feminine: part prey, part goddess. *Minne*[48]. 'Lady'. In every Nordic

---

48 Middle High German: 'passionate love and honouring of another person'. — *Transl.*

man lies a child hidden: the maternal beloved. The Atlantean sibling marriage [is] an extreme expression of pure generation.

102

Atlantis: The female cult of the troubadours—at most aped in Germany and England, but significant in Saracen Spain, is also Atlantean?

103

Atlantis — Matriarchy: 'Matriarchy' is Atlantean, an expression of the genealogical feeling that sanctifies the connection between the womb and the child: not a 'right' (*jus*), but an idea that is already only echoed in the Old Testament. The earth (*chthon*) [is the] *mater*[49]. Here, and not in Kash, [begins] the sexualisation of the cosmos. In Kash [there is] only 'person and thing'. The gods are human personifications of things, but not mother and child, no genealogy(?). Heliopolis[50]: genealogy of Isis [and of] Horus. How is it that heaven is formed as a woman (in what time)? This is a reversal of the sexes.

I want to speak here less of 'law' than of folk 'custom'. It is for the most part quite unconscious order, the conscious shaping of which varies greatly and already signifies decay. A high culture like the Egyptian one shows only traces. Otherwise [it is] alive as a peasant custom in [the] b-culture, village, not urban.

104

Decisive at the time 4000–3000. The monumental construction of the megalithic culture is in Egypt (and from there [on] the Mediterranean in general, Etruria, Lydia) tomb construction, in Babylon (and Egypt, younger, 4th Dynasty) cult construction. In Babylon the sacral tomb is missing!

---

49 Latin: 'mother'. — *Transl.*

50 Heliopolis is the Greek name of an ancient Egyptian city, which was the centre of worship of the sun god Re. — *Transl.*

So the idea of honouring the great dead is victorious in Egypt, but in Sumer the Kash culture has triumphed, the former telluric[51], the latter chthonic. That is why the grave in Kash is without any meaning: one lives and begets (lingam[52]), but forgets the dead, genuine tropical fullness of life and satiety; *carpe diem*[53]. In contrast, the northern megalithic culture became for the first time an idea of duration, of afterlife.

So Sumer is younger than the arrival of the megalithic people. It develops the material of monumental construction, quite external, without depth, for cosmological purposes, whereas in Egypt it has depth. From here, only since 1200 has the ancient masterly spirit used the found forms for its idea of the 'family tomb' in the style of paternal law.

105

Kash and Atlantis have in common the formation from the fear of the world. It is the age of the gods, whether concrete (ancestors) or abstract (cosmos). Heroism uses world-longing and world-love for this. Prostration ceases, the head is raised: I — and you!

106

The god symbolism of Atlantis shows the tendency towards the animal (expression of sexual procreative power or physical strength). Deep meaning of the Atlantean meat-eating: appropriation of the superior powers of the animal (bull). Alongside fertility idols (female statuettes with sexual characteristics). The Kashitic gods are human-like or abstract celestial powers (stars). Atlantis [knows] the gods' fear of the world's demonicity: rage, cruelty, will to kill everywhere. Kash [is] mild, more comfortable: 'ruling' of the numina, celestial laws.

---

51 Related to the Earth. — *Transl.*

52 A phallic object as a symbol of Shiva in Hinduism. — *Transl.*

53 Latin: 'Seize the day'. — *Transl.*

107

The genealogical gaze seeks everywhere to place the primal relations of man and woman, mother and child, in the grounds of being: wherever languages of this style were spoken, they gave things a gender: masculine and feminine. In cosmological language they divided them into persons and things. And even the image of the gods succumbs to these styles: Atlantean gods are couples, fathers, sons, mothers. Kashitic ones are stars. In Egyptian and Sumerian-Akkadian mythology, both styles weave together; in the underclass of Hellenic culture, the family destinies of Olympus are important. In Israel, God has a son.

108

Bull play: Minoan, in Atlantis according to Plato: catching the sacred bull with a net, Atlantean cultic meaning. So also ancient Spanish: how old are the bullfights? The Apis bull[54] in Egypt. The bull bones at Knossos[55].

109

Dionysus: The orgiastic cult belongs to the Turanian-Linear Pottery circle. Hence in Thrace, Asia Minor, in Hellas, Boeotia. The name [Dionysus] must therefore be 'Indo-European' as well as that of his mother Semele, [that is probably] Semlya [the earth]. So also in China. So he is 'pre-Hellenic' and limited to a few areas of the Aegean. Dionysus, in it is Ziu. The 'wild hunter' Zagreus belongs to it, a god in his own right, who was equated with Dionysus only later. The cult originally included orgies in the forests — absolutely Nordic. Only later, Hellenically transformed, did it come to Ionia, the islands, Attica.

---

54 The Apis bull was one of the most important animal deities in ancient Egypt. — *Transl.*

55 Knossos was the capital of Minoan Crete. — *Transl.*

110

The ethical tendency of Zarathustra, quite foreign to the Indo-Nordic, comes from Kash: southern Persia to Indus was 'primeval Elam'. The whole 'Persian' culture except the political form was the heir of Elam.

111

Atlantis: Here belongs the idea of the judgement of the dead, of hell and bliss — Egypt, Catholicism, Dante. Cruel lust to think of the torment of others. The North, on the other hand, has the idea of the end of the world in a grandiose form, world conflagration, the death of the gods. Just as he wanted his life to be 'short but glorious'. The burning of the dead instead of their mummies and 'immortal' souls.

So the ideas of hell in Zoroastrianism come from Semitic fantasy. Zarathustra does not yet know anything about it. In the Occident, this increases to great world humour. Satire: watching the end with laughter. Bullfights, gladiators, Auto-da-fé — Atlantis. The gladiators were heroes like the bullfighters of 1800. Only the people make a spectacle of it.

112

Atlantean thinking revolves around birth and death — mother goddess, tomb-building. What [comes] next? What [was] before? So judgement of the dead, hell, paradise, the Catholic ideas. This includes Tartarus and Elysium, Valhalla (Christian influenced). The Greeks did not know what to do with Tartarus and Elysium. So that is rapidly disappearing. Likewise the 'life after death' and the colourless 'immortality' of the 18th century, just as 'Hades' [is] a mere concept. To the Nordic man (Achilles, Siegfried) the life before death, the struggle with fate alone is important. Luther, Calvin. Only the high cultures ask the question: What is the point of all this? The Egyptian, ancient, Occidental answer.

113

Heroism: Here the *prima causa* of the universe is not felt to be the strongest god as in Kash, but impersonal fate. The hero feels himself to be the supreme personality. And likewise, the hero does not 'build' graves and houses — that is what slaves do — but a life course, a powerful dominion. The desire to build empires, sciences, forms, enterprises is heroic, whereas state and cult in Atlantis and Kash are creations of fear!

114

It has also taken its revenge that professional scholarship has sought to interpret the whole meaning of events from one form of expression. But there is no single one that always and everywhere has the same weight. There are graves everywhere, but it depends on the inner form of a culture, its attitude to the world and to life, whether the grave is, according to its design, a high bearer of spiritual expression or merely a factual necessity. Every c-culture has its choice of means of expression. Not only the use, but above all the selection ensures the overview of the distribution. The Atlantean culture is the burial culture par excellence.

115

The tholos tombs include the idea of a realm of the dead (Hesperid apples, Kerberos, Nekyia[56], Hades, Köre). Cf. the mixture of Celtic (Parsifal, Tristan, Lohengrin) and Germanic legends.

116

It does not matter very much what is found in the graves as a burial object, much less the difference between burial and cremation — as this is treated by the prehistorians. Not only did humans 'bury' before any real culture, but animals did too: bees and ants. They libidinously

---

56 According to Greek myth, Nekyia is the practice of entering the underworld to gain information about the future. — *Transl.*

dispose of corpses in their dwelling place, encapsulate them, bury them, carry them off. Burial has only had a deep meaning since the 5ᵗʰ millennium, since people have been able to speak and think. Then they became aware of the meaning of death and thus of life; thus the way in which the dead are treated takes on the significance of a great symbol. This immediately separates the three great early cultures: South, West, North.

117

Mummy, embalming — preserving the body as long as possible — according to the idea of 'eternity'. To burn — to destroy as completely as possible. For the spirit remained — in name, deeds, memorial, legend; the blood remained in the sons and grandsons. Soul (transmigration). These are the two basic ideas. Highlight the burial as much as possible — menhir, temple — or hide it, inaccessible by heaping it up: so that no one dishonours or robs the dead.

V. EGYPT AND BABYLON

THE ANCIENT SOUTHERN CULTURES

1

DESERT TRIBES ('Semites') are not Nordic expansive, but only striving for living space. Nothing of world power and empire despite all the big words. Egyptian-Babylonian imperialism is still very modest.

2

The hope of 'walking in peace on the beautiful paths of the Western Empire' after death emerges on the threshold of the early period, 4th dyn. In the centuries before 2000, the Book of the Dead with the idea of moral judgement and solar monotheism emerges. EMS 342 ff.

3

At first [the] 'language for the eye' applied instead of [for] the ear. Images, signs whose meaning is known to those who see them. 'Marks' (waymarks, personal marks). But then the series of lines and little pictures no longer become signs for facts, but for words that mean facts. So one can 'read' sentences. Finally, the grammatical element is also clearly drawn: syllables, suffixes etc. The reader, originally a connoisseur of the meaning of signs, now becomes a connoisseur of the reading of signs. One does not understand the meaning of the signs, but the wording.

Egypt: funerary writing, carved in stone, painted on papyrus. Monumental. Babylon: business writing, carved in clay. Cursive.

4

The ancient West in the form of the Kafti Empire [has] penetrated farthest to the East, filling [the] East Mediterranean as a maritime power. [The] Sea Peoples [are] already a subsiding. The North Eurasian inland powers clash here with the West: consequence Antiquity. The old southern culture (highest imprint Babylon, like Egypt originated through the crossing of south and west) in India and China is overlaid by the north. The old southern culture [is] priestly, Brahmanical, still as Buddhism begetting the ruling class of Southeast Asia. [The] Arab culture [is] central, most mixed, [the] North dominant, plus Egyptian and Babylonian civilisation remains.

5

It is not the Egyptian-Babylonian bull that is sacred, but the wild animal in the jungle is a demonic being that is shunned (*sacer*[1]), summoned, destroyed. One 'worships' it in the sense of frightening respect, a formidable enemy. Fear, not love. The evil animal. In Knossos, wild bulls.

6

Egyptian-Babylonian architecture [is] only palace tomb and palace temple. One 'lives' in the open. In the south, the noble house arises from the courtyard, around which lie sleeping, ceremonial and economic rooms. In Egypt ('Way') it develops into columned halls, columned courtyards. In Babylon the gate building — the important thing is the 'entrance' to the god, ruler, life. Courtyards in which the

---

1 Latin: 'sacred'. — *Transl.*

ziggurat is located. The 'palace' is a gate building with rooms behind it. Hence broad building instead of the Egyptian long house (*Klio* 22, 1 ff.). In the case of the farmhouse: in Babylon courtyard wall, in it huts (private law), [in] Egypt courtyard house (state law). The Babylonian priests live in the temple precincts, [the] Egyptian nobility and [the] priests in their own complexes. Egypt: no acropolis, no wall, free-growing; Babylon: palace, city wall, concentrated.

7

The progressive drying up of the Sahara has put pressure on the originally dense population. The rivers become wadis[2], the steppes sand seas. The tribes migrate — to the south (Sudan), south-east (East Africa, South Africa), Egypt, Spain (El Argar), Italy, Aegean. Navigation, known since the 5th millennium, becomes a means of conquest. Pressure on north-western Europe: Bell Beaker.

8

Landscape: Diluvium — desertification, partly caused by humans, forest fires. The great belt Sahara — Arabia/Inner Asia. Originally the most densely populated areas, then emigration from there to all sides, in all forms. Sahara, progressing from east to west. Pressure on Spain, Egypt, Mesopotamia. Pressure from Inner Asia on India, China, Mesopotamia, Europe. Transition from sedentary agriculture to cattle nomads, not vice versa. Hamites, Indo-Europeans — the two language groups that experienced expansion through desertification. Psychologically, the fixed location ('home', possession) is the fundamental thing. The cattle-herding nomads were only driven by hardship.

---

2   A wadi is a river bed or a valley which only carries water after a long period of rain. — *Transl.*

9

Pressure of the desert belt since the end of the 4th millennium. Pressure directions develop thereafter. Sahara to Western Europe (Islam), South Africa, Palestine, Arabia (Akkadians, Islam). Arabia to the north: Akkad, Israel etc. Arabian sea to East Asia. Gobi to east: China; west: Russia, Europe; south: India.

10

In Egypt ancient bulls (power, fertility, roar). In Heliopolis the sun becomes a numen. Later both views are brought together. Several deities became sun and bull gods, Nut the sky goddess became a cow. Originally, the animal form for gods [appears] earlier than the human form. In Babylon: *Reallexikon* 12,438 ff. Ego: Did the bull with the bow come to Babylon through the Akkadians? Only attested since the 2nd millennium!

11

The mother of the gods (often with the son) [is] anciently Western. [She came] to Lydia and Syria from Africa via Crete and Kypros (tholos tombs), oldest layer there. Later — younger stratum — provided with a husband — that is Asian — southern. Hera, Leto, Leda, Baalath [of] Pessinus, the 'great mother', transformation of the Isis type, Madonna. In western Asia Minor and Syria, many layers of religion lie one on top of the other, [they are] always reshaped.

12

Kash, Babylon: The fact that two languages occur in the documents — of life and its language we know nothing — has led to the distinction of 'Sumerian' and 'Semite' as the two formative folk-types, of which Sumerian was considered the 'older' because the [Sumerian] documents are in part older. In fact, many more languages (and dialects!) must have been spoken, of which we know or suspect Elamite and traces of Northern Mesopotamian. But then the question of the

4th millennium remains open: What was there before and beside the 'Sumerian' element? Languages of an inner form related to the type of Sumerian go as far as Etruria and the Caucasus. But we know nothing of Turkestan, India or East Africa from this period. The only certainty is that in the 4th millennium the streams of Kash and Atlantis met here and both brought numerous languages with them.

13

The ancient way of life is: grow up, feed, love, have children, die. The sparrow like the farmer. The awakening makes 'life' lie there in the spiritual light: What is it? What is it for? The great question with which the suffering of the soul begins.

Culture is the attempt to give an answer. All those who know this question participate in culture. Those who create culture are those who ask [the question] more deeply than the earlier ones. All other people are material of culture, raw material. In the younger Stone Age, the question is asked: Where? In what version? The heroes of the 2nd millennium B.C. had the new answer: to live large. Egyptians and Babylonians did not know that!

14

Egypt, Babylon: The relationship to God is fear of his wrath.

Sacrificial thought: Where does animal sacrifice come from and what does it mean? Kash or dolmen? Burnt offering in Nippur[3]? Blood sacrifice. It is rams and bulls — so from the region of livestock and its cause! The Babylonian bloody sacrifice idea entered the ancient world, it is also Israelite, Carthaginian, Etruscan.

15

'People': It is wrong to see in Egypt one people, in Babylon many. It is only in Egypt where the total state was the rule, in Babylon the

---

3   Nippur was an ancient Sumerian city situated in modern-day Iraq. It was a sacred city as the temple of Enlil, the main god of the Sumerian-Akkadian pantheon, was located there. — *Transl.*

exception, as a result of the conception of state law and private law. In reality there were tribes and languages here as well as there, but we only know the written languages.

16

Egypt, Atlantis: The idea of state law made Egypt the best administrative state in history, but incapable of expansion. From this idea, neither an incorporation of the Near East, where it was only brought to control, not to organise, nor the idea of naval rule over Punt or Crete could develop.

17

Kash, Atlantis: Babylonian private law. [The] state [is] meant to be the arbiter. The individual [is] more important than the whole. Hence private initiatives in the economy, competition, hence Babylonian expansion of trade everywhere, with roads, coins, technology, language, calendar and commercial law, custom, usage. Egyptian state centralism, so not beyond the border of the country. Chauvinism for the border instead of private competition.

18

Both cultures [are] in the middle of the high time of taboo. Therefore [here is] the high school of taboo which permeates the whole state (priest-king), [the] society (nobility — taboo). Sowing and breeding are phallic symbols. In Egypt, agriculture is absent.

In the 4th millennium [lives] the magical hero, Gilgamesh, [he seeks] not strife but wonderful experiences. Not until 2000 the northern heroes defy fate. Hence: 3000 the southern nobility, magical, prerogative as a result of [the] stronger taboo, 1500 [the] northern nobility, warlike, as a result of the stronger view of life. This is the step from actual to emphasised self-awareness, to private individualism and defiance of the gods — in the *Iliad* one laughs at [the gods], feels them to be one's equals. The real Sumerians [have] a race strong in spirit: they create the aspect: man is equal to God and can become

God. Gilgamesh: a summit of great taboo thinking. [Is this] perhaps Nordic after all? Having [come] here with the Semitic-Hamitic (6000) or primeval Libyan (4000) stream? Megalithic buildings? In Eridu[4]?

The Akkadians and a corresponding Egyptian lower class (not identical with the bearers of the proto-Semitic!) [are] in contrast soft, whimpering, [have] penitential psalms, dog humility before God, [are] incidentally unseaworthy. Both (Egypt, Babylon) [are] cultures, mixed from these elements: the dog-like and the lion-like, the former remains (late Egyptian world-view in the [imperial] time, primeval Israel). In both [is] the moon cult older. The number 60 is ancient. From the north [comes the symbolism of] 'above and below', from the south [that of] the four cardinal points? Then the six dimensions of man, who feels [connected] to all sides? Perfect tranquillity in space: east-west-south-north-zenith — nadir (heaven — underworld). The mother goddess [is] primeval Sumerian. A northern masculine interpretation south of feminine shivers: thus an exclusive spiritual (masculine) system emerges: four corners of the world, triad of gods much older the polar pairs of gods.

19

Sumerians — '*Caucasian*': I would like to venture a guess here. As I always emphasise, affinity of form in languages is not proof of an 'original language' from which they emerged, but of a kindred spirit of an extended population, i.e. a c-culture, which found an analogous expression grammatically. If today 'agglutive' languages of Caucasian type (to mention the unfortunate word) are spread from the Basques to Ancient Asia Minor to the Near East, we should first make a chronological grouping. We know Sumerian, Elamite from the 3rd, Mitanni from the 2nd, Lycian [from the] 1st millennium B.C., Basque and Caucasian from the 2nd millennium A.D.! That is to say, of the three scriptually preserved of these highly archaic ways of speaking

---

4 Eridu was the oldest Sumerian city, situated in modern-day southern Iraq. — *Transl.*

(Egyptian, Sumerian, Akkadian), one happens to be of this type, and its location is thus important: the younger, the more northerly, the more southerly, the earlier extinct. Thus the direction of movement of this cultural stream is given: from Kash to the northwest deep into Europe and Central Asia. Furthermore, since the dolmen culture cuts across (with Semitic language), the latter is older. Since Sumerian still shows the two-part counting system, it is the primitive type of grammatical thought that has survived to us. The other languages of this kind must be completely decayed, interspersed, mixed, the more so the later they were spoken. If we look at what else was carried on in this direction apart from language, we come to cattle breeding, cult, metal casting.

20

Egypt [and] Babylon [have] extreme written languages. Thus, for the first time, the language in question becomes independent of speech and is based in its existence on a circle of readers. In addition to the vernacular, the 'colloquial language' of society in the cities and the written language of documents are the only language types of the c-cultures.

Up to now, far too little attention has been paid to the fact that the linguistic picture becomes completely wrong if one only concludes or can conclude from documents. From this it would follow that the 'French' and 'Germans' had driven the 'Latins' out of Western Europe around 800, that the 'French' had immigrated to England in 1066 and were later driven out, that until 1700 the Romans had ruled in Germany [then again] and then the French: the diplomatic language [was] Latin-Spanish-French.

If 'Sumerian' is the written language around 3000 and Akkadian next to it a little later, we know very little about the types of folk and colloquial language with it. Languages may have been spoken in Assur, Ur and Akkad which are not attested at all or only in personal names. Similarly, we do not know whether 'Egyptian' was also the vernacular of the whole area, which is unlikely and might be refuted by an examination of proper names.

21

The politics of the early period is urgent idea: in Egypt striving of the Pharaonic style, concentration, closure to the outside. There is no doubt that in Menes'[5] time the influence reached much further, north and south. Babylon vice versa, also no conscious expansion, but a radiation far and wide.

Late period: here begins the real diplomacy with problems and centuries of goals: for Egypt, a continued neglect of [the] West and North, unilateral goal Syria: because now Babylonian policy becomes palpable. The two cultures begin to wrestle.

Akkadian politics is thus more purposeful than Sumerian. In civilisation 'democracy' begins, the formless horde economy: 'Amorites', 'Hyksos[6]'—these are parties of metropolitan type. Not, as naive historians think, 'peoples'. Just as in antiquity the *orbis terrarum*[7] terrorises the peripheries, the old state system, so here: the periphery is more important than the centre: the political style at the beginning of the 'New Empire', Hammurabi[8]. The word ochlocracy can be applied to this.

22

Writing (Kash): Writing was not 'invented' if one understands by it that someone built up a system out of nothing. What has developed is no more a specific system than that of cuneiform writing, for example, but an idea, a principle, namely a sequence of images for the eye,

---

5   Menes was an ancient Egyptian pharaoh who ruled around 3000 B.C. — *Transl.*

6   The Hyksos was a group of foreign kings that ruled Egypt from 1648 to 1530 B.C. — *Transl.*

7   Latin: 'the orb of the world'. — *Transl.*

8   Hammurabi was king of Babylon from 1792 to 1750 B.C. He is best known for his law code which served as the model for others, including the Mosaic Law of the Bible. — *Transl.*

which gives the initiate and connoisseur of language the possibility of reading from it the same sentence that the writer could have spoken: the meaning of phonography. This is only possible in a large context of a whole world of related formations (construction, state) and presupposes the inclination towards the abstract. Consequently, the idea matured in Kash and, having matured, [wandered] from priesthood to priesthood, [from] temple to temple, [from] country to country, and was realised everywhere in its own way.

23

It is characteristic of religion that it develops a very material image of the sky: the gods of early times were 'raised up' and somehow presented 'in' the sky, in constellations, myths and so on. This is quite different from the sky-numbers of the northern cultures (Zeus), which are not images but concepts. Re and Marduk[9] are the sun, likewise Okeanos etc. are 'the' sea. But Zeus-Tien is 'the power from above'. That is why the southern cultures alone have built up concrete cosmogonic systems; the north is no longer creative there, but dissolves the borrowed images into ways of thinking. The soul bird also belongs to this concrete way of imagining.

24

In both religious worlds, the higher principle of society, as an idea, is from the megalithic culture, the lower (peasant, chthonic, related to Dravidian) from Kash. The former must be form-giving, the latter substance-giving (names, cults, localities). Solar monotheism and the astral system are on top. In the 'imperial age' the old comes through again. This explains the 'reversal' of heaven and earth in Upper Egypt.

25

Old Babylon: The Sargon legend contains little that is historical, especially in the younger texts. It is like Charlemagne in the heroic

---

9   Marduk was the main god of the Babylonian pantheon. — *Transl.*

saga. Its great trait is simply epic poetry. In such cases, well-known names of the legend are inserted: Dietrich of Bern, Arthur. Even the Hittite legend of Sargon's train is no more than the *Song of Roland*.

26

Scripture: The designation of concepts (names) by signs is already common in early Neolithic times: property marks 'designating' the owner, signs for certain things and actions. A kind of rebus writing is also possible: this is how the west-east stream of Semito-Hamitic dolmen people will have conceived of painting. Hence the apparent 'decay' of cave painting, i.e. the transition from copy painting to drawing. The Kashites will also have been so far along. But 'writing' as opposed to drawing emerges very quickly in Egypt and Babylonia around 3000, as an idea that is now organised, a system of priestly thought that is to fulfil a conscious task. And the system is finished as quickly as that of architecture, perhaps [in the course of] a hundred years. Written things are to be read (those signs are only to remind!). So signs remind, writing is read. Originally a quite exclusive secret possession. The economic texts of Fara, for example, are of course priestly signs. Did Egyptian writing also originate from a foreign language?

27

Egypt: The sense of self of this race — for that is what it had become in many generations with the Egyptian sun: brown, sinewy, fine-nerved, strong-boned — did not consist in being something, but in being the bodily vessel for something. The individual was, according to his rank, the seat of a divine principle, something alien, from above, raised him up, not his own blood, his strength, his courage. Neither physical strength nor bravery were virtues, but the fact of being the embodiment of Ra[10]. This gave colour and consecration to the individual's world-view: thus he saw his birth, his youth and old age, his death and — above all — his life after death.

---

10   Ra was the ancient Egyptian god of the sun. — *Transl.*

28

Egyptian civilisation: Here it happens for the first time that a nation not only disintegrates into a plurality of influenceless peasants and a ruling urban minority, but that in swollen cities a mass, a rabble arises as dregs, refuse of culture, spiritually devastated and dead, with the instinct of neglected domestic animals, greedy, mean, crude, hostile, envious, [against] everything that is inward, deeper and higher. Whoever promises them something, has them. He who incites them to renunciation has a retinue. And he who knows how to set himself up as their leader has a despotic power such as no single prince ever had. These mass leaders now existed for the first time.

29

Pre-dynastic Nubia: The Nubians [are] like the primeval Egyptians (i.e. the Upper Egyptians). Like them [they have] animal skins (Atlantean) for clothing, bow and arrow, the ostrich feather in their hair. Ancient (Atlantean) are falcon gods with the meaning of the sun. Hero worship is practised. The border between Egypt and Nubia (Cataract region) goes back to prehistoric times, i.e. here lies the border of the Kashitic lower class: the Egyptian has always despised the Nubian, as [the] Norman despises the Saxon. Otherwise the original culture is identical. Thus the Kashites reached the middle Nile through the Red Sea and its harbours.

30

Egypt: From early dynastic times onwards, buildings were made of regularly hewn blocks, instead of the natural unhewn blocks of the entire megalithic culture! A big step!

Masses of megalithic graves in Palestine, Syria: the easternmost main area of the Atlantean culture! As in Egypt, development from crude to hewn block.

31

The Old-Kashite-Sumerian world-thought: [To have worked it out is] merit of Jeremias! Like this: great cosmic-conceptual antithetics. The world is the materialisation of the gods. Night-light, winter-spring, misfortune-happiness [alternate] in a cycle; thus identity of the basic elements in the lot of man, nature, heaven. Heaven and earth [are in] correspondence to each other. What is above is [also] below, according to structure and events. All individual phenomena mirror each other and the whole. Man, who takes himself very seriously, is microcosm, the world is *macro-anthropos*. World domination of the gods, who fight for domination in world ages, who themselves embody individual elementary cosmic phenomena. In ancient Sumer, Enlil of Nippur reigns. In 2000, in the world city of Babylon, [the] rationalist Marduk is made lord. Heaven is the throne or robe of the God-King.

Gilgamesh is [two-thirds] God, [one-third] man, the 'great man'. The king, according to the oldest ideograms, is 'the great man', that is, partly a god. Man is — the great fear and lament! — mortal, but at least on earth the most important and strongest, the lord of plants and animals: idea of 'world domination' older than national thought. The Egyptian idea (grave, ancestors) is political-social, the Kashite idea is religious-social: one state — one mission. Hammurabi says at the beginning of his Code that he received his divine mission to rule the world in order to bring justice to reign, to destroy evil and to protect the weak from the strong; thus something quite abstract.

32

4th millennium: Here, around 3500, an enormous vortex of peoples must have filled the area from Libya to Iran, comparable to the Hun period in Eurasia, at the northern edge of the ancient civilisations, and the vortex around 600 in the Near East, where Lydians, Persians, Medes, Chaldeans met. This is difficult to deduce. But one wave of tribes must have reached the Delta from Kash in the upper Nile, another as far as Sardis and many further, to the Caspian Sea.

Atlantic waves across the Sahara to Kordofan, Somali, Bushman, to Sardinia, Crete, Ionia, to Middle Egypt, to South Arabia and from there to Akkad.

And just now the plant cover, which overgrew the endless area from Sudan to Gobi as a result of Quaternary pluvials, begins to thin: the forest and swamp become steppe and river, desert and wadi, so that a slow moving away of the tribes begins. And a little later, agriculture in Egypt and Babylonia, which had developed naturally when there was no desert, is in danger. And only then did artificial irrigation, the fight against desertification, come into being. It makes no sense to believe that people would have settled here in order to turn desert into arable land with the help of a quickly invented canalisation system.

33

Kash and Atlantis: The power of abstraction of Kash meant that its forms could be easily learned and transferred, whereas the rhythmic aspect of Atlantis could be imitated but not relived. Therefore, Babylonian culture became the great preparator of everything: cosmology, trade, business, law, calendar, astronomy. All Eurasian lines of communication are under the spell of these 'achievements'. Egypt is the high school of state administration, Babylon of private law. Babylon is the great arithmetician (business, measure, weight, rules of procedure, lunar eclipse, planetary orbit, temple levies): construction, number, measure. Here mathematical number has been elaborated, as in Egypt chronological.

34

It is wrong to look for Sumer only in the south. Sumerian principalities, enclaves among tribes of the most diverse languages and 'nationalities', probably stretched along the Euphrates across the mouth of the Khabur[11] to the Mediterranean! Thither the Sumerian god Dagan, e.g. in the principality of Mari (mouth of the Khabur). West of it Jarmuti (Syria between Euphrates and Amanus with Antioch!). But the names of the ancient Mari kings are partly Old Akkadian, partly 'Eastern Canaanite'. So the Sumerians abandoned their language.

Are the 'Phoenician' elements around 3000 Sumerian? All these names have shifted 3000–2000 and changed their meaning: tribal names become land names etc.

35

Babylonian and Egyptian civilisation: The ideas work only in breadth. Politically, it is irrelevant who is ruling, whether Darius, Alexander, Nebuchadnezzar, Hammurabi: it remains a universal idea. The empire is not rationally constructed, neither by the Assyrians nor [by] Macedonians or Persians. The government respects as equally valid language, ethnicity, religion, and confines itself to the 'divine mission' as impartial arbiter. Egypt, however, displays the 'national idea', concentrated, rigid, without expansion.

36

Last, in the fellah stage, the vast fossil worlds of form of Atlantis and Kash on the Nile and Euphrates stand there, weathering but unchanging, the first great example of the petrification of forms that have become formality in conjunction with the emptiness of fellah life.

37

Egyptian-Babylonian art: The ornament is hardly there. One understands the characteristic of living bodies, in Egypt the expression of resting faces and bodies, in Babylon the significant movements, but both serve the construction. Such a poverty of ornamentation has penetrated further, into the pre-ancient Mediterranean world, [to]

---

11 The Khabur River is the longest tributary of the Euphrates. — *Transl.*

Crete, Italy, and it has thus persisted in ancient art, whose ornamentation is very modest. The upper class (geometric style) had it, but soon lost it.

When and where are the high points of strict ornament? What does single, row [and] infinite surface ornament mean? What the constancy of the general character or of the individual features? What richness and poverty, the decoration of ornamental or imitative elements?

38

The epic and the tragedy belong to heroism. Egypt and Babylon do not know such poetry. What is 'poetry' anyway? People confuse it with literary (writing) activity. With purposes — entertainment, instruction. There is no single 'poetry' at all, but many.

39

These amoeba cultures already have an intellectually leading upper class under which the metaphysical ancestry of crystallised b-cultures is weathering away. (Jeremias[12], *Allg. Rel.* 24 ff.) Here a stylised world system (taboo of space) takes the place of direct ancestry. Proto-Sumeric the sacred numbers decimal (finger counting), 6 (above, below, right, left, front, back), 7 of the lunar calculation: 28 = 4 x 7. Pleiades. To this fact clings the number speculation, which is astrological in disguise without being astronomical. Nordic is the moon = 3 x 9 nights. 12 perhaps the lunar number in the experienced year of the recurrence of all natural events.

40

3rd millennium: A mighty push. The Sahara becomes the great divider of peoples. 'Northern Edge'. Tuimah against Middle Egypt. Negroes against Punt and Kash. From Africa to Sardinia (nuraghi),

---

12 Alfred Jeremias (1864–1935) was a German orientalist and historian of religion. — *Transl.*

Balearic Islands. Siculeans. El Argar in Spain. Mauritanian centre? Oldest swords, dagger sticks, flat axes (El Argar).

Separation of Sudan from the Bantu languages at that time? These Kashitic! Negrification of Africa between the deserts? Superior tropical blood, uncreative, assimilating remnants of c-culture. Frobenius: Hamites [via] Ethiopians [as] substratum: [is this] Atlantis and Kash? Kash, on the other hand, is the substratum in India.

CALENDAR

41

The calendar cannot be older than writing. Not only that it presupposes records — that is a very external connection — but that it arises psychologically from the same need is decisive. Memory, which is prolonged by language for the individual until death, is to be established here 'for all time'. But for this very reason the meaning of the Egyptian and the Babylonian calendars is very different. The former is to transmit the memory of the ancestors to the grandchildren, the latter the secret of the universe to mankind in general. That is why the Egyptian calendar links the governments to the obvious appearance, the measure of the year of the Nile, in order to count them by it. The Babylonian calendar, however, takes the measure of the starry sky in order to first get to know the rhythm of the eons. The purpose there is concrete, here abstract, and for this very reason exact measurement is more necessary in Babylonia than on the Nile.

42

Calendar and chronology, astrology: The intellectual (spatial) order of the image of time.

Time is thus also experienced in depth by animals, much more through the cosmic rhythm of the blood than through the testimony of the senses: the change of the moon, the orbit of the sun, the celestial bodies shake the living rhythm, the periodicity of procreation, the feeling of strength, the alternation of waking and sleeping. This was 'known' long before thought. The life of the senses gave the sequence of summer and winter, day and night and the change of the moon, three basic facts of a visual image of the world without all causal judgements. The revival of the sense of numerical order, the seeing of mystical groups of numbers (3,7, north — south — east — west, left — right, etc.) created shaped connections, the number of days in the phases of the moon, the number of climatic changes, the sum of which is the 'year', the number of the moon arranged in the phases of the year, etc. The concepts of year, moon, day were each there for an infinitely long time before the idea of a possible mathematical order emerged. And since cult and myth cling to nature and its image, it was priestly reflection that first used the (mathematical) concepts of numbers to grasp chronological formations, to relate the changing world picture to numbers, without strict logic, without aversion to contradictions, only out of the feeling that something of the numen and its forces lay in these numbers.

It is wrong to assume a need for a 'calendar'. What was needed was known from direct experience of nature. It was rather magic, taboo, a banishment of demonic nature into the numerical order, which created the calendar. It was developed theoretically out of a purely religious-technical need and was therefore not developed logically at all, but adapted to the need. A 'pure' desire for knowledge was far from it. One only wanted to possess the mark of the coming events.

Calendrical thinking is connected with the discovery of the 'future', which the animal does not know. One did not want to order what had happened — that is impractical — but what had not yet happened, in order to have power over it. Thus, delving into the calendar picture of the course of nature is identical with star research — for since the stars exercise power, one must know their intention and methods. Astronomy is only a later aid to astrology.

The rhythmic experiences of the blood, which the spiritual man has long since lost, played a part in it. The first time-ordering experience is that of the 'time limit', a set duration. The measuring was instinctively done by the primeval experience of day, night, the course of shadows, the position of the sun, the phase of the moon, the seasons, the ebb and flow of the tide.

The moon is looked at, the sun is recognised — because it is not 'seen'. The moon is older than the month, the year (summer, winter) older than the sun's orbit, which was naturally assumed to follow the seasons.

43

The idea of the dying and rising sun can only be conceived from the north (solstice). Likewise the dying and returning nature (May — October, blossoming, withering). The south [knows] more drought and flooding (Nile year), withering in the heat, greening in the cool (thus just the opposite as in the north!). So the natural year [is] more Atlantic in a time when Spain was still cool. The 'year' is a cosmic reality: two movements of the earth around the sun, but it depends on the extent to which man notices something of it in the image of nature and how he experiences it. So unmathematical, experience. The moon, on the other hand, is a spectacle of measurable daily number, suitable for calculation.

44

Egyptian calendar (against Meyer): The origin of the Sirius calculation lies not in the observation of the heliacal rising, but in the approximate coincidence with the threshold of the Nile, whereby a day was not important. The first rising (19 July) was taken as the cause of the Nile threshold and counted 36 times 10 days from then on. Then they waited for the 'birth of the gods', about five days: then it came. Thus the number 365 was reached, since only whole nights were counted. This number became sacred and unchangeable: but it was noticed that it was constantly shifting, and was now eagerly awaiting the celebratory collapse in 2781 B.C.

The beginning of this count will be somewhat before the middle, around 3400, still very inexact. The relationship of the Sirius reckoning to the solar year will not have been more accurately explored until around 3000.

Sethe's assumption that one came from a lunar year 36 times 10 and developed the Sirius year as an esoteric cult year next to it, so that the five epagomena arose through the relationship of the two, is quite correct. So four stages: lunar year 30 = 3 x 10 days. Next to it Sirius year = Nile year. Relationship of both: circuit 360 + 5. Relationship to the solar year: Sothis[13] period.

Thus, around 3500, the 'Nile year' was believed to be determined from 19 July with 365 days. It became an established custom, although after four years Sirius rose already one day later than expected, but the only important thing [was] that the Nile threshold occurred. Gradually, New Year's Day became more and more distant from Sirius rising.

Meyer's error is based on the fact that he believes that the New Year must have been on 19 July when it was fixed. But this is not true. We do not know when the calendar was regulated, [say together] with some political epoch, so that the New Year fell on it, and only gradually did people realise that it was approaching the Nile threshold.

Of course, the calendar does not develop from Sirius. In addition, there was the Nile threshold year, which began every time Sirius rose. Finally, this was calculated: 12 x 30 + 5.

Meyer (§ 160) himself says that the civil year begins with the day of the king's accession to the throne and thus has a different starting day under every government. So New Year is not fixed at all. I, p. 32: In the 2nd dynasty Meyer did not recognise that a reform of the 'royal calendar' was attempted. The Sothis dates we know are all after 2000, so — against Meyer — it was not a solar year that was created, but a stretching of the lunar year to Sirius rising.

---

13 Sothis was an ancient Egyptian goddess that personified the 'dog star' Sirius. — *Transl.*

The beginning was therefore the mere observation of the Sirius year — 365 whole days (the error was not seen). This duration was applied to the royal year, first for each king anew. Then, somehow, they stuck with it. So the length of the year is not given with the fixing of the New Year on Sirius, but with the change of throne! Until 2741! The shift is so slow that a generation does not even notice it. New Year's Day has often been moved!

45

Sethe, Society of Sciences Göttingen. Philosophical-historical class, 1920. Egypt [has] three natural seasons of 4 moons each. The oldest names of the months can be proved under Amenophis I., namely as names of festivals in the Sirius year opposite the civil year (Nile year), namely of the festival to which the month leads, which is therefore itself closest (p. 35). The oldest names of the months are everywhere connected with the facts of the natural seasons: blossoming, harvest, rain, snow, etc. According to Sethe (41 f.), the reform calendar with solar year, month names was established at the beginning of the 12$^\text{th}$ Dynasty, because around 2001/1998 the beginning of the change year (normally 19 July) fell on the winter solstice, the 'birth' of the sun, after which the last calendar month is now named. Otherwise, the course of the sun was regarded by the Egyptians as a [life course]: child in the morning, man at noon, old man in the evening! The connection of the sun with astronomical calculations (position of the sun) is already in very late abstract circles, because the sun is never visible at the same time as the stars! The stars are 'born' in the evening and die early. The solstice caused a stir late, earlier in the north. The Babylonians hardly knew the year before the 7$^\text{th}$ century! The Indians in the Brahmana texts (7$^\text{th}$ century), though the High Norse Aryans know the difference of the longest and shortest days: but they did not relate it to the sun!

46

The annual measurement is linked to fixed stars, thus it is night measurement: for half a year the stars 'disappear' because they are not visible during the day. As soon as they become visible again, at dawn (heliacal rising), they are 'born'. However, observation is not very precise for prehistoric man and varies by whole days, depending on cloud cover, etc. Great Bear (China), Pleiades (Mediterranean), Orion (Indonesia), Sirius (Egypt).

The 'seasons' are climatic in nature and by no means sharply measured or even of equal length. They are epochs, not measures. Mostly three. The '4 times' originate from a division of the position

of the sun and are therefore very young. In the north: 'summer' and 'winter'.

The measurement of the annual curve by days is a discovery that only follows from the attempt to measure the peasant year by moons, which does not work out. Natural lunar years do not exist! The seasonal year has 12–13 moons, without both having the same starting point! Incidentally, primitive people are very indifferent to this. If it gets too bad, they 'start again from the beginning' (this is the original meaning of the 'circuit').

47

Primitive man does not think so far back that he would find the position of the sun regularly recurring, except in the far north, where the very dark days and light nights impress the whole of life. There, there is night for half the year. The slight differences between the longest and shortest night in Kash are far too equally valid to primitive people to be remembered. Moreover, as the sun always rises with the dawn and sets with the evening, nothing is noticeable, as just at the moon its exact phases.

In a primitive life, 12 moons is already far too long a time to be grasped as an epoch. In some languages 'measure' comes from the moon (μήν[14], *mensis*[15]). All chronology starts from the moon, without exception. Measuring the moon is far from being proof of a lunar religion. There has never been such a thing! Every cult is causal: the mighty numen is worshipped: but the moon has no effects at all; but heaven (thunderstorm, cloud, rain) and earth (earthquake, fertility) or animals. It is pure fantasy to infer lunar culture from respect for the moon.

48

The Egyptian deals more with *time*: Sothis, calendar, the Dodekaoros zodiac as movement, all this less measuring than counting, cyclical, rhythmic, temporal. Above all, descriptive, artistic. The Babylonians, very abstract, unartistic, treat *space*: heaven and earth, measuring, dividing (one sixth, not six!), hence astronomy, zodiac, fixed stars. Hence for the Egyptians the ideas: birth, death, life after death, youth, old age, creative; for the Babylonians: above, below, circle, angle, orbit as figure. Ground plans already on the Gudea[16] statue, not the architecturally impressive elevations (pyramid). [The] Egyptians' original symbol [is] the path, [that of] the Babylonians distance and angle in space, not cave or width or body, but mathematically divisible extension, legally abstract. Both lead to enormous distant systems, but there the living direction, here the sphere of space.

49

There are two zodiacs: the ancient Babylonian zodiac as a division of the ecliptic [and] the Dodekaoros discovered by Boll[17] (*Sphaera* p. 295 ff.) in the imperial period, since [the] 1st century B.C. Hellenically

---

14   Ancient Greek: 'moon'. — *Transl.*

15   Latin: 'month'. — *Transl.*

16   Gudea was a ruler of the state of Lagash in Mesopotamia, who ruled from c. 2141 to 2122 B.C. — *Transl.*

17   Franz Boll (1867–1924) was a German classical philologist, and a historian of astrology and astronomy. — *Transl.*

attested with specifically Egyptian animals such as ibis, crocodile, scarab, cat, dog-monkey, first appearing in Egypt and Italy, in China in the later Han period (*after* Christ's birth), perhaps only an Egyptian variety of the former.

The way to China is via Bactria and Turkestan (ego: with a religious sect? or by scholars? Turfan[18]? Gnostics?).

The Egyptians divide the full day into 12 hours day and 12 [hours] night, so that they are thus of different lengths with the season. So 24 simple hours. The Babylonians divided the full day mathematically into 12 *biru* (*kasbu*) with a water clock that ran 6 *mana* (mines) daily, so that, for example, the longest day had 4 day and 2 night 'watches', likewise the 12 double hours (*shi*) of the Chinese, attested approximately since Shihoangti[19]. The Chinese and Japanese name these 12 hours, the months and the years of the twelve-year cycle after the animals of the Hellenistic Dodekaoros!

In contrast, Tahiti and ancient Japan have 6 day and 6 night hours of varying length. Similarly, the Chinese have confused their own division of the heavens into 28 lunar stations by what is surely the Babylonian zodiac division of the heavens. The stations may be Indian, very late. So the three northern cultures have tried to order their natural year late by Babylonian measurements!

50

The Sumerians had the sixths abstraction. One-sixth, not six, matters! The system is analytical, i.e. abstracting. Circle division, 6-spoked wheel, sixty as 360: 6. Even the cubit is divided into 60 'fingers'!

In the Egyptian decimal sense lies the finger number, in 12 is the moon number. In Egypt *and* Babylon there is an original common tendency, west-east, Punt and Kash. But the development went

---

18 The Turpan oasis was a strategically significant centre on the Northern Silk Route. It was a centre of Indo-European Tocharian culture. — *Transl.*

19 Shihoangti (259–210 B.C.) was the first god-emperor of the Qin dynasty. — *Transl.*

in different directions. The division into minutes and seconds only appears in 1000 A.D. The ancients, like us, divided into half hours, quarter hours, etc. In general, the counting of hours apparently only appeared after 1000 B.C. in Egypt and Babylon. People did not live so precisely in former times! The 12 night hours of varying length [already] appear in pyramid texts more as a rhythmic measure [than] as a 'unit'.

51

For the calculation of hours, one thing seems to me to have been forgotten: the pre-Kashite culture knew ebb and flow. Only then did they begin to divide the days! That is a fourfold calculation!

52

Calendar: Babylonian astronomy: Does the name for Sirius 'Kakkab misri' have anything to do with the name for Egypt?

Early rising: only when the sun is at least ten degrees below the horizon can a first magnitude star be seen, in a very clear sky. So a distinction has to be made between the astronomical date and the actual being seen, i.e. around 3000, Sirius rising is not a fixed calendar date in the farmer's year, just as little as the first swallow. But it is precisely around 3000 that people will have come to the conclusion that it must be fixed, and will now have fixed the day mathematically, although often enough the star was late. In Lagash (cf. Weidner[20], *Alter und Bedeutung der babylonischen Astronomie und Astrallehre*[21] p. 2), the rising of Sirius is fixed at the 7th month of the calendar of that time, Tammuz (Tammuz is the consort of Istar), at least as early as 2600 B.C.

---

20 Ernst Friedrich Weidner (1891–1976) was a German archaeologist, Assyriologist and astronomical historian. — *Transl.*

21 'Age and Significance of the Babylonian Astronomy and Astral Teaching'. — *Transl.*

VI. MIGRATION PERIOD

CHARIOT AND SEA PEOPLES

THE WORLD OF THE NORTH — LANDSCAPE

1

THE NORDIC LANDSCAPE in the Ice Age is dead, hostile to life, then slowly awakens to life: water-rich, dense forest cover, flocks of animals, people. But it is always hostile to life, due to harsh winters, snow cover, ice masses. Here, life only asserts itself in the struggle against the landscape, sinking into hibernation, bare trees, furry animals. The human soul asserts itself from the beginning against the soul of the landscape, [it is] harder, colder, more wintry than others in the south. The Greek soul thaws and melts in the sun, the Indian soul withers and suffocates, the former casually laying itself down, the latter evaporating into nothingness. For man, whatever else he may be, namely heir of generations, is nevertheless a product and expression of the landscape, surrendering to it, asserting himself against it, for he feeds on the earth, which he becomes again. Not only his body — the side of his being that is reflected to foreign senses, seen, felt, smelled — but also his soul — the way his being is felt, experienced by strangers — is essentially a fruit of the land. Its fate — dying in snow and ice, awakening in spring, lashed by rain, storm, flooded, devastated — is also reflected in human beinghood, which suffers from it and stands its ground against it. The hardship of this fate, of being born here, has formed the strength of the soul, and out of this soul have grown the soul-forms of the individual cultures with their peoples, states, religions, arts.

2

The greatest inland plane of the planets: the piece of earth that forced the creative human beings to come into being. Man of the plain, not of the seashore. Harsh nature, winter, frost, hardship. Rapid alternation of heat and cold.

3

Migration, settlement. Rivers, valleys — routes of dispersal. Also coasts. Mountains hinder, but above all forests, still in the time of the beginning iron axe. Primeval forests, dense undergrowth, are impenetrable, ghostly. Fear. No human being can get into them. Dense forest cover over the continents. It is only slowly being pushed back from the valleys. Rare paths, known only to the natives, secret. Dangerous, as strangers could come from there. So settlements are confined to clearings and coves. Vast areas occupied by forest rather than people.

Traffic: pack animals, ferry, caravans. Small numbers of people. Seafaring. Inland tribes who wanted to conquer forced the owners of the small ships to help them. Etruscans, Pelasgians.

4

End of the Neolithic, beginning of the Bronze Age in the north. Climate change for several centuries: continental instead of Gulf Stream, dry, bleaching mosses disappear from the moors and return later. At that time, the Indo-European advance came from the southeast. The postglacial primeval forest becomes thin or disappears—therefore new settlement possibilities are formed. Afterwards, the forest spreads out again.

BRONZE AGE, CHARIOTS, HEROISM

5

Chariot tribes [migrate] up the Danube to the Baltic Sea. New formation of Indo-European languages, ruling class. Of these we know only what appears much later as a written language: Hellenic—Italic—Celtic—Germanic. [There were] many more. These are new formations. Scattered tribes as a result of the chariot advance fleeing in all directions: to France, Italy, the Balkans. At the same time, in Hellas and Italy, 'Illyrians' lived on both sides of the Adriatic (north). Dorians and Latins—perhaps adopting a pre-existing dialect? What do we know about this?

6

The storm of the *chariot tribes*, comparable in vehemence to the storm of Islam, which we know exactly. Also in that it spread ruling languages:—[there] Arabic –, here Indo-European (besides Altai Uralic). Arabic was a written language, bound to a book, and has therefore survived in relative unity. [The] 'Indo-European', only spoken, immediately disintegrated into dialects.

7

Around 2000: With these primitive peoples of the North, the heroic tribes, of a moral heroism, pathos of detachment, idea of personal bravery, loyalty to followers and manliness, a new flowering enters the human world: in Egypt and Babylonia, human greatness was something with the terrible gods and stars above, the earth beneath. With the sons of cold countries, the hard ones, matured by privation, grown by renunciation, the ideal of their own creation enters: the state, their own people, the fatherland. This is not how Ramses and Hammurabi felt. The sun-warmed souls of the South do not love what they have not learned to respect through privation. Love of one's homeland is love of one's barren homeland. In China, India and on the Mediterranean, this love becomes creative: it is the country of choice, the new homeland, to which the heart is attached. No reverence for the divine changes the fact that there is a deep reverence for one's own creation. One calls the sky god, but one means the god to whom one has inwardly consecrated one's own homeland. Homeric pride: one is related to gods one sees next to oneself.

8

To assume a common ancestral homeland of the Indo-Europeans on the basis of their linguistic affinity is nonsense: as if one wanted to assume that the primeval Spaniards, French, Portuguese, Italians, Romanians had 'sat next to each other' in the Campagna[1] around 500 B.C. and then emigrated: the Romanians, therefore, 'as the name proves', were the former inhabitants of the city of Rome, the Portuguese — *portus* — of Ostia[2].

9

The great northern streams of peoples: Around 1200 formation of the Celtic people — destruction of the Hittites — Phrygian streams — Israel (Aram) from Ararat — end of the Kassites — Troy — destruction of the Mycenaean high places?

Around the middle of the 2nd millennium, the north-south migration of Aramaeans begins (*Reallexikon*), since 1400 more and more down to Syria and Babylon (legend of Abraham). Destruction of Knossos. Dorians. Formation of the 'Teutons' around 1000? Achaeans, Danaans. Middle of the 2nd millennium Mitanni, Aryans as far as Chatti, Palestine, Punjab. Around 1670 (Meyer: *Israeliten* p. 447) Era of Tanis, then Hebron 'founded' around 1700, Hyksos Palace.

---

1   Campagna is the name of the landscape around Rome. — *Transl.*

2   Ostia was ancient Rome's port. — *Transl.*

Middle of the 2nd millennium Assur, Aram, Chatti, Mycenae, Troy. Hebron four times centre, as Kirjath Arba, Philistines (1200), Hebron = Chabiru-ni after 1200. Aramaic by Abram 1500. Hittite about 1700. 1700 Chatti from Chana in Babylon, Hyksos (Chian) in Egypt. 'Cain founds Enoch'.

10

Chariots have meaning only in battle. On the move, the pace of the pedestrian decides, but the horses pulled loads, so greater mobility after all. In the case of equestrian peoples, the speed of the horse. Prerequisite that either the women rode along or followed with the cart or that no women were carried. The speed of the cavalry on the plain is several times that of the pedestrians (at that time not yet 'marching', but slow walking).

11

Bronze Age = chariot. Danube and Vistula roads. Northern European racial types, including the blond ones (at least two, Paudler). 'Teutons' only language designation, like 'Celts'. Sums of tribes which developed the master language of the charioteers with their own vocabulary (sea, ship), [own] pronunciation and accentuation into a group of tribal dialects, while others formed the Celtic, Italic and certainly other, lost ones. Language did not create a sense of community, not even during the migration of peoples, any more than it did among Celts, Umbrians and Dorians. It is wrong to identify finds from the 2nd millennium with such language groups; they can be just as Celtic as Germanic or [other]. They are simply northern European. Equestrian tribes of the I millennium (Scythians, Sarmatians etc.) again [on] the Danube and Vistula — they set Celtic-Italic speaking tribes in motion: Celts, Indo-Scythians, China, Persians, Medes, Amazons, Macedonians?!? The Celts and some Italics thus settled on the middle and upper Danube. Only since then — in the middle of the I millennium B.C. — has the Germanic tribal group clearly emerged, locally, a part of the predominantly Nordic-blond races. Mongoloid types also Western Europe, also language which we afterwards call Finnish, Altaic. Certainly widespread.

12

The chariot tribes also penetrate into Italy and the Peloponnese, burying, [in] central Italy as far as Malta. [In] Mycenae sporadically Old Indo-European languages, close to Indo-Iranian-Persian. As a result of the storm to Central Europe, tribes from there, including 'Hellenic' dialects, on the move, e.g. Dorians and Northwest Greeks. The Arcadian-Cypriot dialect defeats the tholos-tomb people in about the 13th century, very soon after [are] the Dorians Northwest Greeks (1100). Before that, the chariot tribes from which the Illyrians and Thracians [and speakers similar to them] originated (of course, quite different languages were spoken in the Balkans besides, of the Etruscan, Caucasian, Finnish type). The endings, roots, etc. collected in the Balkans belong to many different language families. Venetian, for example (centum), [the] Messapic (satem[3]), [the] Albanian.

13

This tremendous North Eurasian warrior tide is an epoch in world history. The South has become forever passive. The Nordic will makes history from now on. The fact that a high culture spans around a thousand years is not a calculation experiment with exact figures — that would only be mathematics, i.e. abstraction — but it is an expression of the fact that duration belongs to every kind of life. Human life has a normal duration, and therefore the terms youth, old age, childhood, senility are not numerical values, but experienced durations. As with animals and plants. High cultures are sedentary, peasant-like, i.e. plant-like. The peasantry is sedentary (fixed house), the city is it in the

---

3　Indo-European languages have been grouped into 'centum languages' and 'satem languages' since 1890. The canonical satem languages are Indo-Iranian and Balto-Slavic. — *Transl.*

highest rank (cd). The nation [is] therefore a sedentary organisation. Germans have existed since the 10th century. But history is made by the elements (nobility, individual), in which the age-old mobility lives on. Not corals, but fish. High cultures are cities above the peasantry. The city emanates from the castle, the settled nobility. Trends of mobility: crusades, sea voyages, mercenaries (since 1100!), adventurers.

14

North — individualism: Experiencing the self as the centre of the world. Freedom of the will as an ethical matter of course. It is only for this reason that it entered the theology and philosophy of the Nordic high cultures as a problem, where people sought to prove it. This need to prove is a sign of the weakness of the racial instinct. Whether one has proved it to oneself or not, one does not feel secure.

One gives up something of this free will through obligation, loyalty, allegiance — in exchange for reward, booty, honour. More numerous than the example of loyalty in early Norse poetry are those of betrayal (Hagen, Kriemhild, Philoctetes etc.), China, Turks, Huns. Also *Krieg*[4] (from *kriegen*[5], take): each for himself. *Iliad*. Spoils of the individual. In every battle, which had to be planned, because of the chariots, danger that the individual would break ranks, because of the spoils. The account of the *Iliad* is false. The rhapsodes glorify *single combat*.

15

These chariot tribes, wandering, free, conquering, lordly, invaded the Hoangho valley in the east just as they invaded the Danube valley in the west, and here as there they subjugated, dominated and mentally reshaped the sedentary population. For political reasons, we will no longer be able to determine the history, their language (script) perished, in Western Europe they survived and led to the

---

4   German: 'war'. — *Transl.*

5   German: 'to get'. — *Transl.*

creation of languages alongside others, which later disappeared, to the Celtic-Italic, Hellenic, Germanic, which through new historical events formed themselves into language families, of which again the Celtic almost disappeared, the Italic — from a single city dialect! that of Rome — developed into a new language family of world renown, and of the Germanic only the Anglo-Saxon.

16

The chariot marked the beginning of the tactics of fighting as an art, the 'battle' instead of the disorderly brawl. Whoever led a chariot had to think ahead and think about its use, posture, advantages. This thinking distinguishes the 'officer' from the 'crew', separates the noble from the common weapon and way of fighting. The Homeric poets, who certainly never stood on a chariot themselves, describe only out of the primal human joy of killing and making booty and therefore do not give a picture of real fighting, — just as even today poets describe more individual fates than well thought-out battles (this only in Stendhal, Tolstoy, Zola).

17

The [chariot] tribes had a warrior nobility: chariot owners. Rich in booty [meant] noble, poor [meant]
bad. Later peasant tribes have landed nobility — farm owners versus servants, contempt for those who do not own any territory. [The] Egyptian noble [is] official, the Babylonian priest. These original figures of the consciousness of distance have become blurred over the millennia, but still emerged clearly in early Western times: knights, large farmers, officials (justice in France), priests (Rome). [Tension of] nobility [and] priesthood.

18

New attitude to life: West [and] South [are] casual, politically defensive, therefore [here the] priests are the nobility. [The] North [is] expansive, energetic, [therefore the] nobles here are priests. Since then [there is] world history as history of conquest. World history becomes active, purposeful. With the chariots, this spirit also comes to Egypt and Babylon [at the time of] the civilisation [of these first high cultures]: Assyrians, Egyptians, Kassites, Hyksos.

19

Poseidon, the demonic steppe, embodied in the herds of wild horses, which in their swiftness symbolise the infinite. When man took this speed at his service to satisfy his own inclination to roam, also born of the vast landscape, the horse itself becomes some numen. It is not the horse that *is* Poseidon or 'sacred' to him — so logically theologians distinguish, not the primal world feeling of the peoples –, steppe, Poseidon and horse are related in the sense, so experienced. Likewise the sea, the other infinity on earth. The steppe man and the seafarer [have] a kindred soul (race). That is why the steppe tribes make Poseidon the sea god, the horse the river — they experienced their vastness and speed there.

20

We must reckon with a double migration of peoples, 1. from the north from southern Russia (*Reallexikon*) as a result of pressure from Asia, and central Europe as a result of pressure from Russia, and 2. from the western Mediterranean, Spain, North Africa, also from Africa to Spain. For both, the origin is to be sought in the desertification that is progressing. In the East-Mediterranean they meet: shaft tombs and tholos tombs. Likewise in Italy, Sicily, towards Egypt. For the one is characteristic: cave tomb (dome), megalithic building, realm of the dead, goddess of birth, bow and arrow, for the other: burial mound, 'part of the dead', battle axe, chariot, horse. The Tursha and Shardana are northern peoples because they do not wield the bow like the Libyans and Spaniards. The combination of chariot and bow fighting first took place in the Near East and spread from there to

East Asia. Since the Dorian migration, the bow has been considered a cowardly weapon.

21

Idea of using the *wild horse* to increase one's speed. The usual way of talking about the 'pet' obscures what is most important. It is the first and only 'domestic animal' whose movement consists not in striding but in galloping. Others were tamed because they provided meat, wool etc. This was only for the sake of speed. Elsewhere the horse was an object of hunting — it was eaten. Here there is no question of food, only speed. That is why it was ethically perceived not as a beaten slave, not as an object of food, but as a comrade-in-arms, a companion. The only animal of military significance. (Elephant, the wandering fortress. Camel, the burden bearer.)

22

[The] chariot is Indo-European — Central Eurasian. An expansionist tendency that suddenly sees in the chariot the possibility of a weapon. Bronze implements. The battle-axe is occasionally mentioned in the *Iliad*. The war hammer (stone, Thor's hammer) passes metallically into the double-axe. Labrys[6]. Stone-throwing as a weapon (Brynhild, Ajax[7]). Horsemen ignored by Homer, in young Indo-European Central Europe (forest) [they are] of no importance (Romans, Greeks, Celts, Teutons), the more so among the Central Eurasian tribes (Turk, Scythians). Riding as a means of war was invented later than the chariot, but in the same place. Breeding of a light riding horse instead of the heavy draught horse.

---

6   The labrys is a double-headed axe originally from Crete. According to Greek myth, it was used by the Amazons. — *Transl.*

7   Ajax was one of the main Greek heroes in the Trojan War, second only to Achilles. — *Transl.*

23

Here, for the first time west of the Urals, the chariot appears as a weapon, a tremendous creation of tactical thinking, of using the pace of an animal as a weapon. This completely transformed land warfare. Next to the sea-going ship, this is the most momentous invention. This has led to a new idea of power, to new forms of peoples, to entirely new tendencies in history. The world history of the second millennium has thereby gained its predominant significance in the overall history of mankind and has determined the course of history ever since. It has never been seen as a whole. Only pages and parts of this immense upheaval have been treated from individual disciplines, one-sidedly and far too small: the 'Bronze Age' in Northern Europe, the Tripolye culture and its decline, the Hyksos and Kassite periods, the time of the Rigveda, the emergence of Chinese culture, the penetration of Indo-European language systems onto Western European soil — perhaps also of lost systems to which the Caucasian, Ural-Altaic and perhaps other languages bear witness, which have been swept along, in art [the time] of the spread of the ornamental style from Ireland to Korea. But behind this [stands] a phenomenon of the history of the earth, the connection of which with all these facts has not yet been considered at all: the spread of the desert belt, like the Sahara in the west, Arabia in the middle, the desert from Persia to Mongolia in the east. It will be the place later to talk about the time of this phenomenon which human history saw. Suffice it to say here that the same population pressure that goes eastward from North Africa drove northward from Arabia the Akkadians and other tribes with Semitic languages. For the starting areas of the North Eurasian culture lay where the shifting sands later buried the settlement.

24

Professional warriors: Not as if elsewhere a tribe had not hired itself out for pay. The difference is that it wanted to earn so much that it could then live in peace — pensioner ideal. Here, however, war was the atmosphere of life in which one could breathe alone. Peace was empty, wasted existence, straw death was shameful. To lie down. If one had no master, one sought one in whose allegiance one could fight. The chariot was a weapon in which one had to have years of experience, to be a professional warrior. The description in the *Iliad* cannot be entirely correct, because at that time this weapon was already obsolete.

25

Nordic tribes have a different structure than Atlantis and Kash. Christensen[8] 232 ff: Darius calls himself son of Vištaspa (family), Achaemenid (family), Persian (tribe), Aryan (people). Similarly the Romans. The conquests and migrations were partly by individual families, not whole tribes (Achaemenids, Claudians, Anak, Mycenae).

26

It does not sound pleasant to the 'swastika ears', but it is a historical fact that migrating lordly peoples did not exterminate the conquered territories in order to have arable land and pasture for themselves (although they took pleasure in murder and burning), but made the population their subjects. In such realms there are no 'people' but masters and subjects — metics[9], serfs, clients to be *tended* like a herd of cattle so that they yield something. Rebellious and dangerous people are killed (Helots, Israel, Rome), — the beautiful women are taken away, capable men are brought into one's own clan.

27

Around 1500: the heroic peoples: We know nothing of the shining power of these bright people, light in face and soul, of their kings, of the great battles, the death-defying defeats, the sacrificial deaths of the rich villages and blood-soaked plains. Lost are the songs of velvet grief and emerald bliss on the evening of a bloody victory. There the

---

8   Arthur Emanuel Christensen (1875–1945) was a Danish orientalist. — *Transl.*

9   Metics were foreign non-citizens in ancient Athens. — *Transl.*

corpses of friends and sons! The awe of the divine in one's own breast! Hardly does the *Iliad* and some of the *Mahabharata* foreshadow what was experienced before. If ever the springtime of man made souls shiver, it was here. A moral elation forged these races, shaped these faces, this posture of the body, this swing of the arms, this step. Their keel sailed over blue seas, in forests of holm oaks and tamarisk trees they lay down, blissful in the warmth of the sun. They blossomed in this warm land.

28

Not sentimental. First comes the self. Whether a person wants to be a leader or a follower, he decides for himself. Loyalty is a virtue so often mentioned only because it is rare. Betrayal dominates actual history. Also in legend: Siegfried and Baldur. Segestes[10], Henry the Lion[11], Widukind[12] — all [are] great traitors for the sake of their private ends. Rome (Coriolanus), Hellas (Alcibiades). To be master, to look after one's own interest at the price of death. Strong passion. Everything, the Icelandic sagas, the Edda, the German epic, Germanic history, [is] full of betrayal, deceit, assault [and] turning one's back.

29

In the second millennium, the regions around the Aegean Sea were invaded by ever new small bands of conquerors, from North Africa, from Southern Russia, and finally from Northern Europe. From these, ruling classes developed everywhere — Aeolians, Achaeans, Danaans,

---

10 Segestes was Arminius' opponent and betrayed the latter to the Romans. — *Transl.*

11 Henry the Lion (1129/30–1195), from the Welf dynasty, was the duke of Bavaria and Saxony and the most powerful German imperial prince of his time. His campaigns of conquest made him so strong that he eventually became the rival of Emperor Frederick Barbarossa, who could not accept this in the long run and eventually stripped Henry of his power. — *Transl.*

12 Widukind was the leader of the Saxons and Charlemagne's main opponent and was defeated by the latter. — *Transl.*

Dorians, and from these and their subjects finally the 'Hellenes'. This is how it happened, and not through 'immigration of the Greeks' who had previously 'sat' somewhere else.

The brownish Menelaus — the epithet proves firstly that this stood out as an exception, secondly that it was possible. The Negroid types of Olympia! ξανθος[13] taste of the rhapsodes, rarity value. In the pictures without exception brown men with black hair.

30

The first stratum (South Russia, chariots) knows or learns to know the sea. Very mobile. The Libyan period of Mycenae was only maritime. The second Indo-European, Central European stratum, which includes Celts and Romans, was sedentary, arable, landlubbers. (Dorians, Geometric period.) They probably used ships, like the Angles, Vandals, Goths, but they had no seafaring ideal like the North Vikings and 'Ionians'. The Hittites were also landlubbers. The 'Sea Peoples' were not. They resemble the Icelanders. Did they come from the North Sea? The southern Russian stratum mainly horse and cattle herders. Steppe. The Central European were chiefly forest farmers, labouring, peasants, πελαγος[14] — wide open space, steppe, sea.

31

Bronze Age in the North (look up Scheltema, Schuchhardt, *Reallexikon*): Bronze things come from two sides: Atlantic sea culture and Southeast. But the one did not bring a 'style', only the other (?). So the second [movement] was a conquest by new tribes. Not the material, but the new people made the world-view (culture) of the Bronze Age.

---

13 Ancient Greek: 'golden yellow', 'fair', 'blond'. — *Transl.*

14 Ancient Greek: 'sea'. — *Transl.*

32

Three semi-Nordic Eurasian cultures. These chariot peoples are nameless to us. We know nothing of their languages. Only their ethos, their soul can be discerned from their weapons. In India they break in with Aryan language, apparently also the Kassites. But the Hyksos? Mycenae? Compare the confusion of the migration of peoples: Goths a collective name (see Kaufmann[15]), and Alans (Sarmatians) — Gotalans mingling with Huns. Bulgarians!

33

The Westerners as far as Bohuslän, Megalith. So it is wrong to bring the Aegean things together with North German ones by a migration; they are last offshoots from the West. Here the 'Nordic' in general must be treated more closely. Nordic 'race' conditioned and bound by landscape, i.e. unity of life, which assimilates everything foreign to the species (for that is the sign of strong race. Senile ones lose themselves to foreign things!). Indo-European is language = spirit. Languages are grammatically transformed by foreign thought, vocabulary by life, pronunciation by landscape. In addition, there is the North Eurasian culture. In Northern Europe, West and North meet — sea and land, plain. North Sea coast more western, inland more Asian. Master tribes.

34

Pelasgian period: These tribes with their horses since 2000 — 'Tatars' from Carpathians to Arcadia. Non-Indo-European languages. They destroyed the Tripolye culture (spiral, no horse), like Genghis Khan and Lenin. The Tripolye culture, swerving south and west, creating the West Indo-European language by mixing, [is]

---

15   Georg Heinrich Kaufmann (1842–1929) was a German historian. — *Transl.*

mostly lost. πυρ[16] and *ignis*[17] ([is] one of them cult word of burning the dead?).

35

Heroic culture has no religious grace. What is taken for it is reverence for the mighty in nature, for the omnipotence of fate, but not servile fear and contrition before 'someone'. There is no religion in the *Song of the Nibelungs*. Hagen throws the priest into the river. The Lord God is with the stronger battalions. God helps the brave. Help thyself, God helps thee. And likewise Luther: personal justification is the abdication of God. Paul did not mean it that way. Only Calvin! If they will not eat, let them drink.

The ghostly nature, Thor, Wotan, Freya are present, and one honours them, but as powers beside men. Nevertheless, one takes one's fate into one's own hands, even where one feels that one has drawn a bitter lot. But there is no one — for the man — from whom one begs something better. You face the fact and die big.

36

Heroism: To die a straw death — the most contemptible thing for the hero who lifts the dangerous fate. So it was in the second millennium. The *Iliad*, sung among settled descendants, already no longer contains the boldness of worldly pride of the old bardic songs from which the figure of Ajax and Goliath emerged.

What a step: from the deep fear of the finally inevitable death to the love of a death in greatness! This happened earlier than the other transformation: the fear of the gods to the love of God. The hero precedes the saint. The transformation of the highest religious type from the powerful sorcerer and priest to the inner saint follows only from the spiritual transformation of the one whom danger makes brave to

---

16   Ancient Greek: 'fire'. — *Transl.*

17   Latin: 'fire'. — *Transl.*

the one who seeks out danger out of bravery. The saint begins in the 1ˢᵗ millennium B.C., where the hero has prepared the soul.

37

Hero culture: With this, the leadership of human destinies passes to a kind of man who lifts destiny. The high cultures whose best stratum were to discover life as a problem to be tended, and who now lie old and inwardly finished in the sun of eternal summer, are now the object of others who dare to live.

These Shardana, Russian faces, regiments at court, and soon, perhaps, masters, after Pharaoh got the dagger in the ribs. These Philistines, grabbing wife and child on their ox-carts and pulling on it. Were the Hyksos already such Northmen, who first owned castles in Canaan and then in Egypt? An image emerges: the sons of Anak, as distinct as in Norman times. A handful of adventurers.

Since then, apart from states and churches, there has been a third mobile something that counts as a psychic power in history: the 'army', the soul of the army that is created by leaders or begets its leaders, armies that become peoples and states, plough the world with their swords, stride exultantly over the burghers and fellows and make the cities torches of their way: Viking fleets, mercenary squads, all those Mitanni, Chabiri, Kreti. Viewing the world from the back of the horse, not from the steps of the temple, riding, not kneeling. And so it goes now through millennia. Chariot fight, sword, sea battle! Only once has the battle on water been surpassed: the battle of the air. Thus the higher man enters the tragic age: great to end in greatness of soul!

38

[I want to] draw a picture of the way 'peoples wandered' in those days, not the childishness of today's scholars. As an example I take Israel after Wellhausen[18] (Bedouin type), Normans (Viking type),

---

18 Julius Wellhausen (1844–1918) was a theologian and orientalist. He had a
    decisive influence on research into the Old Testament and advanced modern

Goths, Galatians (Stähelin[19]). Depicting, vividly: the 'great heap' sits in the midst of women, people, [so and so many] heads. The individual tribes do not care about each other. There is no mention of 'people', neither in victories nor [in] sacrifices. The geographical horizon reaches three villages away. It is only what comes beyond that which arouses fear.

Examples of how fleeting associations came together for a temporary purpose — these are not 'peoples' but, in the case of the attackers, associations with oaths and names, in the case of the victims 'populations' whose naming is irrelevant. All the 'names' that are considered peoples today are just that.

Race is completely indifferent. Gad, Dan, for example, are not Bedouins, Odoacer[20] does not lead only 'Teutons'; likewise the 'Huns' are all sorts of things. The possession of a language does not even occur to them. They soon get used to learning the language of the natives and do not notice it. Later they conquer new lands, and the new inscriptions show this language.

ON THE INDO-EUROPEAN QUESTION

39

It has become fashionable to extend the name Illyrians — originally a small group of tribes between Dalmatia and Epirus — to the whole of the Eastern Balkans and beyond to the Vistula, to extend the name Ligurians — Iberians, Thracians [in the same way], so that with

---

biblical criticism. He was fiercely opposed by orthodox theologians, and the English minister Gladstone wrote a book against him. However, Wellhausen's views became widely accepted. — *Transl.*

19 Felix Stähelin (1873–1952) was a Swiss historian. — *Transl.*

20 The Germanic Odoacer (c. 431–493 A.D.) was in the Western Roman military service. He was elected leader by mutinous mercenaries in Italy. Together they overthrew the last of the Roman emperors and appointed him, Odoacer, king of Italy — *rex italiae.* — *Transl.*

these names, which have become meaningless, one designates everything that is not Celtic, Greek, Italic [or] Germanic. But first of all, before [the] tribes with Indo-European languages there were tribes with non-Indo-European languages everywhere, and it is nonsense to assume here one language each time (Aegean, Asia Minor) instead of many languages belonging to several very different language families. And secondly, it is nonsense to divide Indo-European languages into the eight languages that are more or less known or not known at all. There have been not eight but a hundred Indo-European languages, most of which have disappeared and a few of which have formed new language families as a result of political and economic events. What is collected as 'Illyrian' roots and endings comes from a great many languages, Indo-European and non-Indo-European, so that this kind of inference becomes nonsense.

40

So, to be precise, the question is whether these tribes who came from the north — by north being understood the whole area from the North Sea to Korea — spoke Greek dialects. This is not the same as 'Indo-European'. It must always be [countered] that linguists make things too easy for themselves. They only know later Greek, Italic, Celtic, Germanic [languages] and reckon as if only these had existed for two millennia. But there have been hundreds of them, of which these remained for historical reasons and united into language families; and there have also been non-Indo-European language types in the north, as the enormously extensive group of Finnish, the countless remains of Etruscan [and] Caucasian prove. It is not permissible to elevate all languages that one does not know to a 'family' because of this common characteristic. Among the tribes (number!) that have invaded what later became Hellas since 2000, there will have been those with very diverse languages, including those of completely vanished 'Indo-European' construction. Possibly [there were] also here and there a tribe with a pre-Greek dialect, but this is unlikely, for these dialects evidently arrived here in closed groups through their bearers. [In] 'Illyrian', roots and endings from a geographical area [are] attributed to a hypothetical language.

41

Indo-European language families: How does such a closely connected 'language family' as Indo-European, the Romance languages, Semitic come into being historically at all? Only through great conquests: *Imperium Romanum*. Thus the Indo-European languages, some of which have survived because they grew into a group as a result of political events, must also have come from a great *period of conquest. Chariot nomads.* What is otherwise called 'linguistic affinity', — e.g. Caucasian with Ural-Altaic 'family', are fleeting similarities resulting from the intercourse of neighbouring tribes with the same living conditions. Similarity and kinship are not the same thing. Mr. Müller is not related to Mr. Schulze because he wears his discarded suit.

The fact that the Lycian, Lydian, etc. languages show some similarities with Indo-European is due to the neighbourhood. Similarity of the phonetic picture is a sign of the situation (type of people).

42

'Nordic' tribes [come] either from Germany or from southern Russia, [they are] very different [according to] language, religion, customs.

Thracians, Illyrians, [these are] artificial names: [the] assertion that these intemperately extended landscape names denote language groups [is] nonsense. 'Thracians' are related to 'Hellenes'. Heros [is] the name of a major Thracian god. 'Illyrians' and 'Italics' — Aeolian and Umbrian. So where does the group of Hellenic dialects come from? They can only belong to one immigration class. The others — Dorians? — have adopted them. The names (personal names) give a completely different picture than the dialects. Grammar and vocabulary. We have to reckon with numerous — Indo-European and other — language groups of which we know nothing.

43

Against the 'Indo-European' problem: It is very naive and, moreover, originates in linguistics, which was formed by the study of written languages preserved in literatures. It gives a fundamentally wrong picture. People talk about 'Greeks' because 'Greek' literature seemed to form a unit. Therefore it is assumed — naively — that 'the Greeks' immigrated as a unit. No thought is given to the fact that there must have been an infinite number of 'Indo-European' language groups which did not develop literature and which are lost to the philologist. One forgets to consider that languages, for political reasons, extend to peoples who are quite different in origin. Because there is a Latin literature, an entirely false scheme of origin is attributed to the Italic language.

44

The Aryan dialect group is at home in Ariana (Turkestan). It was spread by the chariot peoples as a master language, adopted by other racial elements (West, Europe). The original ways of speaking predate the Aryan and Finno-Ugric types. Before there were 'languages', there were ways of speaking: names and rudiments of grammatical form elements.

45

Language: In the beginning there are countless dialects. The 'sound stock' is race plus landscape: mountain, desert, water vocabulary, etc. Grammar is expression of metaphysical world-feeling, [of] religion, poetry, unconscious. The words adhere to the things. With the political-economic events, most dialects disappear, some remain and expand: vernacular, lingua franca. This fading and remaining goes on and on; new dialects of new languages.

Thus the 'Indo-European' we know is a group of written languages that have remained out of thousands of dialects, have spread, narrowed, migrated from tribe to tribe and finally become fixed, *politically* [and] in writing.

Another dialect that was lucky is the one from which the Finno-Altaic languages emerged. Others are left in fragments: Caucasian, Asia Minor, Alpine. By far the majority are lost.

46

Languages that are not bound by writing change rapidly. Especially the most frequently used words change meaning and form and are replaced by new formations. The 'Indo-Europeans' would thus have had a right but no left side of the body (*gauche, sinistra, links*), no horse (*cavallo, Roß,* horse).

47

'Greeks': In the north, a much-divided dialect group, most of which perished, the remainder splitting into new dialects, some adopted by other-language peoples. There is no such thing as 'original Greek'. From the outset [there were] various Indo-European dialects, some of which [became] corrupted, the κοινή[21]. Did one want to reconstruct 'proto-Latin' from today's Romanian, Portuguese, Sardinian, Neapolitan? Likewise, there has never been a proto-Germanic or even proto-Italic. Aryan: 'Persian' was simply an Indian dialect of a few small tribes who had moved to the Persian highlands and called themselves by that name. Other ethnic units also belonged to the 'Persians'. The Indian speakers formed only a part.

48

What we know of older Indo-European languages, for example, are remains of writing. But writing was done by a few, at courts, temples,

---

21   Ancient Greek: 'common'. — *Transl.*

etc. It is the language of the upper classes, not the colloquial language, that developed more rapidly.

49

There is no extant type of language in the whole world which has so developed the verbal sentence element to dominate the structure of speech. Whether there were others besides the 'Indo-European' type, which have disappeared, cannot be known. The distinction between active and passive events, between command and desire, is never so clear. Of course, we only know the forms of the settled tribes in Hellas and India from the written, i.e. late solidified form. The Hittite jargon is out of the question. It is the thinking of conquering, lordly, commanding tribes that is reflected in this system of thought — for that is the grammar. Grammar is the earliest, still completely unconscious expression of a world-view. The habit of speaking in sentence formations and the involuntary conception of life in its forms are the same.

50

K. Classen, 'Die kulturgeschichtliche Bedeutung des Hafers, der Ziege und des Haushuhns[22]'. *Indogermanische Forschungen*[23] 49, 1931, 253 ff.: The words *kakra* = oat, *kana* = cock, *kapris* = goat (Old Norse *hafr*, South German *Habergeiß*) were adopted into Finnish before the first Germanic sound shift, but only became known in the North at the beginning of the Bronze Age. So the sound shift is in the first half of the 2nd millennium. Germanic originated at that time. So [with] oats, rye (?), goat, horse, bronze, [the] Indo-European language reached the Baltic and North Sea at the same time (*Reallexikon!*). The racial phonetic stock of the Nordic race goes back to Germanic.

---

22 'The cultural-historical significance of oat, the goat and the domestic chicken'. — *Transl.*

23 'Indo-European Research'. — *Transl.*

51

The 'Indo-European' languages, starting from Turan — how they *originated* we do not know — are presumably carried by tribes as far as China. The young Indo-European language group — centum-form by the Nordic race — linguistically and mentally transformed. The Indo-European language was then replaced by Turk-Tatarian, Finno-Ugric, etc. — again a stream from the desiccating region. The same paths: Hungarians, Huns, Bulgarians, Roxolani[24], Pechenegs[25] to the west, Turks to the south, others to the east. The race remained down to earth. — Soul of the landscape.

52

It is wrong to equate Nordic people and Indo-European language in the migrations of the 2nd millennium; firstly, 'North' is not Northern Europe alone, but the whole area from there via Southern Russia to Inner Asia. Then Indo-European in the Aegean is not simply Hellenic, in Italy Italian. These are language remnants that have then spread again through *political* decisions. Other, lost 'Indo-European' languages and above all *non-Indo-European* languages from the north are to be assumed as their remains, such as Caucasian, Finnish and those that have completely disappeared: Etruscan, Novilara, Asia Minor — a thousand languages. What do we know, for example, of the languages of the Siculians, Sardinians, Corsicans, Minoans? From which language do the (consistently?) non-Greek names of the 'Greek' heroic sagas originate?

53

Distinguish precisely: 'Germanic' and 'Celtic' are language groups. The race element [is] the same. 'Race' in the usual sense [is] a

---

24 The Roxolani were a Sarmatian tribe that lived between the fourth century B.C. and the sixth century A.D. in what is now modern-day Ukraine. — *Transl.*

25 The Pechenegs were a semi-nomadic Turkic people north of the Black Sea. — *Transl.*

group of somatic types — to the eye — characteristic of a population. 'Germanic' peoples, tribes may have slowly developed from Celtic, Italic and others (lost) since about 1500 B.C. through linguistic differentiation into a consciousness of a special people. But 'Teutons', 'Celts', 'Italians', 'Hellenes' around 500 B.C. only became special forms in Gaul, Italy, Greece, along the Rhine.

54

The Central Asian 'migration' in the 3rd/2nd millennium as a result of the spread of the steppe. Like later Huns, Turks, Mongols.

Displacement of the Tripolye culture by equestrian peoples? Chariots? Indo-European language?

Tripolye tribes as far as Malta, Crete, Syria.

To what do the 'Etruscans' ('language'), Novilara, Teisbas people, Philistines, Shardana belong?

Under pressure from the East, later from Central Europe, here new flows to Italy, Hellas, Asia Minor (1500–1000). Schachermeyer[26], Chronology of the destructions. Counter-storm from Africa, due to the drying of the Sahara: nuraghi, tholos tombs.

55

The *Old Indo-European* strata (in addition the Thracians, Scythians) were mainly cattle breeders, horse, devastating the southern Russian forest (cf. *Reallexikon*: South Russia, end of the Tripolye culture) as far as the Peloponnese. The *Young Indo-European* strata [in] Central Europe [were] peasants. This [includes] not only Italics, but also 'Hittites'. The Caucasian language contains remnants of a pre-Indo-European linguistic world, also Eastern Europe. The 'Achaeans' may have successfully turned to Greece after futile attempts to conquer

---

26 Fritz Schachermeyr (1895–1987) was an Austrian ancient historian. During the Third Reich, he was a dedicated National Socialist and espoused strong racialist views. In 1933, Schachermeyr attempted to interpret ancient history within the framework of 'Nordic world history'. This is why he is considered one of the most controversial representatives of his discipline in the 20th century. — *Transl.*

Crete (1600 destruction). Where did the Sea Peoples come from? Old Indo-European or Caucasian speaking tribes, driven out by the Young Indo-Europeans.

56

The 'Aryans' — according to today's view, these are 'Indians' and 'Persians'. Here one can see the methodology of philology. No thought is given to the possibility that other 'tribes' could have existed without kindly leaving material for philology. One suspects that Scythians, Sarmatians, etc., spoke 'Aryan', but they are therefore only mentioned in a note on the page. In reality, countless tribes must have lived there around 1500, of very different Indo-European linguistic types, mixed with quite different languages. Some of these have preserved a higher history through the conquests in the Punjab, and one or the other of their dialects has developed into a written language. Most of them have disappeared, been destroyed, merged with other tribes (Zhou!). Of the Scythians etc. we have at least obscure information; there were countless tribes of which we have nothing but a few names. One of them had great success in the Persian landscape 1,000 years later.

57

Around 2000 the displacement of the Tripolye people (spiral ornament, cremation or aerial burial, graves are unknown) in southern Russia, by the burying Ochre Grave People[27] (nomads? Only graves, no houses are known), i.e. kibitkes[28], travelling gypsies. The former were scattered from there as far as Sicily and Crete, dragging other peoples with them. Perhaps speaking an old Indo-European language, from which perhaps some verifiable satem dialect originated (e.g. Illyrians). From Tripolye the shaft tombs (but this contradicts the

---

27   The Ochre Grave People were the Yamnaya, a nomadic people in southern Russia and eastern Ukraine. — *Transl.*

28   Kibitkes are Kalmyk skin-tents. — *Transl.*

burning), because of the spiral. But the chariots. Do they belong to the Ochre Graves? Yes.

In the Kuban area, around 2000, there is a much more luxurious culture connected with Fatyanovo[29] (Moscow) and later Armenia, the Hittites: a tribal group. Around 2000 the burning 'Italics' from the Adriatic (language Italic or 'Etruscan'?). The Shaft Tomb tribes have been pushed southwards by the burning tribes from the Danube area. They did not yet know the more easterly burning.

58

The philologist construes on the basis of the following law: what is not *attested* in languages was not *there*. So there are only eight Indo-European 'language tribes'. So in the North there are only Indo-European, Old-Augrian and Caucasian forms. But I say: these are only very special remnants of a great wealth of original forms. Besides the 'Indo-European' form, there were infinitely many other forms, and of Indo-European forms, infinitely many. What we infer as original Indo-European is an erroneous conclusion from a few specialised co-incidences to an original form. (As if one wanted to deduce the 'original riding animal' from the English thoroughbred, mule, dromedary, etc.).

59

Even today, research is burdened by the fact that — for the sake of the sources — it presupposes knowledge of language, and conse-quently, in the manner of philologists, regards language itself as the key to secrets that have nothing whatsoever to do with language. We know the 'spread' of the Hellenic, Italic and other languages through inscriptions and the remains of literature — Homer is a remnant — at best until about 1000. We do not know what existed before that and what existed without writing. If, therefore, written languages are used

---

29 The Fatyanovo culture was an early Bronze Age culture and is named after the village of the same name, near the city of Vladimir in Russia. — *Transl.*

as a basis for drawing conclusions about prehistoric conditions, the picture is wrong. Nothing has survived of the actual literature of the Etruscans, Oscans and other language units. It may have been much more important than the 'Roman' before 200. Even worse is the management of 'folk' names: if we do not know whether the name denoted a tribe, a country or a political unit, whether it was used by the people themselves or by their neighbours, whether it was created or adopted by them, we cannot do anything with it.

60

The understanding of the linguistic context has been prevented by the pigeonhole method of Indo-European philologists: they assume, since the Indo-European 'original language' was invented, half a dozen 'comfort languages' — which they call 'peoples' -, and now everything has to be stuffed into these compartments. Worst of all is the division of all names, endings, pronunciations between Rome and Byzantium into two pigeonholes labelled Illyrians and Thracians.

Hilurii was a small Dalmatian tribe, Thrace was the name of the coast near Salonika. In this area, of course, many languages lived side by side and one after the other, and not only Indo-European, but also those of the Etruscan, Caucasian, Finnish and other types that have disappeared completely. The northern tribes that have invaded Italy, Greece and Asia Minor since 2000 have by no means [exclusively] brought Indo-European language types with them, and Indo-European was by no means [only] either Italic or Greek.

If 'Illyrian' elements were found in Greek, Italic and Hittite, this only proves that many Indo-European and non-Indo-European language types were spread from the Danube. If the vocabulary of Latin and Umbrian is only 10–15% [common], then *after* 1000 Hellenic and Latin dialects were formed on the basis of completely different languages.

Boghazköy may well have been reached by a few hundred warriors from a tribe that also conquered a few places on the Adriatic.

61

The hasty designation of 'the Hittites' as 'Indo-Europeans' proves how naive one thinks in such matters. All that has been established is that the writers of the tablets have incorporated Indo-European inflectional elements and some very common words. Not a single Indo-European name has appeared, as far as I can see, as is the case in Syria and Palestine. How do we know if the ruling upper classes spoke this gibberish as well? The Luic and Hittite were chancery languages in which the actual colloquial language was used incorrectly. Nevertheless, there is no doubt that the empire of 2400 — different in centre of gravity and location from that of 2000 — was the creation of a conquering swarm, as was generally the case at that time, for the architecture of Boghazköy points to Troy and Crete, the feudal forms and stamp seals to the north. The rulers' names, however, are obviously borrowed from the famous ones of the older state (and thus its language). So there is no 'Indo-European Hittite people'. There is also no name for it. The ancient national language is the prefix — Hattic.

62

Germanics: If in the younger Neolithic the Old Norse circle is always strictly separated from the Central European circle (Scheltema and Menghin contradict each other, Schuchhardt also has different views), this [means] the development of the Germanic-speaking tribal group. And if Feist[30] suggests that a third of the vocabulary of this decomposed language comes from an unknown source, it is that of the (Atlantean) megalithic tribes living here, whose blondness prevailed, while the bearers of the Germanic language were perhaps dark-haired, as were [the people] in general in the Danube district.

---

30 Sigmund Feist (1865–1943) was a German-Jewish linguist. He wrote several books on the Gothic language and Jewish racial identity. — *Transl.*

63

[It is] possible that the population of southern Russia-Turkestan, which created the Indo-European type of language and thought, did not know the blond type at all. Only the spread of this language type in the direction of the Danube and Vistula roads leads to the adoption of the language type by the Nordic 'race' (blond, blue-eyed, a completely different hereditary unit is the long skull and the high skeleton). These Young Indo-European languages, of which Celtic, Italic, Latin and Germanic have survived, have many things in common. The Slavic ones still derive from the old Turan type. The 'Aryans' of India, Persia, Turkestan have nothing in common with the Nordic races in terms of *blood*.

64

Centum — satem: This 'division' in the way of pronunciation is a purely racial distinction. Thus, in the second millennium, the speaking of Indo-European languages must have permeated two essentially different populations, two 'races' that can be distinguished purely geographically as North European and North Asian. And this is quite compatible with the fact that in both cases the aristocratic upper class was different. Incidentally, these are not two groups, but two poles with transitions!

65

With reservations I assume that the Indo-European grammatical type originates from the Solutrean and [developed] into certain language groups in the Neolithic Linear Pottery. Since the Norse style is the territory of the soul, not originating from Palaeolithic form, but new, it will have assimilated found languages: so perhaps the Germanic mixed form arose as the latest, almost posthumously. The heroic peoples, however, accepted the Linear Pottery languages of the Indian, Italo-Celtic [Hittite] and proto-Achaic type on the way. The most recent formations on new soil are Persian, Ionian and Dorian, Sabellic.

Corpse burning developed everywhere in the Danubian region (Menghin 815). In the 3rd millennium the Central European circle is formed: Celtic-Latin in the west, Hellenic in the east.

66

The 'Illyrian', satem (*Reallexikon*, Illyrian), [is] a collective term of Old Turanian dialects related to Danubian ornamentation as far as China. They have filled Balkan [and] Italy (Malta? Matera?). In Finno-Ugric there are borrowings from it. All centum languages are juvenile formations. Celtic-Latin originated around 1200, on an Atlantic (Achaian) and a Kashitic (Thessalonian) basis. Kashitic was the widespread substratum (proto-Hellas, Aegean, Asia Minor, Picentes-Villanova, Apulia?), but as a lingua franca, the 'English pidgin' of the 2nd millennium! So 'Hellenic' 1500, Macedonian etc. 'Celtic-Latin'. Phrygian, Hittite, Tocharian 1200. 'Germanic' 600. Lingua franca often become official national languages (Punic, Assyrian).

67

Indo-European languages. 2000: If one considers that the difference between the satem and centum languages is actually limited to the pronunciation, which is always a characteristic of the respective racial carrier, I come to the conclusion that the 'western' dialect types, as far as they have been preserved in writing, originated as Greek, Italic, Celtic, Germanic, in that tribes of other races somehow received this type of language through historical events and spoke it differently: these recipients are the light western human races. The Aryans are black.

What about the Finno-Ugric languages, which have the same territory? In the vocabulary of the individual Indo-European languages, word masses from other, long extinct languages have been preserved.

THE SEA PEOPLES — GENERAL CONSIDERATIONS

68

I do not want to get into linguistic research, but I ask: Is there a connection of the names Agamemnon, Achmemnon; Achilleus, Agis, Aigyptos; Achaians?

69

In those days countries and islands changed names very often: What was Sardinia [once] called? A name long lost. Later it was called after the Shardana, like Etruria [after the Etruscans], Palestine [after the Philistines: Syria *Palaistine*], Sicily [after the Siculi]. These were names of the coastal places and their political masters. No one felt the need to name a large island with a single name.

70

Master tribes: Contrast of sea tribes and land tribes. The former settle on the coasts and plunder the mainland and the sea. The latter rule vast stretches of land with subjects. Both are masters. The coastal tribes of the West were also masters, but only by raiding. Their 'home' was the castle, not the 'empire'.

71

Sea Peoples: At that time southern Europe still had the dense rustling deciduous forests, thus snowy winters, green mountain valleys — not yet bare heights, cactus, palms. With the ancient culture, the Nordic flora, which Homer and Virgil still knew, falls and the Sahara breaks in.

72

In order to understand these times, we must think back from the existence of civilised cities to early human existence, where the sight of spilled blood and killed people was commonplace, where no man grew old who had not killed others, where weapons were necessary day and night and were not merely ornaments but much-used everyday tools, where victory over the enemy consisted in his extermination. The instincts which today are awakened in wars and revolutions were then in the blood. They were *virtus*[31], virtue, manliness. The feeling of peace was felt only in the evening after the destruction of the enemy, when the burning villages illuminated the corpses. Such were the Achaeans, Pelasgians.

73

The Sea Peoples [have] apparently come from the west, indeterminable whence. Their units (*Orlog*[32]) [are] mixed from people of Tunis, Morocco, eastern, western Spain, France, England, all coastal tribes. [They apparently] set themselves in motion by the giant chariot movement to Western Europe, where the mobile tribes made life difficult for the sedentary ones. Their languages — not all tribes will have had languages of their own — [have] 'Etruscan' and 'Pelasgic' swarms changed again and again, adopted new ones (Normans), [they] retain only words of war, of organisation, of the sea. [Some] lose [their] language: Etruscans [in Italy], Phil[isters] in Palestine — the land received their *Orlog* names, the language dwindled. Little religion of their own — such fellows attached little importance to that. They wanted to go to Egypt and Crete, then got stuck in Sicily, Sardinia, Etruria. Also in Caria. From there [they went] to Tyre — Gaza.

74

'Crete' was thus first applied to the eastern tip of the island, then by the Greek seafarers to the island in general. [Similar happened to names] such as Cypros, Egypt, Phoenician. Maritime language. Milatos = Miletos. Sea Peoples in Greece: Pelopians = Pelasgians, Kekropidai = Carians

---

31 Latin: 'manliness', 'courage', 'virtue'. — *Transl.*

32 Low German: 'war'. — *Transl.*

-op [is] the ending in a pre-Greek Norse language. Peloponnesus therefore originally refers to the area roughly behind Corinth, and only slowly to the peninsula when its geographical shape was first understood. With our map memory we presume far too much knowledge of geography among tribes of that time. People moved into the unknown. They never knew where the land ended and what shape it had when *seen from above*. They were also only interested in what was practically close to them.

Then Hellenes instead of Hellopians. Again, another language. Tyrrhenians. The 'Tyrrhenians' rarely showed up here, so Tyrrhopians is missing. The language on Lemnos[33] is *one* Sea Peoples language, like that of the Tyrrhenians, and not their only one.

75

Pel-asgians — Pel-opians?   Cretans — Kekropidai?   Tursha — T yrrhenians — Dryopians?   When?   Where?   Dorians — Doropians. Hellenes — Hellopians.

76

Sea Peoples and migratory tribes: Of course [there existed] no uniform race and language. These are modern political ideals. Just able-bodied fellows. The 'Goths' (S. Kaufmann) [are] a collective term for warriors of all possible origins, among them leading Old Gothic clans, from whom the name Goths comes.

77

What it means to live in danger, we no longer know. Trapped in the prisons of high culture, protected from the rude fist of nature. But in those days one still lived in danger. The fear of life was still creative because it was fertile.

---

33   Lemnos is an island in the Aegean Sea. — *Transl.*

78

The Shardana apparently conquered the land from the south and adopted the Sardinian language. Likewise the Tursha. The Romans of the 5th/4th century had a narrower horizon than the Tarquinians. They only knew the area south of Lake Volsini more precisely. This was 'Etruria' (Caere, Tarquinia) for them. The area of Umbro (Vetulonia) was 'Umbria'. There were other alphabets there. The name Etruria for the whole area was therefore only established as a result of the Roman expansion.

79

Numbers: E.g. Crete. Where was a 'large' city at that time? Knossos 5–8,000? All the Kafti together [numbered] perhaps 100,000, plus 100,000 slaves and bondmen? Philistines, Viking troops of 3–50 ships of 30 men each? The Javonians, a few hundred rich families in Sardis and Miletus? The Dorians, larger and smaller detachments of 50–1,000 war marines, roaming everywhere, staying or moving on, scorching, murdering, slaughtering. In Sparta [lived] a few bands together, from which a tribe grew. A thousand warriors — without wives of their own? Other troops (Anak[34]) perish. Anak — perhaps a hundred men. Defectors joined everywhere. Every able-bodied fellow was welcome. Act of blood brotherhood.

80

Sea Peoples, Italic peoples: Italy [was] sparsely populated, without charm. Forests. 'Colonised' from three sides: from Sardinia into Tuscany (the Tyrrhenian Sea, better the Sardinian Sea). The Adriatic area from the Balkans. The southern, 'Achaean': Sicily, Apulia, Leucas, Epirus. From there, at least from the west (incl. Cyrene) Libyan penetration into eastern Hellas: Argolis, Orchomenos, Thessaly 2nd millennium. From 'Kafti' 1st half [of] 2nd millennium. Alashiya and

---

34 Anak was a giant mentioned in the Bible. His descendants were the Anakim who dwelled in Canaan. — *Transl.*

'Tarshish'. [Tuscany] [became] important only from 1500–1200, therefore [the name came] from the Tursha.

81

If the ancient writers, in claiming that the Siculans migrated out from Italy, are passing on some tradition — which is doubtful, since they treat Sicans and Siculans as two 'peoples' — they were of course not the ancient inhabitants of the island, whose names we do not know, but the Sea People tribes of the 13th century.

82

There is proof against the fact that the Sharden, Siculians, Tursha already came from there [from Sardinia, Sicily, Etruria]: for in this period all the settlements of the natives on the Sicilian coast disappear, retreating inland (*Reallexikon* 12, 200). So they fled from the Sea Peoples. Is it the same in Sardinia and Etruria? Consequently, before the storms, the island [Sicily] was then called something else and the 'Siculians' did not arrive until around 1200. 3rd Siculian period. Orsi about 1000–700, so these are the Siculians? Instead of mass graves with almost the same grave shape 1–2 dead. These Siculians are then pushed inside by Greeks and Carthaginians, like the Umbrians by the Tursha and the X ... by the Sardinians.

83

Among the ethnicities which were peculiar to the Sea Peoples among themselves may be found [the suffix] — sk: Peleset = *Pelasker*[35]. Kyrnes, Kyrene = Korska. Tursha = Etrusci, Osci, Falisci. Perhaps this is peculiar to one group, so that Pelaski and Pelasti point to different language use.

84

Sea Peoples: So far we know nothing of their languages. It is the general rule that warlike swarms of conquerors very soon abandon

---

35　German: 'Pelasgians'. — *Transl.*

their language in favour of the subjugated, as the Germanic migration teaches: Normans, Goths, Franks. The Angles made an exception — because they came only across a narrow sea and therefore not as a detached swarm, but [as a people with] peasant masses. So the Sherden, Tursha, Philistines may have spoken as many languages as they did — Libyan, Aryan, quite different ones — we could only deduce them from proper names and a few titles. What we find later are the languages of the subjugated: just as French is not the language of the Franks, but of the Gallic provinces. So Canaanite is spoken in Palestine, Rasena in Etruria, Tramilic in Lycia, Greek in Danaans' Land, in Sardinia the language of the Nuraghic inhabitants, who must still have left many words in the present dialect.

85

If there were proto-Greek dialects among the Sea Peoples (which must have been distant from written Greek, with a majority of words lost later), they lost them when they took the land. Only the great land-grabbing of the 13th/12th century led to the formation of Greek-speaking landscapes, between which villages speaking other languages must have lain for a long time.

86

Sea Peoples: They everywhere adopted the superior language and culture of the subjugated (Rasena, Canaan, Termulen), perhaps with the exception of the swarm which settled at Novilara and there, among savages, retained its primitive culture, still in the stelae of the 5th century. According to this, the Italic-speaking swarms are even younger than 500! The language of Novilara (5th century, possibly still 6th) [is] perhaps a primitive Indo-European type.

87

Antiquity: How unreliable [are] ancient data! Norden[36] (115 and 125, 127 f.) shows that the description of the Germanic type in Tacitus is taken, except for the wording, from the account of the Celts and Scythians in Poseidonios[37] and transferred to the Germanic peoples.

Sea Peoples: In this colourful mass [are] represented many languages and many races, but with a decided preponderance of a blond, Nordic great race and of a language from which the 'Greek' later developed. The language disappears in individual districts: Phoenicians, Philistines, Etruscans, Sardinians, Lycia. It seems to me quite undoubted that the ancient connection between Troy, Carthage and Rome is historical. The Tyrrhenians once possessed or supported Troy. When one sees how the Germanic tribes fought each other, 300–500, the battles of the Sea Peoples against each other are self-evident. Even today, the [battle] for Troy shimmers through — like the Catalaunian Plains[38].

On the other side [stands] a great fighting community of the Achaeans and Danaans, who ruled the Peloponnesus. These names, like those of the Goths, Pelasgians and Normans, denote a concept. But important [is]: 1200 [was] Troy destroyed, 1100 Carthage founded by the Tyrians, 1100 Tursha [settled] in Umbria, perhaps roamed Carthage before, brought the heroic song of Priam. There is the connection.

---

36 Eduard Norden (1868–1941) was a German classical philologist and religious historian. — *Transl.*

37 Poseidonios (c. 135–51 B.C.) was a Greek philosopher, historian and polymath. He is the only important philosopher of antiquity to have written a work on the history of his time. — *Transl.*

38 In the Battle of the Catalaunian Plains, Attila the Hun was defeated by a Western Roman army, thus preventing the Huns from conquering Europe. — *Transl.*

88

Sea Peoples period: Building a concise picture out of ingenious moves and tremendous syntheses. For the eye. Confusion from which a soul direction quietly rises. To portray a primitive soul.

From Portugal and the Canary Islands to the Caucasus, the Sea Peoples found a mass of foreign languages and language groups, few of which have been preserved in Basque, Etruscan, [in] Boghazköy.

89

If the Sea Peoples, many small swarms, had languages of one type at all, it was perhaps Indo-European, but certainly not of any of the types still known to us. The language of the Lemnos stele, half 'Etruscan', has nothing to do with this. It only proves that a language which was in Italy before the Tursha and was preserved there had some relatives here.

90

Etruscans and Pelasgians [are] Orlog names like Vikings, Geuses, Victual Brothers[39] (perhaps from turan and pelagos). I do not claim it, I only put it forward as possible. If they came from the north of the Black Sea, they brought with them the word *Lar, Larissa* (lord) and *Pyrg, Perga* (castle), which afterwards the Goths found and spread. Perhaps at home in the Caucasus. *Ptolis* [corresponds] not to 'pure' but to 'patan'; *Pteira*; the fortified centre of the tribe.

91

Sea Peoples: Certainly Nordic. I would like to assume [they came] by both Viking routes. The western route via Spain, to the sea (Norman route), perhaps already the T[ursha], then the Shardana, Shekelesha. Certainly to Tunis, Barka, Malta. The Varangian Way, [through] the Black Sea: Etruscan Philistines. Temporarily in Colchis, [then on] Asia Minor coasts, where perhaps the Mermnad dynasty is

---

39 The Victual Brothers were 14th-century Germanic privateers. — *Transl.*

one of their families. Pelasgians may be the men who venture out to the high sea [(Pelagos)] instead of sailing along the coasts. High-sea men. [Are they called] Tursha after the pirate castles by the sea?

92

Greek colonisation, Italic import in Western Europe (*Reallexikon*): The old trade route does not go through the Tyrrhenian Sea to the mouth of the Rhône, but through the Adriatic to the Ticino, Brenner, Semmering. Therefore Epirus, Aetolia, Apulia, Picenum had greater importance than later, also for [the] Sea Peoples invasions (Novilara).

93

Sea Peoples: Their language [is] perhaps 'Indo-European', but not of one of the known types, but [of a] vanished one, like that [of] the ancient 'East Germanics'. But they did sit everywhere once temporarily: Argos, Thessaly ('Larissa'). The Cretans are among them. Anak. Did they form one of the strata of which Wilamowitz speaks? We know much less than we think we know. A great deal is philological construction from the linguistic history into which the archaeological finds have been placed.

If we look at lore, religion, pottery, names, dialects, weapons, according to the experience of earlier historical movements, the uncertainty grows. The picture is not that 'the Greeks' migrated in several waves. There were many other elements involved. Wherever the East Germanic and Mongolian peoples went, their language disappeared. It is therefore probable that in many cases — as in Thessaly — the older language displaced the younger one. It depends on whether the sedentary population was slaughtered or subjugated: Philistines, Normans, Etruscans, Spartans.

94

Pelops Island — the name [was] spread from Argos, first handed down by Tyrtaios[40] (apparently [there is] a contrast to Attica-Boeotia after all, so that the isthmus forms the island bridge). So the Pelopians sat in Argos.

95

1. Dates of the invasion. Language: Phoinikes, Aigyptos — is this Greek? Race. 1400–1200. Trajectories. Names adhere to coasts. Especially against the richest areas, not for agriculture but for booty.

2. What did they find? Complex languages, names, races, form of settlement. West, East, Libya, Balearic Islands. a) Crete. Epoch around 2000. b) Minos.

3. Fate: majority prevails. Names, customs, cult. Rome and Athens emerge.

4. Final push around 1100 ('Dorian migration'), Troy II (Sea People) and VI (Dorians), landlubbers. Dorian festivals in Crete. Origin of [the] Spartiates.

1/2 *Excursus*: method of name research (place, person, countries — migration), covering the whole 2nd millennium. Religion. Sea People and native motifs. What remains? Image of Minoan Crete. Temples. Sacred land. 1600 Chian. Crisis around 2000. 'Krethi and Plethi' since 1400. Kreti Sea Peoples with found names Kaftor, Japhet. *Excursus*: Odysseus. *Excursus*: Sarpedon. The 'Minoan' Viking campaigns to Italy (Daunians, Siculians around 1100?). The ancient west-east direction (Schuchhardt, Frobenius) from North Africa to Crete. Pre-Greek Sicily. Garamantes. Nuraghi. Etruscans and Tyrrhenians. Age of the tribal names — not before 1200? Triumphal words? Epoch 2000. Hittites. 'men' numen from Asia Minor to Libya.

---

40 Tyrtaios was Greek poet of the 7th century B.C. His elegies exhorted Spartan youth to bravery in battle. — *Transl.*

96

Sea Peoples: How to plan:

1. The purely historical. The names (to note that only nobles received grave inscriptions). People, persons, titles, gods.

2. House building, tombs, taste in art (imitation), weapons.

3. Religion. Ornament, cult.

4. Quite independently of this, the question arises: What language did these tribes use? Where did they get it from? Did they impose it on the conquered or vice versa? All this is quite independent of the name stock, which can be foreign to the language despite pronunciation and declension. Example Hans (Aramaic, Greek, Latin, Germanic), Guillaume, Elsa = Lise — Betty (Aramaic).

Even rarer than a completely uniform language of a migrant tribe (Odoacer) is a conquered national language. How often do several languages sit side by side, even more often on top of each other: Philistine over Canaanite, in Rome Etruscan over Latin. It is very difficult to guess which language will win. The Philistines were a master race, they had the superior culture, they were never defeated by the Canaanites. — Why did they adopt their [national] language, as did the victorious Israelites? The same must be true in Rome, where perhaps the Tarquins already spoke Latin. All titles are Latin.

97

Sea Peoples: Luk — Lycia (Bilabel). Lukka lands. It is, in my opinion, the same element of buccaneers which was preserved in the Greek legend as a Lelegian. Whether the name is identical with that of the Lukka and Lycians is a minor matter. Very important is the question of reduplication, which must belong to some language or language group of the 2nd millennium: a collection is necessary. I will give only a few examples: Titans — Giants. Tantalus — Sisyphus. Cecropes. ('Lelegians'. *Philologisches Jahrbuch*[41] 85 [1862] p. 744 ff.)

---

41 'Philological Yearbook'. — *Transl.*

98

Sea Peoples: Where they came from cannot be determined by ornamentation, pottery, etc. Nor the names, because it is not known whether they [were not] taken along the way. Perhaps by weapons, fighting style: Goliath. Their ships — were they their own, built in the native manner, or built in the manner of the Aegean ones found, or captured, forced (Vandals)? If they were a seafaring people at home, unlike Italics, Hellenes, Celts, they can only come from the North Sea and Baltic Sea area or from 'Atlantis'. Bohuslän, Brittany, Spain. In the latter case, the names Tursha, Sarden, Sekelasha could already come from countries on the Tyrrhenian Sea.

99

On the Pelasgian book in general: It contains the heroism, the defiant soul, and this has produced the thunderbolts of high culture, in whose lightning humanity burns. Quite tragic. The ruins are the fellaheen. Here is the grandiose final order of world history: the system of eight cultures. Out of the rubble of the two oldest emerges the fellah concept 'Orient', overlaid by Magian culture. On the other hand, with the Mongol invasion of 1200, the final calm comes to Asia, today overlaid by Russianness. Only the Occident, Mexico and Peru are alive around 1200. This volume must be conceived like Goethe's *Faust*.

100

Sea Peoples: The decisive factor is the fact which underlies the designation 'Arcadian-Cypriot dialect'. If we leave out the misleading name of the country, we find that the language spoken in the interior of the Peloponnese since 1000 has been that of the island of Alashiya. That means 1. that this language was at home on the western edge, if not the whole Peloponnese, until the Dorian conquerors imposed their master language; 2. that it must have been the language of one of the Sea Peoples who went the way of the Philistines. Which was it? Was it the 'Danaans' in Argos with the network of roads into the interior? Was it the Philistines themselves? Their five princes, their Ajax Goliath with single combat and Homeric armour? Their names prove nothing: they came upon solid cities like all Sea Peoples, and adopted the language and religion of the land —like [later] the Normans, like the Dorians themselves, who everywhere adopted the 'Carian' names (Corinth, Tiryns).

101

These maritime peoples [are] inwardly the same, of the same destiny, of the same origin; only the overstratified peoples have brought in the difference. [The name] Umbrians must have been a great pre-Etruscan name: Rasena name?

Age of intoxication, of wine, of visited narcotics and ecstasies: age of grammar, where the waking mind invents world suffering, the gaze full of horror. At that time the tremendous longing breaks out, to cover over again the free spirit just born, the eternally gnawing reflection, the knowledge, the Danaans' gift of that stage. Also [through] art: music, movement, dance as intoxication.

102

Port buildings were completely unknown to the Homeric world. No trace in written or archaeological evidence. The small ships simply sought sheltered anchorages. Hence always river mouths to enter, or deep bays. The shipwrecks must have been countless, hence the scrupulous observation of wind and weather. There is no doubt that the ships were run aground and later pulled into the water.

ETRUSCANS, SARDINIANS, SICULIANS, PELASGIANS

103

Italy: The names Rasena next to Umbrians and Tuscans, likewise Quirites next to Romans, Rutulians of Ardea, etc., show how many tribes sat here after, next to and on top of each other. Of course, one must also reckon with a multitude of completely lost languages. Only the few written languages that were politically widespread have survived. In the settlement on the Tiber, which at some point received the name Roma, more than one language will probably have been spoken before Latin — and Etruscan. It is wrong and shallow to call all names not explained from Italic 'Etruscan' without further ado. Schulze's[42] book has done much mischief. We know so little of 'Etruscan' that we cannot even assert with certainty that all 'Etruscan' inscriptions contain the same language.

104

Numerous types of language [were] introduced onto pre-ancient soil by conquerors, country settlers, mercenaries, traders, [they have] partly disappeared except for a few mutilated words, transformed unrecognisable by the pronunciation of the later ones, falsified by folk etymology, partly written dialects still preserved in later times, in names of gods, persons, places, mountains [and] rivers, partly growing into new language groups, taken over by others. The Etruscan languages may very well be related to several language remnants in Asia Minor, as well as to lost languages in Hellas. This proves nothing for the 'migration'. The assertion that 'the E[truscans]' came from Asia Minor is [a] late combination of trade circles Miletus — Caere.

105

Byblos (*Reallexikon*): Already 3000 B.C. Egyptian colony, even earlier (the name is pre-Semitic) a shipping centre. The name Byblos ships is already conventional in the Old Kingdom for a (non-Egyptian?) type.

---

42 Wilhelm Schulze (1863–1935) was a German linguist and Indo-Europeanist. Together with Emil Sieg and Wilhelm Siegling, the discoverers of the Tocharian texts in Central Asia, he worked out the grammatical functions of this language. — *Transl.*

Aegean import already in the 3ʳᵈ millennium, constant connection since then. A royal rock tomb with sarcophagus c. 2000 (Aegean, Egyptian, native grave goods). Again an example of the rock tombs. It is certain that such nodes of eternal trade routes also existed in Tunis and Sicily, etc., where Phoenicians and Greeks later emerged as heirs.

In addition the Fenchu = Phoenicians, S[idonians], by which are meant the Canaanite inhabitants of the valley plain. Both must have been based on a native country name, which for foreigners denoted the respective inhabitants. They themselves apparently called themselves differently in each of the small city-states. Sidonians, Tyrians.

106

Etruscans: The assertion of immigration from Asia Minor, now fashionable, is based merely on the fact that in the Ionian-Carian coastal towns the name Tyrrhenians is applied wherever there were pirates. They did not like them. And because over there the country was called the same, 'immigration' was a matter of course. But there never was an 'Etruscan' people. This is where the question begins to take on historical form.

107

It is a basic mistake of researchers to simply compile the folk and land names without thinking historically, [so] that if the same name occurs in two different areas, they assume one of them as the origin: Tyrrhenian. But if the name Saxony occurs in Dresden and Leipzig on the one hand, and around London on the other, then neither an English tribe has migrated to the Ore Mountains, nor vice versa [an Upper Saxon to England]. So it is [also] with [the] Tyrrhenians.

108

Shardana [is a] tribe, just [as] Siculians (Sekelasha) or similar. It may have been on the island, but it may as well have been elsewhere, in Libya, Tunis, etc. The fact that it was absent from southern Sardinia and eastern Sicily later on, speaks for a seizure of possession *only since*

1200. Tursha and Pelasgians, on the other hand, are Orlog names: castle and sea men.

109

Coast names: Beginning: Since the occidental historians up to the present day [use] the scheme antiquity — Middle Ages — modern times and under antiquity [understand] the sphere of vision of the Greek and Roman writers — this is only slowly being solved! –, then we have taken the names of the countries of the Greeks, named the language and the people after them, and finally the peoples after the languages.

We all know about Ionia, Phoenicia, Palestine, Syria, Egypt, Etruria, Sardinia, Sicily — but these are Greek names, seafaring names that originally meant the coast on which the trading places were located and the merchants of these places. So this says nothing at all about ethnicity and language. The term Phoenicians and Etruscans, as it is used today, ethnic, has arisen from ancient linguistic usage through false generalisation (like *Allemands*[43]). Today, science is stuck in such errors without exception. The 'Etruscan question' is based on them.

110

The prevailing opinion about the 'Etruscans' is the following: they originated in Asia Minor, 'migrated' (as a whole!) to Italy in various stages since 1000. Evidence is said to be [the] Tursha (Ionian swarm of the coast) [and the] culture of the 8th century (then the Gothic style since 1100 would be the result of the immigration of the Goths in the 11th century!). In reality, everything was quite different.

111

A new type of land names are the coastal names in the language use of seafarers. Thus Phoenicia and Palestine are Greek, Ionian names for coastal places. The 'Phoenicians' called themselves Sidonians

---

43   French: 'Germans'. — *Transl.*

until 1100, then Tyrians (Sidon and Tyre), and from this again a Greek designation has arisen: Syrians [originally applied] only to the coast. When Greek became the language of administration from Alexander the Great onwards, this designation expanded. As an administrative name in the *Imperium Romanum*.

But it must have been the same in the West. Etruria was originally the coastal name, area of Caere. One of the old names (most of which were certainly no longer known to the Romans) was Umbria, but it was pushed back into the Apennines.

Likewise [are] Sardo and Sikelia Greek names. The island as such probably had no overall designation at all, any more than Italy and Spain. The tendency to use such a comprehensive name is late, either scientific (geographical) or political (administration, trade). Then the name of the tribe with which one first comes into contact is extended. Sikelia [was] probably first the area of Syracuse, then the island.

112

Etruscans: The idea of the 'migration' of 'the' Etruscan 'people' from Asia Minor to Italy is inconceivable, impossible, nonsensical. Ask yourself the following questions and try to answer them vividly: How big was the 'people' in Asia Minor? Where did they 'sit'? What was their relationship to the sailors on the coast? Who built the ships (which presupposes long experience)? How many were there, what was the maximum number? (Moving a hundred ships was completely impossible at that time.) Were they captured or rented? Who rowed them, who was pilot, captain, guide? How did one provision a 'people'? One need only ask the question to see its impossibility.

113

Etruscans: The Etruscans [simply] adopted the religion of the land, as well as the language. It is imprudent, and from the point of view of the linguist himself amateurish, to assume of every word of Etruscan inscriptions that it is 'Etruscan'. We know from Greek how many *pre-Greek* words have been taken over. In Latin we simply say that they are *Etruscan* words. But is 'Etruscan' a *uniform* language? How many words from other languages, *pre-Etruscan* words, are there in it? And do we know the language well enough to say that all the inscriptions are written in the same language?

114

Roman myth (suggestion): [Was] Aeneas a Tyrrhenian hero? Hellanikos and Timaeus already know of his founding of Rome. Hesiod[44] (*Theog.* 1011 ff.) knows the king Latinus, with whom Aeneas allies himself against the Rutulians.

Dardana. There was also an Illyrian-Thracian tribe of this name, known since 284. Circeii [is] already known to Theophrastus.

115

Etruscans (Herbig, *Mitteilungen der Schlesischen Gesellschaft für Volkskunde*[45] 1922):

Also uni (Juno)-menerva-nedinus-selvans are not Etruscan.

P. 8: Ancient Etruscan triad of gods to which every city, with three gates and three temples, had to be consecrated: Tinia-uni-menerva (cf. Athens). Nine gods hurling lightning, tinia alone has three [*manubia*[46] (lightning)], thus [all gods together] eleven. The stars of the gods that rise and set daily in the sky.

P. 9: Tinia hurls the 1st kind of lightning *suo consilio*[47], the 2nd on the advice of the 12 gods, the *tertia manubia*, the worst, in agreement with the *dii opertanei*, whose name and number no one knows, who thrones mysteriously and unfathomably over seas — *this* could be from the Tursha! If the noble Tursha dynasties bear Rasena names,

---

44 Hesiod (c. 700 B.C.) was a Greek poet, nearly contemporaneous with Homer. His work *Theogony* describes the origins and genealogy of the gods. — *Transl.*

45 'Reports of the Silesian Folklore Society'. — *Transl.*

46 Latin: 'spoils of war', 'winnings', 'prize money'. — *Transl.*

47 Latin: 'his plan'. — *Transl.*

which, moreover, are often the names of local deities (p. 11), this shows the nature of the land-grabbing: the *gens*[48] carries with its names the dominated territories, villages, castles, while, of course, only the 'first name' applies up to that point. ('Gens of Putlitz'). The Roman *tribus*[49] are also like this: here one met Latin place names and adopted them. However, the conquest of Tarquinia also brought families from there with local names. A part of the oldest first names is therefore the product of the Tursha.

Herbig (p. 11/12) derives the numina from genteel names, but it is the other way around! They became genteel gods with a genteel cult (Kaeso-luperei) because their territory belonged to the gens and thus the cult became their duty. If there was a *gens Rumina*, it had conquered the place where the *diva Rumina* lived on the Lupercal.

Three parts [of the Etruscan sacred books]: *libri fulgurales, haruspicales, rituales*.

116

Etruscan: According to a suggestion by Brandenburg[50] [there is a] close relationship between Etruria and Palestine. Ego: There is no question that Tunis was once a dominant territory. From there the cave tombs and tumuli[51] in Jerusalem, Malta, Etruria, Sardinia, Sardis, Bosporus (Troy I), Crete, primeval Byblos.

Tomb culture. In 'Phoenicia' it can only have come from the west, not from Sumer! The idea of the ancestral tomb is quite sporadic in Palestine. Already Remedello (Po Valley) shows [a] hint of a temple-like layout of the burial ground, influence of Iberian kind. Similar in Etruria.

---

48 Latin: 'clan', 'family'. — *Transl.*

49 Latin: 'tribe'. — *Transl.*

50 Arnold Brandenburg (1868–1946) was German historian and genealogist. — *Transl.*

51 Tumuli are burial mounds. — *Transl.*

117

Etruscans: In this Schuchhardt is right that the Shardana, Tursha and Shekelasha — Sardinia, Sicily, Etruria — already belong together in Egyptian times. If they have the atrium tomb in common, I would have to consider them Libyans. It is nonsense to explain such movements from small towns in Asia Minor.

Obviously, by 1250, a firm foothold had already been established in the three western territories. I must therefore seriously think that these Sea Peoples came through the Straits of Gibraltar. What does Caesar say of the Venetian naval power of Brittany? Surely these are not the Menhir people!

After all, these are not 'peoples' but generic names, like Habiri and Amurru.

Larissa and Pergamos are not names either.

118

The oriental fashion of the Etruscans merely proves the direction of their maritime connections. Otherwise one would have to take the Normans for Arabs and the Japanese for Western Europeans. The Etruscan 'culture' since 800 is Hanseatic taste.

119

The Tursha, a northern people, true Normans with a changing language, after taking land in Etruria, occupied Lemnos, perhaps Athens (prytanis) and Lydia, where they brought Tuscan language and burial customs. Lydian [is] *perhaps* a Libyan dialect. It would have to be about 9th/8th century, post-Homeric, and have traces in the *Odyssey*. Title Prytanis in Etruria and Athens, Maro in Lemnos (Etruscan inscription).

120

Etruscans: In the case of the tombs [it is] to be considered:

1. Partly origin from Spain, Africa, Mycenae, i.e. Atlantic.

2. Partly perhaps Nordic megalithic graves ('Germanic').

3. Since the 8th century with trade the orientalising style and taste. Miletus, Ionia [become] the centre of 'world trade', hence Sardis as a model of noble trading houses. Not the basic type of tomb, but the finer decoration from there. (Criticism by Schachermayer, *Archiv für Orientforschung*[52] VII/3.)

Similarity between Asia Minor and Etruria: [there are] kindred Norse tribes here and there: for instance, Phrygians — Tursha — Villanova. Destruction of the Hittite Empire around 1200.

Novilara!

121

Etruscans: Introduction: All works on Etruria are concerned with the question: where from, when, how? The main thing is not even noticed: What is understood by [the name of] 'Etruscans'! The object of investigation is assumed without [criticism]. The people who inhabit [Tuscany], speak Etruscan, have the Etruscan religion. Does that exist? If one penetrates historically comparatively, the Etruscan concept dissolves. Researchers have believed in an object under the spell of the name Etruscan. Theory: Asia Minor, the North, Spain. What if they were all right *and* all wrong? Language: far too naive. If a word is found in some 'Etruscan' inscription, is it 'Etruscan'? If anyone wanted to say the same of 'the Italic language'! Certainly there have been dialects, in some of them [there are] elements of other languages.

122

Lemnian inscription: On Lemnos the *Iliad* knows Sintians who worship 'Hephestus[53]'. Beloch[54] (*Griechische Geschichte*[55] I, 2, 53)

---

52   'Archive for Research on the Orient'. — *Transl.*

53   Hephestus is the ancient Greek god of fire and blacksmiths. — *Transl.*

54   Karl Julius Beloch (1854–1929) was a German ancient historian. — *Transl.*

55   'Greek History'. — *Transl.*

believes that these Sintians were a Balkan population related to the Etruscans. *Glotta*[56] 7,29 ff. Kretschmer[57] on Adonis. In Phoenician this is never a god, but an appellative. Adonis [is] perhaps from the Cypriot language. [Cf.] 121 ff. Kretschmer, Heracles. He is at home in Argolis. The Theban legend is younger. Ego: Kretschmer forgets the folk etymology, which is without meaning. Heracles is something like that, although Hera is just his enemy. But the name sounded similar. Likewise Menelaus etc. p. 127, in the legend he is originally small in stature but clever. Fairy-tale character of all time. David and Goliath. Etruscan *spural* means something official (*Spurius*).

123

The constant language change of the Normans: [It is] therefore quite possible that Tursha and Peleset would have listened to and carried on the Lydian pre-Greek, which they would then have sacrificed to the Rasena and Canaan. Then what remained of their original language were the personal names, and more the first than the genteel names. The Tarquinians, for example, could be called by the city, the city [could] be called by a god of Asia Minor. Just as everywhere the city name is younger than the numen: *Brunonis Vicus*[58].

124

The 'Etruscan' inscription of Lemnos — perhaps the tomb of a mercenary leader from Etruria, [a] pirate. Like the Viking inscription in Canada.

125

Etruscans, Pelasgians: It is quite possible that Tyrannos means the lord of the castle: *turis, Venus turan*. If Pelasgians and Etruscans

---

56 *Glotta* — *Journal of Classical Philology and Linguistics.* — *Transl.*

57 Paul Kretschmer (1866–1956) was a German linguist who studied the interrelations of Indo-European languages and demonstrated how they were influenced by non-Indo-European ones. — *Transl.*

58 Braunschweig (Brunswick), city in Germany. — *Transl.*

appeared differently, in West and East, where did they get the common words? Were they just Orlog names for the same tribal group? So that they are basically identical?

126

If the Tursha, Sekelesha, Shardana appeared together, this seems to prove that these Vikings had already at that time gained a foothold on the coasts of eastern Sicily, southern Sardinia, southern Tuscany.

Sicans and Siculians differ from each other like Goths and Gotlanders, Scots and Scottish, Japanese and Nipponese, Indians and Red Indians, Franks and French. The suffix -ani is like Lukani, Kampani, the suffix -uli like Tusculi.

127

Etruscans: Were they in possession of Ulysses? Circe? Did they speak Greek like the Philistines? Then the 'Hellenisation' of Etruria was effected by them in 1200, against the Rasena! (Deecke[59] 1, 82 ff.). Matriarchy of the Sea Peoples. (Deecke 1, 376.) Etruscans and Lycians. Tanaquil.

128

Etruscans: The alphabet of the Lemnos statue is close to North Etruscan, not to South Etruscan. There are several a[lphabets], so no Etruscan unit. We know so little of Etruscan that we cannot even say whether it is not *more than one* language.

129

Etruscan, Achaean: Summary 'Pelasgian Period'. The first great compilation. Relationship of the Aeolians with Italics and Celts, the Dorians likewise Aeolian language and literature. Do not talk about 'Etruria'. Each city is its own people, perhaps its own language. In

---

59 Ernst Deecke (1831–1897) was a German linguist and a famous Etruscologist. — *Transl.*

Etruria, 'Etruscan' was only the language of inscriptions. In addition, there are non-identical vernacular languages.

130

Etruscans, Achaeans: When [considering] migrations, the mistake is constantly made of retracing the population speaking *one* language group as a unit. The 'Hellenes' have only existed in Hellas since 1100. The various migratory currents from the north will in part have brought with them completely different languages than 'proto-Hellenic'. Cf. the 'Illyrian' elements in 'Greek'. The enormous difference in the vocabulary of the Latins and the Sabellians proves that one of the two groups did not originally speak 'Italic'. Likewise the difference in the vocabulary of the Hellenic dialects. The so-called 'influence' of 'Etruscan' on Latin!

(πυρ-*pir, ignis*?)

There have been infinitely more 'groups' of Indo-European language than the eight we know, and a great many Norse 'original languages' besides Indo-European. It is childish to determine the extent of 'Illyrian' by place and personal names. There are those of common origin among Italic and Hellenic tribes.

Tonolus, Tumulus. Atavus.

What language did the people from southern Russia (spiral ornament), from central Europe (Megaron) speak?

131

'Etruscan', language: Believed to be [their] origin by sea, because it sits on the west coast. But all Celtic dialects today sit on the Atlantic coasts. If we did not know anything about their prehistory, we would let them come from Spain or [Western France] and put them together with the bearers of the megalithic buildings. But just as these are remnants, Etruscan is 'remnant' of former powerful Balkan language groups.

132

Pelasgian period: And at last it passes through millennia in a jubilant exuberance, in ardent self-confidence, to be human, *above* all that is otherwise called life. Man becomes a *hero*. His soul blossoms, wakes up, high above all. The human form stretches up, the face becomes a sign of powerful forces, mobile, inwardly expressive. What distinguishes the head of the golden eagle, of the lion, lies collected and spiritualised in the heads of the noblest strokes of this blossoming race. In their early ardour they feel akin to all that glows. It was then that the sun-proximity of the soul, the veneration of fire, of the sun, arose as the state of soul in which one knew oneself to be one with the whole environment.

And what scholars, preoccupied with external signs, call primitive man, is the blossoming of the human soul to its richness and depth. Being that feels itself, being awake that understands itself in the universe — from this blossoms a realm of inexhaustible possibilities. Dull animal longing and fear become noble. The wounded pride of captive thoroughbred animals dying in cages, the passion for the beloved being — this is shadowy compared to the primeval age of great passion and capacity for suffering. Everything that the great culture later allows to build up in a wealth of bound forms glows here in primal purity, to which the remains of great myths, frightening ornaments, dark rites bear witness. Where this glows in streams of human thought, there arise races, heroic races, which move over the orbits of the earth, towards the light, out of ice, forests, nights into the light.

133

Pelasgians: They had a goal. What Rome was to the Germanic swarms of the wandering time, that was Egypt to them, a distant, fabulously late and splendid fairy world, full and rich, which a hero might well hope to have as booty. The fame of Rome had reached as far as the far north. They had dark tidings of these palaces of marble and gold. But the north also heard about the fairytale land on the Nile.

Along the ancient trade routes, the merchants of the south-east carried rare trinkets, even news. All these journeys were directed towards the Nile. And only when it remains out of reach does the eye turn to lesser booty somewhere on the coast of the Mediterranean.

CYPRUS AND PHOENICIA

134

'Phoenicians' — an example of how an occasional name can give rise to belief in a 'people' that never existed. In this region, which with a Mitanni word was called Kinachni, Canaan, have sat different speaking peoples. Since the Hyksos period [there have been] city principalities on the coasts and inland. Conquest of the Sea Peoples. And now, after the fall of Egyptian rule and the Achaeans, Sidon becomes powerful, later Tyre, a single city. The Ionian seafarers called them Levantines: Phoenicians.

135

Phoenicians: The ancient peoples of the coast were Mitannic. Semitic was spoken by the conquering ruling class. It became the lingua franca there, widespread, written, thus dominant. When the Sea Peoples moved down the coast against Egypt, they naturally also attacked Tyre [and] Sidon by land and by sea — how else could they have got further? That happened around 1200.

So relatives of the Etruscans, Philistines, etc. are also sitting in these cities. Like them, they adopted the lingua franca and continued to trade, also out of their own talent. Therefore, Ionians, Phoenicians, Etruscans are at the same time Hansa people of antiquity. Carthage [is] in spirit half ancient, half Libyan. Since the conquering lords took the wives of the subjugated, their language prevailed. The political system remained. Phoenicians and Ionians rebuilt empires. The alleged difference in the colonies does not exist. In Etruria there was no such tradition: the coast had been the object of foreign colonisation in the

2nd millennium. Taranto [was] founded by 'Achaean' (tholos tombs), not Dorian [settlers].

136

The Tyrians (Syrians) seek the old bases again since 1100: first Malta, Sicily, Tunis. Then Sardinia (the Cyprian bronze candelabra!), where the naval power of the ancient tribes had apparently been destroyed. From them come the ingots of Serra Ilixi [in Sardinia], the oldest Phoenician finds in the West!

Poulsen[60]: All news about Phoenicians in Spain and Tartessos are late and misty. Tartessos was Tunis. This is where the Kafti sea voyage ended. 'Tyrrhenians' also sailed to Etruria, from Carthage. Old, close connection. The island of Plana near Ibizza [is] 'Phoenician'. Bronze statuettes similar to clay figures from Syria and Cyprus, 8th/7th century (Bosch, *Klio* 22, 365). In the 7th century [the] name Tarshish is transferred from the Tyrians to Andalusia (p. 366).

137

In Cyprus [occur] names like Tamassos and Nemessos. The population [is] related to the Cilician (Luvian). Here the Viking conquest failed: in contrast to Rhodes and Miletus, the ancient Egyptian form of shaft tombs alone has remained dominant (Fimmen[61] 105). Cyprian Arcadian dialect. Epic of the Cyprians was written in the 10th century and later, thus pre-Orthodox, but post-Mycenaean. Ancient cult connection [of] Cyprus with pre-Dorian Laconia, Argos, Achaia. One priestly class was called Achaiomanteis. *Iliad* XI, 19 ff: Agamemnon receives a breastplate from a Cyprian prince.

---

60 Frederick Poulsen (1876–1950) was a Danish classical archaeologist. — *Transl.*

61 Diedrich Fimmen (1886–1916) was a German classical archaeologist who wrote an important book about Cretan-Mycenaean culture. — *Transl.*

'Phoenicians', the redskins = non-Nordic breed? Phoenicians non-Semitic, core: Sea People (see Reinach[62], Wilamowitz, also Evans[63]). Whatever Minoan things appear in the western Mediterranean were carried there by Sea Peoples. Daunians, a Japygian tribe: Herodotus' account of Minos' march to Sicily, where he dies. The men settle in Japygia (VII, 171).

138

When about 1200 the barbarians trampled down everything, slaughtered the population to a great extent, burnt the villages, seafaring, i.e. the existence of some coastal places, military, merchants, sailors cannot have disappeared. These savage tribes, with their delight in bloodshed, were clever enough to see the advantage. They forced people into their service. In the parlance of these circles the terms Tartessos and Alashiya were preserved. Thus 'Carian' became Tartessos [to] 'Phoenician' Tarshian. The 'Carians' (Kereti) were westerners, north of Crete, the Tyrians south. Is perhaps the term Phoenician a translation of Elysium, Orient (Beloch)? [Are] the bird and the palm tree thereby designated as 'oriental'? Orientals, Levantines? Cf. peach, orange, quince.

139

Kypris: In the Viking Age, too, the 'harbour women' were known to the sailors and indispensable. Thus the Kypris temples with their hierodules[64]. Aphrodite [is] apparently [a] Kafti name (Laconia), Kypris the name of a goddess of the Sea Peoples.

---

62 Théodore Reinach (1860–1928) was a French archaeologist and statesman. — *Transl.*

63 Sir Arthur Evans (1851–1941) was a British archaeologist who excavated the ruins of the ancient city of Knossos in Crete. He became thus known as the discoverer of Minoan culture. — *Transl.*

64 A hierodule was a temple prostitute in ancient Greece. — *Transl.*

140

Kypris: This contracted form originated in Aeolic pronunciation and was established by the Homeric rhapsodes. The original form must have been (after Kyparissia etc.) something like Kupara (the *ue* is Ionian pronunciation). Perhaps Kupaera?

141

Kypros was the name given to the island by the Sea Peoples or the earliest Greeks, just as in Messenia the town, river and mountain were called Kyparissiai, because there were brothel temples everywhere. On the Syrian coast the island was called Kittim. Also the old name Alasia was still known. There is nothing to be done with the name Jadnana because we do not know from whom the Assyrian officials heard the name and whether they understood it correctly. (Similarly Kat-patuku. Who is that?)

142

The Greek-speaking tribes did not adopt the name Alashiya. It remained known on the Phoenician coast (Elissa). These seafarers may have made the Kypris sanctuaries the name of the islands (similarly Minoa, Artemision, Apollonia, Athens (?), Delphinion, Potidaia). Kypris is a name that was common in Alashiya.

143

If Zeus, Persian *baga*, (Phrygian *bog* = god), is really connected with *fagus* = beech and *quercus* with Perkūnas, this proves that one did not want to designate the botanical genus, but the demons of the forest mass, of the rustling in the tops — long before personal gods and certain tree species were thought of. Fagus etc. does not (always) denote the same tree. The name of the tree [is] therefore derived from the name of the god, not vice versa! Only late [did one find] an interest in naming the tree species. *Likewise Kyparissos, Cupressus* [= tree of Kypris].

144

There never was a 'Phoenician people'. What is meant is the urban population of a few port cities, among which Sidon, for example, was authoritative until 1200, and later Tyre. These people, or perhaps only the ruling patriciate, called themselves 'Sidon and Tyre'. It is true that they spoke the same Hamitic dialect that was widespread throughout western Syria from Aleppo to Samaria, the Kinachni. This is not 'Phoenician', but rather Canaanite. Incidentally, the region was then called Canaan, as the Tyrians privately called themselves. It was only under the influence of theology that we introduced the name for Palestine, because the Israelite Bedouins encountered it when some of their tribes crossed the Jordan. It was not until the Ionian sea traders from Miletus that the Tyrians were called Phoenicians, the reddish ones, i.e. the Orientals, according to an old common appellative.

145

Hera [is] not a name, but [a] form of address: mistress. Like Freya, Frouwe, Leda, Leto. If in the 'Phoenician' sphere Baal and Baalat are also used, [this] is proof of the fact that the Sea Peoples of the upper class adopted the Semitic language. Tyre is a 'Sea People city'.

146

[It is] quite possible that the Greeks originally placed 'Phoenicians' in Canaan. They meant seafarers from the Orient (red) or [with] red-painted ships or the like. Then the designation shifted to Tyre. [Cf.] Frankistan, West Indies.

147

Kypris: Chased in a storm through the watery desert, failing ... I can think of it like this: the Danaans got to know the goddess Kuparis in the Peloponnese, [in] Carthage, [on] Crete, then, when they came to Alashiya in 1200, they found her again — under the name

'Aphrodite', which sounded different then. Afterwards they called the island Kypros, island of Kupara.

148

Around 1200 [the] Syrian cities were conquered by Sea Peoples, as further south by the Philistines. A ruling class that adopted native language, religion [and] culture. Now Tyre leads.

Politically and socially the class views of the north hold. The leading families then established and organised in the west and in Carthage. Hence the structural affinity.

149

On the coast of Ugarit, at first, as it seems, the name Alashiya sticks, which also remained alive in the Semitic usage (Elissa), without the original meaning being understood yet (a word like 'West Indies'). Then apparently 'Sidonians' appeared [for it]. In Ionian times, however, Tyre was the leading maritime trading centre, and afterwards the coast was called 'Tyrian' = Syria by the Ionians, like Philistaea — Palestine further south.

150

Anak, Pelasgians (Ed. Meyer II, 2, 81): Connection between Lydians, Philistines, Phoenicians. Lydian king Akiamos (Akis Philistine king). 'Foundation' of Tyre in 1198 by the Sea Peoples. -amos: Akiamos Akis, Perrhamos Paris, Pergamos. Ptolemos Ptolis. Lydian naval rule before Troy — there must be some truth in this. They were Tyrrhenians (Pelasgians). Until 1198 Sidon is Phoenicia, from then on Tyre. The Homeric name Sidonians therefore dates from before 1200.

ISRAEL AND PHILISTINES

151

The 'Rephaim' in Palestine are 'Hamito-Semites', with a cult of the dead. They brought the Semitic type of language with them. Akkadians? The Israelites of the 1st millennium B.C. had no belief in immortality, i.e. they had the Babylonian view. Everything Egyptian has disappeared. Nordic is the ancestor cult of the kings, very weak.

152

[The Noah account Gen. 9, 20 ff., which is] the tale of the drunken winegrower, whose original punch line — presumably an inheritance quarrel — has today been replaced by a theological interpretation in which the 'blessing' has been put in the altered sense. This is the work of a priestly editor in the late Israelite royal period, perhaps only after the exile. But the documents of the Hittite Empire do not begin until about 1370 with Suppiluliuma, and the Achaean name, of which we shall speak later, still appears under him. At that time, therefore, the Kafti power had already come to an end, probably a reason for the chaos among the Syrian small states that lured the Hittites and Egyptians to make conquests here. The Noachian saying thus dates from somewhat earlier times, presumably the last attempt of the Kafti to assert themselves, whereby one or individuals may have temporarily established dominions with their mercenaries. The saying shows the same picture as the letters of the city chiefs there to the Pharaoh. When later — around 1200 — the tribal confederation 'Israel' was founded in the mountains between the Jordan and the sea, in order to snatch the land from the small city chieftains (Albrecht Alt[65]), Japheth was understood to mean the Philistines, Canaan the natives. Was it perhaps only then that the name Canaan was transferred to the land, whose name until then had somehow been related to 'Ham'?

---

65 Albrecht Alt (1883–1956) was a prominent German biblical historian. He was considered an expert on Israelite law. — *Transl.*

The Philistines themselves already called the island Crete—hence 'Kreti' –, the Egyptians Kafti; that this was the same word has never been realised. (Cf. Gaul of Celts, Galatians.) To the Philistines the distant island was 'Crete'—hence the 'the Cherethites and Pelethites', the bodyguard of David. The Israelites themselves, of course, being landlocked, had no conception of the geographical conditions of this distance. One cannot imagine the horizon of the writers of the various tables of nations narrowly enough.

153

The pre-Canaanite population of Palestine [was] partly Hamitic (Megalithic), close to the languages of the Nile (most place names, for example). The 'written Egyptian' [was] an artificial language. We know nothing about the dialects of the districts around 3000. They may have been more similar to the early Hamitic.

154

Japhet, Noah: The very old Noachian blessing or curse 9:25 fr. has 'Shem, Japhet and Canaan', Flood. This is connected with the Ararat legend, comes from Harran—Nairi and denotes Shem (Aramaeans), Japhet (allied western states on the coast of eastern Asia Minor, Cilicia) and the south: C[anaan] = Syria. Before 1400? or before 1200? The other version 'Shem, Ham, Japhet' belongs to the author of the Table of Nations, and is therefore made to fit *its* order.

After the fall of Kafti in 1400, hereditary powers emerge: Javonians—Carians and Japhet—Alashiya. We cannot look into the political background of these mere remains of names, because the Egyptians and Hittites are silent, but much can be assumed. I will show this later.

[The biblical author] has no idea that Japhet and Caftor are the same name. He has had to adopt the scheme of the old legend and then divides the names known to him, partly according to the north-west, north-east, south, partly according to political positions known to him. Since the list, repeatedly amended in various versions, was finally combined into one, the oldest scheme, which was perhaps based on a clearer principle, can hardly be reconstructed.

155

The Noah legend (3 sons) [is] an older legend of the origin of mankind alongside [the legend of the] Table of Nations and [the] building of the tower! The legend of the building of the tower proves that it cannot have originated in the S[outh] — complete misunderstanding of the 'tower' and the religiosity that created the symbol. It was people of a completely different religion who created this disrespectful narrative. The Table of Nations knows nothing of the Flood. The Noah legend is older, more northern. It does not think of 'all' peoples.

156

[The Noachian Blessing] is the remnant of a triumphal song, in my opinion, before it gets into the novella of the drunken winegrower Noah, much earlier than this was summed up with the Flood and even the Table of Nations. The song of triumph (like Deborah) of a band of mercenaries who had once triumphed in the service of the Kafti group over a Mitanni state.

157

Both the enigmatic [chapter] Gen. 14, a text so altered by further narration that occasion and original text cannot be guessed, and the series Abraham — N[ahor] — H[aran] show that A[bram] had somehow been a tribal or landscape name before it received this Semitic form. But then it is clear where it comes from: from the Nairi region. Hyksos — Chabiri — 'Aramaeans'. Who then raised the name Aramaean? The Assyrian government. It was then generally adopted, also by the people themselves: cf. *Indios* (Spanish), Indians (English), *Indianer*[66].

---

66 German: 'Amerindians'. — *Transl.*

158

Japetos [has] in H[esiod] a similar part in the genealogy of men, as in the old sagas of Genesis Noah. This must be mentioned here, although it can only be discussed in detail from later contexts: this vivid thinking of human prehistory in the form of patriarchal family trees and genealogies leading down to one's own people as the centre of history. We know it from the ancient tribes, [from] the Hellenic tradition, Hesiod above all, but it must also be presupposed among the Italics, otherwise they would not have adopted the Greek scheme so quickly and applied it to their prehistory when the Hellenistic type of literature became urban fashion. It is the same with the Chinese way of constructing prehistory (Haloun[67]). Before the Confucian scheme, of course, there were folk tribal legends of this kind. Only from the folk [genealogies] has the learned [been derived]. And so it is with that part of the Israelite tribal legends which has this style: it came from the north, so it was [Aramaic]: Chabiri, Hyksos. Nothing of the kind with Akkadians [and] Arabs.

159

The Kafti name, then, [is] respected and feared throughout the coast. In the interior it evidently served as a summary designation of the stranger in the west, northwest, Asia Minor, [in the] islands: Japhet. A very curious testimony to this is the 'legend of Noah' in the Israelite legend, then, when Jahvist and Elohist began to write in the royal period, already old, a dark process that had become incomprehensible. So from about the 15th/14th century. The Flood saga here, hinterland of Ugarit. Likewise the brothers of Abraham. About this later. The Israelites, landlocked people, knew the name Kafti from Tyre. They did not realise that Japhet was the same.

---

67 Gustav Haloun (1898–1951) was a Czech sinologist. — *Transl.*

160

Since Alashiya is only a part of the world of Kafti, it is clear that the name Kafti was still known and used there and on the coasts of Cilicia and Syria. Hence the name Japhet, Kaphtor in the Israelite folk legends, which was created here, in the region of Harran and Naharain, (Abraham-Nahor-Haran). What the Philistines later brought with them was the name of Crete. It was not until the Greeks that the island was called Crete. For the Phoenicians the island name was Kaphtor, and Kreti only the name of a tribe of people.

161

The genealogical is Nordic, the Bible knows only the establishment of ancestors to legitimise nobility, not the mythology of family trees. The ruling class of the Chabiri did that, also Abram, Isaac, Jacob, 12 sons. That is slowly disappearing with the penetration of the southern Bedouin swarm. For patriarchal genealogy is quite alien to the 'Semites', Hamites, Sumerians. The tribes ('Israel') that had long been seated in northern Palestine were 'Aramaeans'. Twelve-tribe confederation with the southern Bedouins (Judah), who would have achieved nothing without this help. Sedentary, intermingling with the natives — thus the Nordic element loses dominance. Japhet refers to the coastal tribes and states that were under the protection of the Kafti. Shem [is] the 'Semitic'-speaking tribe, Ham the other.

162

In the Old Testament Abraham appears as a peaceful old man, an old lord and patriarch. But he must once have been young and passionate. So that image only came into being when he was already the original priest in the theological construction. If Nahor and Haran are states, then Abraham is also the personification of a political concept. 'Aramaeans' and Abraham [are] thus basically identical. Was 'Abraham' the fictitious human ancestor, the 'sense of the people', or the divine power that worked in it?

163

Genesis Table of Nations and ancestral line: Very revealing! It is the only vestigial testimony to the practical-real international significance of the lands to the visual circle of a man in, say, Sidon. In the genealogy of Abraham [is contained] a remnant of the lordly legend which the Habiri had among them. Abiram may have been one of their famous princes. Ancient place names: Haran, Naharain, primeval Chasdim (Chaldea) are Chabiri seats. Nahor = Naharain. Then (ego) the word Abraham is much easily identical with Chabiraim, Abiram. In Hebrew the people is called 'Ibrim'. The genealogical principle still survives late in Israelite thought, where the genealogy of peoples appears in the form of a family tree: the sons of Noah. [An after-effect of] Atlantis.

164

Adonai: appellative: in the Old Testament very often = *pater familias*. Only in Byblos call of the ancient vegetation god, who in Sidon is called Eshmun, among others. [Adonis] only attested

in Hellenistic times! Melek is the lord of the state. Melkart lord of the polis. Baal [is] lord, owner (nobility): Signoria, Senatus. In the Old Testament names of the legend period (before Saul), one has to reckon with a very large number of *non*-Western Semitic names that have been made Hebrew by folk etymology. The many puns prove this. The stream of conquering troops [came] from the north, whose leaders in Egypt are called Hyksos, whose crew as mercenaries in foreign service are called Chabiri (Hebrews), whose nationality is called Aramaeans: 1700 Hyksos; 1300 Aramaeans, Chabiri.

165

Midianites, tribal group of Aramaic language. [The] cult of Yahweh [is] indigenous to them (later the Israelite god). Around 1200–1000 powerful, nomads, since 1000 they disappear, dissolved into sedentary populations. Main grazing areas east and southeast of the Gulf of Aqaba.

166

I now reckon that the 'Israelite royal period' was 'Indo-European', Nordic, in its inner form. Cf. the Indo-European king names since 1400. At that time the whole Orient was flooded with swarms of horsemen. Nordic is heroism, individualism, historical sense — with Jews and Hittites as writing first historical reports and praising the sublime: Samson! With the exile it is destroyed. Now the 'Jews' only continued. But Indo-European is only the upper class: kings, not prophecy! That was the reflex of the Sea Peoples period. The spirit of chess is post-exilic: they are different people. The Maccabees are not heroes, but religious fanatics.

167

Israel and Judah [are] different tribal groups, Aramaic-Hebrew, each with its own tribal legends. When a unification takes place temporarily in the Philistine period (David, Solomon), the committed literature Yahwist and Elohist[68] emerges. Courtly, as a common prehistory. When the Israelites take the land, the nobility of the cities (Indo-European, Harrish, etc.) is also incorporated (A. Alt, 25) — Saul, for example? The northern state was founded by Saul, the southern state by David.

168

Jews 1000 B.C.: These are two 'peoples' that are only brought together externally and temporarily (is the difference between Hebrew and Aramaic perhaps connected with this?). The southern people ('Leah tribe of Judah'), God Yahweh with the empty tent, 'Mosaic' religion, with the Levites (according to H. Grimme[69] the Levites are servants given to the God, in southern Arabia), from Kadesh,

---

68 Yahwist and Elohist are different parts of the Torah. In the Yahwist section, God is called 'Yahweh' and in the Elohist section he is called 'Elohim'. — *Transl.*

69 Hubert Grimme (1864–1942) was a German linguist, orientalist and Semitist. — *Transl.*

imageless. The northern people [is] warlike (Joshua, Deborah), with the God Yahweh Zebaoth and Ark of the Covenant. Tribes 'Israel' or 'Ephraim' or 'Joseph'. Both groups [are] of different religiosity and tradition. Deborah song: any connection with the South is missing. Only the kings created [it], fleetingly calculated, for fifty years. Only the exile creates a history of political togetherness, Ezekiel, and before that the fates of the land since Chaldean times. Jeremiah only feels the kinship of faith. Since then the terms Israel and Judah flow together, which was painfully recognised only after the loss of the tradition of royal unity.

169

History of Israel: In the 2nd millennium [there are] numerous Bedouin tribes of changing connection, sometimes allied, sometimes hostile (blood feud), splintered, forming anew. Larger associations [are] always the work of an important sheikh (Joshua, see Abd el Kader, Senussi, Wahhabis). A number of such tribes, perhaps Hebrew-South Semitic, Israelite, [came] from the south against Canaan (Mosaic legend, Sinai God, Levites), quite another (Israel, Abram legend, Aramaic, Zebaoth) from the north. The danger of the Philistines only led the Sheikh Saul to attempt a larger grouping (12 tribes), which fell apart again with Solomon. But a tradition of belonging together once was maintained. After the exile, only a few southern tribes return, but spiritually they carry both traditions. Only the northern tribes had an ancient 'literature' similar to Hittite. After the exile, Jewish literature is made out of it.

170

The legend of the war of the five kings [Gen. 14] is a remnant of Nordic heroic saga. Just as the Trojan War unites all kinds of heroes before Troy, so here the great names [of the time] are united in one [action] (*Song of the Nibelungs*: Theoderich, Attila). The later literary schools Yahwist and Elohist no longer understood this and transferred it into the 'historical'.

171

Thou shalt not make unto thee any graven image or likeness — this is Nordic sentiment translated into Southern dogmatics. Also the cult horns on the altar in Israel and Crete: the double axe, sign of the Nordic weather god. The male images of the gods are missing in Crete — but the god is [imageless] (Dodona). It is the ancient Indo-European layer between the Danube and the Hindu Kush.

172

Yahweh Zebaoth [means] Yahweh-'hosts' (plural), the numen whose roaring, blood-dripping incarnation is the storming armies, a horrible deity that tramples down and slaughters.

Is not Zebaoth folk-etymologically developed from Teisbas[70]? Zeus Pater.

173

(According to Kittel[71] II, 290 ff.) The Yahwist c. 850, from Judah, great writer. The Elohist 750 (Hosea period) from Ephraim. The Yahwist collected the old legends, preserved them, reinterpreted them in the concept of a heavenly god, of sin, repentance, etc. Yahweh is for him 'God in heaven'. At about the same time, the authors of the king stories.

174

Yahweh covenant god of 'Israel' in Sichern — worshipped by Joshua's clan until then (Joseph). The Aramaean tribe (Leah, Israel), already partly disintegrated, joined in. The covenant must have

---

70 Teisbas was the Urartu god of the air. — *Transl.*

71 Rudolf Kittel (1853–1929) was a German Protestant theologian and Old Testament scholar. — *Transl.*

defended itself against a great danger. Sellin[72] (*Festschrift für Haupt*, 1926): The Deborah Song refers to this. Judah was converted to Yahweh from Kadesh. Moses is the champion of this faith, which was politically transformed at Sichern.

175

There is no Semitic race any more than there is an Indo-European race. These are linguistic designations, nothing more. In reality, from the Near East, from southern Arabia (from Abyssinia) to Armenia, there have been tribes of very different ethnicities and very different somatic types. For historical, political reasons, Semitic languages have spread and slowly displaced the many others. Assyrians, Armenians, Phoenicians are far from being blood relatives of the Arabs.

176

'Tarsis and Elisha' [have] passed into the Table of Nations as a fixed formula. It is quite wrong to suppose there is great geograph[ical]-political knowledge in the Yahwist and Elohist tables. This is a naive compilation into which all names the author had ever heard of was put in order to show off, old genealogies, information from Sidon, names whose meaning he does not even know. 'Tarsis and Elisha' is a rambling expression, which is simply inserted here.

177

The northern tribes (Achlame, Chabiri), who went south before the Armenians, had legends of wanderings which brought them as far as Hebron: of Noah, Abram, Nahor, Haran, etc. Only a few slivers were later, not understood, reinterpreted, adopted by the Jews. These include the single epics, Abram, the wandering Aramaean, etc. In contrast, 'Jacob' sits in the cult place of the later tribe of Joseph. Laban, Esau — these are humanised gods. Canaan (Meyer II, 2, 63) is what the

---

72   Ernst Sellin (1867–1946) was a German biblical archaeologist. — *Transl.*

Phoenicians called their country, even the peasants around Carthage. So originally it means a northern territory.

178

The 'twelve tribes' [is] a fixed term of the covenant of Sichern. The name [is] preserved only in the form which has been fixed since the 9th century. Thus Levi = Levites. Originally [there were] partly quite different names. For example, instead of Levi, Leah. Issakar, 'servant', [is probably] a later mocking name. The actual name has disappeared. Gad and Asser are names of gods. The final version of the name belongs to the time of Daniel. Perhaps the twelve names had long since disappeared and been replaced by others that were Akkadian. Joseph, for example, is not listed correctly either, there are several lists (Noth). But 'Reuben, Simeon, Levi' is old, since the tribes no longer existed. The *sequence* of names must have had meaning once.

179

Sons of Shem (Noah legend), i.e. people who have a name based on the existence of a foreign tribe. The free-living cattle-breeder despises the farmer who clings to the soil. For them, farming is a descent into a slave-like existence. The names of the nomads and cattle breeders, however, are attached to tribe, clan, family, while those of the farmers are attached to place, field, village, house. The Dorian and Aramaic migrations brought such free-living tribes — cattle breeders, robbers, seafarers — into a farming country. They left the peasants to live as bondsmen and the townsfolk to plunder, sitting in between, intent only on their well-being.

180

Israel: In Sichern the covenant of the tribes between Josue (Joseph), the Israel tribes and a few others. The Joseph group used to belong to another Bedouin association, that of Sinai/Horeb. Yahweh [was] the covenant god above the tribal gods. This covenant soon fell into disuse — Philistine times, special kings — with the settling down, the mingling with the townsfolk. Only the number of twelve, the names and the order remained legendary. Many tribes had dissolved, joined together differently. Gradually the geographical connection became more important (Judah, Israel). The earlier special legends of the tribes and places (Abraham, Egyptians, Moses, Joshua) are combined into one tradition by writing priests, contradictory enough. The covenant of twelve did not last long. One event, then only a cult custom.

181

Sethe (*Amun und die acht Urgötter von Hermopolis*[73], § 281) draws attention to the equality of the conception of Amun, the creative breath of air over the primordial waters of Nun, and Yahweh, the breath of God over the waters. This ancient Egyptian priestly conception of the temple of H[ermopolis] — a conception in a wet coastal land — has thus come to Jerusalem through 'Moses' or only since 600. Is Gen. 1. 1. Yahwist, Elohist or priestly writing?

182

Personal names [formed from compounds] with Yahweh [there are five in] Judges' time and Moses' time together; rare, the first 'Joshua'. Since David plentiful (Noth 106 ff.), among the 40 names of kings 21. Outside Israel the name Yahweh does not occur (Noth 108 ff.) The rarity of Yahweh in the time of Moses and Judges proves that it is the god of a tribe that gains ground very slowly. (The five names belong to nobles.) When with kingship the tribes dwindle and the state begins, Yahweh becomes state god.

183

The Semitic personal names with Ab (father) and Ach (brother) thus designate the tribal deity. The own god [appears] as ancestor, protector, comrade of the tribe (Noth 73 ff). This god very often has

---

73 'Amun and the Eight Primordial Gods of Hermopolis'. — *Transl.*

no name, or one avoids naming him. (*Nomina sunt odiosa*[74].) This thus corresponds to designations such as Baal, Melek, Lada, Hera, Frouwe. With the formation of a state (Saul) over the tribes, these names become rarer because several deities are now known to exist. Yahweh is the state god, not the only god. Only the anti-state-minded (followers of the tribal idea) want only *one* tribal god. They do not understand the state idea.

184

Israelites and Greeks [are] the only ones who know genealogical tribal myths: Jon, Hellen, Jacob, Abraham. The only ones for whom professions become fictitious family trees: Orpheus, Daedalus, Homer, Levites, Tubalcain.

185

Bethsean (*Reallexikon II*, 4 and I, 44 ff!): Enormously important: before the Philistines a 'Mycenaean' master race. The name Tursha [is] inscribed! Pithoi as at Knossos, with Mycenaean face masks. Here the Philistines hung the body of Saul. Later (Solomon) with Thaanach and Megiddo one district. Minoan since 2000 in Canaan: Gressmann[75], *Zt. Alttest. Wiss.*[76] 43 (1925) 239 f.

186

The Philistines [are] religiously tolerant (unlike the henotheistic Israelites): they allow land cults everywhere, including the Ark of Yahweh. Around 1080 victory of the Philistines (conquest of the Ark), destruction of the Israelite temple in Shiloh, disarming of the Israelites (no more iron, prohibition of smithing; exactly the same thing was imposed by Porsena on the Romans. So the Sea Peoples brought the

---

74 Latin: 'Names are odious'. — *Transl.*

75 Hugo Gressmann (1877–1927) was a German Protestant theologian and Old Testament scholar. — *Transl.*

76 'Journal of Old Testament Science'. — *Transl.*

iron with them!). Around 1000 defeat and death of Saul. Gad destroyed since about Amos. Gaza flourishing under the Persians.

187

The Iliad in the Old Testament: An excellent account, seen through the eyes of the enemy (Homer is status poetry). This political organisation and mode of struggle, so entirely and therefore strikingly exact [as in the] *Iliad*: council of princes. The Israelites, a primeval and warlike race, were far inferior [to the Philistines] physically and tactically. Both fought for dominion over the native population, from which both borrowed languages and numina. Zeus and Sinai Yahweh. This is what the older legend of the sons of Noah means, as seen in Gen. 9:25 ff. Only from the Philistine victories did a tragic heroism develop among the Bedouin tribes, who were consumed with jealousy: Saul and David. The Sea People were no match for them in numbers. Their victory at Mount Gilboa, where Saul commits suicide in an ancient way when all is lost, the betrayal of David and his band of freebooters, the old skaldic song about the death of the hero — quite Homeric, *Song of Hildebrand*[77]. It is all quite warlike and unpriestly. No revision of Samuel has blurred that. David is a feudal lord of the Philistines, who now rule again as far as the Jordan, and fights Abner, who wants to uphold the house of Saul. Blood feuds, tribal feuds pave the way for David. David seems to have perished in the family quarrel: but he finished off the Philistines. Both were sturdy barbarians, superstitious, inhibited by many religious considerations.

188

Anak: This troop of perhaps a hundred warriors who spread terror had no name. Anakites became the name in the legend. How many inhabitants did Canaan have anyway? The 'cities' [numbered] at most

---

77 *The Song of Hildebrand* is the oldest poetical German text in existence, written sometime in the 830s. It tells the story of a son who does not recognise his father in battle. — *Transl.*

a few thousand inhabitants, a few hundred warriors. Half a million Canaanites [was] already too much. The Israelite tribe, all together, [had] maybe ten thousand warriors. Dan a few hundred. The group of Joseph, again breaking up into Ephraim and Manasseh, a few thousand. Loose connection, which by [Judges] became temporarily a unit for war. Families passing from one tribe to another.

189

Anak's children, in three tribes: Ahiman, Thalmai, Sesai (what language?) around Hebron, later displaced to the Philistine cities. So Sea Peoples. The Sea Peoples [came] along the Norman route Tartessos — Sardinia — Cyrene to the eastern edge of the Mediterranean. Identical with the Dolmen Route! Dolmen in Tripoli (Libyan). Also the Kabyles Sea Peoples Route?

Then the Greeks would have come from the North Sea! Hence the correspondence with [the] Libyan! The landlubbers, on the other hand, are Italic — Dorian. Dorian [is] therefore [an] *adopted* language, not brought along! There are Greek places Thalamai and Seamai (like Perg-amos). Num. 13:22 Hebron built seven years before Tanis. There is the connection: a mercenary colony? 1 Sam. 30 Cretans live between Hebron and Gaza.

190

In Gaza the Marnion, temple of Marna(s), Cretagenes — Zeus (Vita Porphyrii 64)! Marnas is Semitic, but purely Gazan. Cf. also Schürer[78] II, 28 ff. Astarte — the name covers in contrast to Derketo = Atargatis a genuine Philistine deity! Dagon: the name [is] probably a native (Canaan) grain deity; but the numen of the Philistines (fish-tail like Astarte) [is] a sea god (Poseidon).

On the coins Gaza is called: Gaza minca. Gaza mints coins according to Attic foot and often with Greek inscription, while the

---

78 Emil Schürer (1844–1910) was a German Protestant theologian and a scholar of Jewish history. — *Transl.*

Phoenician coastal cities Tyre, Sidon, Byblos had Phoenician foot, Aradus Persian foot. Gaza (in the interior) had a harbour town like all these somewhat inland places. Astaroth (Astarte, not Atargatis!), a generally Near Eastern deity (or category), thus also a genuinely Phoenician deity, is aligned. This has yet to be determined. As Herod had Teutons and Gauls in his bodyguard (Josephus[79] *Antiq.* XVII, 8,8), [so David Cherethites and Pelethites].

191

Enak's children: Aias and Teukros [are] sons of Telamon of Salamis. (Ai — Ahiman, Teucros — Sisai, Zeker; Telamon — Talami). Salamis, Salmoneus, Salmydessos, Salmonia (Crete), Salamander, Salambo (according to Hesych name of Aphrodite in Babylon. If r = 1 [she was probably called] Sarrapa or similar). Teucros [is the] founder of Salamis in Cyprus. Aias and Teucros [are] the priestly titles of Olbe in Cilicia. Teucrians a people (Meyer, § 491).

192

Philistine pottery: It corresponds to the Cyprian shortly before 1000, is a variety of the Late Mycenaean. The counterpart of Goliath is the humorous figure of the tribe of Dan, Samson. A savage, in love, brutal, eternally chasing the Philistine women. The barbarian at the cultural border (Samson, like Jonah, annexed by the Jews! Cf. Grail, Arthur). Under Ramses II 1292–1225 Canaanites still sit in Philistine territory.

193

For the Israelite Bedouins who possessed Canaan (highlands), Crete was a present danger, Japheth a faded Aramaean legend from the north: Shem, Harn, Japhet.

---

79 Flavius Josephus (37 or 38–100 A.D.) was a Jewish-Roman historian who wrote a famous account of the Jewish Revolt of 66–70 A.D. — *Transl.*

194

The Israelite 'prophets' [are] not mystics or ecstatics, but enthusiastic popular politicians who dictated their sayings and speeches, in the fixed scheme of prophecy common in the South. Today's writings, however, are later redactions, composed of many small original texts. This form of demagogy is generally 'magical', since the ruler is also the 'voice of God'. The 'people of Israel' of 1100 B.C. [is] a tribal coalition of very different races.

195

Hebrews: In the royal period [there still exist] clearly two names which Jirku[80] considers to be two peoples; but they are, as often, the cult name of the whole community (Israel) and the status name of the warrior class (Ibrim): cf. Spartiates and Lacedaimonians, Romans and Quirites. Habiru as a status name is also found among other Aramaic peoples.

196

The history of the origin of the Israelites is easy to overlook if one does not have excessive doubt or faith. It is the only surviving example of the fate of semi-nomadic folk formations, as they occurred incessantly in those years.

Everywhere the Bedouin tribes, a few hundred heads, grazed together, had their [tribal] say with arch-fathers, their mountain god. The B'ne Joseph sat in pits, other sheikhs joined, so a somewhat larger group was formed, which allied itself with the B'ne Moab. The B'ne Jacob called themselves [Israel], and as the tribe of Joseph brought the legend of Moses, so another (turnips) brought the legend of Abram the 'Hebrew'. Finally, they all called themselves Hebrews. The covenant, B'ne Israel, came into being for the conquest in Judea. Afterwards it fell into disrepair, but the memory remained as a legend. Four tribes were not originally part of it, so Dan (Samson!), of mixed origin. So

---

80   Anton Jirku (1885–1972) was a German biblical scholar. — *Transl.*

in reality [Israel] was the strong tribe of Joseph (Rachel), and it [was joined by] six small Leah tribes.

The legendary figure of Moses, the Egyptian, belongs to the tribe of Joseph, and it is possible that once an adventurous destiny of this kind [took place], a man [existed] who led this tribe and wanted to [set in motion] a land seizure.

The legend of the Patriarchs is Canaanite and accepted by Israel. Moses, as an Egyptian, will have organised the Egyptian centralisation of tribal culture. The judges (sheikhs) do little. The great Philistine storm leads to the Israelites taking their form: king, army, court, heroic saga!

197

Telling the Jewish story according to Wellhausen: it gives a picture of this kind of history: the Bedouin tribes, united to form the B'ne Israel, then disintegrate again, — already in the Deborah song — cruel, greedy, superstitious. The sheikh Joshua. This is what such migrations looked like: the cities remain Canaanite, of higher culture. The Bedouins have their camps in the pastures, murder and raiding continue, but gradually the Bedouins learn the language of the land (all according to Wellhausen).

But these 'Semites' are Europeans, light-coloured, tough. Like Mohammed. The chiefs of the Canaanites [were] always at odds. So it is all chance until one day a great man comes along. Deborah — a Joan of Arc.

198

The Israelites were shepherds of sheep and goats, the Midianites camel nomads and robbers, the Canaanites farmers, their chiefs still from the Indo-Europeans and Egyptians horse and chariot fighters. The ground smoked with blood, there was murder on both sides, out of blood feud or greed. After all, there was no family in the tribes that was not related to a foreign family. They become farmers; the Bedouin ideal of the prophets is obsolete. That the B'ne of Israel became more than other tribes, they owe to the Philistine wars. Saul becomes the first Canaanite-style 'king', like Arminius, who wanted to imitate the Romans, without success. David has not one tribe behind him, but an army of professional warriors, including many Philistines. He is not an 'Israelite' at all, but an adventurer. Solomon [is] elevated by a palace intrigue.

199

The Babylonian exiled Jews were rich, educated. This was the intellectual centre. In Judea [dwelt] the poor narrow-minded ones. There mixture with the superior Canaanites: cult, marriage. Under Solomon all cults [were] represented in the Temple, for Jehovah [there remained] only a corner. Only the 'second Mosaism' of Ezra created Mecca.

NEAR EAST — AEGEAN SEA — MYCENAE

ARAM AND ASSUR

200

Assur: [Are] the founders 'Mitanni'? The type on the ancient works of Sumerian style [is] not Sumerian. Since 1400 Assyrian art in its own right, reminiscent of Asia Minor, southern Russia in animal reliefs, hunts, etc. The Assyrians [are] the first horsemen. Warrior people. Rock reliefs, facades from Phrygia to E[lam]. Reliefs: landscape painting! Perspective: all this a marginal amoeba of Turanian-Kashitic mixture. The name, originally Asir, [is] probably not Semitic (Eduard Meyer). The Greeks called the Halys region Assyria. Assyrian politics [always] tend towards the Black Sea. Accordingly, Mycenae, Troy VI, Chatti, Assur, Aram are almost simultaneous. Many related traits: warlike, heroism. Dukes with retinue. Nobility of Hittite treatment of opponents, like Abram. Contrast with Judah. Everything 'Phrygian' [is] therefore Assyrian: an East Minor Asian amoeba to which Kussar (Old Hatti), Assur, Phrygia belonged. Home of the mother goddesses: Ma[gna Mater] Kybele. All this is shamanism.

201

Aramaeans: Paradise (Gunkel[81]) is thought to be on the Armenian mountains, from where the four rivers come. Blood revenge (Cain, Lamech) and suicide of the conquered (Saul) are Nordic. Farming is the contemptible punishment of Adam. Cain founds the city of Enoch. Where. Hanigalbat[82]? Gen. 6: sons of gods and daughters of men, giants: a remnant of High Norse (Iranian-Hellenic-Germanic-Hittite) mythology, 'Aramaic', absolutely unsemitic. The Jews deleted all but one verse of it.

202

Aramaeans (*Reallexikon* Ar[am] Ahlame): Starting point (since 1400 approximately) on the northern Euphrates (Naharain, Carchemish, etc. Achlame [is] an older tribal association name).

Advancing from here to the southwest and southeast, forming many small states. Ego: The Aramaic dialect has of course only been adopted and [developed] there. Their earlier language will have been, as in Assur, a 'proto-Artaean' one. From here comes Mos. 22, 20 ff. as the genealogy mentioned there, further Ararat, Noah legends, Paradise, Abram Mos. 11, 27 ff., Harran. These are the Eastern Aramaeans. From the Western Aramaeans came, among others, the Israelite League and the Empire of Damascus. This is a north-south migration of peoples of the first order, which must go back much further — to southern Russia? Can Nordic customs be deduced from the legends of the Fathers? (Kittel? Read up!)

---

81 Hermann Gunkel (1862–1932) was a German Protestant theologian and Old Testament scholar. — *Transl.*

82 Hanigalbat is the Assyrian name for Upper Mesopotamia. — *Transl.*

203

Aramaeans: Chalder, Harrier (Harri-ni = Harran), Mita-ni are structures of Turanian character. The language, too, may be close to the Indo-European type in the spirit of its structure. The same applies to the type of legend formation. This is how (Lehmann-Haupt[83], *Weltgeschichte*[84] p. 147) the Semiramis legend came into being. And likewise Abram and Noah are Turanian figures — may the names and places be what they will. They are personalities and private fates. Gilgamesh, Sargon is different.

204

Aramaeans: The real creators of the Arab culture of northern people — the Semitic language is *adopted*. The older language must have been 'Cassitic' (Gutium, Chaldu, Kassu, Mitanni). Tribal nouns like Harran, Aram, Chald among other gods. They have penetrated as far as Hedjaz. One group has ruled southern Babylon since 1000, (*Reallexikon*, Chaldeans). Therefore [the] Chaldeans of Ur (Nebuchadnezzar) are identical in name with the Chaldeans of Urartu!

Since the Chabiru and Northern Israelites were also Aramaeans, then indeed, as the language proves, in Persian times everything from S[yria] to Southern Arabia and [from] Suez to Babylon is Aramaean! This migration of peoples corresponded to the Germanic (Magian-Faustian) migration.

205

Aramaeans, Israel: A vast ethnic unit with a Semitic language, whose territory around 2000 lay between Assur, Syria and Palmyra, nomads, perhaps of the Armenoid type? (Jirku, Syria and Aram, *Reallexikon*). At the end of the 2nd millennium B.C. they flooded the

---

83 Carl Friedrich Lehmann-Haupt (1861–1938) was a German historian and orientalist. — *Transl.*

84 'World History'. — *Transl.*

whole of Mesopotamia and founded empires. From there (Harran) the Old Testament imagines the Archfathers coming, who were therefore Aramaeans. Perhaps it was the Israelites who spoke Aramaic in the first place. The immigration of the Israelites into Palestine took place in connection with the Aramaic takeover of Syria, where Aramaic kingdoms arose after the general oriental upheaval of 1200 (Damascus). Finally, the Aramaeans flooded the whole of Babylon: Chaldeans! (Cf. *Reallexikon* the blond Amorites, Ammonites.) Finally, the Aramaeans, like the Arabs later, determined the ethnic [character] of the whole area from Palestine to Babylon.

206

Only now can conclusions be drawn from the language. As usual, it would have led to errors if we had started from the language. Most of the Aramaic tribes of which we know — there are very few — spoke a Semitic dialect. We know this dialect from the time of 800 — and call it 'Aramaic'. Immediately the usual false conclusion now sets in in the minds of philologists and historians: so the Aramaeans 'are' Semites. No, they are not. How do we know 'the Aramaeans'? From names, clay tablets, etc. in a small area. The reports of the Assyrians teach something quite different. Hence: the Aramaeans — collective name of tribes — learned to speak Semitic like the Philistines in Syria. This gave rise to a new dialect group.

207

If Hyksos = Chabiri = Aramaean, it is the chariot culture that invades west or east of the Caspian Sea. The end of the 'old Hittite Empire' [is] a consequence of this. Likewise the Kassites.

208

In Syria, not Palestine, a pre-Semitic place-name stratum (Kittel, *Geschichte des jüdischen Volkes*[85], I, 2, p. 52). In Gezer a layer with

---

85 'History of the Jewish People'. — *Transl.*

cremation of corpses. This would have to be the 'Kashitic' current, from Sinear to Central Europe, over which the Semitic current was superimposed in Akkad, here around 3000. Nöldeke[86] (*Die semitischen Sprachen*[87] 1887, p. 11) and Grimme (*Muhammed* 1904, p. 4 ff.) already advocate the African origin of the 'Semites'. The obsidian of the tools at Gezer (Macalister[88], *Gezer*, II, 127) is from Melos — represented in all layers. Palgrave[89] found enormous stone circles in northern Arabia, with triliths in the manner of Stonehenge (Karge[90], p. 500f.). Very similar in the East Bank: the castle of Kurun Hattin (Karge 352 ff.). The Semite migration of the Akkadians thus went east of the Jordan, then still good cattle steppe.

209

Peoples of Western Asia: [Is there a] relationship between the Elamite, Kassite, Dravidian languages? The racially pure inner-Arab Bedouins certainly resemble northern Europeans, weathered seamen (Ungnad[91], *Kulturfragen* [Culture Questions] 1). According to Ungnad, Subaraeans — Mitanni — Hurrians are identical, brachycephalous, from Palestine to beyond Assur. Landsberger[92] (very good,

---

86 Theodor Nöldeke (1836–1930) was a prominent German orientalist. — *Transl.*

87 'The Semitic Languages'. — *Transl.*

88 Robert Alexander Stewart Macalister (1870–1950) was an Irish archaeologist. — *Transl.*

89 William Gifford Palgrave (1826–1888) was an intrepid English traveller, orientalist and diplomat. He converted to Catholicism and became a Jesuit missionary in India and Syria. After narrowly escaping the massacre of Maronite Christians in 1861, he travelled across Arabia. He had to disguise himself as a Muslim, for fear of otherwise being killed by tribesmen. His book about his journeys and observations, *Personal Narrative of a Year's Journey through Central and Eastern Arabia (1862–1863)*, became a huge bestseller. After leaving the Jesuit order, he served in various diplomatic posts. — *Transl.*

90 Paul Karge (1881–1922) was a German orientalist. — *Transl.*

91 Arthur Ungnad (1879–1947) was a German orientalist and Semitist. — *Transl.*

92 Benno Landsberger (1890–1968) was a famous German Assyriologist. — *Transl.*

Zeitschrift für Assyriologie[93] 35, p. 213 ff.) denies the 'primeval people' of the Subaru on a wide area, the Chabiri as Hebrews, the existence of the Amorites as a race.

The 'Four Realms' or 'World Regions' have no geographical reality in Babylon, but are symbolic expressions. P. 218. Amurru, Elam, Subarntu, Akkad are only approximate directional names. The scheme is also young. Incidentally, according to Landsberger (288), Subartu as a geographical term on the part of the Babylonians is not identical with the 'sub-Araean' (Mitanni) language area. There was no sub-Araean people at all. The area was very small (p. 230). In general, it can be concluded from the proper names of the oldest times that many languages were spoken in this area, as in Boghazköy, which we do not know because the documents are written in Babylonian. We only know of the existence of the Mitanni language through the Amarna (?) tablets[94]. Landsberger (p. 230 note 2) assumes that such a language originated from a group of names to which the word Hanigalbat perhaps belongs. Subartu had once been a name for the area east of Assur, i.e. a very vague term, in Hammurabi a 'mountain range Subartu'. The name belongs with Antan, Guti, Lullumi to a north-eastern group of mountains; according to Landsberger (p. 232) the Subartu are the 'Kurds of the Old World', from where swarms reached Syria, Mesopotamia, Asia Minor in the Amarna period — with many other elements, so that the word encompasses more than is right. Perhaps [it was] a generic name like Chabiri = 'gypsy' (cf. 'Tyrrhenian').

---

93   'Journal of Assyriology'. — *Transl.*

94   The Amarna letters are clay tablets inscribed with cuneiform writing that date to the 14th century B.C. and were found at the site of el-Amarna (Akhetaten), the capital of ancient Egypt during the reign of Akhenaten. — *Transl.*

URARTU, ARMENIANS, MITANNI, KASSITES

210

Kassites: There, too, a ruling Indo-European tribe may have led the movement. The language itself is of course that of the subjugated, also the names (as with Chatti), but the sun god is called Surias (Surya), the wind gods Maritas (Marutas), the 'goddess of the snow mountains' Simalia (*sima* Indo-Iranian = snow). [Is] the name related to Kaspi [Lake Kaspi] after all?

211

Armenia: This mountain range, like the other [(namely the Caucasus,)], preserves a lot of ancient linguistic debris. That it has almost all disappeared, in contrast to the Caucasus, is due to the fact that larger political units with written and administrative languages have existed here for millennia. Only the existence of a kingdom of Navarre has [similarly] protected Basque. All Greek accounts suggest that many languages were spoken in Armenia. As late as the 10th century A.D., the Chuth spoke a language incomprehensible to Armenians. So 'Armenian' is one of many debris parts that has had the good fortune to become the sacred language of a sect.

212

The Armenians [are] also proof of how peoples can simply be invented by science on the basis of false methods. The language is the church language of a Christian community — like Manichaean, Nestorian — since [the] 5th century A.D. The name Armenia [is] an administrative title of Darius. The breed [is] ancient Asia Minor, the language some corrupted non-Germanic dialect, perhaps fixed only post-Christian.

213

Mitanni: The old political name, 1/2 millennium, is Hanigalbat, which still lived on as a geographical term, so was significant. The tribal group was called Han. Hanigalbat is a foolish word. 'Mitanni', on the other hand, is an Indian term, either of the Indian troop, or of its state creation: it is identical with Hanigalbat, beginning and ending with the Indian ruler names. Perhaps, then, the tribe was called Mita(n).

214

Armenia: The Chaldeans, a ruling people over subjugated (Armeni[an]) peoples, from Cilicia — Crete. Their stone buildings [are] similar to those of Boeotia, Mycenae, Crete: Libya, Menuas = Minos = Minyans. Where do the names Chaldea and Urartu (Ararat) come from? 'Armenians' = Aramaeans: name of the valley dwellers who liberated themselves. Indo-European Armenian must have [come up] through Cimmerians, Scythians, etc. Around 600 the Chaldean Empire came to an end, around 500 Darius established the satrapy of Armenia. In between, Armenia begins, i.e. an Indo-European people organises the inhabitants of the valley (Medes? Cimmerians?).

215

Hanigalbat, capital Halab (Aleppo), Egyptian 'hrb' [was] a dominant power between the old and new Chatti empires (c. 16th century), from where (according to Forrer[95]) the Hyksos emanated.

Tudhaljas (Tidal, Genesis 14?) around 1500 makes Chatti independent again. Hanigalbat breaks up into Charri and Mitanni (ego: Charri [is] an ethnic name, Mitanni Indo-European imperial name). In the Amarna letters, Tushratta is a 'Hanigalbat' king who also occupies Assur. The name Hanigalbat appears less and less frequently in Assyrian accounts (1100, 900 as a mere geographical designation).

---

95 Robert Forrer (1866–1947) was a Swiss art historian and archaeologist. He was also the director of the Archaeological Museum in Straßburg until 1945. — *Transl.*

(Schachermeyer, *Zur Lage von Mitanni und Hanigalbat*[96], 1921, Festschrift für Lehmann-Haupt). Halab (Aleppo) [is] already mentioned under Thutmos[is] III. (16th century). Subbiluliuma installs his son as king of Halab; middle of the 14th century. Mentioned in the Amarna letters. Harran [is] wine region, place of worship (only mentioned as Sin place in the 14th century!). Accordingly Hanigalbat = Hana — Halab — at. Cain founds Enoch (this is not the fratricide, but the eponym of Hana). Enoch = Haniq?

216

The 'Armenian' language [may] have arisen as gibberish only in Hellenistic times, when Tig[ranes] made a state out of [Armenia], or else we would have some inscription or coin! Or even later, like other dialects, as a dialect of the 'Armenian Church', a corrupted mountain dialect from some lost Indo-European language (cf. Basque, Rhaeto-Romanic).

217

Is 'Ramman' the eponym of the Aramaeans (Araman)? It is the thunder god (Tesub). Mitanni, like Marianni Mitra, must be an Indian word. That the origin of Armenian goes back considerably beyond Augustus is unlikely: somehow one would have to notice something in names and inscriptions. But the 'Kingdom of Armenia' in Roman times certainly did not have the 'Armenian' language. The young Chatti kingdom is contemporaneous with Charri (Armenia) and Mitanni (Mesopotamia and Assur).

218

Armenia: In the Boghazköy period the Charri dwell there. Phrygia [of the] 6th century [B.C.] already contains Greek influence, [is] therefore young. The last Khatti kings are Tudhalijas IV, Arnuwandas IV, Tudhalijas V, with whom the documents break off [around] 1200

---

96 'On the Location of Mitanni and Hanigalbat'. — *Transl.*

(according to Forrer, *Boghazköi-Texte in Umschrift*[97] II, VI). With the Assyrians since 900 the folk name Charri no longer occurs. Achlamê first at Arik-dên-ilu 1323–1311, where they camped north of Nineveh (i.e. from the Wansee[98]!!) on the Tigris with the Suti and Jauri. Their main place Old Aramaic Tilluli, 'the hills', a little east of Nisib! Only Tiglat Pileser I makes [their land] almost a border province.

219

Beginning: The 'immigration of the Armenians' to Armenia is a splendid piece of philologically determined historiography since — Herodotus. One first found the name Armenia. We now know that it first appears in the provincial division of the Persian kings: Armaniya. Earlier, the area was called Urartu, Chaldean Empire. Of course, the inhabitants are now called Armenians, as if they were a people. Then a language of Indo-European type — among others — has been heard here. It is therefore called Armenian. Herodotus claims that the [Armenians] are related to the Phrygians — because he did not know either. So then 'the Amenians' came from Europe.

220

'Mitanni' (*Reallexikon*): It depends on the name which — since when? — appears there. There is a strict distinction to be made: the sub-Aramaic names from an inconspicuous language group and the name Mitanni, which appears with 'Aryan' rulers' names of the Amarna period, i.e. is itself Aryan. Ephemeral empire.

[The] 'Phrygian' deity Mita (Midas!) [often appears] as a proper name! (Forrer, Assur!) — afterwards (ego) Mita-ni? Capital Wassugani. Αουκ -? also Ussikani: it is the 'Mitanni' name of a Subarus city, which may have an Aramaic name afterwards: Nisib? Saussatar, Artatama. Teje and Nefertiti come from this family. Another name of Mitanni: Hanigalbat. Another Artatama [is] lord of Charri!

---

97 'Boghazkoy texts in transcription'. — *Transl.*

98 The Wannsee is a lake in Berlin, Germany. — *Transl.*

The empire existed only about 1450–1300 and spread from the west (Taurus) over the Euphrates to Assur. In the Amarna letters the Egyptians call the empire Naharina (Nahor, Nairi), Nuri [is a] Late Assyrian term, Nahor Early Aramaic (800 to 1200). Tesub [and] Hepa [are] the main deities of the Subaru (Mitanni). The language belongs together with Elamite and Caucasian. Hanigalbat (*Reallexikon*) and Boghazköy [are] great around 1600–1500, mastering Chatti! Disintegrating into Harran and Mitanni around 1500 (Amarna letters), sometimes named by Assyrians after 800. Since Nasibina (Nisib) is missing from the list of Adadnirari I (Forrer 19), it was then called Wassugani!

HITTITE

221

Tavaglavas: It is the only name, as far as I know, that can be partly explained by the Hittite language of the Boghazköy chancery — and it is the name of a man who was not a Hittite. Is this proof that this language of the chancery did not belong to the ruling class?

222

Asia Minor: Indo-Germanic-Phrygian immigration since about 1200. End of the Chatti Empire. New names: Lydians, Mysians, Teukrians (instead of Trojans). At the same time [the] west coast, Pamphylia [and] Cyprus were occupied by Greeks. In the 7th century [came] Cimmerians from the east, [from] the northwest Thracians (Bithynians). The Phrygians will have settled on the ruins of Troy (7th century). Thus the whole of western Asia Minor became 'Phrygian' (according to Strabo). Dialects. 'Carian' becomes the name of the strata which retained the older language (Luvian). Between 2500 and 2000 the Assyrian empire between Antitaurus and the mouth of Halym, capital: Kültepe near Caesarea, where the 'Cappadocian' clay tablets were found. Still the Greeks called the coast near Sinope

Assyria. Besides Assyrian [there were] many once 'Hittite' proper names. Katpatuku (Cappadocians) [is] since Herodotus the new name for the rest of the Hittite population. One must distinguish the Chatti Empire of 2300–2000 and [that of] 1450–1200 (like Achaemenids and Sassanids).

223

How far does -essos occur in Hittite texts? I believe that the ancient inkling of a pre-Troyan maritime rule of the 'Lydians' refers to the western Hittite empire: Old Chatti is East Asia Minor, New Chatti emanates from Smyrna (the pictorial writing!). After 1200, the empire will again have been confined to this area. The Chatti name is absolutely eastern (cf. *němec*[99] and *allemand*[100]), so that in Homer the empire is perhaps called [differently]: Maeonians? Carians? The 'Hittite' ruling people since 1400 comes from 'Lydia', as a thin upper layer of unknown, perhaps Indo-European language. Preserved in the Mermnads? It is pre-Achaic, 14th/13th century, when the Aquaiwasha[101] already sat in Tiryns and Mycenae.

224

I put here only for consideration: If Sparta — Sparten — Saparda derives from the same pre-Greek language and somehow denotes 'warriors', is the castle of Tonolos near Sardis related to Tumulus? Is this the language of tribes that once perished along the Tiber from the north (?)? I have been thinking about the history of the 2nd millennium for years and find tremendous complexity compared to the naive simplification by the p[hilologists].

---

99 Czech: 'German'. — *Transl.*

100 French: 'German'. — *Transl.*

101 An ancient Egyptian term, the Aquaiwasha have been identified with the Achaeans. — *Transl.*

225

Hittites: The so-called younger empire [is] simply an ephemeral entity, founded and ruled by a warlike tribe, [a] colourful mixture of peoples, But which was the central element? Names, languages, weapons. What about Hyksos, Habiri, Aramaeans, Teshub[102]?

226

Hittites: The word 'language of the Hittites' conceals a lack of historical perspective. We know the chancery language of the 14th/13th century archives. I do not know the tablets, but since the few copies with texts of the so-called *Old Kingdom* are probably copies of copies, it is certain that the language is not that of the Old Kingdom. It would have to have changed much more otherwise. Translation. But — quite different languages speak from the proper names, the titles, the names of gods and cults. A chancery language can be quite different from the colloquial language at court (Latin, French in Germany, French in England, today in Alpine countries). And even if this language, a gibberish, pidgin, was the daily language of part of the inhabitants of Hattusas, it was certainly not [the only one]. The king did not understand it at all [or] among others. Ptolemaic. Khedive. Austro-Hungarian. The name Hittite [was] originally a people, then a country name, not belonging to the language of the chancery. What it was called, we do not know. Later, the Hittite name in Syria again denoted [something] else (cf. Achaeans). The naive way of the 'historians' to immediately infer the same 'people' from the name — –

227

Even the Hittite inflection system deviates strikingly from the Indo-European type. In terms of 'antiquity', this language is roughly on a par with Modern Greek: deficient mode and tense system, strange pronoun inflection, absence of most case endings. Ego: All this just proves that this language is Kashitic. (Kretschmer, *Glotta* 14, 300 ff.).

---

102 Teshub was the Hurrian god of the sky and storms. — *Transl.*

228

Hittites, Italics: The long enumeration of all the oath gods is precisely reminiscent of the Roman (Etruscan) type! This is Norse, not pre-Indo-European. Hittite! Indian. In general, the kind of oath that is *sacer* (cf. *Reallexikon* oath — or is that also oriental?). So here a mercenary guard of Goidelic language has used the national language imperfectly. Finally, in the oath formula, whole classes of gods of the mountains, rivers, sea, sky and earth, wind and clouds are invoked, that they may destroy the breakers of the oath: absolutely Indo-Germanic state treaties of the Hatti Empire (Joh. Friedrich[103], 1st part, p. 23f). It is significant that in addition to the present-day gods, the ancient ones (Akkadian: of primeval times) are invoked here. A historical aspect. From this language, a very early state of Goidelic dialects can be guessed, while the 'umbrosa-bellic' language remnants of the 1st millennium B.C. obviously represent a gibberish.

229

On the history of the Chatti: The 'family chronicle' of Telibinus[104] (c. 1775?): reprinted by Forrer in 'Der alte Orient'[105] 24, 3. 'A spectacle of murder and treachery'. Mursilis I, the first to rule in Chattusas, conquers Aleppo, then Babylon, is murdered by his brother-in-law. The murderer becomes king, then murdered by his son.

230

Hrozny: *Über die Völker und Sprachen des alten Chattilandes*[106], p. 39: Hattic and Luish merge in the use of purely local dialects. Sometimes 'Luish' is almost purely 'Hattic'. Since he, like Forrer, calls Luish an even more corrupted Indo-European, it may be assumed to be the purer language of the two. P. 40: according to 2 texts Luigga =

---

103 Johannes Friedrich (1893–1972) was a German orientalist. — *Transl.*

104 Telibinus was one of the deified kings of the Hittites. — *Transl.*

105 'The Old Orient'. — *Transl.*

106 'About the Peoples and Languages of the Old Chatti Land'. — *Transl.*

Arzawa (thus the Arzawa letters[107]!). According to this, this language would be Cilician. But this is precisely where Indian dynasties are located! Luish, however, is the god Sandes, who (E. Meyer I3, 2. 720 ff.) occurs in Cilicia. Furthermore, Luish appears in Hattusas itself and in Kizwadna (Pontos). It is thus the ancient East Minor Asian language which is here just brokenly spoken, in various social classes, while 'Hittite' is not a vernacular but a chancery language. P. 45: The prayers are never spoken in Hittite, but in Chattic, by the singers of Kanes: so either the vernacular there is Chattic or the whole cult still has the old language. Kanes, however, is not Hattusas, but Hegt in the east, and [is] therefore perhaps the old Hattite capital.

231

Above all: if the Hittite language, as is probable, did not inflect at all, but worked with suffixes like Sumerian, people accustomed to thinking of an inflecting language had to bring in *their* inflection! So this is not a decayed Indo-European language, but a decayed *non-Indo-European* language with young Indo-European affixes.

232

Forrer makes a sequence out of his 44 royal names. But we do not know at all whether the kings of 1300 (like the Hyksos etc.) did not revive old names, e.g. Mursilis, which they knew from documents (like Sargon I and II!). The ancient Minor Asian religion (Cybele) was much older, [dates] at least [from] the 3rd millennium: place names [are] also older than Labarna.

---

107 The Arzawa letters, written in the Hittite language, are two letters between the Arzawan king Tarhundaradu and the pharaoh Amenophis III. In the first letter the pharaoh asks for the hand of the king's daughter in order to cement the relationship between the king and the pharaoh. In the second letter the king agrees to the proposal. — *Transl.*

233

Hattusil overthrows the great empire of Halab, Mursilis conquers Halab and Babylon 1800–1750. In addition, battles against the Harriers (but in the meantime, surely, Babylonia has also been plundered by Harri?). Or is Harri Hittite at that time? Besides Halab many small Harri kings also [sit] in Mesopotamia and Syria (18th century).

234

Suppose that the centre of gravity of the original 'Hatti' dynasty without a name (Hatti is the Cappadocian folk name) had been at Ephesus-Lydia: this would explain the proper names in 'Hittite' transliteration, the abandonment of one's own Indo-European language and the stammering of the adopted one. The political term Lydia would thus be a powerful remnant, the Lydian language perhaps likewise. The founding of the Greater Chatti Empire would thus be roughly contemporaneous with the Viking Empire at the castle of Mycenae and Tiryns (and Troy).

The Aramaean world also belongs to this period. The Old Hittite Empire [is] not at all identical with the New Hittite Empire. The former had Boghazköy-Syria as its centre of gravity, the latter Lydia-Cappadocia.

235

If the 'Hittite' chancery language (1400) is centum, then [there was] perhaps a wave at that time which resulted in the formation of the Greek dialects. Before that, however, a Satem-Illyrian-Linear Pottery-proto-Indo-European stratum prevailed as far as the Peloponnese and Malta. See the Linear Pottery traces [in] Thessaly, Sicily, Malta.

236

The great testament of Telibinus: On unity, blood revenge, heroism, something without equal in the Orient! Forrer, *Boghazköi* (in transcription) II, 2 1926, p. 12. Genuine Nordic spirit.

237

The autobiographical memoirs of Hattusil are the oldest in the world! (A. Götze[108], *Hattusilis*, 1/25). He is weak as a child, is consecrated to Istar. Dreams prompt decisions. High ethos, sense of duty, honour, pride in victories, 'manly deeds'. Battle of Hahhas. Pious: all is as in Homer, favoured by Istar.

238

Arzawa (the small ancestral land with a host of vassal states), i.e. 'Great Arzawa', apparently encompassing southern Asia Minor, recognised by Egypt as a great state, official language as in Chatti. Mursilis II wages a bitter two-year war against this empire and detaches the vassal state from it. A real feudal system: the great rulers repeatedly occupied the thrones of the vassal states with their own relatives. There was obviously (Roman!) a developed adoption system. All this suggests orderly genealogical thinking. (Forrer, *Staatsverträge des Hattireiches*[109], 1.96). At court, strict titles and grand offices, everything regulated: steward, cupbearer, marshal. What a difference between this noble policy of pardoning and the contempt of small opponents with the slaughter of the weaker ones by the Israelites, a common people [and] mishmash! (Quoting from Hittite annals: 'For what shall they die?'). Law of succession of Telebinus, according to which, for example, if there is no son, the prince husband of the eldest daughter follows! There were 'cities of God', i.e. spiritual dominions such as Samuchas, subordinate only to the emperor.

239

It is characteristic of the purely political character of the Hittite people that the Greeks had no idea of its existence and that nothing [of it] is mentioned in the *Iliad*. Conquered by Mitanni only around

---

108 Albrecht Götze (1897–1971) was a German orientalist and one of the most important Assyriologists of his time. — *Transl.*

109 'State Treaties of the Hatti Empire'. — *Transl.*

1200, their name and language must have disappeared completely. Are the 'Hittites' of 2000 and 1500 identical at all, or did the latter, like the Rasena, only join them then? Boghazköy was the capital only of the latter empire, whose centre of gravity with quite a different nationality was perhaps to the west of it, the old empire to the east (Carchemish?). 'Hittite' style extends from Boghazköy to Assur — so west of that the Trojan-Cypriot?

The gibberish of the conquerors, or rather their scribes, reaches into Europe. They did not master this language and made pidgin out of it. Boghazköy was a village that only became a residence in 1400. The five great buildings are not Hittite at all, but Western: Troy, Knossos. Were their builders the destroyers of Knossos (1600)? So this was a foreign rule in Hatti, which incidentally replaced the roll seal with the stamp (Sesklo[110], Ukraine — also in Crete?).

The Neo-Hittite Empire [is] a feudal state. Naramsin had Hatti, Kanes, etc. in possession. Around 2000 Kussar is residence, 1800–1500 decay. 1200 destroyed by Mysians, Phrygians. Is the proto-Hattic with its prefixes Libyan? So there is an old real Hittite empire in Syria around 2000 and a new one, as foreign rule, in Asia Minor around 1300. But the flowering of Knossos is the decay of Eastern Crete. 2000.

240

There is a contradiction between the fact that the archival language contains Indo-European elements — such as Anglo-Saxon, French — and the fact that the proper names show no trace of them. If only the diplomatic clay tablets — Babylonian — had been found, the Hittites would be called 'Semites'. If only the Arzawa tablet had been found at Amarna, that would give only the language of Palestine. The Cappadocian tablets prove nothing for the language of Kanis. Official administrative languages prove nothing for the vernacular of the place. Latin and French records in Germany.

---

110 The Sesklo culture in Greece was possibly the earliest Neolithic culture in Europe. — *Transl.*

241

'Hittite' reliefs: According to Herodotus, 2 ('Sesostris' and 'Magna Mater') at Sipylos, a third on the road from Sardis to Smyrna. Further, at Karabel and at Nymphaion on the road from Ephesus to Phokeia. Here must have been a centre of this art. 'Subbiluliuma'. From which language, then, do the names of the Hittites come? Mursilis, Telibinus, Alyattes?

An ancient traffic route [leads] from Boghazköy to Sardis and the coast. That is why the later Persian imperial road makes this turn to the north: it was already established by 1200: (Ramsay[111], *Historical Geography*, 27 ff.). Therefore [is] here the centre of Kafti seafaring, later of 'Lydian maritime rule'. Smyrna [lies] at the mouth of the Hermus valley, Miletos at that of the Meander: the two ways [through] Ionia, there the Sipylos, here the Mycale mountain. Milatos in Crete.

242

The chancery language of the Achaeans in Boghazköy has clear traces of an Indo-European stammering (the older texts are copies, so prove nothing for the existence of this chancery language before about 1500). From this almost the entire scholarly world concludes, with the usual superficiality for historical things, that the Hittites were 'Indo-Europeans'. But who are these 'Hittites'? What are 'Indo-Europeans'? First of all, who was speaking in this record? The court, the nobility, the inhabitants of the capital, the people of some province? Or was it a gibberish of captured strangers employed in chancery service? Or [the] bodyguards who guarded the palace? We do not even know the names of the ruling people, the empire, this language. In any case, among the infinite names of 'Hittite' dignitaries there is not a single one that has an Indo-European sound. So what did the people come as who spoke an Indo-European language and then left the remnants in the quite other languages by corrupting them? Mercenaries?

---

111 William Mitchell Ramsay (1851–1939) was a Scottish historian and classical archaeologist. — *Transl.*

Warriors? Slaves? A tribe or individuals? We do not know. Here lies the great mystery of the history of the great power of Asia Minor.

First the names! Some of them in Lydia later. The language is said to have 'Italic' echoes. But what does that mean? 'Umbrian' or 'Latin'? For these are different languages (Walde[112]). Celtic? Tocharian?

243

In the past, all Minor Asian-Syrian was explained by the Phoenicians; today 'the Hittites' are all the rage, especially since they have been declared Indo-Europeans, because some inflectional elements and a dozen words of the West Indo-European type have been found in the chancery writing of the Boghazköy archive. But who do they mean? The 'Chatti' of Kussar around 1800 or the Chatti of Chattusas around 1300, the gentry class, the chancery people? And what do we mean by 'Hittite culture'? Who spread this language? That pictographic writing is not connected with it is certain. That the art and the building of houses (Bat Hilani) are Syrian [also]. After all, this is a learned fantasy. The Aeolians and Ionians of Homer's time did not hear the name Hatti, although they knew Sidon, Egypt, Caria, Colchis (or does it hide behind a name not mentioned in Boghazköy, such as Aethiopians?).

244

If proto-Hattic is supposed to be reminiscent of Bantu with its prefixes — is it of Libyan origin? Is it the old national language, but not that of the place names? And rightly is the land called Hatti, for these Hatti are the core of both empires, from 2000 and 1300.

---

112 Alois Walde (1869–1924) was an Austrian Indo-Europeanist and linguist. His etymological dictionaries are still in use today. — *Transl.*

CRETE, KAFTI, JAVONIANS

245

The overestimation of Knossos and Phaistos has led to the fact that the picture of the great harbor places in the east remains quite indistinct. And yet that is where the emphasis lay in these two centuries. It is striking how different the noble graves of the masters were from the mass tombs of the bondsmen — that is, of slaves, subjects, mercenaries, artisans. Likewise the accommodation: everywhere the tiny holes stuck together like in Gurnia. But how did the masters live? In the Kamares period there was a castle only in the place of the big Kafti city of Palaikastro, which was probably the seat of an independent chieftain, who was engaged in seafaring and sea robbery on his own. After 1400 the Achaean seats are in the east: the castle in Vrokastro, the other one on the rubble of the burnt Kafti city of Palaikastro. There must have been many more and much more important ones. There is still much to be done here. Where do the temple tombs, the so-called royal tomb of Isopata at Knossos belong? Do they date at all from the end of the Kafti period? Were chief priests or relics buried here?

246

Danaos and Aigyptos (Kafti) refers to the period before 1400. After 1400, the ruins of Knossos are the 'labyrinth' where the legendary Minos dwells, as Minotauros (probably bull on a mural). When the legend of Theseus speaks of Cretans, the Kereti-Peleseti are meant. The Minos of the ancient legend did not emerge from the ruins and from the Kafti empire. Judge of the dead Minos — after that Minos is perhaps the title or name of the priest-king of Knossos — or of an Osiris figure? The legend of the bull sacrifice has developed only from the ruins? Sacred bulls to which human sacrifices were made? Apis (1600–1400)? Other 'Cretan' numina probably possessed first the Kereti, not yet the Kafti. Kafti is either the name of the island or the ruling class or the lower class. Both are of very different race, language and culture. (Libyans over Minor Asians or vice versa?) The temple priesthood did business, engaged in trade — as in Egypt, Delphi, Miletus, Pessinus, with the Catholic orders.

247

To get a picture, one must have an idea of the number. Otherwise one presupposes, without intending it, instantaneous conditions, where great cities have a hundred thousand inhabitants, five thousand are few, etc. Crete, Cyprus, Sicily — how many inhabitants then? Was Knossos, Ugarit etc. 'city' at all? Or a sacred precinct with a large fair (bazaar, storage yard, market)? 'Palace' — this could be a temple with priesthood, or 'steel court', or castle of the ruler with accommodation for the mercenary troops. The word 'palace' gives false ideas.

248

Since when [does the] 'Kingdom of Alashiya' exist? [It is] possible only after 1400. In the state documents in Chatti and Egypt only real political units are mentioned, so Kafti is missing from the Hittites (archive 14/13th century).

249

The old name of the island or the inhabitants, which had remained common in 'Alashiya' and thus over in Canaan (which is not Palestine but all Syria, also the Phoenicians called themselves so, by the way no Semitic word), was Kaftor. The Philistines brought since 1200 the new name Crete, which remained also for the Hellenes the only designation. *Much* older, however, is the form Japhet, which is valid north of 'Canaan' in another language or pronunciation, thus in Cilicia for instance, Mitanni etc. There it has entered the ancient legends, like Mount Ararat. The Israelite writers did not suspect that Japhet and Kaitor were the same. The one was a legendary figure from the north, the other an island in the west.

250

Didymaion, Dithyrambus, Tityros. Kekropians, Titans, Sisyphus, Tantalos (Talos), Daidalos, Leleges.

251

The island was called Crete by the Ionians after the eastern tip, where the Cretans were lords. The conquerors of Argolis may have called it Aigyptos for some time, after the name attached to Knossos and Phaistos.

252

I dare to ask one other question — no more!: on Kypros, only in Phoenician legends, but perhaps older, the name Dido is handed down (Dido and Elissa) (group). This has perhaps led to the fact that Genesis 10 is written Dodanians instead of Rhodians. If Elissa and Dido form a connection of unknown kind, was Didymaion a Kafti word? A name of the gods? Group: on Kypros a promontory Dades. Daidala city in Lycia, Caria, Crete. Daidalos. Mother of the gods. Dindymene. Dindymon near Kyzikos.

253

Possible is the following: the word Kafti could be related to Kpt (Koptos: Min-Minos) as Hamitic. Then it would be possible that Ai-gyptos originally means the Kafti name (Ai-thiops, Ai = E as 'people', Libyan) and in the Danuna language contains the battle of the Danaans against Knossos in 1400. Later identified with Egypt, which was guessed in Crete (India — *Indianer*[113] [is a] geographical error!).

254

Bari Sicily. Carians: This transport barrier, not only geographical, consisted in the fact that in the western Mediterranean Sea seafaring tribes and tribal groups were situated on islands and coasts, which

---

113 German: 'Amerindians'. — *Transl.*

made any penetration through the two roads pointless. This was still true in the Kafti period. Only the seafaring tribes, I believe, organised the same in the west as in the east. In any case, Sardinia was thus [displaced] from its ruling position, Malta too, so that now attempts could be made to penetrate into the unknown through the roads of Tunis and Messina. Rearrangement of the political balance of power from this: the Tursha swarms hold the coast to which their name stuck. The Carians [remained] on the western tip of Sicily. [This is] around 1000 the most important point of the central Italian and Tunisian coast.

255

The name Tart- remained in Tyre and Cypros as a designation of the far west, first of the area of Carthage, Malta; later Spain. In Greece as in Crete, Argos still lived populations, in whose language Tartaros and Tart- meant darkness and wasteland, the word Tart-essos. Nobody had seen it. It was supposed to lie far to the west — a Dorado, to which trains, names [were] soon found/invented.

Pillars of Hercules. Atlas. Moving farther and farther to the west. Tart-essos. Who knows, maybe once = Utika, Syracuse, Gades. The 'Dorians' [were] apparently averse to navigation, landowners with bondsmen. Crete is ruled out for seafaring and colonisation, also Sparta, Argos. [Was] Taranto founded by pre-Dorian formations? [In] Rhodes [the] pre-Dorian element [strikes] through again (distribution of the Ionian dialect). Therefore, the field was open to the west for the Ionians. There was no competition in the Dorian area. Both the Javonians and the Carians must have still known the sense of 'Tart' = west (like [we] Orient [resp. Occident]).

256

Pre-Greek colonisation of the Carians etc., which the Ionians only occupied — continuation thus of pre-ancient movements in old ways. Also the names Odessos and Salmydessos, Tartessos (Carian foundation thus!), Daskylion (Black Sea, Daskylos father of Gyges).

(F. Bilabel[114], *Jonische Kolonien*[115] p. 60 ff, 1920). Consequently, already the Carians-Lydians had developed the Black Sea, the Adriatic Sea and Spain, perhaps also Algiers (where the Sidonians followed them!) during their maritime rule in the 2nd millennium (after Troy's fall?). In part, it is the reverse of the Libyan expansion. Absolute new foundations of Greek cities were almost non-existent. Occupation of old traffic points. The Carian settlement on the Black Sea, at the mouth of the southern Russian streams, shows the ancient Varangian route of the Sea Peoples!

257

Tartessos: In western Sicily -essos. The people called the Carians Elymians [or] Solymians after a similar sounding name in Asia Minor. Near here, [in] Tunis, may have been Tartessos. From this world of maritime traffic after the end of the Kafti period, the legend of the Lydian-Carian maritime rule 'at the time of the Trojan War' developed. And their inheritance was taken over by the Ionians (Miletus) and Sidonians (Tyre). The Hellenic navigators since the 8th century did nothing but attempt [to] re-establish the ancient connection which had started in part from the same coastal places. The road to Odessos [was] blocked by the pirate castle of Troy, which was raided and destroyed during this period.

258

This 'Carian-Lydian' naval domination, of which the Ionian Greeks — the only ones who could and had to know anything about it — may have kept silent out of hostility. If something is missing in the *Iliad* and *Odyssey*, it is not that 'Homer did not know', but that the rhapsodes did not mention it in their songs, because this was considered offensive by the masters for whom they wrote poetry. This is perhaps the reason why the Ionian name does not occur. At that

---

114 Friedrich Bilabel (1888–1945) was a German papyrologist. — *Transl.*

115 'Ionian Colonies'. — *Transl.*

time it was the name of a patrician class of non-Greek origin, which was somewhat deprived of its maritime position. These 'Carians' or whatever they were called — we will talk about this later — knew a lot about the sea route of the Kafti, more than the Hellenes did later. They obviously took over the custom of the syllable writing, then the alphabet writing(?), the shipbuilding and ship type of the Kafti, which then the Greeks learned from them.

259

The name must have been coined by people who at least still heard the sense 'West', even if they should not have understood the phrase anymore — as with us people speak of Orient and Levant and use as title who know neither Latin nor Italian. Here we are talking about seafarers, people with knowledge and wide vision. They knew what was 'Tartessos' for thousands of years. The suffix -essos is attested only for settlements and rivers, or perhaps, since we are talking about river mouths, which were 'ports' at that time, only settlements. So Tartessos was the name of a transshipment point or landing

place in the far west — far for the Carians –, but this does not mean that the same one was always meant. By the 'port of the west' was meant a destination. It will have been epithet. It could be [spoken] today of a place in western Sicily, less in Tunis. This indeterminacy, after all, characterises precisely the location of Tartessos.

260

In this ending of the stem form, which was the only one in use among the Greeks since the maritime trade period of the 8th century, lies the problem that will only be hinted at here. No matter whether the name meant a direction, a country, a market, for the Greeks, who were never there, it meant a mythical Dorado. But if one wants to [reveal] the alleged secret, one should have proved that Tartessos does not stand alone. It is in the west the outermost point with -essos. But in the north [Odessos] corresponds to it. This was later 'Ionian colony', but the ending proves, and this is the most important thing, that *between* the Kafti period and the Ionian seafaring, between 1400 and 800 that is, there must still have been a time of sea powers, with piratical campaigns, emporia[116] — those in which there is the language on all coasts to which the -essos ending belongs.

261

The -essos ports are located differently from the destinations of the Kafti voyages: the Danube and Western Sicily. Tartessos could not have been more distant. So the Carians-Lydians did not know Byblos; for them the west was more important than the east: Calabria, Apulia. So in the Alashiya world another sea power was dominant: Kypros. After centuries, revisit the old landing places, where the huts had crumbled, the fortifications destroyed, the people feral.

262

Also the southern Troad: Marpessos, Lyrnessos. So there sat Carian mariners after Ilios was destroyed and the road to Odessos was clear. These names are the waymarks of the 'Carian-Lydian' seafarers.

Western Sicily ('Elymians', Solymians — native names): rivers Telmessos, Krimissos, Herbessos, so names of landing places at river mouths. The river got its name from the settlement.

Venus of Eryx = *Mater Idaea*: the West Minor Asian mother, originally Libyan! Later the Tyrian-Cretian merchants against the Greek (Ionian?) based themselves on these merchants: the old enmity from Asia. 8th century. So not the natives of Spanish origin (Elymians), but the seafarers. Since the 8th century, the Greeks have been advancing.

If the pirate castle of Troy VI (was it really called Ilios?) was held by Achaean pirates, perhaps there is a relationship with Sicily — Africa. Aphrodite of Eryx (temple prostitution, doves as in Western Asia Minor), Kypros, Carthage, so 'Minoan', Atlantic. Only the Greeks

---

116 An emporium was a centre of commerce. — *Transl.*

(since the 8th century *was* Sicily: around 600 Stesichoros[117]) connected the Western Land (Hesperia = Tarshish) with Aeneas, the opponent of the Ionians and Aeolians. They felt there related un-Greek things: goddess of Eryx, Sea Peoples designations, but -essos — is older. Sea peoples and their legends.

Schmidt[118], Stähelin: Stesichoros (many important things) around 600, before completion of the *Odyssey* and Argonauts, hence the attempt to make Aeneas and Odysseus heroes of a new western mythology. Where was Vilusa located? That is why [Stesichoros has] Aeneas move from the Ida to the Eryx. The real connection is thus Carian '-essos' between Hesperia and Anatolia.

263

But there is one more thing to consider: in the Greek world the name Tartessos has survived, in contrast to the usage on the Syrian coast, where the far west was called Tarshish. The ending is important. Here suddenly the half-obscured indication of early Greek tradition gains value, according to which there had been a 'Carian-Lydian' maritime rule, which still lay between the Kafti period and the Greek Ionian period. And indeed the ending -essos belongs to a language that had its seat here. Above all Odessos, western Sicily. A proof of the factuality of this Carian maritime settlement and its extension after the fall of Troy VI.

So 12th century Sea Peoples period, perhaps Sea Peoples settlement, -essos however denotes [a] settlement. So Tartessos was the name of the city. Only it is not proven that this was the name of a single and always the same city. It could have been also once [a] settlement in Sicily, Tunis, once perhaps Carthage or Utica.

---

117 Stesichoros (632/629–556/553 B.C.) was a Greek epic poet. He was known as the 'lyrical Homer'. — *Transl.*

118 Max Schmidt (1853–1918) was a German classical philologist. — *Transl.*

264

Decline of the Carthaginian-Lydian naval supremacy since the Dorian conquest of the trading places. Since then the predominance comes to the Ionians. Thereby it is very possible that the name Kar-, Ker- was the name of the region, on this side or beyond the roads of Rhodes, perhaps deriving from a much older name from the centuries of the Hittite period, so that the Kereti adopted it, like the Normans of William the Conqueror the name of the subjugated Angles, which had become [the] name of the land. Was the seafaring of the Rhodians the last remnant of the old Carian, which was then in some contrast to the Ionian also for this reason, and not only because the Dorian lords did it, who themselves were mostly not seafarers?

265

The shrines: [In] Pessinus[119] (Stähelin 54) a man next to the goddess. The priests [are] hereditary [and always bear] the same names Attis and Battakos. Likewise in Olbe.

The shrine of Didymaion near Miletus is without doubt a foundation of Kafti. Power of the priesthood on Kypros (group). So [does] Minos mean god *and* the hereditary priestly name? Was the chief priest the incarnation of the deity after the Egyptian model, so that in his name one judged, prophesied, decided? In this direction the key to understanding must be sought — the peasant religion was different.

The Javonians of Miletus, their sanctuary Didymaion. There the seat pictures in the Egyptian style!!! Only when the Greek merchants became the powerful ones in their emporia, they founded their [shrine] of Poseidon, who became sea god here and thus also with Homer.

---

119 Pessinus was an ancient city in Asia Minor, now in modern-day Turkey. — *Transl.*

266

The Kafti — Javonians [were] sea lords of Miletus. From there the name for the ports of the middle west coast had actually become common — so the Greek-speaking sailors of central Greece got to know it. But the country was called Maionia, Asia, etc., the people Carians. A confusion of languages and races as in every trading area. Until finally, politically, the Hellenic merchants of most (not all!) cities got the upper hand and pushed the non-Hellenic ones down into other phyla.

267

Also 'Carians' [is] a genus name, like 'Etruscans' and 'Pelasgians'. They were applied everywhere, where one spoke of original population.

268

On Atlantean-Homeran geography:
Tartaros — Tartessos = West
Elysium — Alashiya — Elisa (Aeneas) = East
Dido — Dodanim (Genesis) = pre-Carthage
Giants — Gyges — Ogygia — Igigi = Zyg (Tsig-) in Tunis?
Reduplication: Sisyphus, Tartarus, Gigas, Ta(n)talos, Dido, Dodona, Didyma.

269

Ionians, Enak: If Madduwattas/Goliath/Alyattes are names around 1200, is then

1. The Lydian dynasty of the Mermnads a Tyrrhenian dynasty? If so, their tombs could be Atlantean-Western.

2. Then, like Enak, Madduwattas could also be a Philistine.

3. The 'Lydian maritime rule' would then be Pelasgic-Tyrrhenian.

4. The Lydian language [would be] either Pelasgian or Sapardian or [an] ancient language from the Hittite period.

Then the connections of Etruria and Lydia would explain themselves casually. The Tyrrhenians would then have occupied a port, such as Ephesus, and attempted to conquer the hinterland as in Canaan. Does the name Lydians come from them? The name Carians/Cretans [certainly comes] from the Pelasgians. The old names are Assuwa, Lukki, Maeonians, Javonians, Mysians.

270

Kafti, Kreti: It would have been a strange occurrence if the name of such a powerful political entity had disappeared without leaving traces. The Huns left their name in *Hüne* and *Hünengrab*, the Goths in Gothic architecture, in places where they had never been. And indeed, the Kafti name has been preserved without being recognised until now. In the legend of Danaos and Aigyptos there are battles for Crete in its basis, but nobody has seen that the name Aigyptos represents the Kafti. And likewise the name Javonians. If we add Japhet, Kaftor, Japetos, it becomes probable that the *Kafti* spoke of themselves with *a*.

271

If Leleges — Lycians, then [are] Kekerians — Carians: Gergithians, Gegarenians, Kekropians, Gerginians. Cherethites and Pelethites = Kekropians and Pelasgians. Gerg-ithians like Lap-ithians.

272

Carian maritime rule: For the time being we have no [knowledge] of this of our own. We possess only the Hellenic late tradition: just as of the battles of the Philistines we have only the Jewish one. But it is possible that during excavations Philistine documents, clay tablets, will be found, which show the intention of Saul on the part of the other party, and likewise something could be found in the Carian language about Tartessos.

273

The feather caps of the 'Lycians' are of course Cretan ('Sarpedon'). The name of the Cretans adheres to the part that remained seated there, Pelasgians were the parts roaming the sea. When Greek tribes entered the island (1400 or 1200?), their most dangerous enemies were the Cretans. That is why the island was called 'Island of the Cretans'. Among the Danaans it was still called Aigyptos.

We know nothing about the Carian language. The few glosses can be loan words. The 'Lycian' inscriptions may be from the ruling class (patriarchy, while the Lycians had matriarchy). It is shown here again how fatal it is to designate the language of inscriptions according to the country name, to identify this with a 'people', and thus to conflate a language and a tribe which have nothing to do with each other. If we knew nothing of the Phrygians, we would call the inscriptions of Phrygia 'Galatian', that is, Celtic.

274

The art of the Kafti was according to the taste of a commercial world — like later Ionians and Etruscans –: a lot of bought foreign things, much imitation of exotic styles, no own creative features. As admired models came into consideration: Syria (Mitanni), Asia Minor coast, Troy?, Shardana (what do we know of their art? Nothing!), Tunis, Libya, Egypt, especially the port cities of the Delta, of which we also know nothing. The archaic Ionian art shows, what has been often noted, a faint echo of Cretan taste, as well as the 'Etruscan' and 'Phoenician'.

275

The Table of Nations [is] according to its basis not a work of a scholar; pointless if today's professors try to figure out the author's intention after modern division of peoples according to languages (Indo-European, Semitic). At that time, one classified peoples according to current political situations or according to custom and costume or geographically or according to their own relationship in friend and foe or according to 'professions': warriors — seafarers — great powers, Javan, Kittim, Rodanim were 'sea powers'. How the Javan, as by far the most frequent in the port of Tyre, also stood for the rare ships of other Greek cities — which should have been these? Rhodes counts after the number of its ships for itself, so Sidon, later Tyre, stood for all ports of the coast which was later called Phoenician.

276

But a part of the Kafti lords must have succeeded in saving themselves by ship from the singeing and murdering. Namely, I believe that they fled to the Asia Minor coast, perhaps because it was the only option, perhaps because they already had bases there. Originally [Javonians] denoted the sea lords, so it was not the name of a 'people' or country, but of a community of rich lords. Then it is adopted by the Greek seafarers, first as a professional title, then as a coastal name, at last as the name of the coastal towns and their inhabitants in general.

277

Javonians: When the political catastrophe struck around 1400 — – Of course [it was], as archaeologists note, not a 'break' or 'change'. These museum and excavation terms have nothing to do with history. But the sanctuaries were destroyed, the cities burned. New state powers took the place of the political entities of the Kafti period, made maritime trade dependent on themselves — it went on quietly. The center of gravity [was] in Argolis, where the skillful potters were massed as slaves. At that time many of the rich sea lords fled to Asia Minor, where there must have been markets and harbors, although nothing has been found so far. Here they probably already had their berths and offices. And here — this is my conviction — their name has stuck, first as a designation for the merchant lords, then for the upper class of the settlements, then for the cities themselves. Javonians of Kafti. The Greek-speaking conquerors found the name.

278

Colonisation, Javonia: This Hansa-period-style expansion occurs in trading cities. Not 'Hellenic' but by a largely un-Hellenic patriciate. The preceding 'colonisation' is naval robbery. Bases, not cities. Agriculture is important only to support trading cities. Phoenicians and Etruscans have been part of this since 300.

279

There was actually no 'Greek' colonisation at all. The East Peloponnesian settling in Crete, Rhodes, Pamphylia, Cilicia, Cypros — the old Alashi direction –, spreading the Arcadian-Cypriot dialect, took place under the name Achaean, which stuck to the Peloponnese since 1500. The language may have been brought by tribes who called themselves Pelopians or Danaans. But the seafarers themselves — for instance from Asine, Amyklai, were probably Kafti. And so was the colonisation of the 8th century. Attica [and] Corinth [did not participate]. Only Chalkis, Eretria (the old Orchomenos area, Aulis!), Miletus, Laconia — old Kafti areas?

280

The base of these Kaf-ones was Miletus, beside it a few other trading ports. Here also by the merchants of the 10th/9th century, whose relations reached to Cyprus, Cilicia, Sicily etc., the letter script of the Syrian trading places was adopted and adapted for the Greek and other languages, which one had to know. In this Javonian script also poems of the rhapsodes were first recorded — thus rhapsodic songs passed into epic literature.

The alphabet then came to the trading places in the west: Corinth, Thera, Crete, where everywhere also the priests learned and used it, not the nobility. For trade in these times had its contractual center in shrines, as once with the Kafti. The 'Etruscan' alphabet (several), i.e. the trade script of the places on the Tyrrhenian Sea, comes, in my opinion, from the Corinthian Gulf — or is it the other way around?

Did the Etruscans establish a market here? Where they met with the Ionian merchants? — The relations are close: Tarquinius marriage, treasure house of the Caerites in Delphi. In any case, it did not occur to these merchant lords to consider the foreign-speaking people as barbarians. The warlike nobility did — in Hellas as well as in Italy.

281

The Lukka [Lycia]: Hittite usage for the southwest. In Greek times the name survives only for the Termilian country. The Greeks call the rest Caria (Dorian) after the new ruling class of the Kereti. This is where Tavaglavas[120] belongs!

282

W. Aly[121], 'Delphinios[122]', *Klio* IX, 1 et seq: Cretan colonisation since 1000 (Milatos): a long chain south of Ephesus to Cyprus and Palestine including Lycia, apparently systematic. Ports without land fortifications. Later the Ionians took over this inheritance. Ego: So the 'Greek' colonisation occurred on ancient trajectories as did the Phoenician. Between both periods there is the migration of tribes to the land around 1200. The Achaeans followed the Philistines to Cyprus, likewise the Greek migration follows the west migration to Sicily told by Herodotus, likewise it must have been in Cyrene. Castles were built by the Greeks only in later times, very high ones like Acrocorinth, Orchomenos. This proves that no hostile seafaring element came into consideration here. The temple-less Delphinios in both Miletus and Athens [is] a chthonic deity. The pre-Greek coast knew sea-gods, partly aged, partly fish-shaped: Triton, Proteus,

---

120 Tavaglavas was an Achaean king. — *Transl.*

121 Wolfgang Aly (1881–1962) was a German classical philologist. In the Third Reich, he was a dedicated National Socialist and published the treatise *Deutsche Revolution im altsprachlichen Unterricht* ('German Revolution in Ancient Language Lessons'). — *Transl.*

122 Apollon Delphinios was the main god of Delphi and worshipped as the god of the sea and the protector of seafarers. — *Transl.*

Osogo, Zenoposeidon, Elitos, Nereus, Phorkys, dwelling protectively in bays, often dolphin-shaped, but not identical with Delphinios, p. 16. Ego: The name has become similar by folk etymology, originally about Telibinus. Malten[123] and Aly reveal that Delph-, Tilph-, Telph-, Thelph- is un-Greek.

283

If my conjecture is correct —: one must have clear ideas. A hazy abstraction like 'the Cretans' 'migrated' to Lydia — is worthless. Who and how? They were merchant lords who [afterward] sat in seaports around the mouths of Hermus and Meander, and who proudly preserved their name when the world was devastated behind them. Perhaps [there were] also priests — what do we know of [the] Branchides, Didyma, the Mater of Ephesus? It would then have been [Javonians, Ionia] not a country name, but the name of the ruling class of a number of cities.

Samurna, Aphasu (Ephesus), Miletus. Later, when a tribe with a 'Hellenic' language, perhaps from the Hellespont, settled there — the Lydians? Because the Lydian language will be older than the name —, numerous settlers come to them from over there. Madduwattas[124] time?

284

The most important area is the estuary of the valleys of the Meander and Hermos. There the Kafti voyage and the internal traffic of Hatti ended. There, as a result, the changes of peoples have been the most intense. The Hittite empire tried to get there: Sipylos[125]. The

---

123 Heinrich Wilhelm Ludolf Malten (1879–1969) was a German classical philologist and scholar of religion. — *Transl.*

124 Madduwattas was the Hittite king of Arzawa. He conquered the whole of western Anatolia. — *Transl.*

125 Sipylos is the ancient name of a mountain in Lydia (now in Turkey). — *Transl.*

kings have names of 'Lydian' character. The Aeolians perhaps there, the Dorians also. Mochlos[126], Pseira[127]!

The 'Ionian' came into the ruling society as a trade language, when the Minoan trade routes were destroyed by the Sea Peoples and new seafarers came from Attica, etc. But Ionian was only the language of rich society, of government, of commerce, of finer intercourse (poetry). These merchants were driven out of Hellas by barbarians (Thessalians, etc.).

285

The double axe: A phallic symbol (phallus with testicles, Thor's hammer at the wedding), as a procreative symbol in the Mediterranean. Female is the *stéatopyge*[128] idol (Willendorf[129]), Crete, Astarte. The Minoan bull is also a fertility symbol.

ACHAEANS AND MYCENAE

286

Achaia has become the country name in Argos and Phthia. Seven against Thebes[130]. The Hellenic-speaking tribes called themselves so because they had become lords in the land. Pelasgians are Sea Peoples. One-track thinking: 'only the' Greek or 'the' pre-Greek language! Everything that sounds Indo-European is to be ascribed to Greek. But

---

126 Mochlos is an island in eastern Crete and the site of a significant Minoan settlement. — *Transl.*

127 Pseira is an island in northeastern Crete and the site of a Minoan town. — *Transl.*

128 With thick buttocks and thighs. — *Transl.*

129 The Venus of Willendorf is a figure of a fat venus, made about 30,000 years ago and found in the village of Willendorf in Austria. It is considered to be the most significant archaeological find in Austria's history. — *Transl.*

130 A tragedy by Aeschylus: the sons of Oedipus fight each other for the inheritance. Polyneices goes to battle against his hometown Thebes. The defenders are victorious at six of the seven city gates, but the brothers are both killed at the seventh gate. — *Transl.*

there were many languages, many non-Greek Indo-European ones, many non-Indo-European Norse ones. Many pre-Greek-Western ones. Why falsify the facts simplistically? Just so that a system comes into being. That is not how history is, and that is not how one learns to understand it.

287

It goes without saying that the Achaeans did not speak Greek. That the Shaft Tomb People spoke a Nordic language is certain. Therefore it need not yet have been Greek, not even Indo-European. The first is as good as impossible, the second I consider very probable.

288

People are bent on calling everything 'Greek', as if that would achieve anything — except the blurring of historical facts. This superficial use of the Greek name — for what can 'Greeks' mean in 1500? Hellene is a cultural term, just as *civis Romanus*[131] was a civilisational term around 200 B.C. Therefore the term Helladic is meaningless.

289

The name Agamemnon comes from the Achaean language, which was that of the lords in 14th-century Argolis. He will have been a widely famous or infamous pirate chief, who may once have made a particularly savage and preying move — against Knossos, Phaistos or the like — what can we know of it! But the image of the army king who marched against Troy is a creation of Greek imagination, which used only those names that had a sound from primeval times. *Reallexikon Homer* vol. V, Karo. Of Mycenae nothing was known but the name. What it looked like — no idea. What old songs in the *Iliad* text show archaic weapons do not nearly go back as far as 1400, but at most [to] 1200. Clytemnestra real, old. Matriarchy. Like Oedipus!

---

131 Latin: 'Roman citizen'. — *Transl.*

290

Whether these Danaans spoke an early Hellenic dialect or an Indo-European dialect at all, or perhaps belonged to one of the other Nordic language groups, we do not know. Is there a connection between this name and those of the great southern Russian rivers Tanais, Danubius? Tanais — Don. Dan — Dnieper, Dan — Dniester. Danubius — Danube.

291

The Hittite chancery scribes were quite careless when they wrote the name Achiyava as they heard it, instead of waiting for a philology professor of today to teach them the correct transcription. It was like a simple maid today writing the word Spain the way it is heard in German pronunciation, if you do not have the typeface in front of your eyes: *Schpahnjen*[132]. If, a thousand years later, someone were to see this typeface without knowing the exact German pronunciation of the letters around 1900, they would guess a completely different country.

292

Face masks [are] only masculine, royal. The face as an expression of personality [is] preserved in the celebration of the dead. Trebenishte — a tribe that has preserved the custom, plaster masks of the Scythians. Portrait? No. It was enough to know that it was supposed to represent 'him' — [which] was later explained, for example, by [an] inscription. One did not 'recognise' him, but 'knew' that it was him. Decomposition, laying out at the act of burial.

293

If 'Cretan-Mycenaean' is already an unfortunate term, from the surface of civilisation, of the arts and crafts, then 'Mycenaean' is in

---

132 German pronunciation of *Spanien* (Spain). In German, the letter s before a consonant is pronounced 'sh'. — *Transl.*

itself completely misleading. [Here] shaft tombs, [there] castle and tholos tomb. Nowhere among the discoveries made so far do two worlds collide so directly in the expression of their sense of the world.

294

The new scheme of three times three 'Helladic' periods on the mainland recommended by Wace[133] and Meyer is quite mistaken. If Evans' Minoan division was already inappropriate, since the historical periods of the Kamares, Kafti, Achaean times were blurred instead of emphasised, here the name of the Hellenes is abused. There are no tribes of Greek language until the 13th century.

295

With the Achaeans, as with the Pelasgians, one must always reckon with the possibility that quite foreign tribes who took part in their enterprises were also called so by those concerned. Cf. the Goths, Huns, Tatars, Arabs. Finally, as soon as the name becomes that of a landscape, the others call every element of the population that dwells here by the name of the land. The Achaeans are therefore by no means a linguistic unit, neither in origin nor in race or ethnicity. The only certainty is that the great upper class neither spoke 'Greek' nor came from the north.

296

The Achaeans came from Libya. The Greeks (Danaans) took the country name of unknown ending as their folk name. The Hittites [quoted it] perhaps still in the Libyan form.

297

Aquaivasha: I am told that according to strictly philological principles a transliteration of Aquaivasha into Achaeans is impossible. This is what one arrives at by scientific method, if one has no historical view. According to such principles, Milan cannot be Milano.

---

133 Alan Wace (1879–1957) was an English archaeologist. — *Transl.*

298

The tholos tomb tribes have no 'empire'. 'They are' individual tribes. Only on the coasts, everywhere from Lesbos to Volo. Their language (or languages?) has disappeared. Many pre-Greek words and names may have remained. The Arcadian-Cypriot dialect has only existed since 1250, [that] of the Nordic barbarians who destroyed everything here but then became seafarers. A hundred years later, the Dorian tribes are formed. 'Agamemnon' is just a name. If there are Agamemnon cults, they originally clung to a tholos tomb in which he was buried. Heroic songs of the Achaeans around campfires — that was everywhere in Africa. Only the names remained. Is Menelaos perhaps even Greek Atreus? Perhaps Schliemann[134] (Agamemnon's tomb) and Forrer (Atreus' house) are right after all?

299

The name pronounced in the Hellenic-speaking countries *achaivoi* (since about 1000) is the country name *achaivis* (Doris, Elis). It was written *achiyava* in the chancery of Hattusas around 1300. From Egypt in hieroglyphics about *achaivasha, sekelasha, mashauasha.* Latin *achivi, achaia.*

300

The name *Aquaivasha*: Unfortunately, it is a learned bad habit today to compare such names sound for sound in order to determine whether they mean 'the same thing'. But such transmissions are never made by scholars in real history, but arise of their own accord in the vernacular, which makes the names it hears fit for its mouth. We too do this in real life, we say Japanese, Moroccan, French, without asking a scholar. Centuries later, the Achaean name was abraded by the Greeks, given its own ending, written. The scribes in Chatti and Thebes wrote what they heard.

---

134 Heinrich Schliemann (1822–1890) was the German archaeologist who discovered the ruins of Troy. — *Transl.*

301

The fact that an appellative becomes a proper name and vice versa happens endlessly. In the Near East, *Chabiri* was the name of warrior troops who sought shelter here and there, became mercenaries, sometimes also lords, without a specific language or race. Last, in Palestine, [during] the time of the kings, the name [Chabiri] is mentioned alongside that of Israel, at first, in the Philistine period, still used differently, then without distinction. So it was here without a doubt. The Achaivasha [are] a tribe from Tunis, which established itself in the Peloponnesus, subdued the population, and then wandered on. Later [their name] became a country name, which was now given to the population without distinction of language and [race].

302

(Meyer 2, 1, 249): The name Argos, Argeians covers the whole Peloponnese, as do the names Danaans and Achaeans. So these are all folk names that have become broad land terms. Perhaps Argos had the meaning of landlubber, and Achaeans seafarer. What do we know? Later Achaeans became the name of various stretches of coast (Thessaly, Italy, Corinth) and Argos the name of the plain of Mycenae, the city last. The Hellenes [were] a tribe in Thessaly, according to Homer, in central Greece, gradually became a collective term. From some passages in the *Iliad* (249 Meyer) it seems that the peoples of this name were not yet identical. But the Aeolic poet considers them all to be 'Greeks'.

303

Achaeans: Originally the name of a Libyan swarm, afterwards the country on the Peloponnesus. Afterwards the tribes on the Peloponnese are called Achaivoi, finally the Greeks. It goes without saying that philological comparisons of letters cannot determine anything. These Achivians were many swarms, probably of very different language and race. No 'empire'. Agamemnon only represents the extensive power of Mycenae over other units. Voluntary, not forced. Also in the *Iliad*, Agamemnon's 'empire' is only Mycenae. One should read the *Iliad* more carefully: not vassals, but allies, very loosely.

304

Danaans: Presumably it was the northern tribes from which the Arcadian-Cypriot dialect derives (1400), who were later subjugated [by] the Dorians. (1200). Labyrinth is the name of the ruins of Knossos. It was haunted, the great wall figures came to life. From the -nth languages (Achaean)?

305

Tholos tombs: The chiefs came from the western Mediterranean. Small raids did not lead to such large tombs. The name Achaean originally referred to the royal tombs of the coasts: Argos, Pylos, Orchomenos. Then, from 1300, it became the general name for sea conquerors, just as Attila became a Germanic hero. So the name A[chaeans] proves nothing for race, language, ethnicity, as little as later the name Pelasgians (cf. *Hünen*, Goths).

306

It is quite possible that the castles of Mycenae and Tiryns (and Troy VI, which is related, 'Achaean') were conquered and inhabited by northern tribes, like the Palatine. Like Theoderic[135] at Ravenna, they had native ([there] Byzantine) architects build. The building history can therefore tell us little about the

time and manner of the displacement of the Libyan Achaeans. Among the Achaean chieftains may have been warriors of any origin, Norse mercenaries, runaway soldiers of the Kafti, Egyptians. Perhaps a troop of national unity once rebelled and subjugated or killed the others. Only this is certain: the Nordic people were not attached to

---

135 Theoderic the Great was king of the Ostrogoths and ruler of Italy at the end of the fifth and the beginning of the sixth century B.C. — *Transl.*

a symbolic design of the tomb. They will have plundered the tholos tombs and perhaps buried their chieftain somewhere in them, for they would not have thought of building d[omes]. As long as that happened, the Libyans were masters. What mattered to them was not the building but [the] burial and the celebration.

307

The original 'Achaeans' who settled in the Eastern Peloponnese were certainly North Africans or Sardinians. Circumcision, dark skin. But the dreaded name of these pirates gradually becomes a generic name for sea heroes — cf. Normans, Tursha, Pelasgians. Around 1400, this name will have been used to refer to the large number of tribes of various origins and languages; even the chiefs were not always of Libyan descent. 'Goths' was a collective name for a mixture, coined by Byzantines. Likewise [the names] Saracens, Corsairs arose. Gradually, or by some great victory, Greek or Indo-European-speaking tribes penetrated the range of this name.

308

If Achaeans took part in the Libyan war against Merneptah in league with S[ards], S[iculians], and Tursha, they were perhaps already in the process of seeking new seats in the Peloponnesus after the destruction of their seats of robbery. A swarm of them placed themselves in the pay of the Libyan chiefs in Barka, others sought to establish themselves on the coast of Asia Minor, in Kypros, certainly in alliance with Greek-speaking corsairs. Perhaps they were also in southern Italy, where the later name of Greater Greece was possibly already there when the first Greek merchants founded their empires in the 8th century.

[The] Theban War [is] older than [the] *Iliad* — some move from the Peloponnese against the rich seats at Orchomenos and Thebes (tholos tombs, -essos names). Whether they were Libyan or Greek Achaeans, we do not know. It is possible that the conquerors or the defeated went to the Gulf of Jolkos, to which the name Achaia is attached.

309

The name Achaeans thus had the same fate as the Tochars and Bulgars, whose relationship has not yet been considered — both were originally names of Turkish equestrian tribes such as Magyars, Khazars, Tatars —, then of the occupied land, then of the Indo-European language that prevailed in them. But just as today 'the Tocharians' are called an Indo-European 'people' simply because a language bears this designation, so it has been done with the Achaeans. Because in Homer this is the name of the Greek-speaking Bel[agerians], so 'the Achaeans' of history are an 'Indo-European' people. And where the name of the Achijava appears, in the Egyptian and Hittite documents, one speaks of 'Greeks'. This confusion of names, languages and people should end here, for only then does the undoubted historical fact come into its own.

310

I. The Shaft Tomb People are ancient Indo-European, South Russian, from steppes. Chariots, wooden construction.

II. Then the 'Achaeans' (African-Spanish), tholos tombs, the names (Agamemnon, Odysseus).

III. Then the stream from Central Europe, destruction of culture, 1400, Megaron, geometry, art, lance, axe.

Which of these layers brings the Greek dialects? I think III. The IIIrd stratum chases the Ist/IInd into Asia Minor. 'Colonisation', Troy. They came from forest areas. Zeus [of] Dodona[136]. Knew neither chariots nor tombs. Burning! Dorian migration.

---

136 Dodona was the oldest oracle in Greece and, after the one at Delphi, the second most important one. — *Transl.*

The Knossians probably had mercenaries. They themselves did not enjoy war and hunting (like the Egyptians, Phoenicians, Carthaginians). This is Atlantean. It is possible that the Libyan layer in Mycenae started from mercenaries who became masters. In any case, the conquest happens by sea, likewise at Orchomenos, Pylos. Libyan mercenaries became masters, as in Egypt, so in Crete last. Merneptah[137].

311

The real problem is already obscured by the fact that one speaks of Mycenaean or today Helladic culture. Of course: the pottery goes on. But it is peasant ware, and the makers remained subjects, as often as the masters changed. But the masters made the history, not the cooking pots.

312

Shaft tombs — this does not include a castle, but a ring wall (refuge castle). Cf. Galatians in Asia Minor (Stähelin 46), Dorians, Teutons etc.

The Galatians [show] no trace of Druids (Stähelin 46), so this is pre-Celtic; the Galatians also adopted the cult of Attis and the Magna Mater. The Hellenes the pre-Greek cults. Likewise the Italics. Teutons: Christianity. It was the 'stronger magic'.

313

The assertion that the 'Mycenaean culture' was created before the 'Greeks' is, when seen in the light of day, the opinion that the chiefs buried in the shaft tombs spoke a Hellenic dialect. This is only a philological point of view. For this tribe could have come from the north without speaking Hellenic. They could have spoken Hellenic without

---

137 Merneptah was an Egyptian pharaoh who ruled Egypt from 1213 to 1203 B.C. — *Transl.*

coming from there. But Hellenes have only existed since 1200, just as Yankees first exist 'over there' and not in Europe.

314

Mycenaean and Helladic are false designations, the latter even more than the former. For what is expressed here dies away as soon as the ancient culture begins. The very diverse tribes that came from the north were very primitive and therefore eagerly absorbed the foreign taste: an area of relatively uniform art arose from Sicily and Etruria to Cyprus and Syria — what used to be called Phoenician, Etruscan, Minoan. But the Minoan world had already been destroyed. In western Crete, Barka, Tunis, Sardinia, other art must have developed.

315

The shaft tombs stand for themselves. The castle is much younger. In the shaft tombs Cretan art (imported, captured craftsmen) stands next to a most primitive own pottery and metalwork, stelae. Where do these come from? (Vase, Frankfort.) The costume remains unique. More details about this. Brooches? The Kafti costume is African. The Kafti style makes the primitive ones wither and die. This is the effect of the 'Achaean' epoch.

316

Were the lords of Mycenae a small band of warlike followers who had established themselves here in the south, the head of a people pressing after them, or had they gone on about the movement further from the north, fighting, destroying, in order to have peace here? We do not know and will not know. But just as little do we know what names they themselves bore or received in the mouths of the surrounding inhabitants. Uncertain, homeless, wandering names of later times such as Pelasgians and Danaans have no meaning for us. We do not know how they originated, where, when, what or how long they designated a living association. The method of research of attaching early names without further ado to later peoples and thus classifying them in their *diarium*, [that is] sticking labels on boxes without knowing what is in them. We do not even know whether the lords of Mycenae lived in isolation, dwelled and died out, or whether they belonged to some great association, whether they felt related by deeds or language or fate. They hardly had an after-effect, for the 'Mycenaean culture' emanated from their heirs, the Achaeans.

317

Because the Greek epic speaks of the attackers of Troy as Achaeans, the Achaeans were 'Greeks'. This has not been a problem in either ancient or occidental criticism. It was simply a fact. Only the historical scepticism of our day sees, or should see, that this is where the questioning must necessarily begin. But instead, as soon as the name Achaeans appeared in Hittite documents, the enthusiasm was loud: Greeks as early as the 14th century! And now they continued to deduce and conclude: a 'great empire of the Achaeans' was there, intervening in Asia Minor.

The basic question is still not: is the name Achiva the same as the Achaeans of the *Iliad*, but: were these Achaeans the Greeks of the 14th century? And further: were there already Greeks in Hellas at that time? Were there Greeks at all? And if not, who were these Achaeans?

318

Tiryns: The round building is ancient Libyan, nuraghi, the palace younger than Mycenae. High point about after 1400 (Atreus tomb), it seems, not a Norse intermediate period. The 'megaron' is really the courtyard (peristyle), then atrium, tablinum, so the old southern form as in Pompeii, with the Moors, in Florence. The real megaron, a farmhouse with a roof, was first introduced by the Dorians in 1200. Dorians, like Saxons and Franks, were a confederation of tribes for the purpose of conquest, named after weapons: shock lance, the sacred lance, *hasta*[138], replacing chariot fighting (throwing spear). Shaft

---

138 Latin: 'spear'. — *Transl.*

tombs existed only in Mycenae, tholos tombs everywhere. 'Palaces' on the castles Egyptianised.

319

Agamemnon: It is forgotten that 200 years lie between the burial of the dead man with the face mask and the building of the castles of Mycenae! Agamemnon was either that dead man or the lord of the castle. He could not have been both.

320

Megaron [was] in Homeric times [the] name of a mansion and especially of its main room. The word is probably taken from a foreign language, and for this reason alone it is [probable] that this type itself is also foreign. But is it a type at all? Rectangular and round, [that] really makes no difference. [In the] North there is a tendency towards the single house, isolated. [From] China to northern Europe. [There is] much less building structure (that is western, plastic) than wall and roof. Decoration, ornamental detail work, microcosm. Whether tent, caravan, log cabin, wickerwork house, [it is a] private house. Not tomb and temple. In the South, the way the individual family lives has not developed any

type at all. People live outdoors. Yard, hay, street, square. Living cells, glued to each other. The 'palaces' of the chiefs (Egypt, Tiryns) are the dwellings of the armed [and] slaves, 'government buildings', not 'house'.

321

Stone building: Still in Germanic all words for stone working and stone building are foreign words from the West, especially Latin (wall, gate, door, tile, roof). Stonemason versus woodcarver. Sculpture — ornament. 'Wall' coiling, wattling, weaving. Nordic: post, timber framing, fur covering, yurt, moveable. Leaving no trace.

322

Defence: Castle, round shield, bow. *Attack*: sword, axe, chariot. Castle, Sardinia, Tiryns. The seafaring West places its dwellings, where it keeps its booty, wives and children, on islands, promontories, hills, which it fortifies. In Egypt, the massive walls around temples and palaces, and the idea of walls made of large stones, are proof of this. The north had 'camps' (chariot forts). They attacked instead of defending. The shaft tombs do not include a castle, at most an earthen wall. Sparta. Teutons before, not in the cities. Gradually the differences become blurred. But in the 2nd millennium they are still very strong.

323

Eteocles takes Thebes Ἑλλάδος, φθογγον, χέουσαν (speaking Greek). The opponents, Achaeans, Argeians, are Ἑτεροφωνοι[139]. This repeated emphasis on the difference of language, what is more, between two territories which belonged to the Greek heartland, would never have occurred to Aeschylus if it had not played an important part in the ancient legends. With the Achaeans, the fact that they were foreign speakers must have been effectively connected.

324

No doubt the shaft tombs are the sign of a single tribe who invaded with its chariots from the north, — a few hundred men perhaps; but this does not say that they were 'Greeks', i.e. that they spoke a very primitive Hellenic dialect. It will have been somehow 'Indo-European', but certainly not one of those which have survived to us as a written language.

325

Since about 1400 Achaean sea chiefs have conquered the Kafti seats, and they are now thinking of further successes. 1350 Hittite Empire, Kypros, Rhodes, for example. These Achaean swarms were

---

139 Greek: 'those who speak a different language'. — *Transl.*

mixed, of many 'races' and languages. Every able-bodied fellow was welcome. But it was not until around 1200 that stronger bands with languages of the Greek type came and conquered the Achaean bases at Kypros. Then the Dorians followed closely behind — cf. in Italy the Germanic swarms: Ostrogoths, Visigoths, Lombards.

326

What kind of invaders were there before the Shaft Tomb People? Around 2000? 16th century these, maybe just a few troops. Spiral ornament? Or was that earlier? 15th century 'Achaeans' everywhere, where tholos tombs, subduing those. 14th century new northern tribes. To what do the names Danaans belong? Pelopians? When did the pre-Greek Indo-European languages come? Who are the 'Aeolians'? 'Dorians'? How do the ravaging peoples of the 'Aegean Migration' relate to the Sea Peoples? Pelasgians, Tyrrhenians? Is it possible that Pel-opians, Pel-esiti, Pel-aski are the same?

327

Shaft tombs: The pottery is silent about such complexes. These lords did not make pots. That had to be done by the subjugated in the Argolis. They lived in a ring wall on the hill and did not want to have any subjects in the neighbourhood. Primitive, uncouth. Captured craftsmen had to make them weapons and jewellery. Where would the Goths and Vandals have built cities? Where they found such and for once did not destroy them, they lived in parts of the mass of houses. When the *Iliad* speaks of cities, the poet had the Ionian cities of 1000–900 in mind. Mycenae, Tiryns, Thebes, however, were not cities, but castles like Troy VI (Ilios. We do not know what Troy II is called). The Mycenae of the shaft tombs probably had no name at all. The name Mycenae belongs to the manor of the tholos tomb lords.

328

Mycenae: The Shaft Tomb People with their chariots could not do much militarily. Argos, the 'plain' is too small. The paved road network is laid out by the Libyans, like the kathabotrons[140] of Lake Copais: for pack animals and foot soldiers. They introduced the donkeys. Arrow, bow — Libyan, Achaean, Ionian, not Nordic.

329

Achaeans: Greek tribes, a) 'matriarchy'. Eroticism. Madonna, b) Dionysus. The Nordic conquerors are too solitary to race inwardly in chorus.

Dionysian is the southern, African glow, Negroid, protesting the Nordic cold. Apollonian domination dissolves in the south. Where the god Dionysus comes from makes no difference. It is a question of race. Not matriarchy, but wild intoxication. Carnival. The Nordic loneliness of the ego dissolves in impersonal intoxication. Ravenous for blood. Likewise in China, India.

330

What we called Mycenaean and Phoenician art style is the 'Achaean'-African taste of the Tholos Tomb People who dominated the Kafti world after the Minoan period (1400) until the seafaring northern tribes subdued it with small conquering troops. A mixed style, handled by indigenous craftsmen of different nationalities. 'Phoenician' is the last remnant of this art after the northern barbarians destroyed everything.

331

Robert I, 298, [represents] the very ancient story of Thyestes begetting the avenger of blood with his daughter πελοπια[141], cf. the Irish Volsunga Saga[142]. [It is] Nordic opinion that the blood of the ancestors must be preserved at all costs if it is to perform the necessary deed. The [sibling marriage] of the Egyptians, Incas, etc., is quite different.

---

140 A kathabotron is an underground water-channel. — *Transl.*

141 Greek: 'Pelopia'. — *Transl.*

142 Written in Old Norse in the 13th century, the Volsunga Saga tells the story of the rise and fall of the Volsung clan. It is actually Icelandic, not Irish. — *Transl.*

The charioteer of Pelops was called Myrtilos (Mursilis Hittite) (Robert I, 212–15). He came from Lesbos, where Pelops carries out the bride-robbery of Hippodameia. King Oinomaos of Lesbos builds a temple to Ares from the skulls of slain suitors.

332

What we call 'Mycenaean' is Cretan imitation. The Kafti were basically Africans — Tunisian, Spanish, Libyan —, who satisfied their taste for the foreign by adopting the Lycian-Minor Asian and Egyptian. Therefore, their style conformed to that of the Tholos Tomb People — this is the fact of the 'Cretan-Mycenaean' koiné[143], which has been rapidly decaying since 1400, when the authoritative centre was destroyed.

333

Aulis must have had significance. Graeian area. Next to it Mykal-*essos*. Narrowest point of the Strait of Euboea. Hinterland Thebes. Are Iphigenia and Agamemnon at home here? Did the lords of Mycenae conquer Thebes (Seven against Thebes)? The Kadmeia? What does 'Thebes' mean? The 'Ionian' colonisation of old Kafti families, Sea Peoples, on ancient routes, [from] Miletus [to] the Black Sea, [to] Phocaea and Euboea [to] the Western Sea. Attica is land without fleet and colonies. The Pelopians and Danaans. If the Ionian amphictyony is 'Kafti', then the 'palaces' of Knossos and Phaistos can also be covenant shrines and [then Minos can be] patron god. Throne of Minos. Javonians [then] is the name of the seafarers dwelling under the protection of the amphictyony.

334

Nuraghi: Castles, belonging to round-hut villages (*biddazze*). The tombs are the Tombe dei Giganti, Domus de Gianas. The size of the

---

143 Koiné was a communal language that developed in ancient Greece in pre-Christian times and was preserved until Roman times. — *Transl.*

nuraghi presupposes [a] strong principality, lords with omnipotence. Perhaps the nuragh type was not developed in Sardinia, but already in Africa from the round huts, because they are immediately 'finished'. The tombs of the Balearic Islands, [on] Pantelleria [and] Sardinia also prove derivation from a formal centre. These castles [are] like the mansions of antiquity, the palazzi in Florence, also inhabited by servants and a general refuge. Feudal relationship. Like the Siculian prince in the Anaktoron of Pantalica.

Massive fortification systems to cover entire landscapes. Time: end of the Chalcolithic to the Bronze Age, 2nd millennium.

So the nuraghi are contemporaneous with the Mycenaean buildings! *Before the Sea Peoples.* But the Sea Peoples themselves experienced *the* last development here. Perhaps the Shardana are really mercenary bands from the nuraghi! Just like the Aquivasha from Tunis!

335

Works of these strata are the irrigation systems at Lake Copa and [at] the mouth of the Pom and the narrow military road behind Mycenae, unusable for chariots, the palaces, tholos tombs: mighty barbarian chieftains who exploited the splendour and technology of southern culture, like Theoderic and others. Was it Kafti prisoners of war who created all this? Or were there treaties like between Hiram and Solomon? Even this landlubber class found refuge castles ('cities') everywhere, so that settlement and numina together with the names remained the same. 'Salamis' on Cyprus!

336

There is always talk of 'Mycenae' and 'Mycenaean culture' — as there is always talk of Knossos in Cretan history — as if this were a unity. But it is nothing less than that.

337

The clay pots cannot go far in this. It is self-evident that the subjugated population continued to shape and decorate their pots in the same way, no matter which masters sat in Mycenae. The graves speak a much clearer language. The pottery, for its part, needs to be interpreted from other historical facts in order to be understood correctly. But these are present here. Grave — weapon (chariot).

338

Shaft and tholos — that sounds simple. One speaks of grave goods, cult of the dead, as if they were the same thing. In reality, the symbolic meaning of the shaft tomb is clearly opposed to that of the tholos tomb. They have nothing in common. The words funerary cult and burial have completely different meanings here and there, or no meaning at all. And furthermore: each of the two symbolic grave forms has an enormous area of validity behind it: [one points] to Spain, [the other] to China.

339

When we speak of 'Mycenaean culture', we think too one-sidedly of Mycenae itself and its tholos tombs. But the 'Iberian-Libyan' form was widespread at the time. Such buildings and traces of them have survived in Leukas, Pylos, Orchomenos. So there is a large number of warrior troops (or tribes with wives and children) that settled everywhere along the old Kafti routes. Since the 16th century [there is] no doubt that the Achaean name applied to them. If they were Vikings, it is likely that they came as men and fathered children with captured women. But then it is also possible, as has often happened (Turks), that the language of these women gradually penetrated while the 'race' was newly formed.

340

Today, when the prehistoric and early times of the Hellenes are spoken of, the images of the shaft tombs of Mycenae with the gold treasures of the dead, and the castles of Tiryns and Mycenae, Agamemnon and his Achaeans immediately rise before the eyes, and the name of the Hellenes for all this readily presents itself, the Hellenes who from then on made 'Hellenic culture' and history. And the scholars are eager to accept all this. But still missing are the tholos tombs in between, architecture of the first order, and the much older enormous round building of Tiryns (28 m). I have already shown that here the early historical culture of the old West and the somewhat younger northern Eurasia meet. Here historical order must first be established. If 'Agamemnon' was buried in one of the shaft tombs, he could not have sat in the castle of Mycenae, which is 200 years younger. Either the 'Achaeans' had shaft tombs, then they could not have built the tholos tombs that begin exactly where those end. I start from the two very different types of burial, in which two world-views are expressed. Shaft tombs only exist in Mycenae, tholos tombs everywhere. There a single tribe, here a large number, a tribal group.

341

Wilamowitz also confuses tholos and shaft tombs (I, 309). The funeral games were not a sacrifice to the dead, but were held in honour of the dead; prizes were offered from the property of the dead, the heir to the property had to prove the munificence of the dead. When corpses of wives and servants lay in Nordic graves (Ur, Scythians), they were not sacrifices, but the property of the dead that was given along.

342

The Homeric epics know only one solemn method of burial: the burning of the corpse and burial under a mound of earth. There is not the slightest mention of shaft tombs and still less of the enormous tholos tombs all around in the Peloponnesus, in Phthia, etc. It is therefore certain that these poets had no idea of the time before 1200, the Achaean period. At that time the domed buildings were so-called 'treasure houses', i.e. they were plundered, and that there were tombs under the ring of slabs was forgotten — otherwise they would also have been plundered.

343

Ring of Plates: It would be possible that the Shaft Tomb tribe, nameless to us, was not destroyed or driven out, but subjugated, so that it still sat in bondage in the neighbourhood of Mycenae, and received permission to tend the graves of its chiefs. In any case, however, and this is the most important thing, the Achaeans had the idea of this care, for they included the ring of plates in their castle: for them the dead were living on, had become heroes of the land, and they had to be appeased if they were not to bring mischief.

THE TROJAN WAR

344

Trojan War: A glance at the *Iliad* and the accounts of the lost epics should have shown that here the deeds of a *naval war* are at the basis, worked on by poets who knew only *land wars*. The great exodus of the attackers — Achaeans — presupposes *naval battles*. But where is the fleet of the Trojans? Did not Paris go to sea to steal Helen? The *land war* depicts *chariot battles* — the weapon of the landlocked. The legend of Troy is the invention of entire *generations* of poets to an extent that no one has ever *dared* to imagine. The Achaean voyage went against the Kafti. On Crete, the Ida cherishes, where Aphrodite and Idaios sit. Ilios on the Hellespont was a castle, not a city. So it had no 'army', but it did have a fleet. The 'destruction of Ilios' — is that even the name of the castle? — Vilusa. In the Saga of the Nibelungs, the historical Hun campaign to the Rhine, in which the conquest of Worms was an insignificant event, has become the campaign of the Burgundians to Attila's camp, which never existed. Here Greek-speaking tribes from 'Achaia' (that in the Peloponnesus and that in Phthia) brought the foreign Agamemnon legend, the legend of Vilusa, the Achilles legend, and some rhapsode sang of the raid of the buccaneer fortress of 'Troy' so well that the motif became the focus, the magnet for all other songs.

But who destroyed the castle? In my opinion probably Odysseus, the 'castle-breaker', of whom we shall now speak.

345

Trojan War: We are talking about 'Homer', and even the specialists are always seduced by the name into imagining a single poet as soon as the word slips from their pens. In the 'epic' ages of the Occident there are also points of crystallisation of epic poetry: not the Saga of the Nibelungs, which had been popular as far as Iceland, but was not claimed as a theme for poetry of status, but the 'Matière de Bretagne' — the Arthurian legend (Erec, Iwein, Lancelot and Ginevra), the Grail legend (Parzival) and between them Tristan. Lohengrin, Roland! So were the historical events at Thebes and Troy (Aachen, Worms, Charlemagne) and pure myths (Paris, Helen, Grail, Nibelungs, Aphrodite). In the Gothic Occident, individuals wrote poems in imitation of others, but here the older poems were combined by younger ones in a mosaic-like manner. Even more so in India (*Mahabharata*). The 'Homeric' epics — one must never forget that there were many of them, of which the *Iliad* and *Odyssey* slowly came to the fore as the most popular — are collective poems.

346

The early history from about 1200 onwards is repeatedly attempted to be elucidated by two circles of legends which we know only from the works of epic poetry: the Trojan War and Seven against Thebes. The latter is usually unjustly neglected, so that a skewed picture emerges. But how much can we learn from such legends? Where would we end up if we had the Nibelung poems from the German Song of the Nibelungs to the Greenlandic Atli's Song[144] as our only source for the history of the migration of peoples? We would take Siegfried and the Nibelungs for historical greats. Aetius and Atli. The Burgundians did not perish, did not move against Attila. Theoderic has nothing to do

---

144 *The Lay of Atli* is one of the heroic poems in the Norse Poetic Edda. — *Transl.*

with them. What is at all true of the moves [against] Thebes and Troy? Troy was not a city, but a pirate castle.

347

Trojan War: (v.d. Leyen[145], *Deutsche Heldensagen*[146].) Several motives:

1. The typical story of a Viking stealing a chieftain's wife and treasures: also Germanic, Celtic, Indian, fabliaux[147]. The name Paris/Priamus probably belongs to this. Mycenae, Ida.

2. Fact of a great naval war against Kafti: Agamemnon, historical name.

3. Aeolian voyages against the Trojans: Achilleus.

4. Destruction of a pirate castle by cunning (Odysseus).

As in the Germanic sagas, names (persons, peoples), facts, motifs change context.

348

There was no epic 'of the Trojan War' at all, just as little as one of the war of the Huns against the Burgundians. The rhapsodists and skalds do not deal with such things. There was a poem about the anger of a hero who loses and avenges his dearest friend; that this fate was baptised in the name of Achilles is not so important. Another poem is about the return of a seafarer — whether this was Odysseus or Jason is a minor matter. Kypria etc. It could also have adhered to the Argos saga. Hagen was in the service of Attila (Walther? Thidrek). Kriemhild

---

145 Friedrich von der Leyen (1873–1966) was a German medievalist and folklorist. — *Transl.*

146 'German Heroic Sagas'. — *Transl.*

147 A fabliau was a comical fable in verse in medieval France, often obscene or scatological. — *Transl.*

avenges Siegfried or Günther. Atli, the non-German, is the centre of attention everywhere. The 'Hun country' had various camps.

349

Finally, practically everything that the ruling class of the Hellenic tribes believed about their origins, their deeds and their conquests from about the 10th century onwards has flowed (been carried) into the story of the 'Trojan War'. If one therefore subtracts everything that certainly has nothing to do with Troy, nothing at all remains but the fact of landing attempts in the Troad, which may have had nothing at all to do with the destruction of the pirate castle of Ilion. Ilios was not a city, Priam belongs in the Peloponnese, as do Paris and Helena. Ida is in Crete. Agamemnon, Achilles were not 'Hellenes'.

350

The 'Trojan War' is predominant in the epic not because it was the most important, but because it was closest to the Ionian poet. It is not true that it was a great event — it only became so in poetry. Other motifs, figures, names were added. The *Odyssey* was only the vessel for collecting the Ionian ship legends, and not because Odysseus actually had anything to do with the castle on the Hellespont. The epic of the Occident lost sight of the Germanic migration of peoples. The occidental Christian, Celtic-Germanic knighthood was more enthusiastic about the Crusades and the battles in Spain; Tristan, Arthur, Grail, Roland. *The Song of the Nibelungs* stands lonely in between, unbalanced between migration and courtly mores. There were no epic poets in Italy, on the Rhine. There were Bavarian, Swabian, Breton, Provençal poets. The Cid romance did not become an epic.

351

The *Thebaid* in its old part was older than the *Iliad*, wilder, bloodier: skull-drinking, slaughter, cultureless. This must have displeased the Ionian nobility — as the material of the migration of nations displeased the nobility of Germany. But for this very reason the battles for Thebes are to be taken more seriously historically than those for Troy. There really must have been a war between the Achaeans in Thebes and Mycenae, in which Thebes was defeated. That is why the name Achaeans has been displaced northwards from Thebes. From there come the Greek-speaking conquerors of Lokris and Aetolia, whose grandfathers had perhaps still fought through these battles. The *Iliad* was written for chariot fighters, the *Odyssey* for sailors. It is the difference between the legend of the Nibelungs and the legend of Gudrun.

352

All the great ancient legends adhere to the main places of the Mycenaean period: 1) Tiryns, Mycenae, Pylos, Athens. 2) Thebes, Archomenos, Jolkos (Volo). 3) Sparta. Only not the Calydonian hunt. (Odysseus is a sea legend, has nothing to do with Ithaca.) So there must be a historical connection between the legends and the fates of the rulers' seats. In Laconia the cults are largely pre-Dorian, partly pre-Achaic. Homer [is] Ionian, which the Dorians ([to whom the] Herakles legend is peculiar) found strange; Herakles [in turn is] alien to the sea! Primeval Achaean: the voyage to Troy and the voyage to Argo. Troy VI was attacked in long arduous battles: in the *Iliad* there was originally hardly any mention of the plan of conquest. Achilles' moves against Lesbos, Chrysa etc. in the *Iliad* also point to long, small feuds. The Aeolian Achilles is also the hero of the oldest *Iliad*. The fleet gathers in Aulis.

1) Argonauts. Homer already knows them (primeval Achaean). 2) Theseus.

353

Psychology of the weapon: Chariots in Homer. An infinite amount has been written together with infinite naivete about 'Homeric weapons'. Mostly it has been talk about the shield of Achilles. The most important weapon has always been forgotten: the ship. Where were the ships of the Trojans? Then the chariot.

354

It was not the 'Greeks' who destroyed Troy, but the Sea Peoples. The figures then became popular. But the 'Homeric' poets of the Aeolians wrote differently, for Agamemnon's campaign was unsuccessful. Persis is much younger. The fact of the ruins then affected the poetry and merged with the legend of the Atrides. The robbery of Helen is again a completely different motif, mythology of the Asia Minor kind. Wilamowitz, *Odyssey* 180 ff. So the songs of Odysseus were at home everywhere with Pelasgians and Turshas and did not first reach Italy through the *Odyssey* with which we are familiar!

355

Iliad: A historical trait lies in the quarrel between Achilles and Agamemnon; it is without doubt a matter of two historical tribal princes who have become legendary, both Achaeans and conquerors (the *Iliad* still contains remnants of Achilles' moves against Lesbos and Thessalian places such as Lyrnessos, Pedasos, Thebes), who come into conflict over booty, in reality probably over Lesbos. Briseis from Lyrnessos — where?, actually 'the one from Brisa'. [Is] Chryseis therefore 'the one from Krissa'?

356

Homer: What myths were known in north-western Asia Minor from the Achaean country originated 1. from the Kafti (Minos), 2. from the Sea Peoples (Odysseus), 3. from the Aeolians (Achilles). But 4. much must also have been known of the Danaans and Achaeans. Consequently, the Achaivasha and Danaans brought much with them. But what were they doing in Asia Minor? Agamemnon is Libyan. The heroes come from wherever there are tholos tombs (Nilsson[148]). The great power of the Achaeans, many individual tribes, partly of Greek language, 1400 ff, appropriated by the Danaans.

The Aeolian talent was song — single song of heroes, gods. From the primeval songs before Homer to Sappho. The Ionians were story-tellers, from the epic to the prose of the historians (Schmidt-Stähelin 74). Milesian fairy tales. The primeval songs contained deeds of individual heroes or individual deeds from the destruction of Troy, in short, sung. The epic is performed without song. The Odysseus material [is] genuinely Ionian. The Argonauts material [is] Thessalian, but only shaped in Ionia for the journey to Pontus (instead of [to the] mythical West).

357

Troy: What was the name of this pirate castle anyway? Quite apart from Troy II, whose name — if it had one — must have been lost by the time of Troy VI, we know nothing of this one either. The image of the city of Ilios in the poem is a free creation along the lines of Ionian cities of the 8th century. A glance at the ruins should have taught us that there was no question of streets, temples or palaces in this castle. The name Ida has been transplanted here by the poets, from Crete, so probably with a story of an Achaean campaign against Crete. The names Paris, Perrhamos, Hekabe are not from here, because there were no 'kings'. So the name Ilios must also have been transplanted here as part of another legend of a conquered city. Vilusa. The original fact, which forms the core of the whole mass of individual legends that later grew together, will have been the raid and [the] destruction of the castle — by trickery (wooden horse!). Odysseus, the buccaneer, is called πτολίπορθος[149] because his name [is] connected with the de-

---

148 Martin Nilsson (1874–1967) was a Swedish historian of religion and classical philologist. — *Transl.*

149 Ancient Greek: 'city-destroyer'. — *Transl.*

struction. Probably a brilliant stratagem, which led to an improbably great success. Thence long told everywhere.

358

In the material of the *Iliad* a historical event shimmers through, even if we disregard Troy, something that must have deeply moved the world of the Aegean: a fleeting great empire of an Achaean hero, like Theoderic and Alaric, to whom the heads of countless tribes pay homage, but who almost or entirely perishes from the jealousy of *another* Achaean tribe.

359

World of legends: 'Odysseus' [is] a Homeric name. Originally Olykos. Only located in Ithaca by Hanseatics in 900, when Viking times were forgotten? Danaids. Fall of the sons of Aigyptus, a typical motif (at the same time Pharaoh in the Reed Sea).

Two Philistine legends: Samson [is] (while Goliath [is] the depiction of a historical person) a fairy-tale figure, quite un-Israelite in his manner. One still recognises the path. Last [he is] a 'judge', before Da[nite], before quite religionless, still earlier an enemy. It is [a form of] Heracles. The 'Cherethites and Pelethites' of David may have told the story. The core of the Book of Judges was not compiled until around 600, and it came into its present form much later still. The analogous Nissos legend from Gaza! Aeneas?

The epics have only been in circulation since [the] 6th century. Until then [they were] known only to small local noble circles, while the vase painters used the orally [handed down] legends (group 609 f.). First the Kypria, still later the *Iliad* and *Odyssey*. Oldest parts of the Troy legend: Aias (historical person like Goliath?), Achilles (god of healing), Epeiros (wooden horse), Helen. Odysseus is introduced very late (group 624 ff.).

360

Bethe, *Sage vom Trojanischen Kriege*[150], review [*Deutsche*] *Literatur-Zeitung*[151] 1927, 43, 2343 ff. Ego: the real form of the 'wars' of the Trojan period shines through in the *Iliad* in Achilles' military campaigns, typical Viking journeys with small troops. The 'campaign against Troy', in whose heroic song the whole heroic poetry was gradually incorporated, was also one such campaign. Achilles and Agamemnon belong together as little as Günther and Dietrich von Bern.

361

Odysseus, the legendary hero of the time of the Sea Peoples, [is] cunning, unscrupulous. That is why [he] was later despised by the Nordic tribes. There they told mean stories about him (Wilamowitz: *Odyssey* 184). He *was* already the cunning one before there was an *Iliad*. He probably took Troy by surprise. He was a famous archer — that is why his son is called Telemachus, already in the *Iliad*. In the *Odyssey*, [Odysseus] only uses the bow in the practice shot. But this was the weapon of the pre-ancient Aegean. His ships are in the middle of the camp. The Ithacans will have settled last on the islands, any one of which retained the name. Originally they had no homeland. Ithaca was actually called Kranae. Ithas [is] a Titan. Prometheus at times Ithax. Was this a 'speaking' name in an unknown language?

362

Did the name Odessos (Odessa) influence the form 'Odysseus' when [the hero's] adventures were partly transferred to the Black Sea?

363

City-destroyer Odysseus: These Nordic peoples — also Galatians, Celts, Teutons — understood nothing of sieges. They devastated the

---

150 'Legend of the Trojan War'. — *Transl.*

151 'German Literary Newspaper'. — *Transl.*

area and thereby tried to force the population to make a treaty. Here Odysseus is a man who once succeeded [in taking a fortress]. But where?

364

Iliad II: Under Hector are the individual tribes. Dardans (Skamander Valley, Ida). II, 821–7 Other Trojans under Pandaros, son of Lycaon (*Iliad* V, 105; 73 is called Lycia). These Lycians are different from those of Sarpedon. So again a 'host name'. Apollo is the tribal god of the south-western Minor Asian tribes. The army cry of Troy was 'You Trojans, Lycians and Dardans'. The catalogue further names Pelasgians (Larissa), Leleges (Pedasos), Cilicians (Thebes), Mysians, Phrygians of the Ascanian Lake, Maeons (Tonolos). This is a geographical line around Troy: Trojans, Dardans, Lycians, Pelasgians, Leleges, Kilicians, Myians, Phrygians, Maeons. From this it is evident that, as with the Teutons, two 'Hellenic', at least Indo-European tribes were on the foreign side (Attila!) [and] that the 'Cilicians' were perhaps a swarm that had come from Arzawa and had Indian names there, that the Phrygians were at that time on the Galatian road to the east, that perhaps the name Thebes came from there to Boeotia (Sparten, Saparda). Here, as everywhere, a distinction must be made between the name of the larger tribe, the name of the army, which had only a mythical-heroic meaning (Achaeans, Tyrrhenians), and the name of the small individual tribe, often identical with the field name of its settlement at that time ('Rutulians of Ardea, Quirites of Rome, Pelasgians of Larissa, Cilicians of Thebes, likewise Etruscans of [Caere]'). Ramses' [as] Homer's accounts of victory list the name that happened to catch their ear most strongly at the trial.

365

Priam (Perrhamos): The name seems suspicious to me. It is [compared] with Paris as Lygda*mos*, Imbra*mos*, Perga*mos*. So which of the two was the original one that once had a reputation somewhere on the west coast? Perrhamos, Perrhaean in Thessaly. Aeolian pronunciation, then.

366

'Trojan War': Most such events, even very significant ones, are soon forgotten. But when a song describing an insignificant encounter remains popular by its drasticness or merely by its invigorating rhythm and tone, the event grows at last in memory into a tremendous deed. So it was with the walls of Jericho, the death of Roland, and so it has been with the fall of Ilion. The time and place can change completely, the name can be linked to a completely different event. It is not at all certain that the castle which Ulysses destroyed (a famous pirate and chief of the Ithacans) is identical with the two castles at the Dardanelles and the place called Vilusa.

367

Late sea robbery: The pirate castle of Troy (II, VI), which made shipping unsafe in the Dardanelles, naturally delivered 'metal treasures'. They testify to nothing more than the fact that these things were sailed past there. Under certain circumstances, a skilled blacksmith (Wieland) or potter was also robbed and had to make the things himself in the castle. From this, in the eyes of prehistorians, a 'Trojan culture' of wide spread originated. How these pirates would have laughed at the use of their booty for scientific conclusions!

368

The legends of the Trojan War [arose] from very different elements. 1. The happy raid of Odysseus, the sea-folk hero, on Troy. 2. The departure of Agamemnon for a mighty campaign into Asia Minor. 3. Journey of Menelaus. 4. Move towards Aulis.

The Argonaut legend ties in with ancient Kafti and Cretan voyages to the Black Sea. Miletus, the Kafti city, knew Colchis and resumed the voyages (-essos) in the interim period ('Lydian maritime rule'). The original form of the legend (Robert II, 709) directs the voyage to Aiaia to the west. The return journey through the Okeanos and Pontus Euxeinos. The departure from Aulis (Boeotia) reveals that another move was merged with it.

Achilles' move against Lesbos. The move against Lycia (Sarpedon) and Rhodians against the mainland. Move against Thebes from Argos to Kypros. Move against Calydon.

From these massed battles only a few circles of legends remained, which drew the others to themselves (Burgundians).

369

What then was the Trojan War! If the fact of the fall of Ilion is certain, we must free ourselves entirely from the image of the *Iliad*. This little castle, in which dwelt a few hundred weather-beaten fellows, accustomed to murder, of every origin, fugitives, former enemies, with a handful of slaves, and the pomp of a successful pirate — gold, women, wine, blood, and torture — perhaps 10 to 20 fast ships — this was a great power then! — [was] raided while the band was away, or raided and massacred them in the field. What lasted was only the feeling of liberation on all coasts when the nest was burnt down. The image of the Trojan War is poetic creation like the end of the Burgundians in Attila's Hall. This is how war was waged in the 9th century, and not even there, for the fantastic numbers — a thousand ships, 10,000 men — are fantasy.

370

Is there priesthood in the *Iliad*? There is the seer, the *gode*[152], like the physician and singer as a trade. That is Nordic. What about Hesiod? The Greek epic, like the Indian epic, is swollen by continued work into it. In the *Iliad*, the chariot no longer plays a role in active battle. It is foreign to the Javonians.

---

152 Old Germanic term for a priest. — *Transl.*

371

The poets of the Homeric epics call the attackers in the 'Trojan War' mainly Achaeans — and more rarely Danaans, Argeans, Pan-Hellenes (late). From the 8th century onwards — when the *Iliad* may have been written, but the *Odyssey* was still a long way from its present form — the educated were convinced that these Achaeans were their ancestors. At that time, the usage of calling the Greek-speaking population Hellenes developed. It is by no means certain that the poets of the individual cantos, from which written literature then arose, also believed this.

VII. VIEW OF HIGH CULTURES AND CIVILISATION

RISE OF ANTIQUITY

1

Tyros, sidon, carthage also belong to antiquity. [They are] poleis. It was only the fact that the present history of 'antiquity' grew out of philology that brought in the difference between 'Semites' and 'Indo-Europeans'. In truth, it is the difference between West (sea, Sea Peoples) and North (inland peoples) out of which antiquity grew: Tyros, Miletus, Corinth, Athens, Etruscans, Ionians, Phoenicians, Carthage, Sparta, Rome, Macedonians, Dorians, Italics. This is the difference of Dionysian and Apollonian, matriarchy and patriarchy, sea and land, trade and dominion, Aphrodite and Poseidon.

2

Ancient Rome: There were several noble clans from which the king could be chosen by acclamation — for war — to whom the individual warriors then pledged themselves (*lex curiata*). Quarrels between the families, in Sparta. Followed by the double kingship. Germanic, Chinese, Indian. Extensive clans (China, Fabians, Tarquinians,

Claudians, Alcmaeonids). Was Numa also 'Etruscan'? Western priest-king. Tarquinians therefore not army kings but hereditary dictators, un-Nordic: lictors (executioners). Costume (red stripe), *sella*. Fasces. Religion. People as property (Virginia, Lucretia). [It was the] fortune of the Romans that they retained dictatorial power (Imperium) (West and North).

3

K. Latte[1], *Nachr. Ges. Wiss. Gött.* 1934, *Phil. hist. Klasse*, p. 59 ff. (p. 64) Lex originally binding (of the retinue to the leader) to a vow, i.e. to the power inherent in the vow. Mitra Varuna[2]. So 'power' is luck, magic, spell (as in handshake, ring, in brotherhood). Magical act: oath of allegiance of army, retinue, spouse. — Sparta, Germanic tribes, Macedonia the ruler (also the hereditary ruler) swears an oath to the people, whereupon the people recognise him. If he breaks the law, he can be 'recited': originally voluntary bond of the men to the army king, duke. 'Allegiance' is mutual, reward. Ego: In the West there is a theocratic bond of subjects to the god-ruler: pope, pharaoh, Louis XIV [were] anointed in the cathedral. In the North, individual: each individual swears. The Homeric Greeks (around 1000) thought the same way: vows of the heroes to Agamemnon for the march to Troy. Originally, anyone in the state could undertake privateering expeditions (*coniuratio*). Fabians on the Cremera (Mommsen correctly says that the later formulation of the Fabian legend expresses displeasure with these private raids, because the state had actually taken over the monopoly of warfare). But even Scipio offered his private retinue (*clientes*) in the Spanish war. Solon includes in the law of associations the groups of ἐπὶ λείαν οἰχόμενοι (buccaneers). To the state, *coniuratio* appears as a crime (Latte 68, 71): the '*lex curiata*' comes from the

---

1   Kurt Latte (1891–1964) was a German philologist. — *Transl.*

2   Mitra and Varuna are two deities that appear in the Rigveda. They are regarded as twins and symbolise the intimate friendship between men. They are gods of law and order. — *Transl.*

immigration period, the earliest kingship, which was also very dependent on warriorship. Private trust of the individual in the person of the leader.

4

Apollonian is the Nordic, Dionysian the Western spirit in antiquity: the two forms matured in their opposition. But with this it is said that Apollonian is the form of the ruler, the chivalrous upper class; Dionysian is the life of the numerous subjects, which comes into its own to the extent that the ruler adapts himself to the culture. Apollonian is the patriarchal, male attitude to life; Dionysian the matriarchal: in the former man stands against fate. The struggle ennobles him. Dionysian [is the] flight from the meaning of life somehow. Dionysian is the matriarchal, life as a fact between birth and death; the joy of sexual life, the fear of the hereafter.

5

Ancient peoples: There were no 'Greeks' at all around the middle of the 2nd millennium. There were tribes who spoke very different languages of Nordic origin, among them certainly Indo-European languages, some of a lost type. Only the Aegean migration resulted in the formation of a relatively uniform linguistic area, whose inhabitants since then slowly learned to feel themselves as a unit, as 'Hellenes'. This ideal unity emanated neither from the Dorians nor from the Aeolians, but from the centre, the Ionians, Attica, etc. It was the unity of the lords, the nobility over foreign-speaking, subjugated people.

6

Eteocles: Then other, apparently Greek names, such as Heracles, Dionysus, Menelaus, are also suspected of being of foreign origin. We should finally be beyond the time of philological enthusiasm, which wants to explain every Greek name from the Greek, because to assume something else as possible is a crime of majesty. It is precisely the names that are easy to explain that are suspicious, namely of folk etymology. *Plumbum* — plum tree. Hans and Liese are Hebrew names. If you want, you can of course explain the syllables of each word from your own language. But if one explains *Spektralanalyse*[3] with *Speck*[4], *Tralala*, Anna, Liese, one has not finished an interpretation but a silliness, and no better is the case with the interpretation of very many Greek-looking names. What then is Aphrodite — 'foam-born' — but a silliness? Professional patriotism. Heracles, Hercules, Herkle: Which name is older?

7

The diverse and different linguistic northern tribes, originating from different areas between northern Germany and the Aral Sea, but still northern Eurasian in their basic conception of the soul, individualistic, spread out here subjugating, exterminating, intermingling among much more numerous and equally diverse populations of an old western character. Thus arose the ancient soul, ahistorical, Euclidean, given over to the moment — the first of the southern journeys attested to us by their works, as we know them from our own culture from Otto the Great[5] to Nietzsche.

Northern ice on a tepid sea, slowly gnawed and broken until, in imperial times, the old West and the young Arab soul reign alone, the former as the keynote, the latter as the dominant. It was different in India, where the Indus region belongs to Iran as a habitat, not to the actual India of the Ganges and Deccan. There, the soul melted away completely in tropical glow.

8

(*Glotta* 11,195. Kretschmer): Ares is appellative (The Avenger), not a proper name.

---

3   German: 'spectral analysis'. — *Transl.*

4   German: 'bacon'. — *Transl.*

5   The Holy Roman Emperor Otto I (912–973). — *Transl.*

In the oath formulas of the Arcadian synoecism[6] treaty appeared as the oath gods Ζεύς[7], Ἄρης[8], Ἀδάνα[9], Ἄρεια[10] and Ενυάλιος[11], Ἄρης, Ἀθηνη[12], Ἄρεια. In Smyrna and Pergamum [appears] behind Ares Ζευς Ἄρειος in the oath of the Epirotic kings, is thus named after the (chthonic) avenging principle — hence the connection with the avenging Erinyes. Enyalios [is] a war god in Thrace-Northwest Asia Minor. The epithet Ares becomes the name of a war god because the northern peoples originally had none — as did Hera. It was not a person, but originally the avenging power in space, somewhere, mysteriously. The powers were called upon to avenge the broken oath ('Mithra Varuna', Romans, Teutons, Persians). Likewise, Zeus, Hermes, Poseidon are not names, therefore not gods. God [is] *neutrum pluralis*. Zeus is 'the above'. Γη[13], Δα, Ποτιδαν[14] the 'below'.

Here, with Romans and Teutons, the transition to personal gods can still be seen. [There are] no ancient theophoric names, but 'I-names'. Thor in names of the Viking Age is protest against Christianity. When Αιδης[15], Νυξ[16], Ωκεανος[17] and others become

---

6 Synoecism is the merging of several villages into one town. — *Transl.*

7 Ancient Greek: 'Zeus'. — *Transl.*

8 Ancient Greek: 'Ares'. — *Transl.*

9 Ancient Greek: 'Adana' (a city in modern-day Turkey — originally an ancient Hittite settlement, Adana is one of the oldest continuously inhabited cities in the world). — *Transl.*

10 Ancient Greek: 'Areia'. — *Transl.*

11 Ancient Greek: 'Enyalios' (another name for Ares, but also sometimes portrayed as a separate god). — *Transl.*

12 Ancient Greek: 'Athena'. — *Transl.*

13 Greek: 'Earth'. — *Transl.*

14 The Dorian term for Poseidon. — *Transl.*

15 Ancient Greek: 'Hades'. — *Transl.*

16 Ancient Greek; 'Nyx' (the goddess of night). — *Transl.*

17 Ancient Greek: 'Oceanus' (a Titan in the form of a river circling the Earth, he is the source of all fresh water and father of the oceanids [nymphs]). — *Transl.*

persons, marry, have children, it is a sign of the progressive advance of the lower class.

9

The Dorians immigrated as *ver sacrum*[18], without family. Men's house, therefore homosexual, which the Ionians did not know at all. Therefore they adopted the language of the subjugated, the women. This is the later 'Dorian'. It is ridiculous to infer origin from language. Jews, Haitian Negroes.

10

Among the Germanic peoples the large farmers kept horses and cattle, the small farmers mainly sheep and goats. Hence Thor travels with goats. Likewise Dorians: Karnos — Dionysus? The 'Dorians' were farmers and hunters. The cattle breeders come from southern Russia with the chariot and the ox. Is the word Dorian from a non-Greek Norse language and only later related to spear? Thor — Dorian?

(Grönbech[19], 571st group, Crete.)

11

The peasant has become a slave to the soil, rooted, immobile. His kind of work never attracts him. His soul is dull and humble, proud only of the possessions he seeks to increase by avarice, cunning, violence. The transition to a cattle breeder frees him mentally from work, from being bound, from fearfulness. All conquering tribes originated from cattle breeders, none from peasants. Sea robbery and hunting are part of it. All Nordic culture arose when such conquering tribes seized the land together with the peasantry rooted in it, into which

---

18 The *ver sacrum* (Latin: 'sacred spring') was an ancient Italic custom: a group of young men was expelled from the tribe to conquer new land and found a new tribe. — *Transl.*

19 Vilhelm Grønbech (1873–1948) was a very influential Danish historian of religion and a professor at the University of Copenhagen from 1915 to 1943. — *Transl.*

they themselves partly sank. *Not* the Spartans, the patricians, the lords of antiquity. The Attic, Messenian, Latin peasant was partly, often entirely, of a different stock.

12

As far as the early ancient treasure of legend and myths is concerned, one has by no means yet become so conscious of its manifold origins that one would really have based one's investigation on it. As regards, for example, the legends which, according to Nilsson's observation, adhere to the 'Cretan-Mycenaean' main domiciles, there are three kinds of legends:

1. that of the original inhabitants of these domiciles,

2. those linked to the fact of their defeat and conquest,

3. those connected with the ruins.

To 1. may belong Minos, to 2. Danaos and Aigyptos, to 3. the Labyrinth. — Furthermore, the legends of the Sea Peoples — Pelasgians, Boeotians, i.e. those brought with them and new ones, which are linked to the odyssey. Legends of the land tribes. The subjugated population. Finally, new legends of the Geometric period.

13

The Hellenic language (obviously some dialects perished early) penetrates about 1400–1200. Last wave of 'Dorian' tribes, which were not then called that. Pelopians [were] perhaps the conquerors of Argolis, Sea People: Kekropians. Before that the African Achaeans, even earlier the 'Iranian' Mycenaeans. (Chariots, spiral, little sedentary, hardly any agriculture, but herds of cattle?) The name Peloponnesos must have been coined by seafarers — when? Danaans and Pelopians — how does this relate? Danaos and Aigyptos. Pelopians and Pelas-gians.-opian [is] therefore ending that comes from a Medieval Greek, not Western Indo-European language. Pel-opians,

Hellopians; Pel-asgians, Etruscan; Pel-eseti, Ker-eti. Geographical distribution of these endings? Chronological distribution of these endings?

14

The problem is: How did the folk originate that became the bearer of ancient culture? As a result of the exclusive valuation of 'Greek' and 'Roman' literature, the 'motherland' and the city of Rome are usually placed at the centre of considerations. This is wrong. Around 700, for example, Ionia [and] Tuscany were more important than Attica and Laconia and Latium. Later Boeotia, Argos — i.e. seats of the former Mycenaean culture. The Oscians earlier than the Latins. The area of culture in the beginning reaches from Tuscany to Cyprus and from the Hellespont to Cyrene, and behind it lie the ancient cultures in Egypt and Indus and Babylon and Syria, and the great movements of peoples from the north to southern Europe and the Near East, and from Africa and western Europe to southern Europe.

15

Against the rich world of Tartessos and Alashiya, tribes from the south and north broke forward (cf. Saracens and Vikings, Celts and Parthians). Against Egypt: Libyans and Aithiopians, against Babylon in the 1st millennium B.C. [in the] northwest Arameans, in the south Arabs. The incursion of the oldest layer of Nordic (perhaps not yet Hellenic?) tribes: shaft tombs, *satem*? Then Achaeans, then pre-Dorian Greeks. 1200 lastly 'Dorians', from whom the preceding ones fled to Asia Minor: 'Ionians' and Aeolians, and to Cyprus. Achaeans was then a country name for Peloponnesus, etc. The Cyprian (Arcadian) Hellenes thus fled from the Eastern Peloponnese about 1200, on the old track to Alashiya.

16

In the fact that the Hellenic languages lost the Indo-European word *rex* and [acquired] instead foreign words, such as βασιλευς[20] [and] τυραννος[21], [lies] evidence that the migrating northern tribes were subjugated by foreigners (Achaeans, Lydians, Carians) — tholos tombs. Like the Goths by the Huns (*Hünengrab*) and the Romans (Emperor). Hence the non-Greek names of the heroic saga.

17

Just like the misuse of the words *people* and *state*, that of the word *city* has caused mischief. There is no city in c-cultures. City and state belong together, as do writing and administration.

Troy was a castle, not a city. Perhaps with a few villages in the neighbourhood, likewise Mycenae. There were markets with transient populations, villages, manors and refuge castles. 'City' leads to misconceptions about [the] population size. Knossos and Chattusas were cities. There were only remnants of ancient cities in the Occident around 1000. The Germanic tribes stayed outside. So the northern tribes also settled next to the remains of the Mycenaean, Mi[noan] cities around 1000 B.C. An ancient city did not come into being before 900. What Homer calls άστυ (settlement) and πτολις (castle) is not meant as a city. In the more recent parts of the *Iliad*, the dwelling of the poets in Ionian cities has created the image: 700. Only the real city forms the state, the nation out of the primitive bond of tribes and families. Nation is state-organised and urban-dwelling people. Rome (Gregorovius) [was] around 1000 a ruined area in which a number of castles and rural settlements lay. The idea of a city only begins since then (Hansa, Lombardy). Senigallia, Siena, Florence: castle-like palazzi, construct[ions], markets. Only administration, officials,

---

20 Ancient Greek: 'basileus' (king or chief). — *Transl.*

21 Ancient Greek: 'tyrant'. — *Transl.*

bourgeoisie make it a city. Urbs[22]. oppidum[23]. Cité, ville, town (dunum: Autun). Συνοικισμος, thus the πολις[24] comes into being, as city and state at the same time. It gets government, law, administration, instead of council and custom.

18

Parts of Crete [were] occupied by other Greek tribes before [the] conquest by the Dorians. As in the shaft tombs of Mycenae, also elsewhere Nordic, not Hellenic-speaking tribes ('Aryan'? Southern Russia). Still others with the Cyprian-Arcadian dialect (is it the one that lies below Dorian in Crete? Probably). That would perhaps be the Danaans who fought against Egypt. 1400. Destruction of the palaces. The later dialects gave an unreliable picture of the conquest. How, for example, can phonetics separate what reflects the pronunciation of the subjugated and what that of the conquerors? Who wrote and set the orthography? Stonemasons had to learn it or have it recorded.

19

On πτολις[25]: no Indo-European language has as many accents with πτ, κτ, σθ, σβ, χθ, φθ, γδ as Greek (but, ego: they are to be found in pre-Greek Asia Minor — and in Africa!). This, then, is a phonation of a foreign race. So the words πτολις and πτολεμος[26] passed through a foreign race before they came to the Greeks. The 'Greeks' first added such affixes to some Indo-European words because they fit their mouths: Σδεύς[27], cutis skin, scutum[28], σκυτος fur shield. Are these after-effects of prefix pronunciation? (Proto-Hattic, Hamitic?)

---

22 Latin: 'city'. — *Transl.*

23 An oppidum was a walled Celtic settlement. — *Transl.*

24 Ancient Greek: 'polis' (city). — *Transl.*

25 Ancient Greek: epic form of 'polis'. — *Transl.*

26 Ancient Greek: epic form of 'polemos' (battle). — *Transl.*

27 Dorian: 'Zeus'. — *Transl.*

28 The scutum was a long rectangular shield used by Roman legionaries. — *Transl.*

Similarly in a special area of Germanic languages pf for p: Pfote[29], Pfeffer[30], Pfau[31], Pfister, Pflaume[32], etc.

20

Pre-Greek personal names: The many two-stemmed names with a non-Indo-European element are striking: i.e. an Indo-European layer of the same heroic thought, but of very divergent vocabulary. Some Hittite names are apparently formed in this way, e.g. Sipylo-liuma, Ma-yssolos. The large number of personal names (heroes, gods) of epic times are non-Greek and folk-etymologically adapted. Genuinely Greek, for example, is the group Heros — Hera (heroine, army woman). (Heracles does not come from Hera, but [from] Hrapa, hero.) The features of the strong Hans, Samson, Gilgamesh are peculiar to the primitive people; what is Greek is the tragedy of it, as Parsifal reinterpreted, the great helper, always for others, victim of his ethos. The Sea Peoples, like the Normans, have often changed languages. [The] Philistines [perhaps] came to Canaan with the Lydian-Carian language. In Homer Σ 288–292 Hector complains of the poverty of Ilios in comparison with Phrygia and Maionia. Perhaps the older Lydian name only reasserted itself with Gyges: by then the Indo-European master class had been overthrown. Assurbanipal speaks of Gugu, king of Ludi, whose name his predecessors would not have heard. Very often people (e.g. the Greek and Carian mercenaries in Egypt Egyptian ones) still take a name in the newly learned language (Normans French, Jews).

21

Etymology: The tendency to declare every ancient name genuinely Greek or Roman if it can be explained from that language is fatal.

---

29 German: 'paw'. — *Transl.*

30 German: 'pepper'. — *Transl.*

31 German: 'peacock'. — *Transl.*

32 German: 'plum'. — *Transl.*

On the contrary, any name that can be explained all too well should be suspect, suspect namely of folk etymology. Names like Milan, Nijmegen, Braunschweig, Neumagen are genuinely German, are they not? But the same is true of Eteocles, Diomedes, etc., all of which are adapted from common Greek word elements, without regard to meaning. No Greek, for his part, will have formed such silly names as Alexander, Eteocles. Likewise, the endings are subject to the fashion of language: earlier we said *Japanesen* (*Chinesen, Indonesen*), now *Japaner* (*Amerikaner*). Agamemnon is similar to Memnon. Always to common words, especially word endings, without regard to the sense.

22

'Greeks': These are really two questions: Who were the light-skinned swarms that formed the upper class of most Greek cities, and who were the bringers of the language or Indo-European dialects that later gave rise to the Greek dialects? The conquerors in the 2nd millennium, always new ones, Vikings, vagabonds, swarms of robbers and peasants, were no doubt multilingual and of very different 'race'. There were no 'Greeks' at all, for each people only becomes what it is on the new soil.

The languages that could already be called pre-Greek, however, certainly only came along in the 12th/9th century and through densely successive swarms of land-hungry settlers. The proper names in Homer and [in] Chatti are not Greek, even if they have long since acquired a Greek character through folk etymology in the mouths of the singers: Andreus, Agamemnon, Eteocles, Alexander are just as assimilated to familiar word sounds as Etzel, Bern (Verona), Milan.

23

A Hellenic dialect was spoken by a part of the population of the Peloponnese, which was subjugated by Libyan Achaeans. This language of the peasant class held firm and prevailed. It was the Arcadian-Cypriot dialect. 'Achaia' perhaps corresponded to the whole

Peloponnese. At last the name stuck to the north coast. But if in Lower Italy the name Achaia became dominant, it was certainly because it denoted seafarers in the first place. An Achaean campaign in this sense was the raid on Troy. The event itself, the conquest of a royal city by an army, may have taken place somewhere else entirely. In the real Troy there was only a pirate captain.

All the Sea Peoples were gradually drawn into the legend. List of Trojan names. This happened before Homer, perhaps in the 12th/11th century, where the memory of these wild peoples was still alive and resounding in old songs. The names Agamemnon, Odysseus, Priam are certainly genuine. So are the names of the Teucrians, Dardans, etc. Perhaps also the inner-Russian, Iranian horsemen of the Amazons, among whom perhaps women really fought occasionally, as among the Teutons, Turkmen, [in] Novilara.

24

Among the connoisseurs of early Greek history, one has long since racked one's brains as to how the southern Italian coast came to be called Great Achaia. For the colony there was established (more precisely!) by Ionians, Spartans, etc., among whom the name Achaean was not common. But it did not come into use at all, except for two small landscapes (Thessaly, Peloponnese). Homer adopted it with the legendary figures of Mycenae, and already in the younger epic (*Odyssey*) it becomes rare. In the 7th century it would not have occurred to any Hellene to call himself Achaean. So perhaps the possibility must be admitted that the name already adhered to the coast before the Hellenic colonies were founded, i.e. that Aquivasha also landed here and there in the 12th century and left their name here and there. The name may have taken on a completely different form in the course of the centuries and would then have been rendered by the Ionians with the Homeric form Achaeans (cf. Galicia). It is possible that the group of Aquivasha landed everywhere, from Apulia to Pylos, Tiryns to Orchomenos (cf. Normans), that the name, the meaning of which we do not know, was also applied to other tribes of the same fearfulness — what is all called Vikings or Goths! Their attempts in Asia Minor were then thwarted by Hittites. A proud height is reached by the tribe that conquers Argolis.

25

[Sardis] City 'Lydian' (Herbig, *Reallexikon III*, 138). It will rather mean castle, fortress. A confusion has arisen because Greek writers used to refer to West Minor Asian languages by their country name, which was the most common in their time, and today's philologists have accepted this without criticism. The inscription from Sardis is therefore considered to be Lydian, because the Greeks had experienced a Lydian empire whose capital was S[ardes]. But this city, once Hyde, was later called Swart (like Sparta) after a tribe, Saparda, which may have played a role there as a swarm of mercenaries. The Homeric poets also knew the region as Maionia, the southern part was also called Caria, the northern Asia (Hesione). And how many names do we *not* know?! So whose language was that of the inscriptions of S[ardes]? We do not know. The 'Carian' mercenaries left behind a small number of graffiti, which are thus described as 'Carian', although with brevity it is not even certain whether it was always the same language. But what does 'Carian' mean?

26

If Tavaglavas comes from a pre-Greek, non-Hittite, perhaps one of the countless lost ancient Indo-European languages, then this could — because of the 2nd element glavas — also apply to Heracles (this has already been suspected!), thus for instance Saraglavas. Is this perhaps connected with the Latin *atavus* or the ancient Italian cult of Hercules? Then Herk and Herak would be later forms from a very early one — similar to Odysseus and Ulixes. I am not claiming anything, just asking. Are there several more ancient names on -kies? So Tavanannas could be from the language of the ruling class, not from the so-called 'Hittite'. Only Hellenes, Teutons, Celts have two-letter names(?).

27

Eteocles, [the name comes] from one of the pre-ancient languages — it could therefore have been Indo-European after all, from a quite lost group of Indo-European languages. Perhaps it was related to the element that spoke the chancery language in Boghazköy — which is not Indo-European — so badly that its own inflection and a few vocabulary words got into the texts. But then the ending kies = glavas is also suspicious of non-Greek origin, as are almost all epic-Greek names of this kind.

28

Mediterranean, 3ʳᵈ/2ⁿᵈ millennium: No doubt: Egyptian shipping [is] economically (state-organised, thus bureaucratic, weak) not significant: Kafti, Byblos, Punt. More export than private enterprise. All the stronger [is] the shipping of 'Atlantic' coasts and island ports dominating the whole Mediterranean: Tarsis — Elisa, Atlantis — Massilia, Minoan since 2000 in Syria — Canaan. Tart-essos. Odessos; tholos tombs. Tursha in Bethsean. Nonsense, [that] the Sargon train [came] even as far as Cyprus — on whose ships then? A burial culture in Canaan from the west: Ain Shems, Bethshean, Gezer. In the Old Testament, the Antigone of Rizpah.

29

Javonians: There has been a strong maritime trade (and maritime robbery) from western Asia Minor, between the collapse of the Kafti world and the emergence of 'Hellenic' orientalised trade, with a non-Greek language. When the ancient culture began to become mentally a new entity, from Etruria to Cyprus, at first the new ruling class was landowning, [a nobility dominating the] peasants and townsfolk, who despised trade. This was true of Tursha and Pelasgians as well as of the Greek-speaking families of the Aegean. Trade, however small it was until the 6ᵗʰ century, was thus largely driven by population elements that were subjugated and despised, in Italy by the bearers of the 'Etruscan' language, in Ionia by Kafti and Asia Minor. There were warrior nobles from northern Europe in Italy and Hellas, who formed the Dorian-northwestern Greek dialect and Italic. It played no role in Ionia. There is no unified Greekness. The 'motherland' with its ruling class did not understand the Ionian Pelasgians mentally. They resembled the 'Etruscans', i.e. their upper class, which formed and traded from Tursha and Rasena from the 8ᵗʰ century onwards.

30

Ares, Laran, Mars: Such peoples do not have a specific god of war. War is far too self-evident: likewise that all their own gods help in war. Arne (according to Noack the fortress of Gla, Boeotia) [is] a frequent castle name. Perhaps related to Ares, who was especially important in Boeotia? Everywhere the names Mars and Ares have attached themselves to all fertility numens, i.e. the principle of male power, often alongside the corresponding female numen of the fertile earth. Only with Homer does Ares become the 'warrior' — but Apollo, Artemis, Athena are [warriors] too.

31

[In] the 8ᵗʰ century, Saparda [appears] alongside Scythians and C[immerians]: these are the people of Sardis whose army name was Lydians (like Romans, Quirites). Likewise Spartans and Lacedaimonians. Sapardes, Spartes, Sparta [is] a group of names [formed] probably in the 11ᵗʰ century: Homer knows Sparta, [but] always calls Sardis Hyde.

32

Saparda, Sardis: The tombs [were] thus evidently made by the people of Gugu (Mermnads, from whom the name Lydians comes). All western warrior dynasties. The Saparda [had] all become horsemen (mercenaries), lords: they called Hyde the Saparda city.

33

The 'Lydians' [were] also certainly linguistically equal to the Carians, while their popular name is Phrygian. The priest-princes in Olbe (Cilicia) [have] constantly the names Aias and Teukros (*Archäologisches Jahrbuch*[33] 1909, Anzeig. p. 435), Hellenised from Jan- and Tarku.

34

The massive amount of warrior statuettes of lead with round shield in Sparta, c. 1000–700. What does this mean? [Are they] 'Dorian'? Where [did] the lead come from? Where else [did it occur]? Sparta, Saparda, Sparten.

35

If Pel-opian = Pel-asgian, Pel-eseti (root Pelas?), then perhaps the bearers of the 'Arcadian' dialect were these people? Sons of Enak? Who, for example, bore the Achaean names? What then does the distribution of dialects mean? It is not languages that migrate, but speaking people who change languages that can corrupt. The conquerors of Laconia, nameless to us, may have been five hundred strong. The inhabitants of the country perhaps three thousand, Amyklai, Sparta perhaps two hundred.

The name Dorians clings in Argos, Sparta [is] pre-Greek. The people triumphantly took the name of the conquered main domicile. 'Dorian' only became party-political fashion later. Does Herodotus know it at all? And Homer? The Dorian dialects [developed] only by Nordic tribes from the found language, as the Franks transformed Romance into 'French', the Normans Saxon into English, the Tartar Bulgarians Slavonic [into Bulgarian].

---

33 'Archaeological Yearbook'. — *Transl.*

36

The so-called Orientalising period (8th century), which follows the Geometric: it is the difference of the village-peasant chivalric period, where there were no towns yet, and the beginning of refinement in commercial towns (patriciate). The Ionian-Phoenician-Etruscan patrician culture is a unity, not taken over from Tyre as Poulsen believes. Egyptianising everywhere — as in the Occident since the Crusades the late Islamic civilisation influenced the Gothic.

37

Rise of the ancient peoples: Ionians [are] a nation of their own. Various tribes of Asiatic and African origin. Many pre-Greek languages, then Kafti, Sea Peoples, Saparda, a mixture of names (folk, country, city names), then in the commercial cities a Hellenic patriciate, whose language does not rule exclusively, but nevertheless as a lingua franca. Here, where Hittite, Babylonian, Kafti, Egyptian things were known, the Ionian column (Musasir[34]) arose, a mixed style like the Phoenician and Etruscan. All three [are] patrician. Merchant taste; science, historiography, dissolution of the heroic epic into the travel novel (Odysseus).

Also political opposition of the Ionians against the other Greeks, Persian period. 'Late nationalism' leads to revolt. Since when did the Ionians feel themselves to be 'Hellenes'? Does the division into phyles also reveal the difference of the Hellenic patriciate in other parts?

38

(After Javonians = Japhet has been shown:) After the wild time of the Sea Peoples, who had undoubtedly plundered, exterminated, and temporarily occupied all coasts, the remnants of the seafaring families revived in the most important empires. There must still have been some Kafti families in Miletus. But elsewhere it was

---

34 Musasir was an ancient kingdom located between Urartu and Assyria in what is now modern-day Iraqi Kurdestan. — *Transl.*

people from the Greek-speaking northern tribes who learned sea-faring. A centre of these young seafaring circles was in the area of Boeotia — Euboea — southern Thessaly — northern Attica, for instance. From there they sailed from one island to the other and finally settled at some points of the Javonian world — for example, Etruria etc.

It is nonsense and shows the lack of historical perspective to speak of 'migration' as a result of 'overpopulation'. At first there must have been only a few thousand who perhaps felt threatened as a result of the wild events of the 'Dorian' migration. They came over, perhaps gladly, bravely, because their lives were at stake. They were the protectors in the ancient empires, and very slowly their language began to become the language of trade, then the vernacular of the nascent 'cities'. In the countryside, Ionian certainly did not have any validity even in Herodotus' time. The old name of the Ionians stuck to the trading circles, perhaps in Greek pronunciation.

39

Carthage [has been] powerful since 700, protective power of the Phoenician settlements, founds an empire, turns against the Ionians who rule the Tyrrhenian Sea and Massilia. With and against the 'Etruscans', i.e. the southern Etrurian ports and Rome. The treaty of 509 will also have been concluded with Caere and Tarquinii. Carthage, founded only in 804, is the first city with an ancient state spirit and Semitic language. All the others are powers, cities. Ionian-Dorian influence from the beginning.

40

If it is true that the names Athens and Attica, Assuwa, Asia were identical, then the relations between the shores of the Aegean must be very ancient. Since, therefore, there was maritime traffic there, the conquest of the coastal places of Asia Minor from Attica by Greek-speaking expeditions would have been on account of this relationship, perhaps on account of internal struggles in Javonia, where one party called on the Greek fighters over there for help, took them into pay, or the like.

41

Athena [is] a general Hellenic goddess in the *Iliad*. So she can hardly be named after a city (but Hera of Argos, Pallas of Athens?). But if Attica, Athens (Assuwa) is to be named after the goddess, it becomes even more difficult. Would [then] Hesione be Athena?

42

If Sara and Milka ([to masculine:] Sar, Melek) are Harrian god-titles (Melchisedek, Abimelek), then they occur in Hellas as Hera, Zeus, Meilichios (etc.). Meilichios — Melek; Dephinios — Telibinus. Sipylos, Sibyl — Subbiluliuma.

43

The 'Ionian'-speaking Hellenes set off there in about the 12th century, at the time of the fall of Chatti, [were] perhaps first called to help in wars, then taking dominion in some cities under *condottieri*[35] (phyla division). The Hellenic language [was] at first only that of the small ruling class in these cities, besides very many others (among them Kafti? The later so-called Lydian, Carian, etc.). The area retained the old Kafti name.

44

Greek colonisation: One has to distinguish sharply between two colonisations, which are better called differently. The first is a land-grabbing: the foreign city was destroyed, subjugated, the inhabitants [were] partly murdered, the women taken into one's own harem: here heroism is the motive. Herodotus 1,146: allusion to the hatred of the subjugated. From them remained underclass, name, cults, customs. Before the planned conquest [there was] certainly already

---

35 *Condottieri* were leaders of mercenary troops. — *Transl.*

Achaean individual immigration. All crafts remained in the hands of pre-Hellenic strata. 'To the victors the plain, to the vanquished the mountains!' After the land-grabbing, the hostile [opposition] between the coast and inner Asia Minor arose, so that the Hittite traffic routes were closed off: the Aegean and Cappadocian worlds for themselves, prerequisite for the history of Urartu, Phrygia, Assyria — and for the westward expansion of the Greeks. The style of this colonisation is pre-Greek, as are names, trajectories, tendencies.

45

Heracles [is] a peasant ideal: to become a god through toil and labour (Wilamowitz 11,241 *Heldensage*[36]). Achilles [is an] ideal of the conquering tribes: honour and battle death. Odysseus sea-people ideal: cunning, merchant-like. Heracles: Dorian, peasant, dumb. Achilles: Aeolian, chivalrous. Odysseus: Tyrrhenian, piratical. Odysseus [is] before the *Iliad* the castle-breaker, pirate; *afterwards* [a] flying Dutchman.

46

Tartessos, Etruscans, Sea Peoples: The Greeks [are] not 'born' seafarers, [but] landlubbers. (Wilamowitz 224.) They took the ships of the subjugated peoples. Their seafaring [was] only imitation of that of the 2nd millennium. Colonies [are] only reconstructions of older trading places. The seafarers [were] mostly the subjugated population. Since 800, the interest, the boldness has been slowly waning. If Euclidean antiquity had had the slightest will to discover, to conquer in the distance, it would have extended the knowledge of the 2nd millennium instead of inventing fairy tales about it.

47

The High Song of the Doers. Heroic time. The immeasurable longing of being judged on deeds. The expansion barely awakens.

---

36 'Heroic Saga'. — *Transl.*

Direction is everything. That rushes forward, into the wide foreboding world and also into life. Danger is the air in which one lives. The daily sight of blood on gaping bodies, the daily hearing of how the sword cuts in, how groans and gasps end a life. Behind it all, something unfathomable, as if it all speaks a secret — and the foreboding now translated again into an image of gods. If one wants to know the nature and direction of this wild seafaring of small, manly swarms, one must know this ethos of the travellers, under a warm sun, a homeland of Azure and Atlas never imagined, a daily fairy tale, a jubilant exuberance of southern nature. *Incipit tragoedia*: down here sat another humanity, psychically a creation of the old-possessed soil. The soul of the travellers resists — and succumbs. This spectacle is what we call the historical image of ancient culture. The most powerful symbol stands in its midst: Aeschylus' Oresteia, and here Bachofen[37] saw what lay in the depths of the world. The right of the father is victorious, Apollo! But this victory is a defeat. Apollo tames Dionysus, but it is the tamed Dionysus who precedes the following period as a symbol, the bonds become looser in the growing cities. In another place: in Rome ... There they fall: the imperial age begins, dull fellahdom, primitive earth-sun cults, renunciation, extinction.

48

Antiquity:

---

37 Johann Jakob Bachofen (1815–1887) was a Swiss legal historian, scholar of antiquity and philosopher of history. He wrote the groundbreaking book *Das Mutterrecht. Eine Untersuchung über die Gynaikokratie der alten Welt nach ihrer religiösen und rechtlichen Natur* ('Mother Right. An Inquiry into the Gynaicocracy of the Ancient World According to Its Religious and Legal Nature'). Although Bachofen did not yet use the term himself, his study triggered a huge discussion about 'matriarchy', i.e. about the power of women who were supposed to have ruled over men in the early days of cultures. Bachofen had reconstructed such a stage of early history by interpreting ancient myths and thus creating a new myth himself. He influenced a lot of later feminists with his theories. He is famous for the quote: 'The history of the human race is determined by the struggle of the sexes.' — *Transl.*

1. Chapter primeval times. Here the history of the soul. The cosmic currents of the pendulum swing. Man, animal and plant. Forest time, steppe time. Ancient trade routes. The first 'personality': the pathfinder of these ways. Trade was sacred. The great giver and mediator. The idea of the hospitable [is] ancient. The eternal guests from horde to horde. The ideal nomads. A powerful image of the awakening of the human soul, the skeleton of which is the Stone Age. Frobenius only shows maps, but I show the 'direction' into time and the future. This is where the arc begins. So what wanders? What rests?

2. Sea Peoples. Mystical migration to the south, to the sun. The soul of such swarms of men. Here the ideal of comradeship, of the right of fatherhood. Here an enormous outline of the soul-image, whose intersection with what is found is [the] emergence and withering of 'antiquity'.

    Parallel of antiquity and India, fertilised here by the same migratory swarms. 'Aryans', cremation. Arya and Agathoi. Heroes. Stoa and Buddha — Minos, Dravida and reaction.

    The 'races': since when do people in East Asia look 'Mongolian'? It is not bone structure, it is expression.

    Their world-view. The myth was there. It is proto-Nordic, Turanian. From China to Ireland. In China it evaporates, in the West remnants are rebuilt into a 'mythology'.

3. Apollo and Dionysus. Homer. Birth of the ancient soul. Opposite soul. Divide everywhere like this.

    a) The inner form of the soul. Its expression in grave and house, form of tribe, estate, clan, family, custom. With the reception of destiny (for history is the image of how one bears destinies). Imitation ('dance').

    b) Understanding. Tool, myth, morality, ornament ('art'). To b) belongs language, namely vocabulary of names and grammatical system, which are not firmly connected. Transformation by the race, namely pronunciation and syntax. Human style and dialect by interbreeding. 'Dorian.'

Name hoard: Polynesian and Aryan grammar: Basque and Indian. Sea Peoples (Iron) to the Mediterranean and Horse Peoples to India, thence to Mitanni, where they meet the Pelasgians. Goliath of the Pelasgians.

We hardly know the vocabulary of the Sea Peoples' language. Among the ancient names are Pelagos, Goliath, etc. With the Apollonian soul a new naming arose, also in Etruria. Without doubt, geographical sound shifts since 1100.

49

Antiquity: If Wissowa [comments] against the Minerva Acropolis, this is philologically correct, but wrong in terms of religious history. The numen worshipped on the Acropolis was, however, not identical with the Minerva on [the Capitol]. But neither was she identical with the Athena of the epic. In Rome and Athens the cults are purely local and state-bound without any connection to the great early mythology.

This link is rather of literary origin and was, say from 500 B.C. onwards, common property of the educated. But this is still true only for Rome. There is no doubt that the Homeric poems, which originated in Aeolian and Ionian territory, from the noble chivalric culture along the edges of the northern Aegean Sea, were very soon familiar not only to the Dorian knighthood from Crete to Sicily and lower Italy, but also to the Etruscan nobility.

This is evidenced not only by the Etrurian version in the *Odyssey* and [in] Hesiod, but also by a name formation such as Ulixes. Homer was as well known at the court of the Tarquins as at that of Peisistratos. And the genuinely ancient relationship of these myths to the numina of the local cults occurred everywhere, in Athens, Sparta, Rome, Veji (vases!). What strikes us in Roman poets is precisely the same thing that has taken place everywhere. It is quite certain that the Etruscan poetry, which has disappeared without trace, and of whose existence we have evidence enough, connected the Etruscan Minerva with the Athena of the Trojan mythology as early as 500, about the same time that the same thing happened with the Athena in Athens. It is very regrettable that the linguistic term 'ancient history', which was very common in Goethe's time and still is, for example, in France (Fustel[38]), was eliminated by Mommsen. Only since then have we been accustomed to treat Greek and Roman as *two* worlds instead of one.

50

In the prehistory and early history of ancient religion one has to distinguish (carefully!): the names of the gods — are they local or introduced, do they belong to the language of the worshippers, or what else? Thus Zeus — Jupiter's name Old Norse, Aphrodite perhaps Achaean, Artemis Dorian? Then the numina! The old natives of the place, then those of the established population who do not stick to the place but to the tradition of the people, finally those who come into the country with new streams of people. All these numina are newly formed, and the question now arises again as to what the names for them will be.

Finally, there is an enormous difference between the popular faith, which finds expression in the official city cults, e.g. Rome, and the religion of a higher order, which has been formed in the priesthood since 1100 and leads to a philosophy and world-view. The development of both is very different. For example, despite Wissowa, 'Juno' in the Roman state cult may have meant a house-numen (genius), in the higher faith the female deity [besides] Jupiter.

---

38 Numa Denis Fustel de Coulanges (1830–1889) was a French historian who developed the scientific approach to the study of history in France. His historical thinking had two main tenets: the importance of complete objectivity and the unreliability of secondary sources. He established the modern idea of historical impartiality at a time when few people had any qualms about combining the careers of historian and politician. — *Transl.*

Thus one has to distinguish the Old Norse Zeus (e.g. oracle of Dodona) very much from the Cretan deity who received this name — from the Achaeans, i.e. [the] Sea Peoples.

51

Zeus — deivos c. 2000.

a) Noun *djaus* — Zeus — *dies, diespiter.*

b) Adjective *deivos*: the divine — *tiwaz* — *Ziu* — *Tyr, deus.*

Slavs and Lithuanians also had the *deivos, tien, tinia.* The ancient thunder, thunderstorm and oak god (the oak attracts lightning, 'before the oaks shalt thou depart'). Zeus Keraunos. Lithuanian Perkunos, Perkus (lat. quercus), later Perkunas. Slavic Perun (thunder). Oak: is this related to Zeus Herkaios? Dodona. Then Herkaios would later be reinterpreted as protector of the house, when the Indo-European word for oak disappeared as in Lithuanian and Slavic. Brückner[39] (*Chantepie II* 520) assumes the following as Lithuanian-Slavic stages: a) Perkunos period. Jupiter tonans. Keraunos; b) Dazbog period. Sun cult; c) since Metal Age fire cult. Japan, Aino layer. Sun goddess.

52

Hephaistos, pre-Greek, in Lemnos. Athens: Poseidon (Erechthonios) the elder, Athena the younger numen. Poseidon, originally not sea god, is pre-Greek, dwells in the castle (1400) as well as in the Panionion, the Ionian covenant shrine. For the primeval Hellene of the 2nd millennium, perhaps Zeus is [the] celestial power, Poseidon [the] earth power (shaker), both numina of action, [of] power, of will! Athena is only victorious in Athens when she is already city goddess and Poseidon already sea god, i.e. late Athenian. Athena belongs to the Rasena layer!

---

39 Alexander Brückner (1856–1939) was a Polish professor of Slavic Studies at the University of Berlin. — *Transl.*

53

Athena: The 'Minoan' Athena is a mother deity, especially in Crete, in Hieraphythra the Corybantes[40] are her children. Thus she appears in Ephesus, Priene, Miletus, in Homeric Troy. Only the Greeks made her (status poetry) the lance-wielding virgin. Tritogeneia, Athena and Triton — Libyan? Nothing to do with '3'.

54

Hellenes: The name probably spread from the small tribe of Achill to all the others because its legendary princes Peleus and Achilleus were the most famous (as was the Achaean Agamemnon before). Thus Zeus of Olympus became the ruling god of the ruling class. Their ancestral pride made, between Homer and Hesiod, the skaldic guild, all princes descend from Zeus. This was the ancient expression for 'primitive nobility'. In Thessaly (Aeolian) the 'troubadour age' must have had its centre, and Homer's Ionian guild only formed the conclusion with the beginning of writing. Alkaios [is] the last Aeolic knight and troubadour, Archilochos and Simonides [are] the 'Ionian poets'. At the court of the Sun King Peisistratos, Orphic-mystical court poetry flourishes. Athena (cow, bird, serpent) [is the] Mycenaean domestic goddess: the palladion is the sacred image, with the wresting of which the numen escapes from the palace. Apollo (name type like Sarpedon) is Lycian, bitterest enemy to the Greeks before Troy, later received as god of disease and healing. Hera especially among ancient Ionian tribes. Poseidon in Thessaly, Arcadia, Boeotia god of horses and earth, and from Libya god of the sea.

55

Before antiquity: 'Romans and Greeks'. Map image.

---

40 Corybantes are half divine, half demonic beings. They are orgiastic ritual dancers who accompany the goddess Cybele. — *Transl.*

Overthrow of Tarquinian gens by a small group of leading families. There were always some gens with democratic leanings: Alkmaeonids. Agiades? Aemilians?

By the way, the kings in Sparta are not called basileis, but [archagets[41]]. That gives a deep insight (= consul). The 5th century in Rome knew party fights in the form of the creation of offices. First Praetor-Judex, then Tribune, then the Decemvirs, Consular Tribunes, like a coup d'état. Did the consultative title first emerge from '*consulari potestate*[42]'? And where did it come from?

Epoch of family factions. Much later only 'parties'. The nobility [is] connected by the phyles of the polis. Thus [is] Porsena, who takes Rome, no doubt connected with [the] Tarquinians, cf. Kleomenes after the fall of Peisistratos. Likewise the old connection Cumae — Rome, Sparta — Syracuse, Marcius — Coriolanus.

Mommsen [is] harmful: 1. formal instead of historical (see the Roman offices where he is interested in competence), 2. irreligious: religion as a formal state matter, 3. anti-Greek: he has made discord a method.

With the victory of the polis, the formerly quite general *conubium*[43] within the phyles from city to city ceases.

I combine politically, not philologically, and beyond [that] soulishly-religiously, not philologically. The fact is that the poleis have a life of their own, and the more decidedly so the more mature they are. The Etruscan city, just like the Dorian city, did not form a unified political power. On the other hand, the family interest of the great families passes through phyla in the same way as the party interest does later on.

---

41 The archagets were two kings at the same time. — *Transl.*

42 *Tribuni militum consulari potestate:* 'military tribunes with consular power'. — *Transl.*

43 According to Roman law, the *conubium* was the right to enter into a recognised marriage. — *Transl.*

56

Antiquity, problems and methods: Any consideration of the political structure must start from the core question of the agnatic kinship. The individual means little, and the whole is a sum, not a unity. Here is the basic form. Only through phratry does the individual belong to the phyle, only through this is he part of the state.

And thus arises what can never be meant as a form by the ancient name of the Dorians, Ionians, Etruscans: not a 'nation', but the sum of the noble phyla. The names originate from a cityless and therefore purely noble time. What exists outside the phylums is appendix and object.

Plebs. Until 350, these were very rich merchant families who wanted to penetrate the old basic nobility. Fathers and plebs [correspond to] landed and funded interest.

Religion: Wissowa says: Aphrodite is Venus. This is true, but it is true of all antiquity. It has everywhere confused religion with literature, and the most famous and worst case is at the beginning: Homer. An attempt must certainly be made to gain ancient religion to the exclusion of Homer.

57

The two Spartan kings were originally called archagets. This sounds like a title in the manner of the Athenian archon and the Roman praetor. Was the original royal house overthrown by the nobility, as elsewhere, and a governor appointed from each of two leading, equally powerful families, who gradually received the title of king, but never even remotely royal power? The Roman consuls have authority of their own accord. Likewise, in Rome, the praetor must have stood opposite the king before 600, before the Tarquinians.

In the Phaeacian city, 12 archoi ruled with the title of king alongside the actual king. In Athens, the Kodrids are said to have renounced the kingship to become archontes[44]. The four 'first' Roman kings — before tyranny — bear Etruscan names. Since a much larger number of personalities were involved in the fate of the city during these at least 200 years, these names, which are very ancient and yet probably all genuine, must for some reason have stuck in the legendary memory: Numa perhaps like Teiresias as a saint and priest, others perhaps through the power of the family of the same name. But it is doubtful whether the name Numa was really that of a king.

<h2 style="text-align:center">58</h2>

It is possible that in Sparta the ephors[45] were installed in 754, but of course not with the omnipotence they possessed at the time of the Persian Wars. When the archagets had really secured royal power for the two noble houses, the jealousy of the others was probably explicable. Ephors also existed very early in other Dorian states. Between 700 and 500, power must have passed from the archagets to the ephors, who became the natural advocates of the non-nobles and took on the role of tribunes.

<h2 style="text-align:center">59</h2>

Antiquity: How closely connected this whole world still felt around 700/600 is shown by the Italic-Etruscan data in Hesiod and Herodotus. Not only do they betray a precise knowledge of the Italic situation and tradition even in Boeotia; participation in it must have been so great as to justify mention. But then follows the blockade of the sea [by] Carthage (500?); that the ancient world let it happen without rising up together against it; that it spoke so little of it that it must actually be discovered today as a historical fact first — this proves how Euclidean ancient being is increasingly becoming. And when the great Roman decisions were made: the 1st Punic War — even the Tyrrhenian

---

44 The archontes were holders of office. — *Transl.*

45 The ephors were five elected leaders in ancient Sparta. — *Transl.*

Sea was taken from the inhabitants of the Aegean at the same time, and this gigantic war was hardly heard.

60

As far as the ancient myth is concerned, we have to distinguish between a popular one, which remains alive and changing everywhere, and a great one of the Homeric period, which came into being once and has been preserved ever since. As for the former, it is at home wherever ancient men live, in every village, on every mountain, in every river, whether we know of it or not, in Rome as well as in Miletus or Tanagra. And if it is claimed of the Roman one that it is a literary make after famous models, the same has happened to it as to every other: in Hellenistic times they have all, so far as they occur near a poetical or learned literature, been dressed up literarily, in Athens as in Rome. The great myths, however, are not linked to a place or a 'people' but to a society, and that in Homeric times. They are therefore at home in five or six courts, which were the centre of chivalric life around 1200: they did not include Sparta [and] Corinth any more than Rome, but they were later sung everywhere, whether in Dorian, Latin or Etruscan. The legend of the Rape of the Sabine Women is as genuine or spurious as that of Midas, Lycurgus [or] Kodros.

61

Apollonian [is] the world-view of the masters, Dionysian that of the vanquished, that of the 'land' which bursts forth again with tyranny. Not to be confused with Orphism, the greatest priestly religion of antiquity.

62

Antiquity: Here, too, write the great history as the history of war (Delbrück[46]). It begins with Ajax. The peasant legions. The general

---

46 Hans Delbrück (1848–1929) was a German military historian and politician. He wrote the influential work *Geschichte der Kriegskunst im Rahmen der politischen Geschichte* ('History of the art of war in the context of political history').

conscription of the citizens, on which heroism dies (as on the mass armies of the World War): the born fighter comes into his own again at last, not the pressed one. The great moments of human heroism here too. Thermopylae. Hannibal.

63

Prehistoric times: Already here it must be noted that from the moment when swarms do not evade each other, but peoples subjugate populations, the ruling minority preserves only the forms of race: the political, in addition — for itself — the custom and form of the family, the political part of the economy (possession, right to things), while theory and technique in religion, art, science are mainly accepted as something which the victor makes use of, which he partly respects and fears. The religion of the Homeric period was the pre-ancient one, with cults, sites, myths, names; the religion of the victorious generations was, in some non-local features (Zeus!), its own ancient one. The religion of the Homeric songs is what the skalds were allowed to mix into the poetry of the ranks, because it was common in this circle and in a form that corresponded to the custom of the circle and was therefore pleasing.

The warlike gods and goddesses did not really exist in any religion, neither here nor in India or Germania; but the masters liked it that way, and so it was written that way. Hesiod is quite different; he tells what was mixed from the priestly doctrine of the temples and the peasant faith. But Heraclitus and Aeschylus, both of whom grew up in ancient priestly families, know the primeval, pre-ancient priestly theories in the thought-out version of the time. Heraclitus even reproduces the sibyllic style of the formulae.

His fact-critical approach to source texts, which relativised previously held views of military historiography, was attacked by the military historians of the Prussian-German general staff. This work, which also attracted attention abroad, received numerous translations and served as a textbook in various military academies. Its main focus was on antiquity and Frederick the Great, in whom Delbrück saw the perfector of the art of war in his time. — *Transl.*

64

Family, phyle, state (Busolt[47] 135 and 256): These phyles in their developed form — about 600 — are something unique to only ancient people, but not to all here either. Here an investigation would be of value: When did these phyla form? Did synoecism only bring them to maturity or already decompose them? What is their origin? Do their very ancient names teach anything about it? Their sum represents the nobility. But the tribe is older. Such blood associations must have formed in the Viking crowds, which held firmly together with custom, name, *conubium*, even when the swarm sat in far conquered lands. It is a sign of decay when they became local, with new land division or by revolution like the *tribus* of Rome (replacement of blood phyles by local ones in Sparta etc. Busolt 257). They are absent in the Aeolian and most of the north-western Greek (Thasos, Paros) colonies.

Between phyle (*tribus*) and γένος or πάτρα (gens, *pater familias*) stand familial associations, phratries (Busolt 133). Very deep reaching. In Rome perhaps evidenced by the mutual exchange of adopted sons! What families are connected there? Common cults (Fustel, Münzer[48]). In Homer: a man without phratry is *hostis* (135). The phyla form the original state (feudal state): 3 tribus: council of the three hundred (Rome); 4 [phyla]: council of the four hundred (Athens).

65

Phyles: It is too little said that these blood unions 'occur' everywhere. The 'cities' of that time are nothing but common settlements of phyles-phratries. What other 'people' lived there did not really come into consideration around 1000. The 'Ionians' are not a people, but a word for the sum of the nobles who belonged to the four phyles.

---

47 Georg Busolt (1850 — 1920) was a German ancient historian who wrote a handbook about Greek civics which is still used today. — *Transl.*

48 Friedrich Hermann Münzer (1868–1942) was a German classical philologist who researched how family relationships in the Roman Empire were linked to political struggles. — *Transl.*

The so-called Phoenician colonisation: in Homer there is not even a hint of Phoenician maritime expressions, and without heavy wars Phoenician associations would not have been tolerated in these aristocratic settlements of the great Phylon period. No: when the Sea Peoples had come to rest and the ancient culture [experienced] its rise, Phoenician merchants settled in the markets everywhere, like the Spanish Jews since 1000 in the Occident. They may have built small forts around their warehouses, but there is no question of a Phoenician sovereignty or even a Phoenician state. They enjoyed the protection of powerful kings, who appreciated these merchants in weapons and jewellery; they brought many a Semitic name with the goods, perhaps also many a cult, if they inhabited a ghetto somewhere in larger numbers. These merchants also brought writing with them — as merchants! — and just as their superior accounting system — late Babylonian — attracted these barbarians to imitate them, so did the more spiritual cults. We know how many crusaders succumbed to the Islamic magic — not to mention the Sicilian Normans. But these merchants remained subject to the kings of Tyre and Sidon.

66

Important: The similarity between Persian and Ionian architecture is not due to borrowing, but to development from a common substratum from Miletus to Persia. This is evidence of the 'Hittite' character of Miletus and Ephesus. Elamite things throughout Persia!

67

Antiquity: Forest is domination of the plant over the animal, steppe vice versa. Environment of humans thus rooted, green at that time, later mobile. The forest is unassailably superior before the Iron Age. People avoid it, they fear it. Animals are solitary, the forest is infinite.

68

Antiquity: Investigate: [are] the seats of the ancient heroic saga — (Danaids) of the Minoan cults (Orchomenos) and the

Mycenaean castles identical? The hexameter first developed in the courts of the nobility (from Sea Peoples or native metre?) as the measure of a distinguished society. All heroic songs originated in ancient metrics.

69

The ancient temple is Dorian, first a mere temenos, then a quadrangle, only much later a megaron (not yet, for example, [that of] Artemis Ortygia in Sparta, [that of] Apollo at Gortyn, hardly [that of] Dictaean Zeus on the ruins of Palaecastro, [nor the] Heraion on the ruins of Tiryns). These temples on the rubble of the destroyed Sea Peoples' cities [are] the first 'Dorian' ones. The 'Oriental' style of the $8^{th}/7^{th}$ century then brings forth the elegantly patrician of the Ionian column, with subtle hints of the foreign.

70

Antiquity: Homer and Orpheus are status poetry. As the 'Renaissance' penetrates as patrician taste into the corresponding circles of the northern commercial cities, so the Orientalism of the Ionian period penetrates into Etruria.

71

Antiquity: Hansa period in Etruria. Here begins the 'oriental' style of the city patricians, the 'founding' of Rome, Tarquinia, Caere. Rome from Vetulonia? Burial in sarcophagi.

72

History a sea of suffering, drawn from knowledge. The highest that is possible is heroism and holiness: the great affirmation or renunciation. The ascent [to this leads from] the 5th to the 2nd millennium: from the fear of life to heroism: the victory of the Nevertheless. Summit of the soul. Most balanced in antiquity.

73

Antiquity: In the foreground the deep principles: a dense population long indigenous. From the north the Viking swarms of strong race, forming a master race everywhere. Their race ideal has a breeding effect, through living with the ideal image, seeing, choosing a husband, through fine art, dreams and desires, all of which shape the body.

And here in the small plain between hills and sea, the new ancient world blossoms. The landscape, overpowering in its language: the sunlight, the dominant colours (yellow-brown and blue), the lines of the hills, the power and costume of the flora, the wind and [the] clouds create the human character. Certain traits all immigrants take on; they are 'assimilated'.

But something else is ancient language of the blood: the Apollonian of the ruling conquering race, the Dionysian of the obeying natives. Both have the style of one soul, the ancient one, and both struggle for supremacy within this soul of a great culture. Bachofen saw this first: Oedipus, and clothed it in the opposition: matriarchy and patriarchy. Nietzsche followed and created the words for it.

This struggle pervades all of politics: the polis was founded by the Apollonian lords, but the Dionysian demos conquers it and gives it the lord in Divus Augustus[49]; in religion: the great myth arises in the ruling class, but the peasant cults penetrate it and subjugate it in the emperor cult. In art: for the struggle, waged in Aeschylus' Oedipus not only for two rights but also for two ideas of art, is decided in Hellenism in favour of the rustic one.

This is the story of antiquity as the fate of a uniformly seasick human world. At the beginning, in the Mycenaean castles from the Arno[50] to Rhodes, the new lords sit over a populated land; tyranny follows against nobility, Athens against Sparta, tribunes against

---

49 Latin: 'God Augustus'. — *Transl.*

50 The Arno is a river in central Italy. — *Transl.*

senators, Caesar against Pompey; at the end, a lord sits on the Palatine again, and the population lives as it did a millennium before.

74

In Rome, in the 2nd century B.C., capital punishment and corporal punishment were abolished for the *civis Romanus* — that is, at the same moment that the mob exercised its death penalty. Military service at that time made people flee the country. It no longer appealed to them. From 150 onwards, it is the international urban rabble that demagogically creates the 'empire'; by then, Rome is only the plaything of Asian-African and Nordic instincts. In any case, it is the 'Roman spirit' as a wonderful idea that continues to leave its mark on diplomacy for a hundred years, although the plague of civilisation: big city, Jacobinism, nomadism, capitalism, prevails.

75

[The] Dorian migration (c. 1100) [was] a sharp crushing cut. Apparently a coarse, brutal, illiterate mass, trampling down everything: music instead of eye art. That looks rather Russian. That is how the word Sparta sounds to us today. In Sparta, the primeval Dorian shrine of Artemis Ortygia is quite un-Achaean over the rubble of Menelaion, which is pure Achaean. At the same time, Thracian-Phrygian tribes go to Asia Minor, Illyrian ones to Italy. The colonists of southern Italy spoke Dorian, called themselves Achaeans — they were the descendants of the sea bears, the subjugated and linguistically assimilated, in whom the old blood still existed. That is why they called the country Greater Greece after the small landscape Hellas in Phthiotis — only then did 'Hellas' become a collective name like Ionia. (Ego:) These seafaring Dorians came from Phthiotis.

76

Antiquity: Arcadia [was] the main seat of ancient maritime cults: it was here [that] the Dorian onslaught was most terrible, which is still belatedly attested by the energy of the Spartan state. It was precisely here, then, that the Sea Peoples element was partly devastated, partly pushed into the mountains, where fate made it hard and conservative. This is precisely why the Arcadian forms in cult and state are particularly valuable. (Arcadia in Pauly-Wissowa.) Everything anciently Arcadian is therefore 'Danaan' good.

77

Greek Hansa period: Miletus colonises Pontus, that is, the Carians had previously settled there, and Miletus laid its eggs in the foreign nest. But this is evidence of maritime routes from southern Russia. Miletus, Ephesus, Samos, however, is an ancient Hittite centre. Assyrians and Egyptians had influence there. In general, it was the Ionian barbarians who first occupied and devastated this flourishing coast. Then they mixed with them, and in the patrician colonisation the lower class of the natives picked up the old threads again.

Shift in the centre of gravity of ancient history: area around 1100 Aeolis, Thessaly, crossroads period Dorian-Etruscan, Hansa period Milesian, Renaissance Athens, possibly Corinthian.

One should abandon the term 'motherland'. The 'mainland' was by no means the ancestral seat of the conquering population, Asia Minor by no means merely the daughter foundation.

CHINA — INDIA — EQUESTRIAN PEOPLES

78

Equestrian Empires: The oldest of these nomadic empires is the Median-Persian — small equestrian tribes similar to the Celtic empires. The Scythians in Hungary. As a result of these events, the Celtic language became a tremendously widespread one for half a millennium, similar to Persian. Later, Sarmatian, the Turkish dialects, Arabic. With a favourable fate, Hunnic [and] Scythian would also have found a lasting spread.

79

Equestrian tribes — iron: The extraction and processing of iron requires quite different techniques from those of copper. The former was first used somewhere in the western Mediterranean, the latter certainly somewhere between the Urals, the Caucasus and the Altai — for weapons-sword, lance, dagger, axe.

80

Gobi, Sahara: The great land conquerors came from Central Asia, the sea conquerors from Western Europe (from the 4th millennium until today). Did they perhaps move from Central Asia (via India?) to the South Seas? Are the Malays — Incas chased away from there?

81

India: The North Eurasian element is found in India only in the Rigveda. The priestly caste, the theologians are South Asian. From Brahmanism onwards — as in antiquity since Orpheus and Dionysus — the subjugated element determines religion. South Asia: stars, astrology, astronomy, divination. The Western 'oracle' is something else: not calculating, but getting the god to say something. Fear of the future.

82

Since the 1st millennium B.C. [the] sea ship has been in general use. In the 2nd millennium B.C. it was still little known in the Indian Ocean. River navigation. As late as 0 [there is] the connection between China and India partly by land. The Persian Empire made a great deal of difference. At that time there was no navigation. The three chariot cultures [are] typically inland. Greek, Indian, Chinese navigation [is] insignificant, retrograde, made by foreigners.

83

The Nordic conception: Ancestor worship, memory, glory and perpetuation through the blood of descendants, embodiment of the ancestral soul in the grandson, all lead to theological-philosophical views in the transmigration of souls (antiquity, India, China). The path of the soul through the body of descendants is morally shaped as a path up and down (to animals) until liberation in Nirvana. Part of the funerary temple is matriarchy, i.e. the emphasis on birth before procreation. Bachofen has made a distorted picture of the facts from late ancient writers. Hatshepsut.

84

'India' — this is a prejudice of the Indologists. In cultural history the Indus region belongs to Persia, Elam, Amu Darja; the Ganges region to Burma. The Deccan is a world apart. Names for it? The writing of the Harappa seals is reminiscent of Chinese characters. 'Turan' is a territory in itself. Assur belongs to Asia Minor, Caucasus, southern Russia. Sumer? The tombs in Ur? *All high cultures* on the border of several c-cultures. Also in China. One element related to Tonkin, another to Turan. Ainu?

85

Eastern Persia and the Indus region are historically and geographically one unit. 'India' only begins with the Ganges and the Deccan, which belong to Burma. 'The Aryans' sit here in the eastern steppe from the Dniester to [the] Amu Darya. Scythians, Sea Peoples, etc. belong to it.

86

Expansion of the Turanian master nomads, physically perhaps very different 'race', mentally not. To China, Sunda, Europe: hence the kinship of certain elements in North China and [among the] Malays with the 'Teutons' (Bali, Borneo — Polynesia).

87

Turanian expansion corresponds to Saharan expansion. Transformation of sedentary people into wandering herd owners who only occasionally cultivated food crops. Expansion to the east (China), south (India), west (Europe). Relationship or identity of 'Germanic' ornamentation with Turkic and Bornean. Human types, mixed. Aino, Mongoloid. Likewise languages: Ural-Altaic, Indo-European, Caucasian, other families. In the north the pale type of people, Nordic = 'north-west'. Invasion of Atlantis (Bohuslän) and Turan (Indo-European language). The young Indo-European languages of the West (in Europe), of which [the] Greek, Celtic, Italic, Germanic have survived — of course there were more –, are based on the adoption of this type of language by people who pronounced differently and thought linguistically differently.

88

It is nonsense to talk of 'Indo-Persian' pre-culture. Genuinely philological, to combine the two philologies into one historical unit! Product of method.

Linguistically, of course, most of the languages of the 2nd millennium are lost! We only know more about religion from the Vedas. From the late Gathas (6th century) we can deduce a few things! From the Balkans some other things: Helios, Eos, Ignis come from there. And also the Zhou religion of the Chinese. The burning of corpses and chariots are much more revealing. With the chariot everywhere the designation of the upper power, patriarchally, as Tien, Teisbas, Tinia, Juppiter. 'Chariot peoples', 'equestrian peoples'.

89

The 'Aryan' language group of Central Asia does not break down into Persian and Indian, but into a large number of languages, of which the 'Persian' of the homeland of the Achaemenids is only one, which happened to gain great historical importance. But Parthian, Sogdian and many other languages also belong to it, as well as Vedic and Sanskrit, 'Indian', and beyond that 'Scythian', 'Slavonic', 'Baltic', i.e. in the 2nd/1st millennium [a flooded area] from China to the Baltic

Sea and the Indian Ocean. To judge this vast mass of languages by the accidental remains of Old Persian and Vedic and to try to trace them back to a primordial Indo-European is like trying to extract a 'primordial Roman' from Romanian and Portuguese.

90

'Persians': (see Lehmann-Haupt, König, Christensen): Zarathustra certainly born in Elam (ego), Babylonian effects — priesthood, theology, formalism. Nordic is the belief in impersonal numina (*Amesha Spenta*[51]), also in India, Rome, Germania. Drag, Kant's 'primordial evil', transformed in the West into the figure of the devil. Zarathustra sect, opposed to magicians (more Nordic?), supported by Darius for political purposes. Soon again (Artaxerxes) [subdued] in favour of the other world-views. Never been strong. Zarathustra represents the cattle cult against the horse cult! The peasants against the Bedouins. This is the 'reform' of the North by the South. Compare Israel (Christensen 219).

91

India: The whole polytheism of the Vedas is of the subjugated. Likewise in China. Pantheism always allows itself to be bribed by the concrete ideas. It remains in feeling but not in seeing-thinking. And the organised priesthood of the natives contributes to this. A spiritual power.

92

Landscape and tribal names can be very lucky in some circumstances. The small landscape of Persis gave the name to the few Indian tribes who dwelt there among those who spoke other languages, then to the Persian Empire. [Compare:] Prussia, Italy (Vitalia southern tip). Indians, Spaniards.

---

51 In Zoroastrianism, the Amesha Spenta are the six immortal sages who fight together with Ormuzd against Ahriman. — *Transl.*

93

The Arya encountered a higher culture in India, like the Italo-Celts in the Mediterranean. The Vedic world of gods, like the Hellenic, is predominantly pre-Nordic.

94

Indians in the Aegean: It must be reckoned that in the 2nd millennium tribes with Indian dialects also arrived here and that many an archaic Greek name and place name would be easily explained if it were traced back to ancient Indian forms. (Brunnhofer[52], *Arische Urzeit*[53], p. 26, cuneiform S(a)parda [corresponds in the] Rigveda Sprdha.)

95

If Arya is the self-designation of the 'Indians' and Hind the name of the Indus, i.e. native words, then the folk-name Indian-Hindu is only the product of the accomplished culture (as 'Hellene' already means the mixture!). Further, Hind and Sind are distinguished like Ahura and Asura?

96

Foundation of the three heroic cultures China — India — Antiquity: ruling class. Polis. *Amor fati*. Awe. Human heroism. Three new battlefields of the master spirit against satiety. Geographical-historical horizon. Ancestral pride and defiance of the gods. Homeric mockery.

a) China: continental, inland, 'The Way'. Miao[54].

b) India: tropical, inland, 'The Uncertain Vastness'. Dravida.

---

52 Hermann Brunnhofer (1841–1916) was a Swiss orientalist. — *Transl.*

53 'Aryan Primeval Age'. — *Transl.*

54 The Miao are linguistically related peoples from the mountains in southern China. — *Transl.*

c) Ancient: warm, sea, 'The Body'. Encounters ancient civilisations. Concept of fellah-like 'Orient': old, rich, tired, wise: first example of fellahdom.

97

Heroism — proto-China: On the Chinese clans of the 2nd millennium B.C.: *Reallexikon XII* 177 ff. It is said that in Sumer, too, the lower class was spoken of as the 'black-headed', just as here the 'hundred clans', [i.e.] the nobility, stand in contrast to the black-headed. So the Zhou were blond. The 'phratries' (haloun) are a number of clans with common ancestors (= Ionians, phyles, tribus). The Chinese language was previously in the country. The clans spoke a rapidly lost Aryan language (Tien).

98

North 2000 B.C.: Has a difference between Persian and Indian already been established in the Near Eastern inscriptions? Otherwise Persian is just a younger (500 B.C.) dialect of Indian, transformed by other tribes speaking it. In China, on the other hand, a dialect group of a south-east Asian nature has penetrated and caused the old northern languages to disappear! Another northern group (Ural-Altaic), perhaps very late (post-Christian?), carried over to the Baltic Sea, a small tribe? The Hittite language reveals that a northern-speaking people adopted a southern language or vice versa, like the Normans in England.

99

Proto-China and proto-Indo-European (Wilke, Krause): The inner kinship of the less mythological than metaphysical world-view, which in China is embodied in the dualism Yang-Yin, while Tien is older and more southern. In any case, the primordial opposition of the landlocked countries: heaven (male) and earth (female). This applies to Hittite, Dravidian, Taoist, thus creating three world ideas. Likewise, Indian belief in spirits and ancestor worship is Indo-European.

Around 2200 from Babylon [from] (Anau, Indus) a conquest, with calendar, bronze, etc.? According to Rosthorn[55], the Miao had helmets and swords in 2200 B.C., as opponents superior to the Chinese (South)!!! The mythical primordial emperors did not sacrifice to the Tien, but to the five planetary spirits from which they originated! Chinese historians at that time have proved matriarchy, while from North comes patriarchy (clan names female).

From which stratum comes the writing, from which the language? The emperor beaten by 'Hoangti[56]' was said to be the inventor of forged weapons (i.e. South Asia?). At that time [there was a] close relationship between Central Asia and China, which was then lost (torn apart by the Pelasgian period?)!

100

3 Northern cultures: All three [are] distinguished by the fact that they leave no remains: we possess absolutely nothing from the post-Homeric, [the] Vedic, [the] early Zhou period. Expression first found spiritual-abstract forms, the visual arts took place in wood and fabric. There is no talk of great architecture at all: very unlike the two southern cultures, which thought in buildings, in stone-heavy mass (the Gothic negates mass!), that is, in monuments of optical art; while the northern culture created ideas of space, but in the most ephemeral writing: the north just yearns. Hence [in antiquity] the 'body',

---

55 Arthur von Rosthorn (1862–1945) was an Austrian sinologist. He was chargé d'affaires at the Austrian embassy in Peking from 1895 to 1906 and envoy from 1911 to 1917. During the Boxer Rebellion, his wife Paula (1873–1967) became famous for her tireless efforts, like taking care of the wounded and helping to build barricades. — *Transl.*

56 Hoangti (259–210 B.C.) was the first god-emperor of China. Also known as the Yellow Emperor, he is considered the common ancestor of all Chinese people. — *Transl.*

but without monumentality, [in] China the 'change', [in] India the 'confusion'.

101

Primordial Indian religion: The Rigveda religion is already syncretic, half Dravidian. Dyaus, heavenly father, usually as complement of Prithivi, earth. Varuna, the more concrete, younger sky god, to whom most Rigveda hymns are addressed. Epithet Asura. Indra, weather storm, who gradually becomes chief god (Apollo). [What did the] natives call him? Sindara? To Varuna clings the first idea [of a] cosmic-ethical order. An intra-idol as a fetish against enemies! Un-Aryan. Asura is also the name of the god-opposing powers (Titans) — perhaps infiltrated from the Brahmi language into Aryan? Ahura mazda. Then the inversion in Iranian, where ahura means the good, deva the evil god, would be the original non-Aryan sense! Otherwise we learn nothing more about the gods here. Everything else is later.

102

If Indus Sindh Sindu later Hindu, [is Indra called] Hindar? In Amarna texts Induruta. Likewise Surya, with Kassites: Suwardata; an Old Aryan god who later ceased to play a role.

But Indra appears among the Boghaz king gods! So [is he] to be separated from Indus — Hindu?

Mitra, Varuna, Indra are secured [in] Boghazköy as proto-Aryan — but also the fact that this exhausts the main gods. Surya and Dyaus are already receding, the others are Dasa[57] gods.

103

Primordial Indians. Rigveda: Strictly patriarchal, usually monogamous. Above the *familia* in the Roman sense is the *grama* (village community as a male association, patriciate, phratry), above that the

---

57 The Dasa were the indigenous people of South Asia before the arrival of the Aryans. — *Transl.*

viš (*Gau, populus*), above that the *jana* (people). But this is not strict. The Bharatas are called jana, then grama — [similarly] Homer! Viš be gens, grama more military: the men; Višpati for instance praetor, duke, consul, anax. Viša often = subjects, followers. In a later hymn, classes, not castes, appear (in Purushasukta): priests, nobility, commoners, barbarians. Only in the Bramavarta did the strict priesthood, pre-Aryan, come through! But the texts come from just that! Likewise [are] the Brahmins etc. ancient priestly dynasties of native origin! Old Aryan: the house priest: the head of the family, the king sacrifices. Next to it the Kalchas type (purohita, royal house priest). The main weapon [is] the bow (next to it probably the spear), cocked at the ear. Aryans and Dasas were pastoral peoples; cattle are the domestic animal; horses and chariots; oxen for drawing; cows [are] milked three times a day.

104

Japan (Krause, Chantepie): First inhabitants Ainu ('Russians'?). Second stratum Mongoloid from Asia: with them the present language long before Chr. (Finns?). Third, post-Christian, from Kiushiu the warlike ruling class of Oceanic (Malay) origin, [an] upper class, like the Normans [absorbed into the people], but politically determining the character of the people: pride, war, honour.

The grammar is 'Asiatic', the phonetics largely Oceanic. Cult and higher myths mostly oceanic (core of Shinto). Centres of legend circles: Kiushiu, Yamato and Izumo (the centre of ancient Mongolian folk beliefs). In Izumo (west) the moon god rules, in Yamato (east) the sun goddess. The conquest by Satsuma — Oceania — must have been around 500–0. Incidentally, [the conquerors] had wooden tokens and knotted cords as writing (Easter Island, Peru). The idea of Hades, Eurydice, Jason, Medea: Izumo. Oceanic the sea saga of Izanami and Izanagi (sibling marriage) whose children [are], among others, sun goddess and moon god (this pre-oceanic). The original couple is Polynesian and grafted onto the Izumo myths.

Japan: the c-culture of Oceania, so in the 1st millennium B.C.

105

Ancient India: In South India (Buschan[58] p. 530) women's freedom, Couvade[59], matriarchy spread like in Libya. Also veneration of the dead. Also menhirs in the South Indian temples (p. 530) as the seat of the death demons. Among the Mundas, menhirs at burial places. During the Portuguese period, ritual regicide is attested on the Malabar coast (12-year cycle).

106

Indos: Old Kashitic will still be found all along the west coast of India, as well as South Arabia and East Africa. Almost the entire Indian pantheon is 'Dravidian' and thus related to 'Sumerian'. Kash is the temple culture of abstract high mythology, whose slowly dying remains lie as a counter-soul in antiquity and India, Dionysian and Brahmanic, slowly penetrating, already secularised. In Babylon, however, it is at home.

107

'Iranian' ([according to] Hüsing[60], *Völkerschaften in Iran*[61], *Mitteilungen der anthropologischen Gesellschaft*[62], Vienna 1916, 46) has always been only Western Persia, Indian-Sakic, on the other hand, the East (Afghanistan, Belujistan). This agrees with my theory that the 'Persians' developed from Indians only in the Zagros, likewise the Medes, not before 800, only around 700 the Persians.

---

58 Georg Buschan (1863–1942) was a German doctor and ethnologist. — *Transl.*

59 During their partner's pregnancy, men sometimes complain of symptoms that are similar to those of the pregnant woman. Scientists refer to this as Couvade syndrome. — *Transl.*

60 Georg Hüsing (1869–1930) was an Austrian historian, linguist, Germanist and mythologist. — *Transl.*

61 'Ethnicities in Iran'. — *Transl.*

62 'Communications of the Anthropological Society'. — *Transl.*

108

North 2000: One obstacle is the previous treatment of Indian history, which is based exclusively on the philological treatment of the texts and thus arrives at the strange conceit that the Indians had nothing better to do than philosophise. Next to this, prehistoric soil research stands completely unnoticed, separated from it again by linguistic research. One day we will have to start combining Vedas and Neolithic soil finds; only then will there be a view of Indian facts.

109

Amoeboid cultures in South Asia: 'Dravidian' = Kash. Earth mother service. 'Munda' = South-East Asia, pre-Malaic; the stratum which the Aryan masters subjugated and to which they owe their lower religion.

These are two ancient intercourse worlds of the monsoon zone. India has been the most poorly researched ethnographically! This is the place to start! The amoeboid cultures down here must have withered away early. Proof: that the Babylonian-Egyptian knowledge of the southern sea was little and that Buddhism came to China purely by land. Proof, by the way, that this navigation was and remained a fearful coastal voyage.

Buschan p. 514: the wandering numina are Nordic, the earthy demons Dravidian.

110

Antiquity: Sea Peoples: if one wishes to delve deeper, one must get a clear picture of two traits: the custom of naming and the population figures of the time. For both, the Gallic campaigns against Rome, Delphi and Asia Minor can serve as a comparison.

In *Galatia* one can see how first the religion and language of the conquerors succumbed: the old Phrygian cults remain, and the Pessinus priests are called Galli. But the conqueror's name clings to the land, as is usually the case, the tribal name perishes, and personal names last longest.

Around 400 Po Valley, Etruscan power broken, 387 Rome destroyed, 300 settlements in Illyria, Thrace. 279 Delphi, around 250 Galatia. There is the great parallel. Landlubbers.

111

Galatians (F. Stähelin, *Geschichte der kleinasiatischen Galater*[63] 1907): The old lines Delphi — Bosporus. 278, 17 chiefs, 20,000 heads, 10,000 men recruited as mercenaries, then wandering all over Asia Minor, separating into three 'tribes', with names that probably existed long ago (Teutonic legends also existed in Gaul and Germania), finally settling in the middle, where they hold on and try in vain to expand. Despite the number and cultural level of the country, it was possible for this small group to take part in all wars as mercenaries. Around 230, the decisive Gallic victory of Attalus I[64].

In the 2nd century, three tribal areas under pseudo-chiefs and nobility, a common council in Drynemeton ('sacred cove'). Each tribe has four districts (much like Caesar's Helvetians and the Old Irish clan constitutions). This makes one think; three, four phyles! With the tendency to segregate themselves locally! So one district [is] more than 1,000 men!

They certainly adopted the native cults: Attis, Mater. According to Jerome, the Gallic language was still spoken in the 3rd century A.D. — but only by peasants. Not *one* Celtic inscription exists, all educated people speak Greek.

112

The Medes emerge around the 8th century, with small castle dominions (according to Hüsing) arising from Kassite and Indian followers (the Indians founded smaller baronies around 1400), such as that of Ramateja of Arazias. Indian names are the last remnant

---

63 'History of the Galatians of Asia Minor'. — *Transl.*

64 Attalus I was the ruler of Pergamon, in what is now modern-day Turkey. — *Transl.*

of the origin, as is the dialect. According to Hüsing, the castle lords in this mountainous country become twenty 'kingdoms', which under Assyrian pressure (as in Israel, ego) give rise to the kingship of Hagmatana (Ekbatana) (Hüsing, OLZ 1915, 33 ff.). Nebuchadnezzar already marries a Median princess. Median mercenaries and captains enter the service of the old great empires (as again and again: Teutons in Byzantium). Teisbas also founded a Persian empire in the old Elamite Anshan, from where 550 Media was subjugated. Only then was there — not a Persian people, but a Persian sultanate. There is no question of an Iranian race next to an Indian one. Zarathustra only became important through political ascendancy.

113

Around 600, a complete transformation of the political situation of the Near East begins, three great empires arise anew: Lydians, Medes, Persians. Chaldeans rise and fall, Assur collapses, Egypt is taken, the Cimmerians found an empire in Cappadocia, the Scythians follow: the deeper meaning of this mighty movement is that the Nordic c-culture between the d-cultures of antiquity and India pushes incessantly into this fellah world without procreation: but in this period the foundation is laid for the rise of Arab culture. This movement about 600 prepares the soil, as in antiquity that about 2000, which Chatti Minos etc. ephemerally stimulated. The result is the barbarian empire of the Persians, without culture, containing only the latest civilisation, without style and soul, a mere political shell with changing content.

Such was also the vortex of peoples of the Hun period from China to Rome, whose fertilising thrust lay half a millennium later in the West. The pseudomorphosis of realms and humanity, which until then had only been objects in their souls. Around 600, the enormous movement of the entire North. Then, at the same time as these Scythians, Cimmerians, Medes, the great Celtic expansion into Spain, probably that of the Sabellians in Umbria, a similar catastrophe in China, in India. There is a connection! Read up North (Tacitus),

Menghin (pottery, Iron Age), Haloun (oldest Indo-Europeans). At that time the pre-Arab prophecy of the Jews, Zarathustra.

114

Migration of peoples, around 600 B.C.: An enormous chapter, to be switched on at the end of the early Nordic times! Heroic expansion, in the middle Cimmerians, Scythians, Medes, in the west Celts, in the east Indo-Europeans in Zhou. A Germanic defensive area must have formed then. And what about the Finnish-type tribes? Languages of this type have reached from the Baltic to Japan, the Hungarians and Huns to France, so their distribution is the same as that of the late Indo-European languages of Celts and Tocharians. When did this confusion arise?

115

Schmidt, *Die Mon Khmer Völker*[65]: What is important, what he did not see at all, is that these languages penetrated from the south-east into nothing but river regions: Munda into the Ganga Valley and the Mon into the Saluën and perhaps [into] the Irawa Valley, Khmer into the Mekong region. Ego: The Aryans encountered Munda cultures in 1500 B.C., which dominated the Ganges region at that time. Therefore it should be possible to prove that cult, festive custom, etc. in the Vedic are in fact products of the Munda. On the other hand, since these peoples also overshadow the entire Australian island region, connections between Vedas and M[alaia] would be very natural!

'Dravidian' forms of irrigation, threshing, grain storage (silo), cultivation tools, the type of courtyard house including furnishings, jewellery (typically the same from Morocco to Hind India), food preparation, trade, traffic, technology [are] closely related to southern Persia and Mesopotamia. The South Indian maternal law with polyandry = loose mating is chronologically even older.

---

65 'The Mon Khmer Peoples'. — *Transl.*

Among the Munda and in Hind India skull cult, stone worship. The Munda gave the 'Aryan culture' its light customs, spring fights, the cult in general (up to the 'slaves'). In contrast, the original Dravidian earth mother cult is from 'Kash'!

LATE ANTIQUITY AND MAGIAN CULTURE

116

Jesus (pseudomorphosis): He may only be mentioned in one line. Here, too, the armour of Germanic legions clanked, and next to the great altar of the Herodian temple gleamed pillars of the palace in which Varus, Pilate commanded — at the time when on one day the carpenter's son Jesus of Nazareth chased away the sellers in the forecourt and died on the cross the following morning because of his sedition.

117

In the Arabic pseudomorphosis, the heroism of the Nordic type is set against the southern cosmological serenity: the type of the religious hero and martyr emerges: *Jesus*. Here the stream of people from 600, all Nordic, has had a testifying effect: already the Mitanni hero, then Persians, Medes, Hellenes. The heroes of the consensus peoples are the blood witnesses. The more heroic, the greater the people: Christians, Manichaeans, less the Jews (but 70 A.D.[66]!).

118

Jesus — World History, Introduction: The great tragedy here is the struggle of a deep individual with his experiences and conclusions against the great breath of the world, which remains 'nature' in people and also in himself.

---

66 In 70 A.D., the Romans destroyed Jerusalem and its Temple. — *Transl.*

Nature against culture: for Jesus has cultural feelings. The logic of the world, the organic one, triumphs over the logic of mind and spirit of the do-gooder. But by developing the idea of 'cultural man' to the extreme, it has created this lost type itself. It is in him and against him.

What Goethe (*Gespräche*[67] 126) said about the elective affinity is true: the sensual and the moral (nature and spirit) in irresolvable contradiction. Gethsemane, monstrous, there he senses the hopeless entanglement. The dreadful in vain.

119

Christ and Augustus: The last act of the ancient world-view was the cult of the ruler: space is nothing, bodies alone form the cosmos. The most perfect bodies are gods. Since the body was burnt — this connection has not been suspected until now — the genius, the divine breath could only show itself in the living body: this is how Alexander felt when he called himself the son of God, this is how Caesar felt — which was compatible with deep scepticism. If one immerses oneself in the ancient world-feeling — which only a few of us can do — one understands that precisely the finest minds could at the same time scoff at the old gods and honestly acknowledge the cult of rulers. Thus Caesar and Augustus became *divi*, Ptolemy, Seleucus received the title '*soter*' — saviour — and '*epiphanes*' — sent by God — and here the profound act of world history is revealed: dying antiquity rendered the last service to the flourishing Arabic culture by once more accomplishing the deification of a man. Jesus became '*soter*', '*epiphanes*' in the first two centuries after his death in the way the rulers had become: it was the last act of Hellenism: he — Jesus — remained the only god-man. When Constantine made him the god of the empire, the emperors were his servants: the monotheism of the ruler who was ruling at the time merged into that of the ruler who would rule forever.

---

67 'Conversations'. — *Transl.*

120

[The] northern 'Teutons' [are] the mobile ones, not only as Vikings. Goths, Vandals, Burgundians [also come] from there to Asia Minor, Spain, Africa. The inert masses — Swabians, Franks, Saxons — remained seated.

121

Everywhere the great political combination: China, Antiquity, Arabia, Occident, namely state systems, groupings, the great current questions that lead to wars. Thus in antiquity the rich old East is the magnet, afterwards the group of peripheral countries. Thus in Arabia the never before discovered great combination that guides Byzantine and Sassanid politics, Umayyads[68]. The ideas of Holy Byzantium, the orthodoxy, the nations of the Magian complexes. Show how Byzantium has traits of youth!

122

Pseudomorphosis 0–300: Arrange like this: first the great politics of Rome, Byzantium, Ctesiphon, then the new religions become nations and political powers. There is no 'Christianity', but historically first anarchistic sects, then city and state, finally the Christian state. World-historically, only this active side comes into consideration: the formation of the political units of Magian style.

123

[The] early period [of Arab culture] may be called Aramaic with the same justification as that [of] Faustian Germanic: a people with a unified soul and language for its expression begins to build up a new world under the folk formations of the A[rabs], Israelites, Chaldeans.

---

68 The Umayyads were the first Muslim dynasty. — *Transl.*

124

Pendulum of Christianity: From the mighty centre of a new solar monotheism (Mithras, Baal) to Ireland, where the slowly progressing Celtic or Germanic is overtaken. Then setback: from pre-Celtic Ireland the idea of the papacy, the *Conceptio* etc. to Rome. Boniface.

125

Beginning of Arab culture: What gives the political church its superiority is its organisation, which is ingenious compared to [the cultures of] Mithras, Sol, etc. But who created it? Partly Paul. But the hierarchy? Cf. Karl Müller[69], *Kirchengeschichte*[70] I (1926), excellent! On this Harnack[71] in DLZ 30 April 27. *Kunst der alten Christen*[72] DLZ 1927, p. 804. Important new thoughts. Kittel[73], *Die Probleme des palästinischen Spätjudentums und das Urchristentum*[74] — cf. OLZ 1927, no. 4.

126

Antiquity: The grandiose pendulum swing: 200–0 the mysterious flare-up of solar religion west of the line Pontus — Petra (Mithras, Baal) everywhere. All religions are turned solar and carried westward

---

69 Karl Müller (1852–1940) was a German Protestant theologian and church historian. — *Transl.*

70 'Church History'. — *Transl.*

71 Adolf von Harnack (1851–1930) was a German Protestant theologian and church historian. About Oswald Spengler's *The Decline of the West*, Harnack wrote that it could be 'thrown overboard' with a single name: Augustine. — *Transl.*

72 'Art of the Ancient Christians'. — *Transl.*

73 Gerhard Kittel (1888–1948) was a German Protestant theologian, as well as a passionate anti-Semite and active National Socialist. In his book *Die Judenfrage* ('The Jewish Question') (1933), he wrote, 'The violent extermination of Jewry is out of the question for serious consideration: if it was not possible for the systems of the Spanish Inquisition or the Russian pogroms, it will be even more impossible for the 20th century. ... But killing all the Jews does not mean mastering the task.' — *Transl.*

74 'The Problems of Late Palestinian Judaism and Early Christianity'. — *Transl.*

to Iceland, Mithras by the army, while the east stream Edessa — China remains entirely free of it — lunar? — so Jews and Parsees. The west stream skips the top of the Germanic and the Celtic invasion (Thames, Picts) and goes as far as Ireland, which has remained primeval Nordic. In this stream, Christianity, which had become solar, goes with the substance problems of father and son, at the same time patriarchal (Sea Peoples fading out).

In primeval Ireland, however (from where Iceland was fertilised), the counter-current sets in, matriarchal (the Mother of God instead of Theotokos or Theogonos, Christ overcome by Mary). Here the most secret primeval ground of the old Norse soul, deep, fairy-tale infinity, Arthur, Parzival, Grail legend — pre-Celtic, genuinely Norse, an essential trait in Faustianism. Faustianism is therefore primeval Nordic and Celtic and Germanic. The new mystical idea of Catholicism emanates from Ireland: the papacy, the cult of the Virgin Mary, infinity. The Irish missions also convert Rome, from Byzantinism. So there is deep Nordicism in the papacy too, wherever its idea is new. This counter-current begins in 500 and pushes forward in the Crusades — the real upsurge of pre-Celtic North, not Germanic — to the exit of the Sun religion. Rome becomes matriarchal, Rasena.

127

Gothic campaign: They went south, small brave swarms without a secure geographical horizon. Scorched skies, corpses along the way, smoking cities mark the way, stolen women went along, ravished, mothers of future heroes. Thus they broke into the rich and late world of antiquity, which lulled itself into peace and whose world-view hid the course of the world from them: as it does today (Böcklin's picture!). From Sulla to Actium a mighty brief picture of spiritual greatness: contrast with the phrasiness of today.

128

Late antiquity: Now the territory from Spain to the Euphrates covers itself with white cities alike; all with marble halls, amphitheatres, temples in a washed-out Greek style, innumerable statues, fountains. With a crowd speaking Latin or Greek, though mixed from peoples from the North Sea to the Indian Ocean, raceless, tired, pleasure-seeking, superstitious. The old languages are dying out or are spoken in lost villages, a mishmash religion is superimposed on the peasant faith.

The forests become rare, the rain too. The peasants disappear. The big cities have absorbed them. Freed slaves from all continents live sparsely on the vineyards. The great life of the spirit goes on only in four or five cities and in these only in a small social upper class. If this disappears, there is nothing left. And it disappears. New families, who lack maturity inwardly, replace the extinct blood, but their great constitution is external. They imitate the Romans, they are not Romans.

SOME OUTLOOKS

129

With the cultural soul begins the set of insoluble tragic conflicts, which are also fought out by the heroic culture, tragically, while the South avoids them. For heroism exists not only in the face of bodily enemies, but also in the face of spiritual situations. Heroism includes loyalty to one's husband everywhere, loyalty to one's fiefdom, loyalty to one's oath, in China, India, [the] ancient world, [the] Occident. Loyalty to the death in the face of duty to fatherland, ruler, cause, party, religion, family, idea, enterprise. Comradeship. Poetry of the wandering clergy, Landsknechts, guilds, nobles, students: Germanic or 'heroism' in general. Part of this is that the 'family', the woman, takes a back seat to the status, the man. Patriarchy actually means 'male culture', not 'men's right', but 'men among themselves'. Rationalism (*code civil*) deliberately destroys all these forms.

130

At the beginning of high cultures there usually awakens the consciousness of togetherness, which expresses itself more or less strongly in the tendency towards political unity. In Egypt, unity has acquired [such] strength that disintegration into the original tribal units (districts) is the exception; in Babylon, it is the rule; in [the] ancient world, it is a desire expressed in the name Hellenes and in the shaping of the Troy legend as a pan-Hellenic enterprise. [In] China, the idea of emperorship [stands] at the beginning of the Zhou dynasty. [In the] West, Charlemagne. If he had had a gifted, long-lived successor (Augustus, Louis XIV), there would have been no Germany, France, Italy, Spain, but a Western unity with some (Latin-Rustic?) unified language and among them landscapes: Saxony, Bavaria, Lombardy, Burgundy, Aquitaine, Franconia, etc.

131

Russia [stands] between d-culture and c: Middle Asia since the Varangian period. Spirit of China, India. [The] migration of peoples [has continued] to America. Partly Atlantic — navigation –, partly Turanian — land-grabbing. Chivalrous [and] mercantile.

132

Introduction: c-culture (short): 3 c-cultures. This is the beginning of 'world history'. Why? Conclusion: frantically short overview of the history of high cultures from 3000 to the present. Ingenious, short, deep, brilliant. In addition, very briefly the history of languages, peoples, races, war and states. Tragedy of the human will, the imperative of its total life to the end. Like d cultures.

133

Western European socialism is either the will of the masses to op-press the others — cosmopolitan city, physiognomyless, compulsion –, or nobler: religious spirit — voluntarily expressing itself, for the sake of a goal, allegiance for reward. Loyalty, betrayal.

134

Godless destiny: A god has a fixed form that can be depicted, a character, a way of thinking; body and soul therefore. God the Father has a full beard, Mary breasts, a face. All the artificiality and empti-ness of modern thinking in the question of 'whether God exists'. As what? To the Western Catholic [it is] quite clear: as a person. Theism: to him God is an empty sound: world, world-soul, nature, universe. Belief in a personal God is always belief in several such beings. 'God' today is an empty word behind which hides the insincerity of modern souls to themselves. *One* God is not a God.

135

'Europe' is not a continent at all like Asia and Africa, but a pen-insula of the first, opposite the other. If the cultural world of the Occident, since Charlemagne, conceived of its area of residence as the centre of world history, it was increasingly right: the history of the world has had its centre of gravity more and more there since 1000. But if her scholars constructed the entire development of human his-tory, art, language, race, from this horizon, it was nonsense and ar-rogance, the same arrogance that dominated the thinkers of all high cultures, for the Egyptians, Babylonians, ancients, Chinese saw the past precisely in the same way from their geographical location. Only today, when the Faustian spirit embraces the globe, has this become too narrow. We must not only understand, but also draw the conclu-sion that Western Europe is not a natural centre and was very small in its importance for world history *before* Western culture.

136

It is naive to assume that 'Europe', a small peninsula of Asia, has been the centre of world history since prehistoric times because we sit on it today. Admittedly, since all works on prehistory show European maps of Europe and [since] mostly only Western Europe, and since the geographical thinking of the Western-educated ones today depends on the habit of seeing maps, the horizon of thinking ends in the territories of Russia.

137

Grandiose image: The old West and its seafaring (c) slowly decaying. Flourishing of the great buildings: Egyptian culture, i.e. about 3rd millennium. Seafaring world in the 2nd millennium from the Mediterranean and Bohuslän to the east urgently, here a late moonlight flowering: Kafti. Now the huge inland expansion: Asia with the peninsula of Western Europe. Pushing back the sea power: Antiquity, *Imperium Romanum*, purely inland. But since the birth of Christ, seafaring 'Teutons' from the ancient sites of the West, Megalith. In the east, Japanese, Pacific Ocean. Arabs and Normans dominate the Mediterranean. Malays. A ring of maritime peoples forms around the continental block. While Genghis Khan attempts a summary of this block, the old megalithic areas unfold their tendency once more: Vikings, Portugal, Spain, Holland, England — the Venetians only in their pond –, advance to India, East Asia, to America ([first the] Vikings). The sea powers are now greater than the land powers. The latter are firmly locked in. All internal wars since 1700 are also a naval problem — Thirty Years' War, Seven Years' War, Napoleon, World War. America, Japan. Now come the decisive battles of the future: aeroplanes! Russia [is now] Asia.

138

Russia: Without will, without heroes, but a mass that believes and is ready to sacrifice, a terrible instrument in the hands of a great leader, for whose hordes Europe and Asia already lie ready as prey today.

139

Nordic religion: The 'divinity' of the whole world, therefore [is] man also divine. Self-feeling. No other gods beside himself. Machine — man as god, the machine as world. Around 1500 the crisis: abolition of the Catholic Church — of Christianity — of religion in general.

140

Language: History shows everywhere that the spirit, 'intellectuality', is an end, the form in which extinct races pass away. Expiring nobility is expressed in the fact that the last sons go to the *variété*, write monographs, witty novellas. The French nobility in the 18th/19th century: it was not the guillotine that destroyed it, it died from within. Esprit was the outward sign of it. And the most extreme rabble of the great cities, something last, dying, is literacy, these novelists, newspaper writers, orators in popular assemblies: in 1789 they made the revolution and incited the mass of peasants to become masters themselves. The Petersburg rubbish has made Bolshevism since the Decembrists, the German literary rabble made 1918 in order to make money out of it.

141

Soul or better civilisation: A terrible psychology of civilisation. The tragic soul is given. Its negation takes the meaning, the content out of human existence. The fulfilment of time (through great history, heroism, suffering) becomes an intelligent killing of time. And then the end breaks in, not from the outside, but from the disembodied life, from the depths. And the spectre of boredom rises hugely above the stone masses of the world's cities, the life that has become empty without danger, without blood, which is now to be filled by business and entertainment, an intelligent vegetation in technology for comfort. Eroticism without children, circus, intoxication, travel, idle literature, substitution of art, exhibitions, poetry, feuilleton, radio, cinema, records. Until nature takes revenge through sterility from within and barbarians from without.

142

Nor forget the downfall of religion: below, peasant faith, the god Sixtus, above, the swamp surrogate of literate Buddhism. Draw with immoderate contempt the literati who have done away with poetry. Likewise the animal faces and dirty hands, flat feet, dripping mouths of the thieving alley politicians of today. A sword of Caligula, a Mussolini chasing them into the lair with castor and dagger!

143

H. Trimborn, 'Der Kollektivismus der Inkas in Peru'[75]. *Anthropos* 18/19, 978 ff: 'Communism' is nonsense. A distinction must be made between the economic council of the subjugated and the exploitative system of the victorious Incas. The Kechua word *ayllu* [corresponds to] the Germanic '*Sippe*[76]'. These tribes may have settled in northern Europe by kinship, so *ayllu* is also a local term. Division of tribes into hundreds (all as in Germania and Rome. Gens, centurie, where also the clan is politically, militarily, economically, cultically the cell of the people's body). The clans had their ancestor god (huaca) and myth. Hundreds is never meant literally, not even in Rome, but approximately the maximum. The clan [consists] of common owners of land and cattle.

The social division in the Inca Empire [is] very natural: 1. ruling family, 2. men of the Inca tribe, 3. subjugated clan chiefs, 4. 'common

---

75 'The Collectivism of the Incas in Peru'. — *Transl.*

76 German: 'clan'. — *Transl.*

free' *tributarios*, rest of the clan members. Cf. Normans. The clans-men were periodically allotted land by the clan, free wood, hunting and fishing rights; house and farm were special property, as with the Teutons built by the clansmen in the '*Bittwerk*'. This resulted in the relative impossibility of being rich or poor — in the clan. The Incas were different.

144

Imperium: The world is getting old. The luxury streets decay, grass grows in old temple courtyards. On the deserted Palatine, the roofs of the palaces are collapsing. Freed slaves of the Orient become peasants of Italy.

145

Language: The growing intellectualisation of the generation suc-cession, which is rapidly disappearing in high cultures [and] world cities, means the isolation to the point of suffocation of life, in the form of barrenness. Intelligence is an end. 'Progress' in the sense of the 19th century is an end: rich in words and ideas, poor in children, at last tremendous spirit, but childless. This is how culture goes out.

146

The great course of politics in d-culture is always that in the begin-ning a sacred or exalted form reigns, in which all are relatively free, but that with 'freedom' begins general slavery with the horde of stealing professional politicians, from which only Caesarism then redeems.

147

High cultures: What distinguishes each later and earlier one is the degree of spiritual tension that leads to catastrophe. The division in life between the element and the spirit grows. The birth of culture already takes place under terrible inner convulsions. And everything that emerges in form, political, religious, economic, is charged with more and more doom. Something that began around 5000 is coming to an end, like an avalanche. The thunderstorms [are] becoming louder and louder, more and more violent. The cities are becoming more and more blatant. The faces ever sharper, more jagged, heightened to the most personal. The passions more terrible, even more cruelty and pity: What did the Egyptians suspect of the inner torment of Heraclitus and Buddha? What did Buddha suspect of the torture and contrition of the 13th century? How benign were the wars of the Romans, their revolutions, against ours! And if Russian culture comes to birth at all and does not die in the womb, what blood and suffering does it already have for its daily needs!

High culture is the great shaping of suffering. What one suffers in oneself and from others, what one inflicts on oneself and others or takes from others, already exhausts the meaning of high culture.

148

From heroism to decomposition! Here the appearance of world humour since the migration of peoples. Don Juan with the grandiose mockery of universal law: what I have enjoyed, even God will not take away from me. Don Quixote. This is different from wit, esprit, jest, which only nails the illogical of the logical.

149

Thus meanness grows to giant size. Animals and primitive men are not mean. There is no rabble. But now, at these heights, humanity breaks down into heroes and rabble. The mental possibilities expand upwards and downwards. With it grows veneration and contempt, disgust.

150

If in every noble animal race — not in lice and fleas, but in horses, dogs and eagles — good and badly turned out specimens are very different, in great history this grows to the extreme. Great history is the elevation of an ever smaller number of people above a high average, below which the great majority sink ever [more]. There are lice and eagles there too; tragic culture is the fact that only the eagles have them and are them, and that the lice eat them.

151

North: The new feeling that shines forth here, from a new soul, a new countenance, is contempt for death. More than that: contempt in general, contempt for the rest who cling to life, for whom life is something supreme, not life as hero, as strong, but life in general as duration. As Achilles feels: short, but great. In Egypt, where something of Nordic blood still shines, one occasionally encounters a disdain for life by a sage who has tasted it and finds it stale; but this Solomonic contempt in the corners of the mouth — all is vain — in a Wen-Amon[77] is late, aged. But here it is youth that despises, and not life, but life without heroic greatness, and not death, but death in bed. Here the highest of humanity is reached, its splendid flowering, for which it was well worth thousands of years to soak the ground with blood, to build up what fell to pieces again.

Marks of heroism were these epics and cathedrals, marks of heroism are henceforth the books of history with their countless battles and great names. And there should be no doubt today that with the heroic soul, humanity also loses its rank and is once again placed in the history of an animal species that lives, eats and dies, in deliberate forms that are called the progress of humanity.

152

Creative, that is, determining the inner form of all that happens — happening is an expression of the soul — and thus the result of history itself, is only the *idea*, not the programme. I would like to make this difference, which is decisive for history, quite clear. We are currently living in a time when people are weak in ideas and rich in programmes and confuse the two.

---

77   The Travelogue of Wenamun, a report of his trading mission to Lebanon, is an untitled work of ancient Egyptian literature. — *Transl.*

Idea is the primordial vision of the whole, which underlies all expression without entering into conceptual thinking. If one is practised in thinking, one can reflect on it, i.e. make the attempt to put the idea into words and thus make it comprehensible to others, which hardly succeeds. But action is instinctively controlled by the idea, all the more completely for that: it can never be defined. So I am talking about an 'Atlantic world idea' that cannot be defined, but can only be made tangible in its practical expression: state, religion, grammar. A programme is only a conceptual determination based on causal reasoning, e.g. Marxism. Practically, [the programme] is worthless, because instinct still decides: the instinct of whole cultural masses, the will of individuals (drive) does everything; it makes use of the programmes in which its thinking 'believes'. But the creative is instinct after all, the programme is only the costume.

153

Culture and civilisation behave like the young and [the] old Goethe: the former changing, always developing new forms inwardly — Werther, Faust, Tasso — the latter absorbing everything that comes from outside in a fixed, detached form. *Diwan*, *Faust II*. Thus civilised China, Egypt, India.

154

History — private fate: The significant man (take 'signify' literally, his private experiences signify fates of time) [is the one] whose private existence absorbs the whole existence. The case of Napoleon is the strongest, Caesar far weaker.

Above all, however, the cases of the great intellectuals. Here the modern standpoint is quite correct: their philosophy, art, etc., is a private matter, to be explained out of nerves, dispositions, race, self-defence. How, for example, did Kant and N[ietzsche] arrive at their philosophy? Completely privately. So one may also derive their results privately (which is what the psychoanalysts do). But the greatness lies precisely in the fact that the thinking of the time is absorbed in these private events and gains form in them for the next generation.

N[ietzsche] in particular, through his bizarre appearance, has handed down the thinking of 1880 in bizarre form for us, the next generation. If a calm systematist of Kant's type (i.e. à la Mommsen, Helmholtz[78]) had appeared in his place, we would have had the substance of the time in a different form and instead of our journalists, reviewers, literati, the style of our scholars would have been shaped on the technical level. The core of Nietzsche's thought could also be understood, instead of from Wagner and Dionysus, from modern technology and the money economy. It would have been better for us to have a great national economist instead of a great actor. Our fate was Nietzsche. What a pity; otherwise we would have had an official German philosophy around 1914, which every one of our industrialists, politicians, national economists would have known and which would have intervened in our scientific and practical work in a normative way. Thus, unfortunately, Nietzsche has become a matter first of all for literati and journalists.

155

On the political dynamics of Faustian culture: from Columbus onwards, its setting is planetary. This has led to the very comprehensible aspect of 'world history'. Its 'modern age' is merely the late period of a single culture, and its extension over the surface of the planets is a symptom of Faustian spirit and thus bound to its lifetime.

---

78   Hermann von Helmholtz (1821–1894) was a German physiologist and physicist. He was one of the most versatile natural scientists of his time; his scientific results in the fields of physiology, optics, acoustics and electrodynamics provided fundamental epistemological advances in the 19th century. — *Transl.*

156

The tragedy of great talents [lies] 'between the times'. There a riddle of the great misunderstood is solved. I am thinking of List[79], our greatest statesman, who was superior to Bismarck in g[enius]. He should have been in the full force of his creative powers in 1800, then he would have dominated the politics of 1815. Or 1860 — then the Bismarck era would have been filled with his much more generous ideas. But he was born in 1789 and shot himself in 1846 after all his intentions had failed in that 'interim' period.

157

The older forms persist, apparently, prevailing among antiquated peoples. The French and Italians will no longer get beyond the political form of a nationalism that becomes more comical from year to year. The Frenchman and Italian does not travel — as a sadist — he knows of the other for lack of distance and sense of proportion: that is chauvinism. The 19th century is that of the national form of the public sphere: parliaments, incorporation of foreign peoples. But the older form of the dynamist principle (subject, territories, 'my' people) is for the everyday man the only thing he sees, lives in and acts upon. Today the stage of economic complexes is beginning, but everyday feeling will continue to pretend that the national stage exists for a hundred years and more, and fragments of peoples like Poles and Czechs will be absorbed into [the economic complexes] without noticing that their actions have long since become quite insignificant.

---

79 Friedrich List (1789–1846) was an important German-American national economist. He espoused the doctrine of the independence of the national economy. To realise his goals, he called for the implementation of protective tariffs and the expansion of the railway network to improve the infrastructure. He is considered a pioneer of the German Customs Union. To this day, his ideas of creating large economic areas with a corresponding transport structure have not lost their relevance. — *Transl.*

APPENDIX

DISPOSITION I ON 'WORLD HISTORY'

hat is history (versus nature)? Time-space. Fate. Causal. World-weaving, current. Fact, unique.

Antiquity — Middle Ages — Modern Times. Bronze Age, cultural area. Earth history, biohistory, human history. Horizon.

Historical thinking: seeing, experiencing, writing.

Epochs of world historiography. Philosophy. We the last. Retrospection. Symptom.

1. *What is man?* Roaming predator. Instinct, senses. Swarm, horde, small. Liberation from the constraint of the species. Hand-tool. List-weapon. ab-cd. 'Life'. Plant, animal. From within. Cosmos-microcosm/macrocosm. Will/Fate. Stream of generations. Number. Life is struggle. Deed is struggle.

2. *When does world history begin?* Fifth millennium. Speech — thought. Idea — ideal. 'Spirit'. Reflection, Consciousness. Enterprise, organising. Conscious community organised, meaningful, purposeful, speaking connected. Goals. Scale between cruelty and compassion. Sharing rather than instinct. Farmers: farming, animal husbandry. Work, deed. War.

3. *What is world history?* Struggle, fate of thinking man, tragic, self-destructive. Two hundred generations. Depth, meaning.

Primordial phenomenon. World feeling, metaphysics; powers of thinking. Powers as tendencies. Tempo, duration. Domination against the world. Will/fate. 'Politics' and 'economy'. Facts, unique. Epoch, episode, chronology.

4. *What is culture?* Inner form, growth, life course. Idea of the form of change. Sedentary, house, fetter; d vegetable, c amoeba. Early and late cultures c-d group: type, pace, duration. Above, not after. Emergence — decay (primitive peoples, civilisation, fellaheen). Peasantry and society. Village, town. Tribe, state, class. Nobility — priests. Symbolism. Original symbol. Expression of religion and politics. Works, deeds. d-city, parasite on c-village.

5. *Culture vs. nature:* Earthbound. Race (nature: peasant races, culture: status races). Man nature ravager (forest). Nature transformation. Geology, climate. Soul of the landscape. Blood against soil. Race. Desert, forest, sea, mountains. South, North. Fire, ice. Sahara — Arabia — Gobi. Larger versus smaller history: World — Man.

6. *Three early cultures:* Tombs, temples, later Nordic house culture. Sense of the world. Types of 'life'. Metaphysics. Genealogy, cosmological destiny. Art, religion, thought — not works but actions. Style of the soul. Seeing the mystery. Symbolism in thinking. Inner form, seen shape of deep life.

7. *Three early cultures:* Life, deeds, history. Historical events. External struggle: actual life itself. Tribe: patriarchal, matriarchal. Clan, house, village. Dominion. Historical powers and tendencies. Possession, content of life. West: bow, axe. Priestly politics. War, law, rule. Politics, economy: robbery, trade, traffic. Power as booty. South, North. Purpose in life: passive, active. Peoples, races, languages not identical.

8. *Sedentary and mobile life:* Freedom, bondage of land, peasantry, culture, society, bohemian. Master life. Nomads (hunters, herders,

robbers, a-d), sea nomads. Fourth millennium. Above [the] peasantry. Culture as dungeon. Swarm, corporation. Protest against society, class, city, state. Ship. Sea routes and land routes. Traffic, trade. Metals, tent. Adventurers, criminals, artists. Protest against culture. 'Barbarians'.

9. *Egypt and Babylonia:* Contrast and stratification in the south. Semito-Hamites. Akkadians. Rephaim. Ur, Guti. Growth and style of these high cultures. Third millennium. Emergence, early period — late period. Civilisation. Tomb, temple. Maritime history in the Mediterranean. South Asia. State and private law, economy. Tombs and temples.

10. *Chariot:* Horse. Turan. Soul of the plain, late awakening. Inland, Nordic. Desert. Conquering as purpose of life. Caucasian language. Second millennium. Indo-Europeans, Turk. Hyksos, Arameans. Kassites, Zhou. Young Indo-Europeans. 'Empires'. Sea Peoples, Kafti, Bohuslän, Tursha. Oldest sea power. Patriarchy, master tribes, warrior ideals. Idea of being a lord. Egyptian-Babylonian civilisation. 'World power', empire. Hittites. Individualism.

11. *Three northern cultures above south:* Warrior status. Priesthood. Form of state, nations. Land — sea. Carthage, Etruscans. Apollo — Dionysus. Aryan — Dravidian. First millennium.

12. *Equestrian tribes:* Persians, Scythians (Aryans), Cimmerians; Celts, Galatians, Tocharians. Assyrians, Medes, Amazons. Malays. Even more passionately expansive. Zarathustra. Israel. Protest of the Semites (West) against the Arameans (North): prophets against kings. Seafaring South Asia. Vikings.

Three empires. Huns, Germanic tribes, Indo-Scythians, Parthians. Disappearance of Egyptian and Babylonian civilisation. Frankistan. Culture of the Middle.

13. *Arab culture: Pseudomorphosis. First millennium:* Pacific: Japan. Mexico, Peru, Polynesia, Malaya. — Christianity. Nations. Catholicism. Islam. — Magyars, Turks.

14. *Occident: Nations, Dynamics. Second millennium:* Crusades. Slavs. Normans. — Genghis Khan. Mongols. Russians. Turks. — Sea powers West. Columbus. Expansion. Japan. — Catholic Church. Levant.

15. *Present: Civilisation. 19th/20th century:* Danger. All or nothing. Fellaheen, uncreative. — Crisis, technology. New weapons. Dostoyevsky. End of world history. — Religious storm. — Coloured. Russia. Islamic civilisation. — Decay of the c-cultures ('primitive peoples').

APPENDIX

DISPOSITION II ON 'WORLD HISTORY'

S HORT, deep, transparent, clear, infinitely superior.
Essence of the knowledge of history (against Kant). Looking, physiognomy, figure, destiny.

What is time, chronology, direction? Facts, truths, time — space.

Writing history, poetry. Historical thinking. World as history.

Against antiquity — Middle Ages — modern times, Bronze Age, cultural area.

What is history, historiography, knowledge of history?

Little metaphysics, only a few broad lines. Short! More psychological. Against 'Stone Age'.

1. What is man?

Experienced from within: freedom, will. Predator, hunter. 'Life', plant, animal, flame. Appropriation, struggle. ab-cd. Compulsion of the species. Hand. Individual and flock, specimen. Rare animal among massed others. (Like a genius among the mass of inferiors.) Questionable life among later species. Brought up to cunning by harshness. Weaponless, powerless, hence 'mind' as weapon. Instinctive, inventive. Fire. Infantile. *Bête incompréhensible*[1] (Pascal), noble beast. Earthy life. You shall become earth!

2. When does world history begin?

---

1   French: 'incomprehensible beast'. — *Transl.*

Fifth millennium. Speaking — thinking. Enterprise. Organise. Aim. Fateful investment. Idea and Ideal. Deepening of life. From south to north. a-b historyless. Why? c-d conscious community. Reflective soul. Writing, war, weapon, device. Streams of existence — waking connections. Drive. Speaking thinking *over* understanding feeling. Power of the human being. Master of the world — slave of the world. Pride, despondency. New depths of the soul.

3. *What is world history?*

Organised, language-bound, purposeful action among several: political-sociological-economic. Life currents in spiritual compulsion. Happening, history. Deep, sense. Powers and tendencies. Conscious, instinctive. Facts, not truths. Unique, date. Style, ethos. Chronology. Generations. Organising power, goals. Inner conflict. Power and spoils. War [as] enterprise among several.

4. *What is culture?*

Inner form of history. Culture a life stream in generations. Heredity. Expression. Soul. Life stream of higher order like clan, school (art), style. Plant, rooting. Shape. Early and late cultures. Underneath, not after. Pace, duration. Group of cultures: 3–8. Original symbol. Style inside/outside. Works, deeds, persons. Way to the North. Birth, civilisation. Decay ('primitive peoples'). Civilisation is predominance of metropolitan 'intelligentsia'. Peasantry, society. Village, city. Tribe — state, class, nation. Nobility, priests. Citizen. House (rooting), domestic animal, cage. Peasants: cattle breeding, agriculture. Culture — inner form of a struggle to annihilation.

5. *Culture against nature:*

Blood vs. soil. Soul, power of landscape. Climate. Forest, desert. Ice Age. Drying. Sea, mountains. South, North. Race, number. In man, in the will, the two powers remained fighting: earth-bound (from earth are you) and heritage-bound.

6. *Three early cultures:*

Idea, metaphysics. Tombs — temple — house. Genealogical — cosmological. Style of the soul, of life. Pantheism, polytheism. Fate,

God. South earlier on, art (imitation, ornament), religion, thought. Noble — priestly: North — South.

7. Three early cultures:

Deeds. Political-economic-social history. Tribe, power, property, war, weapons (bow — axe), law, rule. House, village. To have race. Will. Historical powers. Borders, homeland. Traffic, trade, cattle and plant breeding. Noble — priestly: North-South.

8. Sedentary and mobile life:

Instinct of the free predator vs. culture. Dungeons. Peasants. Seafarers and land nomads. Ship (fourth millennium), tent. Nomads ancient (a-b). Ship new. Tribes. Style. Master life. Robbery, trade. Protest against the bondage of life: against village, peasantry c; city, society of anarchists, bohemians, adventurers, travel.

9. Egypt and Babylonia. Third millennium:

Opposites of the South. Hamito-Semites and Dravidians. Type of stratification. Early period, late period, civilisation. Estates, revolutions. Maritime history of the Mediterranean. Akkadians. Ur, Guti. Desert.

10. Awakening of the North to Action: Chariots. Second millennium:

Indo-Europeans, Turk. Desert. Inland vs. sea. Sea Peoples, Kafti, Hyksos, Kassites, Israel. Egyptian-Babylonian civilisation. Hittites. Arameans.

11. Three civilisations: China, India, Antiquity. First millennium.

Perfect strictest form of 'culture', clear construction, stricter than Babylon-Egypt. Origin, place, time, types. Southern, chivalrous, priesthood, sea — land, social, economic. Own — foreign.

12. Meanwhile equestrian tribes:

Persians, Scythians, Celts, Malays, seafaring in South Asia. Three empires. Barbarian attack. Internal crises. Huns, Germanic tribes, Indo-Scythians. Zarathustra. Israel.

13. Arab culture. [First millennium:]

Byzantium, Sassanids, Islam (horsemen). Sea: Vikings, Japan. Pacific: Polynesia, Mexico, Peru. Christianity, Nations. Magyars, Turks.

14. Occident. Second millennium:

Islam, Russians, Genghis Khan: coloured people all around. Japanese, Turks. Sea power, expansion. Columbus. America, colonies. Church, State, Crusades. East, nations.

13. Situation in 19th/20th century:

Civilisation: crisis. Technology. New weapons. Land and sea. Coloured people. Russians. Japan, Africa. End of c-culture: 'ethnology'.

The Club at Bremen

16th Lenzing (March) 1935

Atlantis-Haus,

Böttcherstrasse 2

Invitation No. 32

Thursday, the 21st Lenzing, in the evening at 8.30 p.m,

speaks in the lecture hall of the Atlantis-Haus, Böttcherstraße 2:

Dr. Oswald Spengler:

'Shipping and its influence on world history'.

Transition from Palaeolithicum to Neolithicum: the emergence of language. Tribes as language-linked organisations. Language-led enterprises: stone building, mining, shipbuilding, etc. Shipbuilding and navigation emerging on the Atlantic coast in the fifth millennium. Idea of seafaring, liberation from land. Type of ships. Hazards. Emergence of early historical cultures. Sedentariness. Animal husbandry and plant cultivation. Three early cultures: in the West (shipbuilding, grave construction, death cult, etc.). In the south (temple construction, plough). In the north (timber construction, house, ornamentation).

Against the sedentary tribes revolt of the original human soul. Mobile tribes: hunter, robber, seafarer tribes. Emergence of the sea tribes: seafaring in fleets, maritime powers, coastal monopolies.

Around 2000, the other great idea of movement emerged: inside Asia the chariot. Basic idea. The horse. Around 1000 equestrian tribes.

Speed as a weapon. The high cultures arose from the movements of these mobile tribes against the sedentary ones, sedentary tribes overlaid by master tribes.

Overview of world history from the fifth millennium to the present, where the old means of movement, oars, sails and horses, are replaced by mechanical forces, to which movement in the air is added. Revaluation of sea and land in the present age.